The
Fun Seeker's
North America

Alan S. Davis

Greenline Publications

In 1998 Alan Davis wrote and published *The Fun Also Rises Travel Guide North America,* followed in 1999 by *The Fun Also Rises International Travel Guide.* Together, these books covered the world's most fun places to be at the right time— from the Opera Ball in Vienna to the Calgary Stampede.

The success of these guides persuaded Davis of the need for a different approach to travel book publishing—*extraordinary guides for extraordinary travelers.* Greenline Publications was re-launched as a full-scale travel book publisher in 2002 with the introduction of the first book in the Greenline Historic Travel Series, *The 25 Best World War II Sites: Pacific Theater.*

The Fun Also Rises Travel Series is being introduced in 2003 with this updated version of Davis' first two books—now called *The Fun Seeker's North America* and *The Fun Seeker's International*—to be followed by destination guides for each of the five-star cities on *The Fun Seeker's Gold List,* beginning with Los Angeles, Las Vegas, New York and San Francisco.

Like Ernest Hemingway's *The Sun Also Rises,* which helped popularize what has become perhaps the most thrilling party on earth (Pamplona's Fiesta de San Fermín, also known as the Running of the Bulls), *The Fun Also Rises* travel books will take readers to the world's most fun places.

Greenline's guiding principle is "never settle for the ordinary." We hope that a willingness to explore new approaches to guidebooks, combined with meticulous research, provides readers with unique and significant travel experiences.

To reach us or for updated information on all Greenline books, visit **www.Greenlinepub.com.**

Back Cover Photo Credits: Calgary Stampede (left); Alan S. Davis (middle); Richard McMullin, Office of the City Representative, Philadelphia, Pa. (right).

Recycled paper including not less than 20% postconsumer content

ISBN: 0-9666352-7-2 Library of Congress: Catalog Card Number 2002095528

Distributed in the United States by National Book Network (NBN).

Second Edition. Printed in the United States. All rights reserved.

Copyright © 2003 Greenline Publications, Inc.

GREENLINE PUBLICATIONS
Extraordinary Guides for Extraordinary Travelers
P.O. Box 590780
San Francisco, California 94159-0780

THE FUN ALSO RISES TRAVEL SERIES

The
Fun Seeker's
North America

THE ULTIMATE TRAVEL GUIDE TO THE MOST FUN EVENTS & DESTINATIONS

Alan S. Davis

Edited by Chuck Thompson

GREENLINE PUBLICATIONS

In memory of my parents
for their support and for passing on the travel bug

To ML
for her love, companionship, and humor

And to Jaimee and Paul,
who have lovingly tolerated their father's endeavors

Acknowledgments

Both editions of this book benefited by the contributions of hundreds of people, including friends, tourist-board and travel-industry representatives, and the many people I met attending events, who are what make these events fun. I must thank the staff at National Book Network, who have been incredibly patient and helpful, in particular Miriam Bass and Vicki Metzger. Roger Migdow has made it possible for me to get through the difficulties of both writing and publishing. And Chuck Thompson has been the rock upon which Greenline has rested—there could not have been a person more responsible or effective to work with, or one from whom I could have learned so much about writing. There would be no second edition if there hadn't been a first edition, and there would not have been a first edition without the support of James Marti and Mitch Rofsky.

Credits

Editor	Chuck Thompson
Managing Editor	Kristin Poss
Book Design	DeVa Communications
Production	Yalitza Ferreras, Samia Afra
Research and Administration	Roger Migdow, Vene Franco, Harry Um, Diane Weipert, Kurt Wolff, and Paul Zemanek

Table of Contents

The Fun Seeker's North America Destinations .... Inside Front Cover
North America Map 7
Introduction 8
How to Use This Book 10

Destinations in the United States	Events	Map #	Page
Scottsdale (Phoenix), Arizona	*Phoenix Open*	A01	14
Los Angeles, California	*Academy Awards Weekend*	A02	18
Napa Valley (St. Helena), California	*Napa Valley Wine Auction*	A03	22
San Diego, California	*Street Scene*	A04	26
San Francisco, California	*Black and White Ball*	A05	30
San Francisco, California	*Exotic Erotic Ball/Halloween*	A05	34
Aspen, Colorado	*Ski: Aspen*	A07	38
Washington, D.C.	*Inauguration*	A08	42
Daytona Beach (Orlando), Florida	*Bike Week*	A09	46
Key West, Florida	*Fantasy Fest*	A10	50
Lake Buena Vista, Florida	*Do: Disney World*	A11	54
Miami, Florida	*Cruise: Carnival Victory*	A12	58
Miami (Miami Beach), Florida	*Calle Ocho*	A12	62
Tampa, Florida	*Gasparilla*	A14	66
Savannah, Georgia	*St. Patrick's Day Celebration*	A15	70
Honolulu, Hawaii	*Aloha Festival*	A16	74
Chicago, Illinois	*Taste of Chicago*	A17	78
Indianapolis, Indiana	*Indy 500*	A18	82
Louisville, Kentucky	*Kentucky Derby*	A19	86
New Orleans, Louisiana	*Mardi Gras*	A20	90
New Orleans, Louisiana	*New Orleans Jazz & Heritage Festival*	A20	94
Baltimore, Maryland	*Preakness*	A22	96
Boston, Massachusetts	*Boston Harborfest*	A23	100
Detroit, Michigan	*Detroit Auto Show*	A24	104
Black Rock City, Nevada	*Burning Man*	A25	108
Las Vegas, Nevada	*Las Vegas Rodeo*	A26	112
A Whale of a Good Time	JUNO: About Gambling		115
Las Vegas, Nevada	*Super Bowl Weekend*	A26	116
Albuquerque, New Mexico	*Balloon Fiesta*	A28	120
Santa Fe, New Mexico	*Fiesta de Santa Fe*	A29	124
New York, New York	*New Year's Eve New York*	A30	128
Cincinnati, Ohio	*Oktoberfest-Zinzinnati*	A31	132
Philadelphia, Pennsylvania	*Fourth of July*	A32	136
Charleston, South Carolina	*Spoleto*	A33	140
Memphis, Tennessee	*Memphis in May Barbecue*	A34	144
Nashville, Tennessee	*Country Music Fan Fair*	A35	148
Austin (Dallas/Ft. Worth), Texas	*South by Southwest*	A36	152
Galveston (Houston), Texas	*Dickens on the Strand*	A37	156
San Antonio, Texas	*Fiesta San Antonio*	A38	160
Park City, Utah	*Sundance Film Festival*	A39	164

(cont.)

Destinations in the United States (cont.)	Events	Map #	Page
Seattle, Washington	*Bumbershoot*	A40	168
Milwaukee, Wisconsin	*Summerfest*	A41	172
Cheyenne, Wyoming	*Cheyenne Frontier Days*	A42	176
Two Much Fun			180

Destinations in Canada — 181

Calgary, Alberta	*Calgary Stampede*	A43	182
Montréal, Québec	*Montréal Jazz Festival*	A44	186
Québec City, Québec	*Québec Winter Carnaval*	· A45	190
Toronto, Ontario	*Caribana*	A46	194

Destinations in Mexico — 198

Acapulco, Guerrero	*Party: Acapulco*	A47	199
Aguascalientes, Aguáscalientes	*Feria de San Marcos*	A48	202

JUNOs (More Fun Things) — 206

G-Wiz, You Call This Fun?	About Amusement Parks	207
More Barbecue To Chew On	About Barbecue	208
Running of the Bowls	About Bowl (Football) Games	209
Start Your Engines	About Car Racing	210
Living Fantasies	About Fantasy Camps	212
If It's Tuesday It Must Be Alligator Lasagna ...	About Food Festivals	213
Real Swingers	About Golf	216
All That Jazz	About Jazz Festivals	218
Larger Than Life	About Movies, Giant Screen	· 220
See And Be Seen	About Parades	221
Meet Me At The Fair	About State Fairs	222
Beautiful People	About Supermodels	223
High Times	About Tall Buildings	224
Christmas Nuts	About The Nutcracker Ballet	225
Tourist Boards		226

The Fun Seeker's Gold List (FSG) — 227

Making the Fun Seeker's Gold List	228
The Fun Seeker's Gold List	230
FSG: The Mating Rating	240
The Fun Seeker's Gold List Travel Planner: Travel Dates and Ratings	242
The Fun Seeker's Gold List 2003 Calendar	247
The Fun Seeker's Gold List 2004 Calendar	248
The Fun Seeker's International Destinations	250
The Fun Seeker's International Maps	251
FSG: Changes Since 2000	252
Index	253
About the Author	255
The Fun Seeker's North America Events	Inside Back Cover

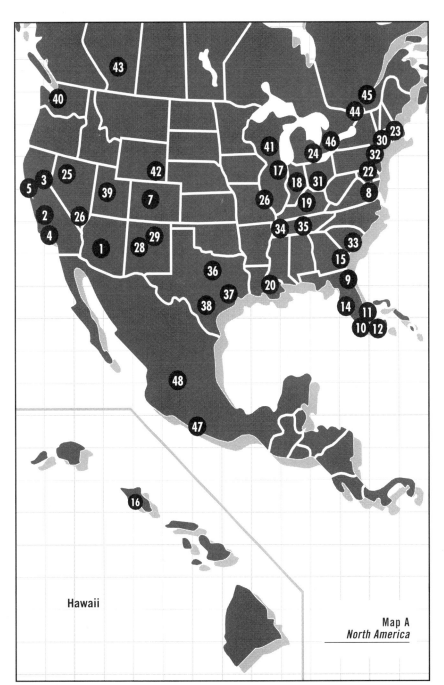

Hawaii

Map A
North America

Introduction

More than a few years ago, while enjoying the beauty and quietude of Point Reyes National Seashore, just outside of San Francisco, I realized I was ready for a change. Rather than escaping and communing with nature, I wanted to commune with people. Lots of people. I felt a need to inject some excitement into my routine and it became apparent that one thing was missing from my life—fun!

I reflected on all the fine meals I'd eaten at great restaurants. (San Francisco is a lot of things, but maybe a great eating city most of all.) Rather than focusing on food and conversation, I now wanted a different kind of stimulation—the buzz of animated, downright noisy people, spectacular surroundings and nights on the town that ended with the sunrise, not *The Tonight Show*. I wanted to be in places where and when people came together to have the most fun times of their lives. My thoughts naturally turned to travel, which has been in my blood since childhood. Could my lust for new experiences be satisfied if I chose not another beautiful beach or mountain, but some of the wild festivals around the world I'd often heard about?

My search for fun began in the travel sections of local bookstores. Skimming through the pages, I quickly realized that, beyond insubstantial one-line references to events in various guide books, a reliable, comprehensive source of information for fun events simply didn't exist. As an avid reader of travel magazines I knew that the multitude of available lists of events make no critical distinctions between, say, a potato festival in North Dakota and *La Tomatina* (the incredible tomato-throwing festival in Spain). According to *Event Business News*, there are more than 45,000 annual events just in the United States! But how are you supposed to know which are the best?

Even tourist boards were of little help. Call the Dutch tourist board and ask about the most fun time to go to Amsterdam—"We're not interested in promoting fun, we promote tulips." That was the point at which the need for this book became apparent.

The opening scene of *City Slickers*, in which Billy Crystal gets chased by the bulls, led me to Pamplona, Spain, for my first event, one which subsequently gave birth to this book and **The Fun Also Rises** travel series. (The name is derived from Ernest Hemingway's *The Sun Also Rises*, a book that helped popularize what has become perhaps the most thrilling party on earth—Pamplona's Fiesta de San Fermín, also known as the Running of the Bulls.) However, it might not have been such a spectacular, life-changing experience without a bit of luck. Every guide book on Spain, even the Spanish Tourist Office, listed the beginning of the event as July 7. I arrived in Pamplona on the 6th. While waiting for a taxi at the airport, another traveler told me to skip checking into the hotel and hurry to the town square. It turns out the event actually kicks off at noon on the day *before* the running of the first bulls. What's more, it's one of the most incredible moments one can ever experience!

That moment—one I could easily have missed—highlighted how important it would be for me to diligently research and accurately inform readers about the many unseen details that, if planned right, can turn good experiences into unforgettable ones. To get the maximum from each event, travelers need to know how to *be in the right place at the right time*. Thus was born *The Fun Seeker's Gold List* (the world's most fun events), my selection of the best travel dates, and the day-by-day itineraries found in this book.

Since the Running of the Bulls, I've been to more than 140 annual events around the world, immersing myself in the experiences, but also assessing the various elements that make something "fun." Of course, everybody has some idea of what constitutes fun. But ask them to describe it or define it and, as with pornography, you end up with a Supreme Court interpretation: You'll know it when you see it. Well, I did see it—fun, that is—at its best.

Whereas Pamplona is a twenty-four-hour party, most events are not. This meant that I had to search out other necessary components to complete the fun seeker's package—hot restaurants, the best hotels (in the most convenient locations), top sightseeing opportunities and, maybe most importantly, the best nightlife. Say what you will—looking for fun is hard work. Showing up at a club in Madrid at 2 a.m. and being told to come back at 4 a.m. when it fills up isn't easy when you've got a museum scheduled for that morning. Perhaps that's why most travel publications virtually ignore the most fun part of the day—night! Despite the fact that there are millions of single people over 30, ask a concierge for advice on where to meet singles, and it's likely you'll be directed to a Hard Rock Cafe (or if you look as old as I do, to a strip club). *Zagat* doesn't even have a "fun" category. My perseverance paid off with the simple, up-to-date catalog of only the best each destination had to offer—what I now call the *Hot Sheet*.

My goal has been to choose events that can be enjoyed comfortably and appeal to a broad range of interests, while not requiring one to be an aficionado of any-

My job has simply been to improve your chances of having fun.

thing. After all, if you're a tennis fan, going to Wimbledon would be your idea of heaven. But if your primary interest is fun, not tennis, would you rather watch two guys whacking a ball back and forth, or grind to calypso music with beautiful, costumed people in Barbados? To encourage you to go to Barbados, or Burning Man, or Frontier Days in Cheyenne, I've done everything possible—with tips, ticket information, detailed itineraries, *Hot Sheets*—to remove the intimidation factors from attending big-time or unusual events.

I've made the itineraries concise, the information easy to find; but you won't meet my criteria for fun just by reading the book. You've got to participate, smile, laugh and move some of your body parts—you've got to go. Even preparing for events is a lot of fun. My companion and I took Viennese waltz lessons to get ready for the Vienna Opera Ball. We outfitted ourselves in Wrangler jeans and Stetsons and learned the two-step for the Las Vegas Rodeo; and for the Exotic Erotic Ball in San Francisco, well ...

While it is often true that life draws meaning from its journeys, not its destinations, *fun seekers* also know the importance of being in the right place at the right time. My job has simply been to improve your chances of having fun. It's up to you to break out of the ordinary, ignore the accepted. And if I've been successful, **The Fun Seeker's North America** will help you experience the world in the sensuous flashes of color, light, sound, flavor and motion that describe some of the best moments of life.

—Alan S. Davis
San Francisco, January 2003

How to Use this Book

These chapters describe the 48 North America events and destinations on the *Fun Seeker's Gold List (FSG)*. To help you choose an event we've also provided the following:

- **The Fun Seeker's Gold List** (page 230), alphabetical by event, allows you to quickly see the details about all 96 events: key month; weather; events to go to on U.S. holidays; ratings; event type; and even what to wear (to get a sense of the event style).

- To find an event appropriate for a particular date (a birthday or anniversary celebration, your vacation, or holidays), The *Fun Seeker's Gold List Travel Planner* (page 242) has exact dates for each year. See also the *FSG Calendars* (page 247)

In addition you can find:
- **North America Cities**, alphabetical by rating (inside front cover) with map (page 7)

- **North America Events**, alphabetical by rating (inside back cover)

- **FSG Mating Rating** (for singles), events by mating rating (page 240)

- **International Cities**, alphabetical by country (page 250) with maps (page 251)

The Key to the Chapters

1. Popular name of event

2. Official or secondary name, if applicable

3. Event location (if chapter includes a city in addition to the event destination it will be indicated in parentheses)

4. State (or country for Canada and Mexico)

5. The month(s) to go to the event/destination

6. Ratings, one- to five-star for the event

7. Mating rating

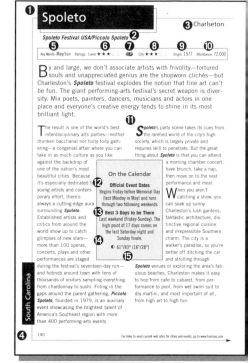

8. Ratings, one- to five-star for the city

9. First year of event

10. Most recent attendance figures

11. Explanation of event and overview of destination

12. How official event dates are determined (for exact dates each year see The Fun Seeker's Gold List Travel Planner, page 242)

13. The day/dates that are the absolute best three days to go, and the reason chosen

14. Other Times To Go, if applicable, describes another major event in the same destination

15. Average high and low temperatures during event in Fahrenheit (and Celsius)

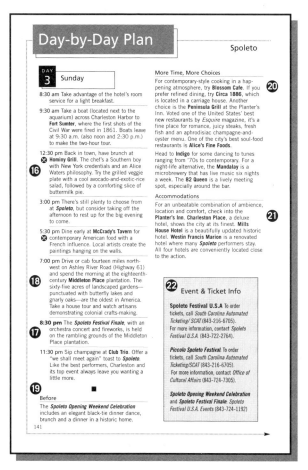

Day-by-Day Plan

Spoleto

DAY 3 Sunday

8:30 am Take advantage of the hotel's room service for a light breakfast.

9:30 am Take a boat (located next to the aquarium) across Charleston Harbor to **Fort Sumter**, where the first shots of the Civil War were fired in 1861. Boats leave at 9:30 a.m. (also noon and 2:30 p.m.) to make the two-hour tour.

12:30 pm Back in town, have brunch at **Hominy Grill**. The chef's a Southern boy with New York credentials and an Alice Waters philosophy. Try the grilled veggie plate with a cool avocado-and-exotic-rice salad, followed by a comforting slice of buttermilk pie.

3:00 pm There's still plenty to choose from at *Spoleto*, but consider taking off the afternoon to rest up for the big evening to come.

5:30 pm Dine early at **McCrady's Tavern** for contemporary American food with a French influence. Local artists create the paintings hanging on the walls.

7:00 pm Drive or cab fourteen miles northwest on Ashley River Road (Highway 61) and spend the morning at the eighteenth-century **Middleton Place** plantation. The sixty-five acres of landscaped gardens—punctuated with butterfly lakes and gnarly oaks—are the oldest in America. Take a house tour and watch artisans demonstrating colonial crafts-making.

8:30 pm The *Spoleto Festival Finale*, with an orchestra concert and fireworks, is held on the rambling grounds of the Middleton Place plantation.

11:30 pm Sip champagne at **Club Trio**. Offer a "we shall meet again" toast to *Spoleto*. Like the best parties, Charleston and its top event always leave you wanting a little more.

■

Before

The *Spoleto Opening Weekend Celebration* includes an elegant black-tie dinner dance, brunch and a dinner in a historic home.

141

More Time, More Choices

For contemporary-style cooking in a happening atmosphere, try **Blossom Cafe**. If you prefer refined dining, try **Circa 1886**, which is located in a carriage house. Another choice is the **Peninsula Grill** at the Planter's Inn. Voted one of the United States' best new restaurants by *Esquire* magazine, it's a fine place for romance, juicy steaks, fresh fish and an aphrodisiac champagne-and-oyster menu. One of the city's best soul-food restaurants is **Alice's Fine Foods**.

Head to **Indigo** for some dancing to tunes ranging from '70s to contemporary. For a night-life alternative, the **Mandalay** is a microbrewery that has live music six nights a week. The **82 Queen** is a lively meeting spot, especially around the bar.

Accommodations

For an unbeatable combination of ambience, location and comfort, check into the **Planter's Inn. Charleston Place**, a deluxe hotel, shows the city at its finest. **Mills House Hotel** is a beautifully updated historic hotel. **Westin Francis Marion** is a renovated hotel where many *Spoleto* performers stay. All four hotels are conveniently located close to the action.

Event & Ticket Info

Spoleto Festival U.S.A To order tickets, call *South Carolina Automated Ticketing/ SCAT* (843-216-6705). For more information, contact *Spoleto Festival U.S.A.* (843-722-2764).

Piccolo Spoleto Festival: To order tickets, call *South Carolina Automated Ticketing/SCAT* (843-216-6705). For more information, contact *Office of Cultural Affairs* (843-724-7305).

Spoleto Opening Weekend Celebration and *Spoleto Festival Finale: Spoleto Festival U.S.A. Events* (843-724-1192)

About the Day-by-Day Plan

Day-by-day plans usually run Thursday through Saturday (when destinations are most lively) unless the high points of an event justify being there on a different days. The itinerary typically begins after breakfast on Day One and ends when nightclubs close on Day Three.

The Key to the Day-by-Day Plan

16. ❌ Indicates the itinerary's meal times

17. Bold times and bold-faced, italicized entries highlight an official activity connected to the event

18. Bold-faced recommendations for where to eat and what to do (more detailed information, such as phone numbers, addresses and price guides, can be found in the Hot Sheet at the end of the chapter)

19. Noteworthy happenings before or after the three days we've selected

20. Bold-faced recommendations for alternative places to eat and things to do that didn't fit into the itinerary

21. Hotel recommendations

22. Detailed information, such as phone numbers, addresses and prices (CD indicates a charitable donation included) for main events (bold-faced) and subevents (bold-faced italic)

About the Hot Sheet Selections

Hotels – When available, only hotels equal to U.S.-standard first-class or deluxe hotels are selected. These hotels should, in priority order: fit in with the events (convenient location to recommended events is important); be hip or classy but not stuffy; and capture the character of each city.

Restaurants – The food must be good, but ambience is as important as the meal. Otherwise, the criteria are the same as for hotels.

Nightlife – The bars, nightclubs and entertainment (generally excluding the performing arts) are the hottest places for the over-30 crowd. The bias is toward Scotch over beer, classy over funky.

Sightseeing – These indicate the best each destination has to offer, but shy away from zoos, natural-history museums, botanical gardens and shopping destinations (there's no time for shopping) unless they are unique.

The Key to the Hot Sheets

23. Numbers indicating the day on which a corresponding description can be found in the itinerary. "A" indicates alternatives in the *More Time, More Choices* section

24. Prices for each hotel's best nonsuite double room during each event: $, Up to $100; $$, $100-$200; $$$, $200-$300; $$$$, $300-$400; $$$$+, More than $400

25. Rms, indicating number of rooms in each hotel

26. Best Rooms, indicating rooms to request when making reservations

27. Restaurant prices indicating average cost of one entree for the recommended meal (Cover and Entry Fee indicate prices at nightspots and attractions): $, Up to $10; $$, $10-$20; $$$, $20-$30; $$$$, $30-$40; $$$$+, More than $40

28. Rec, indicating the recommended meal in the itinerary at each restaurant followed by other suggested meals, if applicable:
    B – Breakfast; L – Lunch; D – Dinner;
    T – High tea or snack

29. Food, indicating each restaurant's cuisine

30. Rec, indicating the scene at nightspots:
    M – Live music; P – Party atmosphere or dancing;
    S – Show; R – Bar only; (F) – Food available

31. Type of music featured at nightspot

32. Convention and Visitors Bureau (CVB) information

33. Local time relative to New York City

34. Local airport name, three-letter airport code and approximate time and taxi fare from the airport to our recommended hotel, rounded up to nearest $5

35. Recommendation on whether or not to rent a car: Yes, No, or Yes/No (could go either way)

36. Map code refers to North America Map on page 7

*In 1995 I began a journey to determine the world's 100 most fun places to be at the right time (**The Fun Seeker's Gold List**). Of the 96 events and destinations that every fun seeker should experience (yes, there's more work to be done!) 42 are in the United States. Read on ... have fun!*

Events and Destinations in the
United States

Phoenix Open

Scottsdale (Phoenix)

Key Month: Jan	Ratings: Event ★★★☆☆ **V** City ★★★☆☆ Origin: 1932 Attendance: 470,000

"They had a party—and a golf tourney broke out!" That's how the organizers of the world's most well-attended golf tournament, the **Phoenix Open**, explain its origins. You don't need to know your way around a nine-iron at this seven-day fiesta, because the **Phoenix Open**'s main appeal is its status as the best party this side of a golf course. It's the only Professional Golf Association (PGA) tournament big enough to compete with the Super Bowl for an audience.

Golf isn't the only game being played at the Stadium Course of the Tournament Player's Club of Scottsdale. The PGA circuit's VIP and party tents are infamous for their "meet market" appeal, conducive to both sightseers and more interactive thrill-seekers. The best places to watch and be watched are the sixteenth hole, where up to 20,000 fans gather daily, and the **Birds Nest**, a party tent with a capacity of 8,000, plentiful beverages and live music.

There's more than enough to keep you occupied at the **Phoenix Open**, but beyond the greens, the Valley of the Sun offers everything from swank cigar bars to no-apologies honky-tonks, fresh sashimi to scorching Mexican cuisine and spectacular desert scenery. Phoenix, Arizona's capital, is the sixth-largest city in the United States with 1.2 million residents (and still growing steadily), many of them transplants from America's Cold Belt. With Arizona State University in adjacent Tempe, Phoenix maintains a youthful feel. In fact, the bulk of the area's nightlife isn't in Phoenix at all—it's concentrated either around Tempe or Scottsdale. The latter is an upscale burb that's also known as Snottsdale to the locals, but don't worry about reputations. Even the locals descend on Old Town Scottsdale to take advantage of the great restaurants and bars.

There couldn't be a more appropriate venue for attending a golf tournament. With more than 140 golf courses, the region is considered to be the golf capital of the world. In fact, for many people who come to Phoenix, not spending a few days on the links would be like going to Italy and not eating pasta. But you don't have to be a golfer to enjoy the Phoenix Open—you don't even have to like golf, for that matter—because three days of fun in the sun will no doubt suit you to a tee.

(For more on golf, see page 216.)

Excluding some shopping and restaurant areas, attractions in the Phoenix area are spread out and blocks are long. Unless otherwise noted, plan to drive between each itinerary destination.

On the Calendar

Official Event Dates

Three practice and four tournament days, ending on Super Bowl weekend

Best 3 Days To Be There

Wednesday-Friday. The Celebrity Round on Wednesday is golf as fun. The partying on Thursday and Friday beats watching the final rounds.

☾ 43°/65° (6°/18°)

Arizona

DAY 1 — Wednesday

10:00 am Get acquainted with the magnificent Sonoran Desert with a visit to Papago Park's **Desert Botanical Garden**, the world's most extensive collection of arid-land plants with beautiful displays of cactus, wildflowers and desert trees.

Noon Drive to the Royal Palms Resort for lunch at **T. Cooks**. Request one of the tables at the back of the restaurant for gorgeous views of the Camelback Mountains. Keep an eye out for celebrity diners while you enjoy the ambience of Old World elegance and New World sophistication.

1:30 pm The pros teed off long before breakfast, but afternoon is the best time to catch golf action on the course and extracurricular action in the beer tents. The largest party is around the sixteenth hole, a short par-three where thousands hang around the huge grandstand waiting for holes-in-one. (Tiger Woods hit one here in the 1996 Phoenix Open.) The highly animated crowd is not what you'd usually expect to see at a professional golf tournament, but most of the tour players enjoy the enthusiasm as much as the spectators.

5:00 pm The *Birds Nest* was moved away from the golf course to Westworld (a short shuttle ride) because "course marshals kept unplugging our amps." But it's still the venue for one of the best parties on the planet.

7:30 pm Enjoy a leisurely dinner at the Scottsdale Princess' **La Hacienda**, an elegant ranchero with all the charms of Old Mexico—even strolling mariachis. Another option is **Roaring Fork**, a meat and fowl American West hangout with a casual but decent bar scene.

9:00 pm With two-steppin' boots on, head out on the town for a night of Arizona culture. In Scottsdale, stop at the **Handlebar J** for a high-end honky-tonk with a fun-loving Western atmosphere.

DAY 2 — Thursday

7:00 am For the ideal perspective of the Sonoran landscape, enjoy the Valley of the Sun's perfect winter weather with a sunrise balloon ride with **Hot Air Expeditions, Inc.** Coming back down to earth means a ceremony of induction into the ballooning society and a champagne breakfast.

8:30 am If 7 a.m. is too early for you, make a reservation with **Cave Creek Outfitters** for an early-morning horseback ride through nearby canyons and mountains. Relive the legends of cowboys and Indians and soldiers and outlaws as your guide recounts the history of the desert.

Noon Drive to Phoenix for lunch at **RoxSand**, which has a hip environment with transcontinental flair.

2:00 pm The galleries and courtyards of the **Heard Museum** feature dramatic collections of prehistoric, ancient and contemporary Hohokam, Apache, Hopi and Navajo art. Be sure to see the world-famous Kachina Doll Gallery.

3:30 pm The **Phoenix Art Museum** displays Asian, European and Latin American art, as well as an excellent collection of Western art. The nearby sports arenas and new buildings are part of a 1990s downtown reclamation project that has been one of the most successful in the country.

5:00 pm If you're not rushing back to the *Birds Nest*, unwind with a cocktail at **The Merc Bar**, a sophisticated retreat where the beautiful people go to be with each other.

7:30 pm Return to Scottsdale for dinner at **P.F. Chang's China Bistro**, a popular spot that almost always has a line out the door. Call a half hour in advance to avoid a long wait. A hotel restaurant option is the Sanctuary Camelback mountain's **elements**, which along with Asian influences in food and décor offers a community table for a shared dining experience. Before or after, enjoy the restaurant's **jade bar**.

10:00 pm Continue your evening on the town at **Axis**, where jazz is served in a supperclub atmosphere. Adjacent is **Radius**, where funk lures the dress-to-kill crowd.

DAY 3 — Friday

9:00 am After breakfast, visit Frank Lloyd Wright's famous architecture school, **Taliesin West**.

11:00 am Be back in Scottsdale in time for a stroll through Old Town, where you may get sidetracked by the extensive up-market shopping.

Noon At **Old Town Tortilla Factory**, get a ✪ head start on margaritas—choose from more than eighty tequilas—and great Mexican food.

1:30 pm Head back to the TPC Stadium Course. Several spots allow you to view driving tees and putting greens simultaneously, but most spectators hang out in beer tents or on the lawns, soaking in liquids, sunshine and intoxicating views of the opposite sex sporting desert tans in midwinter. It's the second day of the tournament, with two more days to go, so most of the excitement centers around the desperation of the still-date-less denizens.

6:00 pm Be sure to get to the *Birds Nest* by this time. Otherwise, it may be too crowded to gain admission. Drinks, conversation and lots of golfing stories and ✪ jokes flow until 11 p.m., so snack food will have to suffice for dinner.

10:00 pm Leave the nest for additional nourishment and partying. The hefty cover is worth the experience at the huge **Cajun House** in Old Town Scottsdale. You'll feel as if you've been transported to New Orleans' Bourbon Street, complete with theme bars and live music. If you prefer something more hip, a lounging option is **Six**.

■

Before and After
Tuesday's draw is the invitation-only dinner, but during the day there's the Shoot-Out, where pros bond with celebs in a ten-team, nine-hole contest. There'll be plenty of birdies in the final rounds of the tourney on Saturday and Sunday, not to mention in the *Birds Nest* Saturday night.

More Time, More Choices
Breakfast on eggs with French toast stuffed with orange marmalade and cream cheese at **Mimi's Café**. For a quiet evening, drive to **Mary Elaine's** for gourmet continental cuisine in a formal setting. Also gourmet, but with an Asian-inspired flair, is **Restaurant Hapa**. A trendy option with a party atmosphere, is **Roy's**, a Hawaiian-chain transplant specializing in Pacific Rim cuisine. **Harris'** steak house consistently receives superb reviews.

The Famous Door has a supper-club ambience. At **Marco Polo Supper Club**, Italy meets the Orient. **Barmouche** has earned a reputation as a great meeting place. The four rooms at **Sanctuary** (not the hotel)—including Voodoo and Moroccan—have made it an area dance favorite. There's usually a good crowd at **Madison's**.

Accommodations
The two new kids on the block are probably as good as it gets in Scottsdale: the very zen-cool **Sanctuary**, and the desert classic **Four Seasons Resort Scottsdale**. As the official home to the Phoenix Open's TPC Stadium Course, the **Fairmont Scottsdale Princess Resort** is in the heart of the action. It offers luxurious accommodations amid breathtaking desert surroundings. The **Hyatt Regency Scottsdale at Gainey Ranch** has ten interconnecting pools, golf and a spa.

Event & Ticket Info

Phoenix Open (Tournament Players Club, Scottsdale Princess Resort): Admission: $20 at *TPC* (480-585-4334), or in advance from *Ticketmaster* (480-784-4444). Golf enthusiasts may prefer more elaborate packages, starting at $150. For more information, contact the *Thunderbirds* (602-870-4431).

Birds Nest (Westworld, one mile east of the TPC): Admission is $10 at the door, or in advance from *Ticketmaster* (480-585-4334). VIP tickets at $150 is also available. For more information and tickets call 602-843-6378.

Scottsdale (Phoenix)

Hotels	Phone	Address	Price	Fax	Rooms/Best
Fairmont Scottsdale Princess Resort	480-585-4848 800-257-7544	7575 E. Princess Dr.	$$$$+	480-585-0086	650/A casita
Four Seasons Resort Scottsdale	480-515-5700 800-819-5053	10600 East Crescent Mood Dr.	$$$$+	480-515-5599	210/Premium casita w/vw of valley and pool
Hyatt Regency Scottsdale at Gainey Ranch	480-991-3388 800-223-1234	7500 E. Doubletree Ranch Rd.	$$$$+	480-483-5550	493/Back of hotel w/vw of resort or mtns
Sanctuary Camelback Mountain	480-948-2100 480-483-7314	5700 E. McDonald Dr.	$$$$+		98/Deluxe mountainside casita

Restaurants	Day	Phone	Address	Price	Rec	Food
elements	2	480-948-2100	5700 E. McDonald Dr.	$$$	D	New American w/Asian accent
Harris'	A	480-508-8888	3101 E. Camelback Rd.	$$	D	Steakhouse, continental
La Hacienda	1	480-585-4848	7575 E. Princess Dr.	$$$	D	Mexican
Mary Elaine's	A	602-941-8200	6000 Camelback mountain (The Phoenician)	$$$	D	Continental
Mimi's Cafe	A	602-451-6763	8980 E. Shea Blvd.	$	B/LD	American diner
Old Town Tortilla Factory	3	480-945-4567	6910 E. Main St.	$	L/D	Mexican, Native American
P.F. Chang's China Bistro	2	480-949-2610	7014 E. Camelback Rd.	$$	D/L	Chinese
Restaurant Hapa	A	602-941-8200	6204 N. Scottsdale Rd.	$$$	D	Fusion
Roaring Fork	1	480-947-0795	4800 N. Scottsdale Rd.	$$	D	American
RoxSand	2	602-381-0444	2594 E. Camelback Rd.	$$	L/D	Transcontinental, fusion
Roy's	A	480-905-1155	7001 N. Scottsdale	$$$	D	Pacific Rim
T. Cooks	1	602-808-0766	5200 E. Camelback Rd.	$	L/BD	Rustic Mediterranean

Nightlife	Day	Phone	Address	Cover	Rec*	Music
Axis/Radius	2	480-970-1112	7340 E. Indian Plaza	$	M(F)	Jazz, '80s, techno
Barmouche	A	603-956-6900	3131 E. Camelback Rd.	None	R(F)	
Cajun House	3	480-945-5150	7117 E. 3rd Ave.	Varies	P(F)	Varies
The Famous Door	A	480-970-1945	7419 E. Indian Plaza	None	M	Jazz
Handlebar J	1	480-948-0110	7116 E. Becker Lane	$	MP(F)	Country, rock
jade bar	2	480-948-2100	5700 E. McDonald Dr.	None	R	
Madison's	A	480-949-8453	7108 E. Stetson	None	M(F)	Varies
Marco Polo Supper Club	A	480-483-1900	8608 E. Shea Blvd.	None	M(F)	Classics, contemporary
The Merc Bar	2	602-508-9449	2501 E. Camelback Rd.	None	R(F)	
Sanctuary	A	480-970-5000	7340 E. Shoeman Ln.	$	P(F)	Techno, hip hop
Six	A	480-663-6620	7316 E. Stetson Dr.	None	R(F)	Varies

* M=Live music; P=Dancing (Party); R=Bar only; S=Show; (F)=Food served. For further explanation of codes, page 12.

Sights & Attractions	Day	Phone	Address	Entry Fee
Cave Creek Outfitters	2	480-471-4635	31313 N. 144th St.	$$$$+
Desert Botanical Garden	1	480-941-1217	1201 N. Galvin Pkwy.	$
Heard Museum	2	602-252-8840	2301 N. Central Ave.	$
Hot Air Expeditions, Inc.	2	480-502-6999	7500 E. Butherus Dr., Ste. F	$$$$+
Phoenix Art Museum	2	602-257-1222	1625 N. Central Ave.	$
Taliesin West	3	480-860-8810	12621 N. Frank Lloyd Wright Blvd.	$$

Greater Phoenix CVB	602-254-6500	400 E. Van Buren, Ste. 600

Scottsdale area code: 480   Phoenix area code: 602

 NYC -2   Phoenix Sky Harbor (PHX) <30 min./$20   Yes   Map Code: A01

Arizona

Academy Awards Weekend

Los Angeles

Key Month: Feb/Mar   Ratings: Event ★ ★ ☆ ☆ ☆   City ★ ★ ★ ★ ★   Origin: 1929   Attendance: n/a

Whether you consider action, romance, comedy or adventure the most fun, you can always count on Hollywood to deliver a damn good show. And the show it puts on for itself—the *Academy Awards*—grabs the attention of the entire world. With film-industry luminaries, screen superstars and major media clamoring about, Hollywood in springtime is the destination for glitzy partying and world-class glamour.

Even celebrities who normally avoid Los Angeles like the plague swarm into town for the February ceremonies. Star sightings are never more frequent—you may find one sitting next to you at lunch or strolling on Rodeo Drive, the shopping street that epitomizes luxury. Everyone within six degrees of separation from Tinseltown dons their finest, making the weekend a celebration of beauty and fashion, as well as cinema. The *Oscars*-night parade of stars—a two-hour procession of filmdom's biggest names arriving at the show—rivals the Milky Way for sheer star power.

If you're lucky enough to score a pass into the Kodak Theater, you might witness a bizarre, pop-culture acceptance speech that will endure for decades—such as Sally Fields' "You like me, you really like me!" moment of self-affirmation, or James Cameron's unseemly "I'm the king of the world!" outburst. And though getting into after-show parties such as the *Vanity Fair* bash or Elton John's annual shindig requires extraordinary finesse, the surrounding scene is still a first-class tourist attraction.

On the Calendar

Official Event Dates
Last Sunday of February

Best 3 Days To Be There
Friday-Sunday. Catch the weekend and awards day in a very hot L.A.

☾ 49°/69° (9°/21°)

Los Angeles is a city, county and geopolitically confusing place. Beverly Hills, Burbank and Santa Monica, places that people associate with L.A., are independent cities within the vast county. But along with the smog and road rage of the valley, they help create its indelible image.

Musts among the city's movie-related attractions include the campy Mann's Chinese Theatre and Universal Studios, where you can tour movie sets. Beyond Hollywood glitter, the billion-dollar Getty Museum is the brightest star in the cultural firmament, with its vast holdings housed in a hilltop complex. The area boasts the largest collection of ultrahip restaurants and nightlife in the world. Though tickets to the *Academy Awards* come by invitation only and the cost of scalped seats runs into the thousands of dollars, February is still a blockbuster time to be in Southern California to celebrate the magic of cinema and its celluloid Eden of Hollywood.

For links to most current web sites for cities and events, go to www.funrises.com

Academy Awards Weekend

Day-by-Day Plan

Friday

9:00 am On the other side of attitude is the Farmer's Market (Fairfax and 3rd Street), a series of food shops and small restaurants. Breakfast at **DuPar's Restaurant and Bakery** is a must.

11:00 am Thirty minutes away, the pristine **J. Paul Getty Museum** contains a huge collection of master paintings, but the main attractions are the architecture and grounds. To park, you need reservations two weeks in advance. Take a cab and get there early.

1:00 pm Backtrack a bit to the **Ivy** for lunch. This pioneer of California cuisine is a meeting place for film-industry insiders.

3:00 pm Drive thirty minutes to Santa Monica and the Santa Monica Pier (at the end of Colorado Avenue). The pier offers sweeping views of the coast, as well as cotton candy and a giant carousel. Continue north on the legendary Pacific Coast Highway to Malibu, where the Santa Monica Mountains meet the Pacific Ocean in a series of dramatic bluffs and many Hollywood types seek weekend refuge.

6:00 pm Stop at the bar of the gorgeous **Casa del Mar**, just blocks south of the Santa Monica Pier. The buzz in the lobby bar sets the stage for cocktails and a view of the sunset.

7:30 pm Santa Monica's ultrachic **Chinois-on-Main** is a blend of East and West, with a Sino-French menu and décor combining European and Asian elements.

9:30 pm Third Street Promenade is a great people-watching hangout. Plant yourself at one of a number of restaurants/bars within its pedestrian zone.

11:30 pm Join celebrities back in Beverly Hills. The popular **Conga Room** showcases big-name Latin acts for a slightly younger crowd. Or you might want to try getting into **Beauty Bar**, with décor a la '60s hair salon.

Saturday

9:30 am For brunch and star-gazing, you can't beat the chic **Campanile**. Friendly servers bring wonderful pastries in a covered courtyard with Moroccan accents.

11:00 am Attracting the sportiest cars and dressiest crowds, Rodeo Drive is the shopping mecca to America's rich.

1:00 pm Go for Mediterranean-influenced cuisine on the large patio at **Le Petit Four**, where pretty people and young starlets gather.

2:30 pm Ten minutes away, **Mann's Chinese Theatre** is an essential stop. The theater resembles an opulent Asian palace. The sidewalk out front, known as the Hollywood Walk of Fame, is covered with plaques commemorating hundreds of entertainment-biz greats. Squeeze in a visit to the **Frederick's of Hollywood** flagship store, which includes a fun museum of bras and other intimate apparel.

4:00 pm You might enjoy a stop at the West Coast branch of the **Museum of TV & Radio**. View an exhibit or an old tape of your favorite television show.

7:30 pm Dress stylishly and drive to **Spago Beverly Hills**. The original one rocketed chef Wolfgang Puck to stardom and put California cuisine on the epicurean palette, but the real reason to go is the Hollywood A-list clientele.

9:30 pm After dinner, stroll to **Le Dome**. The round bar has served many celebrities at post-Oscars parties. An alternative would be a visit to the **House of Blues** with its fun and intimate showroom setting.

11:00 pm By now the **Garden of Eden** should be packed with beautiful creatures. You won't see the Tree of Knowledge, but there's plenty of forbidden fruit on display, especially on the crowded dance floor that thumps with house music.

Day-by-Day Plan

DAY 3 — Sunday

9:00 am Breakfast on **The Argyle's** terrace ✖ before driving to **Universal Studios**. Take the tram tour of some of Hollywood's artful illusions. You'll pass the miniature lagoon where a new and improved Jaws attacks a fisherman. Don't miss the exploding boiler room from *Backdraft* or the *Back to the Future* cyberride.

Noon Have lunch in one of Universal Studio's ✖ outdoor cafes, then take in live shows. Favorites are the *Waterworld* scene reenactment and Old West stunt show.

4:00 pm Allow half an hour to reach the new Kodak Theater in Hollywood, park and claim standing space across the street in time for celebrity arrivals to the **Academy Awards**. Along with a huge crowd of gawkers, you'll see a two-hour parade of limousines and stars dressed in outrageous and classy fashions.

5:30 pm Return to the hotel to dress for the big night. Flick on the television to see the first award-winners on stage.

7:00 pm The hip crowd watching the ceremonies on television at the casual **Barfly** makes being there more fun than being at the show. With industry types all around, you'll hear exclamations such as "I did her hair!" and "He always mumbles—we had to get him a special mike!"

9:00 pm For a different twist on local Asian-✖ fusion, try the Mondrian's **Asia de Cuba**. Dinner also gets you into **SkyBar** next door, but the food and chic surroundings are enough of a draw.

11:00 pm Cruise the post-Oscars parties. Locations vary, but your hotel concierge should know where this year's are. Stars without parties might appear at **Las Palmas**, a dance club with a packed floor. Since its opening in May 2000, it's become L.A.'s latest place to go and see beautiful people in sexy outfits.

1:00 am Either because you're staying at the right hotel, or you have connections, script yourself a happy ending to the weekend by checking out the talent at **SkyBar** or **The Whiskey**.

More Time, More Choices

Los Angeles has so many hip restaurants and clubs it requires a separate guidebook (*The Fun Seeker's Los Angeles*). Hot restaurants include **Chaya Brasserie**, **Linq** (try to sit near the hopping bar) and **Moomba**, a still-trendy New York transplant. You'll probably see someone you know (from the movies) at **Matsuhisa**, a local institution that *Zagat* called the best restaurant in L.A. Also high on the sushi roll is **Sushi Roku**.

Two more hotel bars that are difficult to gain entry to are **Bar Marmont** and the **Standard Bar**. At the Grafton Hotel, **The Bar** is intimate but may be more accessible.

The **Kodak Theater**, home to the *Academy Awards*, gives backstage tours (but check to see if they are open the days before the awards ceremonies). The **Los Angeles County Museum of Art** has a fine collection of masterpieces and contemporary works.

Accommodations

On Sunset Boulevard, the cozy, art-deco **Argyle** makes a glamorous base, complete with celebrity guests and glorious views. The exclusive **Sunset Marquis Hotel** is a favorite of celebrities, who enjoy the private garden and excellent room service (and admission to The Whiskey). Similarly, many people stay at the ultrahip **Mondrian** just to get into its SkyBar. The newest kid on the block, and right next door to the Kodak Theater, is the **Renaissance Hollywood Hotel**, offering simple but stylish rooms at moderate prices.

Event & Ticket Info

Academy Awards (Kodak Theater at Hollywood Boulevard and Highland Avenue): It's nearly impossible to get invitations to the ceremony or post-Oscars parties without fame or serious connections, but you can call *The Academy of Motion Picture Arts and Sciences* (310-247-3000) for Oscars-night details.

The Hot Sheet

Hotels		Phone	Address	Price	Fax	Rooms/Best
The Argyle		323-654-7100 800-225-2637	8358 Sunset Blvd.	$$$	323-654-9287	64/City vw
Mondrian		323-650-8999 800-525-8029	8440 Sunset Blvd.	$$$$	323-650-5215	238/Balcony suite city vw
Renaissance Hollywood Hotel		323-856-1200 800-627-7468	1755 N. Highland Ave.	$$	323-856-1025	637/Hollywood sign or city vw
Sunset Marquis Hotel		310-657-1333 800-858-9758	1200 N. Alta Loma Rd.	$$$$	310-652-5300	114/Garden villas

Restaurants	Day	Phone	Address	Price	Rec	Food
Asia de Cuba	3	323-650-8999	see the Mondrian hotel	$$$	BLD	Fusion
Campanile	2	323-938-1447	624 S. La Brea Ave.	$$	B/LD	California, Mediterranean
Chaya Brasserie	A	310-859-8833	8741 Alden Dr.	$$$	D	American, Asian
Chinois-on-Main	1	310-392-9025	2709 Main St.	$$$$+	D/L	Asian, French
DuPar's Restaurant & Bakery	1	323-933-8446	Fairfax and 3rd St.	$	B	American
Ivy	1	310-274-8303	113 N. Robertson Blvd.	$$$	L/D	American
Le Petit Four	2	310-652-3863	8654 Sunset Blvd.	$$	L/BD	Mediterranean
Linq	A	323-655-4555	8338 W. Third St.	$$$	D	New American
Matsuhisa	A	310-659-9639	129 N. La Cienega Blvd.	$$$$+	D	Japanese
Moomba	A	310-652-6364	665 N. Robertson Blvd.	$$$	D	New American
Spago Beverly Hills	2	310-385-0880	176 N. Canon Dr.	$$$	D/L	California
Sushi Roku	A	323-655-6767	8445 W. Third St.	$$$	LD	Sushi

Nightlife	Day	Phone	Address	Cover	Rec*	Music
The Bar	A	323-654-4600	8462 W.Sunset Blvd.	None	R(F)	
Bar Marmont	A	323-650-0575	8171 Sunset Blvd.	None	R	
Barfly	3	310-360-9490	8730 W. Hollywood Blvd.	None	M(F)	
Beauty Bar	1	323-464-7676	1638 N. Cahuenga Blvd.	None	R	
Casa del Mar	1	310-581-5533	1910 Ocean Way	None	R(F)	
Conga Room	1	323-938-1696	5364 Wilshire Blvd.	$$	M(F)	Latin
Garden of Eden	2	323-465-3336	7080 Hollywood Blvd.	$$	P(F)	Hip hop
House of Blues	2	323-848-5100	8430 Sunset Blvd.	$-$$$	M(F)	Blues
Las Palmas	3	323-464-0171	1714 N. Las Palmas Ave.	None	P(R)	Varies
Le Dome	2	310-659-6919	8720 Sunset Blvd.	None	R(F)	
SkyBar	3	323-650-8999	see the Mondrian hotel	None	R	
Standard Bar	A	323-822-3111	8300 Sunset Blvd.	None	R	
The Whiskey	3	310-657-0611	see the Sunset Marquis Hotel	None	R	

* M=Live music; P=Dancing (Party); R=Bar only; S=Show; (F)=Food served. For further explanation of codes, page 12.

Sights & Attractions	Day	Phone	Address	Entry Fee
Frederick's of Hollywood	2	323-466-5151	6608 Hollywood Blvd.	None
The J. Paul Getty Museum	1	310-440-7300	1200 Getty Center Dr.	None
Kodak Theater	A	323-308-6363	6801 Hollywood Blvd.	$$
Los Angeles County Museum of Art	A	323-857-6000	5905 Wilshire Blvd.	$
Mann's Chinese Theatre	2	323-464-8186	6925 Hollywood Blvd.	None
Museum of TV & Radio	2	310-786-1025	465 N. Beverly Dr.	$
Universal Studios	3	818-622-3801	100 Universal City Plaza	$$$$

Los Angeles CVB   **213-624-7300**   **685 S. Figueroa St.**

 NYC -3   Los Angeles (LAX) <60 min./$40   Yes   Map Code: A02

California

21

Napa Valley Wine Auction

Key Month: Jun   Ratings: Event ★ ★ ★ ☆ ☆   ⓗ   City ★ ★ ★ ☆ ☆   Origin: 1981   Attendance: 2,000

The planet's largest charity event focused on food and wine, the **Napa Valley Wine Auction** pours a world-famous party into a gourmet extravaganza, creating one spectacular, waistband-expanding three-day gathering. The event raises millions each year for Napa Valley's health-care institutions, but even if you don't make a single bid, you'll come away with a new appreciation of food, wine and fun.

The schedule varies from year to year, as do participating wineries. What's consistent is scores of epicurean events that keep crowds happy and full from morning until night. Constant rounds of gourmet meals are prepared by celebrity chefs. Tastings of rare and fine California vintages continue through the weekend. Dozens of events include appearances by celebrity impersonators, boccie ball, art tours, nature walks and live jazz, zydeco and rock music.

The social centerpiece is the fancy **Vintners' Gala Dinner**, held at the gorgeous Meadowood Napa Valley resort in St. Helena. Guests are wined and dined with course after course of delicacies prepared by world-renowned chefs. Also held at Meadowood is the *auction*, a sky's-the-limit nail-biter where some wine lots go for upward of $150,000. Thousands cheer as the bidding paddles go to battle and prices are pushed into the stratosphere.

Think you spend a lot on wine? The top bidder at the 2001 auction was a self-described "regular guy" named Ron Kuhn from Wheaton, Illinois, who dropped $955,000 over the weekend, including $650,000 for the top lot—eight three-liter bottles of Screaming Eagle Cabernet Sauvignon.

The *wine auction* makes June the perfect time to visit famed Napa Valley. This lush and fertile area annually attracts hundreds of thousands of gastronomic pilgrims with its outstanding restaurants and opportunities to sample vintages from more than 200 wineries—more wineries than in any other region of the world, outside of France. British statesman Benjamin Disraeli might have been disappointed by the **Napa Valley Wine Auction**—"I rather like bad wine," he said. "One gets so bored with good wine." But a few days in one of the world's premier wine regions is never boring, and it should turn you into a connoisseur of fine wines and great fun.

On the Calendar

Official Event Dates
Four days covering first weekend in June (Thursday-Sunday)

Best 3 Days To Be There
Thursday-Saturday. The Thursday night winery dinners are a must. You can miss the Sunday anti-climax.

☾ 52°/86° (11°/30°)

DAY 1 Thursday

9:30 am Drive to St. Helena for the excellent ✖ pastries and cappuccino at **Model Bakery**. Take time to read through your program of auction activities and related events.

11:00 am Stroll through the nine colorfully decorated tents pitched on velvety lawns at Meadowood. Barrel tasting allows you to sample great wines straight from the fermentation casks. In a preview of Saturday's main auction, bids are taken on selected wine lots and proud vintners present fascinating explanations of how they brought their product from vine to wine. During a silent auction, you get first crack at wines, books and collectibles created by Napa Valley artists.

1:30 pm In various tents, Napa Valley pur- ✖ veyors offer creative gourmet specialties such as herbed grilled prawns, rabbit strudel and smoked salmon in pastry cones. Choose the perfect wine accompaniment from the wide range of excellent bottled varietals on hand.

3:00 pm Squeeze in a visit to **COPIA, The American Center for Wine, Food and the Arts**. This beautiful and unusual museum has exhibitions of the two things—wine and food—that brought you to Napa in the first place. Alternatively, drive to **Sterling Vineyards**, two miles south of Calistoga on Route 29. Take the aerial sky tram to Sterling's tasting room. The awesome panoramic view of Napa Valley is by far the best at any winery in the state.

6:00 pm Choose one of the reliably fun and delicious hospitality events offered at thirty Napa Valley wineries. You can flirt with impersonators of Hollywood stars while enjoying a gourmet dinner and ✖ champagne tasting at **Domaine Chandon**. Or go to Far Niente winery to dance to live zydeco music and feast on Southwestern barbecue grilled by a celebrity chef. The **Napa Valley Wine Train** is always a popular selection—wine, dinner, music and stunning scenery highlight the trip through parts of the thirty-mile stretch of flower-covered ground and lush hillsides that make up Napa Valley.

DAY 2 Friday

10:00 am Prepare yourself with a room- ✖ service breakfast as another forty vintners open their wineries and homes for feasting, wine tasting and music. Study your schedule, because you must narrow the options to one.

Noon You might choose a vineyard tour, barrel tasting and lunch at Acacia Winery, overlooking San Francisco Bay. Or go for a game of boccie ball with the Anderson family of Conn Valley Vineyards, followed ✖ by a lunch of barbecue and select wines. Other options include a visit to **Clos Pégase** winery. Proprietor, art collector and winemaker Jan Shrem takes you on a tour of his art collection (it's mildly erotic and loads of fun).

2:00 pm To get a close-in experience with the natural wonder of Napa, put on your hiking boots and trek to the summit of the mountain behind **Pine Ridge Winery** (where winemaker Nancy Andrus is an experienced Nepal hiker). Local naturalists and birdwatchers give a wildlife tour along the way to the mountaintop, where you're welcomed with a picnic featuring California cuisine, chilled wines and live music.

6:30 pm At Meadowood, arrive at the **Vintners' Gala Dinner**—the fanciest event of the wine auction—dressed to the nines and sparkling like the vintage champagnes served. This party is the keystone event of the auction.

8:00 pm After oysters, shrimp and other seafood hors d'oeuvres, chefs from all over the country prepare an exquisite ✖ four-course meal. Dine inside the giant auction tent, which has been decorated with fantastic sculptures adorning tables and flowers and vines climbing the twenty-foot tent poles.

10:00 pm In another series of tents, sample a grand array of desserts, from mousses to truffles to ice-cream sundaes. You can dance to live music provided by a big-name talent such as Grammy winner Narada Michael Walden (performing artists change each year).

DAY 3 — Saturday

9:30 am At **Meadowood Grill**, start your day with a fresh and bountiful breakfast that includes bagels with smoked fish, breakfast burritos, hot chocolate and coffee.

Noon The first gavel crashes down at noon sharp, unleashing the **Napa Valley Wine Auction** at Meadowood. In the big tent, nearly 200 barrel lots are on the block. Auctioneers from Christie's exhort bidders to make paddles fly and credit cards jump. Silent auctions continue in nine smaller tents. In another tent, wine and auction-related souvenirs are sold to people who love wine but don't need it in barrel lots. Music, dancing and other revelry take place throughout the auction, and a festive picnic for all guests accompanies the bidding.

3:00 pm Take a break from the auction action to stroll around the grounds, perhaps stopping for a cappuccino and cookies at one of the food booths. Many guests use this time to socialize, network or sit beneath a shady tree to chat or nap.

6:30 pm The last gavel falls and the final banquet begins. Tables are set up in a grassy area under the trees at the base of Meadowood's south hill. A band plays as guests dance between courses that include roasted lamb, fresh and marinated vegetable salads, goat cheese, crusty herb-flecked breads and homemade fruit pies. This final, perfect evening brings the three days to an earthy, casual and sensual finish.

■

More Time, More Choices

The three days of auction events are so filled with gourmet food you probably won't want to eat anywhere else. But if you stay longer in Napa Valley, try **Mustards Grill**, one of the first major eateries in California to emphasize small side dishes (think tapas) in lieu of standard entree meals. **La Toque** was recently named one of the top-twenty restaurants in America by *Wine Spectator* (fourteenth, actually). **Brix**, **Catahoula** and **Terra** are three more favorite spots. The vine-covered courtyard at

Ristorante Tra Vigne provides a perfect setting for excellent Italian food.

Napa Valley isn't known for its nightlife, but for the three Bs: ballooning, bicycling and bathing (that means mud bathing). There are many choices for each, but Calistoga's **Mountain View Spa** is one of the area's best places for massages, hot tubs and hydrotherapy mud baths.

Accommodations

With 250 acres of manicured grounds containing pools, fitness and spa facilities, golf course and croquet lawns, **Meadowood** is a dream resort. Check into a suite with cathedral-beamed ceilings. High on a hillside, **Auberge du Soleil** in Rutherford is another of Napa Valley's most elegant and romantic hostelries. Spa facilities, a pool, tennis courts and a romantic restaurant occasionally lure guests out of their suite's immense two-person hot tub. The **Inn at Southbridge**, in downtown St. Helena, is the Meadowood's charming little sister. Each of the twenty-one rooms has homey touches, such as a fireplace and fresh-fruit delivery. Waterways and fountains gurgle through the lush grounds of the **Vintage Inn** in Yountville. Rooms on the ground floor feature rosebush-bordered patios. Upstairs rooms have cathedral-like beamed ceilings and open verandas—all have fireplaces.

Hotels	Phone	Address	Town*	Price	Fax	Rooms/Best
Auberge du Soleil	707-963-1211 800-348-5406	180 Rutherford Hill Rd.	(R)	$$$$+	707-963-8764	52/Cottages
The Inn at Southbridge	707-967-9400 800-520-6800	1020 Main St.	(S)	$$$$	707-967-9486	21/Maryville winery vw
Meadowood	707-963-3646 800-458-8080	900 Meadowood Ln.	(S)	$$$$+	707-963-5863	85/Cathedral cottage
Vintage Inn	707-944-1112 800-351-1133	6541 Washington St.	(Y)	$$$	707-944-1617	80/Inner courtyard

Restaurants	Day	Phone	Address	Town*	Price	Rec	Food
Brix	A	707-944-2749	7377 St. Helena Hwy.	(Y)	$$$	LD	California Asian
Catahoula	A	707-942-2275	1457 Lincoln Ave.	(C)	$$$	LD	Southern-inspired American
Domaine Chandon	1	707-944-2892	1 California Dr.	(Y)	$$$$	D/L	French-California
La Toque	A	707-963-9770	1140 Rutherford Cross	(R)	$$$$+	D	French
Meadowood Grill	3	707-963-3646	see Meadowood Hotel	(S)	$$	B/LD	California
Model Bakery	1	707-963-8192	1357 Main St.	(S)	$	B/L	Bakery, American
Mustards Grill	A	707-944-2424	7399 St. Helena Hwy.	(Y)	$$	LD	American grill
Ristorante Tra Vigne	A	707-963-4444	1050 Charter Oak Ave.	(S)	$$$	LD	Italian
Terra	A	707-963-8931	1345 Railroad Ave.	(S)	$$$	D	Italian-Asian

Sights & Attractions	Day	Phone	Address	Town*	Entry Fee
Clos Pégase	2	707-942-4981	1060 Dunaweal Ln.	(C)	None
COPIA, The American Center for Wine, Food and the Arts	1	707-259-1600	500 First St.	(N)	$
Mountain View Spa	A	707-942-5789	1457 Lincoln Ave.	(C)	$$$$+
Napa Valley Wine Train	1	707-253-2111	1275 McKinstry St.	(N)	$$$$+
Pine Ridge Winery	2	800-575-9777	5901 Silverado Trail	(N)	None
Sterling Vineyards	1	707-942-3300	1111 Dunaweal Ln.	(C)	None

Napa Valley CVB   **707-226-7459**   **1310 Napa Town Center**   **(N)**

* C=Calistoga; N=Napa; R=Rutherford; S=St. Helena; Y=Yountville

California

 NYC -3   San Francisco (SFO) <120 min./NA   Yes   Map Code: A03

Street Scene

Key Month: Sep   Ratings: Event ★★★☆☆   **P**   City ★★★☆☆   Origin: 1984   Attendance: 85,000

There are a lot of people out there who think San Diego is California's best-kept secret—and they haven't even been to **Street Scene** yet! It's scary to imagine how many out-of-towners might pack up and move out to this mainland paradise once they get a three-day **Street Scene** peek at all the music, food, culture and natural beauty that makes San Diego unique.

Street Scene is unusual for being a raging, over-twenty-one-crowd party on Friday and Saturday that turns into a mellow family event on Sunday. But no matter what day it is, the festival's combination of food, music and cultural celebrations keeps happy crowds buzzing around San Diego's turn-of-the-century Gaslamp Quarter. There's a mix of mini-festivals that includes the Wine & Garlic Festival, Via Caliente (a jalapeño heaven or hell, depending on your tolerance), Taste of San Diego (samples from the city's finest restaurants) and the Microbrewery Festival.

A major festival component is music. In fact, for some, **Street Scene** means music. Lots of it. Jazz, R&B, rock, swing, reggae, zydeco, hip hop, reggae, funk and even gospel music propel revelers through reliably beautiful Southern California nights. It's no wonder MTV has called this the best music festival in California.

A lot of fun contests throughout the weekend help keep partiers interested, even when they've reached the breaking point. Prizes typically include vacation packages and plane tickets, but also blind dates and tickets to other events.

Just south of Los Angeles and just north of the Mexican border, San Diego has a look and feel all its own. The ubiquitous Spanish and Mexican architecture is a point of civic pride. Balboa Park is one of the most beautiful city parks in the world. Old Town and the Gaslamp Quarter preserve the city's history. The San Diego Zoo is internationally recognized as the best in the world.

Coastal weather patterns bring sunny, warm days all year. Gorgeous white-sand beaches along the city's coast are perfect for swimming, surfing, diving and ocean fishing. San Diego's harbor is home to fishing boats, yachts, clippers and the U.S. Navy's primary Pacific Coast fleet.

Tequila shots, tacos, tank tops and tans, however, are the primary lure in September. At **Street Scene**, you won't find a shortage of any of the local specialties.

On the Calendar

Official Event Dates

First weekend after Labor Day (Friday-Sunday)

Best 3 Days To Be There

Thursday-Saturday. Street Scene Sunday is family day—doesn't compare to Thursday night in San Diego.

☀ 62°/76° (17°/24°)

California

Day-by-Day Plan

DAY 1 — Thursday

10:30 am Head for San Diego's jewel, Balboa Park. Its lush gardens and Spanish architecture house fascinating museums of all kinds. The largest museum in the city, the **San Diego Museum of Art**, includes an impressive collection of European, Asian, American and contemporary California art. Visit the **Timken Museum of Art** next door for a sampling of Russian icons.

12:30 pm Just across from the Museum of Art is **The Prado**, a Latin-Mediterranean restaurant with indoor seating as well as an outdoor terrace overlooking the "Wedding Bowl" garden. Salads, pasta and seafood are all good here.

1:30 pm Wander Balboa Park's exquisite gardens and visit some of its many other museums. The **Museum of Man** exhibits Mexican history and Indian culture of the Americas. The **Aerospace Museum** spans the history of flight from gliders to the Wright Brothers to space.

4:30 pm If you're staying at the Hyatt, the view from you room is good, but it's better with a cocktail at the **Top of the Hyatt** lounge.

6:30 pm The trendy Gaslamp Quarter started out as the 1867 vision of Alonzo Horton, who offered lots to people who promised to build houses. Renovated in the 1970s, it's now a thriving district for music and food, sometimes referred to as "the New Orleans of the West Coast." Though *Street Scene* doesn't begin until tomorrow, get your bearings by wandering its streets and alleys and popping into a pub for a drink.

7:30 pm **Fio's Cucina Italiana** has earned more than fifty dining awards. Executive chef Robert Gaffney's innovative Italian dishes add California, French and Pacific Rim influences to entrées such as lobster ravioli with saffron sauce and chive oil.

9:30 pm Jim Croce and wife Ingrid used to serve grand dinners to their friends Jimmy Buffet, James Taylor, Arlo Guthrie, Bonnie Raitt, and The Manhattan Transfer before retiring to all-night jam sessions.

9:30 pm (cont.) Croce hit the big time with songs such as "Time in a Bottle" and "Bad, Bad Leroy Brown," but died shortly thereafter in a plane crash. Ingrid, who moved with Jim to San Diego just a month before he died, opened Croce's as a tribute to her husband. **Croce's Jazz Bar** features live jazz every night. Its **Top Hat Bar & Grille** is the place to be for live rhythm and blues.

Midnight **Ole Madrid** may be the hottest club in San Diego, judging from the fashion-plate lines outside. You can beat the lines by having dinner there. The food isn't Spanish or all that great, but the views from the balcony tables are a treat.

DAY 2 — Friday

8:30 am Try one of the hearty breakfasts at the Horton Grand Hotel's **Ida Bailey's** restaurant, named for the Gaslamp Quarter's most notorious madam at the turn of the century.

10:00 am Morning is feeding time, so get to the **San Diego Zoo** early to see the animals at their liveliest. An aerial tramway and narrated bus tour give good overviews of one of the world's largest collections of animals exhibited in natural landscapes.

2:30 pm Back at the Gaslamp Quarter, have a late lunch at **Osteria Panevino**. Tuscan ambience and brick-oven pizzas have made this a popular restaurant for lunch and dinner.

5:00 pm Dive into *Street Scene*. It doesn't really matter where you start. Pick your favorite type of music and head for a stage, then dance your way past festival and food booths into the night.

8:00 pm Walk to one of the trendiest spots in the Gaslamp Quarter. The **Dakota Grill & Spirits** offers mesquite-grilled and wood-fired meats and pizzas, along with micro-brewed beers.

10:00 pm *Street Scene* will be packed with people drinking and enjoying the parade of costumed revelers through the streets.

Day-by-Day Plan

12:15 am The city's best underground (literally) dancing is at the **Blue Tattoo**. The location for television's "Silk Stalkings", it requires "proper dress," but is worth the effort.

DAY 3 *Saturday*

9:00 am Mexican food fanatics praise the **Old Town Mexican Cafe**'s pozole soup for breakfast. If pork and hominy don't stimulate your appetite, you're sure to find a breakfast dish that will at San Diego's favorite Mexican restaurant.

10:00 am Visit **Old Town San Diego State Historic Park**, which commemorates the first Euro-American settlement in California. Plaza Vieja was the center of town and the scene of bullfights. Casa de Machado depicts everyday life in early, Mexican San Diego.

Noon Relax in Southern California style. Head to La Jolla (pronounced La Hoy-ah) for a Mediterranean lunch at **Trattoria Acqua**. Choose between pastas and sandwiches on fresh Italian rolls.

1:30 pm La Jolla's white crescent beaches, warm ocean and great surfing are irresistible. Swimmers head for the southern end of La Jolla Shores Beach, while surfers take over the northern end. La Jolla Cove is a natural tide-pool area where starfish, hermit crabs, sea cucumbers and other sea life abound at low tide.

5:30 pm Head back to **Street Scene** for a few late-afternoon beers and maybe some chips, salsa and mariachi music.

8:00 pm If you haven't filled up on festival food, try **Blue Point Coastal Cuisine** for seafood and a hopping bar scene. Return to the festival for closing acts and rub shoulders with a large and lively crowd.

12:15 am Wind up the night dancing to Top 40 and disco music at the **E Street Alley**.

More Time, More Choices

Head to **Mission Basilica San Diego de Alcala**, the first mission in American California. It makes for an interesting visit. Another mission you may want to visit is Mission Beach, a wide, sandy ocean beach. Black's Beach is decorously referred to as Clothing Optional.

Taka has been voted one of San Diego's best Japanese restaurants by both diners and restaurant critics. **Rainwater's**, an intimate downtown restaurant known for its prime steaks, is a good dinner alternative. Greek food is excellent at the **Athens Market Taverna**, where the owner fusses over her customers. The classic Italian food at **Salvatore's** gets absolute rave reviews ... and deserves them.

Opened in 2000, **On Broadway** is a 27,000-square-foot Vegas-style nightclub with beautiful people and long lines. Tables in the VIP lounge go for $150 to $500. If you skipped the festival Friday or Saturday night, you can listen to a mariachi band and then dance to salsa bands at **Casa Guadalajara** in Old Town. **Cafe Sevilla** offers a Flamenco show with dinner and a Euro-Latin disco afterward. Or you can drive to La Jolla, where **George's Ocean Terrace** provides a wonderful ocean vantage point. The restaurant downstairs is more formal and popular with locals.

Accommodations

Admire San Diego Bay from your room at the **Hyatt Regency San Diego**, where all rooms have bay views. You're also close to the **Street Scene** here.

The **Horton Grand Hotel**, an elegant Victorian hotel complete with a ghost and horse-drawn carriages, also offers modern amenities. Its Gaslamp District location makes it either noisy or convenient, depending on your perspective. The beachfront **Hotel del Coronado**, an imposing Victorian National Historic Landmark, recalls turn-of-the-century, high-society summer holidays. The **Sheraton San Diego Hotel & Marina** offers luxury in a resort setting on Harbor Island.

Event & Ticket Info

Street Scene (Fifth Avenue at Market Street): Tickets ($35) are available at the gate for Friday or Saturday. A combined ticket ($60) for Friday and Saturday is sold in advance through *Ticketmaster* (800-488-5252). Sunday tickets ($35) should be purchased at the gate. For Sunday tickets and more information call *Street Scene* (619-557-8490).

San Diego

Hotels	Phone	Address	Price	Fax	Rooms/Best
Horton Grand Hotel	619-544-1886 800-542-1886	311 Island Ave.	$$	619-239-3823	132/Courtyard vw
Hotel Del Coronado	619-435-6611 800-468-3533	1500 Orange Ave.	$$$$	619-522-8262	681/Ocean front vw
Hyatt Regency San Diego	619-232-1234 800-233-1234	1 Market Pl.	$$$$	619-233-6464	875/Bay vw
Sheraton San Diego Hotel & Marina	619-291-2900 800-325-3535	1380 Harbor Island Dr.	$$$	619-692-2337	1,045/Ocean front vw

Restaurants	Day	Phone	Address	Price	Rec	Food
Athens Market Taverna	A	619-234-1955	109 West F St.	$$	LD	Greek
Blue Point Coastal Cuisine	3	619-233-6623	565 5th Ave.	$$$	D	Seafood, American
Cafe Sevilla	A	619-233-5979	555 4th Ave.	$$	D	Spanish
Dakota Grill & Spirits	2	619-234-5554	901 5th Ave.	$$$	D/L	American, Southwestern grill
Fio's Cucina Italiana	1	619-234-3467	801 5th Ave.	$$$	D	Northern Italian
George's Ocean Terrace	A	858-454-4244	1250 Prospect St.	$$	LD	American
Ida Bailey's	2	619-544-1886	see Horton Grand Hotel	$$	B/D	American
Old Town Mexican Cafe	3	619-297-4330	2489 San Diego Ave.	$	B/LD	Mexican
Osteria Panevino	2	619-595-7959	722 5th Ave.	$$	L/D	Italian
The Prado	1	619-557-9441	1549 El Prado	$$	LD	Latin-Mediterranean
Rainwater's	A	619-233-5757	1202 Kettner Blvd.	$$$	LD	Chop house
Salvatore's	A	619-544-1865	750 Front St.	$$$	D	Italian
Taka	A	619-338-0555	555 5th Ave.	$$	D	Japanese
Trattoria Acqua	3	858-454-0709	1298 Prospect St.	$	L/D	Northern Italian

Nightlife	Day	Phone	Address	Cover	Rec*	Music
Blue Tattoo	2	619-238-7191	835 5th Ave.	$	P	Dance
Casa Guadalajara	A	619-295-5111	4105 Taylor St.	$	P(F)	Salsa
Croce's Jazz Bar	1	619-233-4355	802 5th Ave.	$	M(F)	Jazz
E Street Alley	3	619-231-9200	E Street Alley btwn. 4th and 5th Aves.	$	P(F)	Top 40, funk, '70s, '80s
Ole Madrid	1	619-557-0146	755 5th Ave.	$	P(F)	House, Latin
On Broadway	A	619-231-0011	615 Broadway	$$	P(F)	House, hip hop
Top Hat Bar & Grille	1	619-233-4355	802 5th Ave.	$	M(F)	R&B, swing
Top of the Hyatt	1	619-232-1234	see Hyatt hotel	None	R(F)	

* M=Live music; P=Dancing (Party); R=Bar only; S=Show; (F)=Food served. For further explanation of codes, page 12.

Sights & Attractions	Day	Phone	Address	Entry Fee
Aerospace Museum	1	619-234-8291	2001 Pan American Pl.	$
Mission Basilica San Diego de Alcala	A	619-281-8449	10818 San Diego Mission Rd.	$
Museum of Man	1	619-239-2001	1350 El Prado	$
Old Town San Diego State Historic Park	3	619-220-5422	Twiggs and Congress Sts.	None
San Diego Museum of Art	1	619-232-7931	1450 El Prado	$
San Diego Zoo	2	619-234-3153	2920 Zoo Dr.	$$
Timken Museum of Art	1	619-239-5548	1500 El Prado	None

San Diego CVB		619-232-3101	11 Horton Plz.	

California

 NYC -3   San Diego (SAN) <30 min./$10   Yes/No Map Code: A04

Black and White Ball

San Francisco

Key Month: May	Ratings: Event ★★★☆☆	**H**	City ★★★★★	Origin: 1956	Attendance: 12,000

Leave the color film at home and prepare yourself for a weekend in monochrome: The **Black and White Ball** turns San Francisco's Civic Center into a set from a glamorous black-and-white film, starring you and 12,000 or so other beautiful people. Too special to happen every year, the biennial ball is the largest one-night arts fund-raiser in the United States—benefiting the San Francisco Symphony—and is probably the world's largest indoor-outdoor black-tie ball.

After a four-year hiatus, 1999 marked the return of the **Black and White Ball** to the Civic Center (many of the buildings were being retrofitted for earthquake safety), meaning that, once again, the party can take advantage of the beautiful City Hall, Opera House and Symphony Hall. Local professionals and socialites drink, eat and dance away a night made dreamy by the bayside fog and twinkling lights of one of the world's most romantic cities. Chinese lanterns hang from trees, balloons float through the air, champagne flows freely and a laser-and-fireworks show lights up an already-glowing crowd of exquisitely dressed people. Sixteen related venues host more than fifty musical acts. Entertainment typically ranges from Tito Puente Jr. to techno-pop from Berlin to symphony-orchestra dance music in the City Hall Rotunda.

If your image of San Francisco is of a gritty, counter-culture bastion, you're right ... and also very wrong. San Francisco was built on Gold Rush fortunes and there always has been an element of style and wealth here. In keeping with the theme of this first-class event, a weekend itinerary should allow you time to discover the City by the Bay's most elegant diversions. Victorian houses, bay views, parks and the Golden Gate Bridge are all on the daytime schedule. So is Muir Woods, one of North America's most impressive stands of ancient forest.

The upscale side of San Francisco's after-dinner scene is in flux, as the hipper crowd moves to the Mission District (see Exotic Erotic chapter, page 34). Not so with dining—San Francisco is the place where California cuisine originated and the number of outstanding restaurants is extraordinary. You may not leave your heart in San Francisco, but you'll definitely give it a workout.

On the Calendar

Official Event Dates

Last Saturday in May or first Saturday in June (held every two years)

Best 3 Days To Be There

Thursday-Saturday. The Ball is Saturday. Thursday and Friday set the mood.

Other Times To Go

See *Exotic Erotic Ball*, page 34.

☾ 50°/69° (10°/21°)

9:30 am Grab a coffee and pastry at **Rose's** ❌ **Café** and people-watch along Union Street and nearby Chestnut Street.

Noon Drive to the scenic Pacific Heights and Presidio Heights areas and check out San Francisco's finest homes on your way to ❌ **Garibaldi's on Presidio**. This hottest neighborhood restaurant in San Francisco offers upscale Mediterranean lunches.

1:30 pm Drive through the Presidio to the Marina. Pass the gorgeous Palace of Fine Arts, circle the entrance to the Golden Gate Bridge, and look for the stately, columned **California Palace of the Legion of Honor**. Views from the art museum and the Rodin sculptures make this a worthwhile detour.

3:30 pm Returning from Golden Gate Park, stop for a drink and ocean view at the **Cliff House**.

7:00 pm Begin the evening at the city's most comfortable drinking spot, the **Bubble Lounge**. The rest of the evening's venues are within walking distance, so taste various champagnes without worry.

8:00 pm Eating at **Bix** makes you part of the ❌ San Francisco scene. French-accented American cuisine is served in a supper-club atmosphere and the active bar and live jazz make it a popular meet market. For a high-end Greek alternative, try **Kokkari Estiatorio**—the only thing missing is dancing on the tables.

11:00 pm In the thick of North Beach, ❌ **Enrico's Sidewalk Cafe** bar has live blues and jazz and a heated sidewalk patio.

9:30 am On the patio of **Il Fornaio**, have break-❌ fast looking out on one of the nation's most attractive urban office parks. The fresh breakfast pastries are a treat.

11:00 am It's time for awesome. Drive past Pier 39, Fisherman's Wharf and Ghirardelli Square. Across the Golden Gate Bridge, pull off at the vista point at the north end of the bridge.

Noon Drive to **Muir Woods**, seventeen miles north of San Francisco. If a noted conservationist says, "This is the best tree-lovers monument that could possibly be found in all the forests of the world," you should name the place after him. The national monument includes 560 acres of redwood forest, with some trees more than 200 feet high and 1,000 years old.

2:00 pm On the way back to the city, stop in ❌ Sausalito for lunch at **The Spinnaker** restaurant. The main attraction is the view of the water, but the seafood is good.

4:00 pm Browse downtown Sausalito's shops or drive into the hills and marvel at houses built on stilts in one of the world's earthquake centers. Wind up the hill (Conzelman Road) for spectacular views of the bridge and city.

5:00 pm Back in San Francisco, stay on Lombard Street. The corner of Hyde and Lombard provides one of San Francisco's most magnificent views. It's also the start of the drive down the world's crookedest street.

7:30 pm Have an aperitif with well-groomed minglers crowding the bar at Wolfgang Puck's **Postrio Restaurant**. Many consider Postrio San Francisco's best restaurant, but ...

8:30 pm Nearby is the San Francisco edition ❌ of New York's **Asia de Cuba**. The communal dining experience has earned it a reputation as the place to be. Also downtown, a bustling dining experience awaits you at **Scala's Bistro**.

10:30 pm High above Scala's (on the top floor of the Sir Francis Drake hotel) is **Harry Denton's Starlight Room**, where house musicians play big-band or Latin music as the champagne-sipping dancers take in Union Square views.

DAY 3 | Saturday

9:00 am Have breakfast at the **Grand Cafe** in ❌ your hotel's art-nouveau restaurant.

10:30 am Cab to the **San Francisco Museum of Modern Art**. The imposing modernist structure is the second-largest in America devoted to modern art.

12:30 pm Dive into the underwater theme at ❌ **Farallon** for outstanding seafood.

2:00 pm Browse through San Francisco's premier shopping area, Union Square.

4:00 pm On Union Square in the St. Francis Hotel, custom detailing and museum-quality antiques and artifacts deck **The Compass Rose**, which serves afternoon tea with silver service that includes finger sandwiches, scones, cream, berries and petits fours.

6:00 pm You can't dress too elegantly for the **Black and White Ball**. But while changing, consider the challenge presented by an indoor-outdoor event with five hours of walking and dancing.

7:30 pm Start the evening with a meal at **Stars**, ❌ where new chef Amaryll Schwertner has added to the excellence of this California-style brasserie.

9:00 pm As soon as you arrive at the **Black and White Ball**, consult a schedule and map to plan your dancing and music agenda for the evening. Then get giddy on all the complimentary bubbly, live music, finger foods and mingling. And when you meet some locals, give them some tips on what they should see and do in their great city.

■

More Time, More Choices

You'll want to find time for the **Fifth Floor**, a chic restaurant serving beautifully presented French dishes. **Boulevard** is one of the hardest reservations in town to get, but the art-nouveau décor and outstanding American cuisine make it worth a shot. Nearby, **One Market** also serves delicious American

cuisine in a contemporary setting. In the Italian-flavored, bar-studded North Beach area, **Moose**'s has a thriving social scene. For a gourmet dinner, San Francisco's best is **Aqua**, which serves beautifully prepared and presented seafood. Across from Il Fornaio, the famous **Fog City Diner** serves hearty plates of upscale comfort food. **Jardiniere Restaurant** has become a popular addition to the Civic Center. (You might want to go here before the Black & White Ball.) It serves inventive American cuisine. **Azie** is now on the city's hot restaurant list. The décor recalls a Hong Kong street scene, but the Nine Bites appetizer and beef ribs braised with sake are straight from the French-Asian penthouse.

At the top of Nob Hill, near the landmark Grace Cathedral, the **Top of the Mark**'s nineteenth-floor views of downtown make it a fine place for a nightcap.

At the corner of Mason and Halleck (in the Presidio) is Chrissy Field, an area with a trail starting at Fort Mason that heads toward the Golden Gate Bridge. There are beautiful vistas all along this trail which, after a $6-million renovation, opened to the public in its new form in 2001.

Accommodations

At the French-inspired **Hotel Monaco**, your small but gorgeous room includes a canopy bed. Intimate, luxurious and always rated among America's best hotels, the newly renovated **Campton Place** is located on Union Square. Rooms are small but elegant. **Inn at the Opera**, in the Civic Center (and near the Black and White Ball), has classic European furnishings. The **Clift** hotel has been taken over and updated by Ian Schrager—the famed hotelier has brought a new sense of cool to San Francisco.

Event & Ticket Info

Black and White Ball (Civic Center, Van Ness Avenue at Grove Street): Admission tickets ($175 CD) should be purchased in advance from *San Francisco Symphony Ticket Services* (415-864-6000).

San Francisco

Hotels		Phone	Address	Price	Fax	Rooms/Best
Campton Place		415-781-5555 800-235-4300	340 Stockton St.	$$$	415-955-5536	117/City vw
Clift		415-775-4700 800-652-5438	495 Geary St.	$$$	415-441-4621	329/City vw loft
Hotel Monaco		415-292-0100	501 Geary St.	$$	415-292-0111	201/Dntwn vw
Inn at the Opera		415-863-8400	333 Fulton St.	$$$	415-861-0821	48/7s series

Restaurants	Day	Phone	Address	Price	Rec	Food
Aqua	A	415-956-9662	252 California St.	$$$	LD	Seafood
Asia de Cuba	2	415-929-2300	495 Geary St.	$$	D	Fusion
Azie	A	415-538-0918	826 Folsom St.	$$$	D	French-Asian
Bix	1	415-433-6300	56 Gold St.	$$$	D/L	French, American
Boulevard	A	415-543-6084	1 Mission St.	$$$	LD	New American
The Compass Rose	3	415-397-7000	450 Powell St.	$$	T	High tea
Farallon	3	415-956-6969	450 Post St.	$$	L/D	Seafood
Fifth Floor	A	415-348-1555	12 Fourth St.	$$$	D	French
Fog City Diner	A	415-982-2000	1300 Battery St.	$$	LD	California diner
Garibaldi's on Presidio	1	415-563-8841	347 Presidio Ave.	$$	L/D	California
Il Fornaio	2	415-986-0100	1265 Battery St.	$$	B/LD	Northern Italian
Jardiniere Restaurant	A	415-861-5555	300 Grove St.	$$$	D	California, French
Kokkari Estiatorio	1	415-981-0983	200 Jackson St.	$$	D/L	Greek
Moose's	A	415-989-7800	1652 Stockton St.	$$	LD	American
One Market	A	415-777-5577	1 Market St.	$$$	LD	Contemporary American
Postrio Restaurant	2	415-776-7825	545 Post St.	$$$	LD	California
Rose's Café	1	415-775-2200	2298 Union St.	$	B/L	New French
Scala's Bistro	2	415-395-8555	432 Powell St.	$$$	D/L	Mediterranean
Stars	3	415-861-7827	555 Golden Gate Ave.	$$$	D/L	New American
The Spinnaker	2	415-332-1500	100 Spinnaker Dr., Sausalito	$$	L/D	Seafood

Nightlife	Day	Phone	Address	Cover	Rec*	Music
Bubble Lounge	1	415-434-4204	714 Montgomery St.	None	R(F)	
Cliff House	1	415-386-3330	1090 Point Lobos Ave.	None	R(F)	
Enrico's Sidewalk Cafe	1	415-982-6223	504 Broadway	None	M	Jazz, blues
Harry Denton's Starlight Room	2	450 Powell St.	415-395-8595	$	MP	Euro jazz, Motown
Top of the Mark	A	415-392-3434	1 Nob Hill	$	M	Jazz

* M=Live music; P=Dancing (Party); R=Bar only; S=Show; (F)=Food served. For further explanation of codes, page 12.

Sights & Attractions	Day	Phone	Address	Entry Fee
California Palace of the Legion of Honor	1	415-750-3600	Lincoln Park	$
Muir Woods	2	415-388-2596	Muir Woods Rd. off Hwy. 1	$
San Francisco Museum of Modern Art	3	415-357-4000	151 3rd St.	$

San Francisco CVB	**415-391-2000**	**900 Market St.**

California

 NYC -3   San Francisco (SFO) <30 min./$30    Yes   Map Code: A05

Exotic Erotic Ball / Halloween

San Francisco

Key Month: Oct   Ratings: Event ★ ★ ★ ☆ ☆   **P**   City ★ ★ ★ ★ ★   Origin: 1979   Attendance: 15,000

For San Francisco, being ground zero for **Halloween** isn't enough. When the annual Castro Street party comes around, the City by the Bay also throws a one-night, everything-goes-sexual extravaganza known as the **Exotic Erotic Ball**, an event that somehow pushes the envelope on the city's already rarefied reputation.

The raunchy festivities take place at the infamous suburb-dwelling Cow Palace, which fills up with 15,000 straight, gay and bisexual revelers from up and down the social strata, the sex industry being particularly well-represented. All comers are jazzed up in creative, expressive, explicit and illicit costumes, many of which mock the nature of the word "dressed." It's such a wild affair, sartorially speaking, that people who show up in street clothes might feel more naked than, say, a couple wearing nothing but body paint. Even the warm-up party—in the flamboyant Castro district—is wilder than any tricking or treating you've ever experienced.

At the Cow Palace, you'll find yourself smack dab in the middle of a sexual festival of contortion acts, catfights, lapdancing, flogging and heavy petting, to name just a few diversions. Various stages host musical groups—Sugar Ray, Chris Isaak and Joan Jett have played here—burlesque shows, S&M shows and strip acts, as well as the Mr. and Ms. Exotic Erotic and Best Costume contests. Half the attendees are voyeurs and exhibitionists, and the other half are suburbanites who come to blow off a little steam. The sexually charged atmosphere builds as the night wears on, and the dance floor gradually turns into an undressing room of sorts.

What had started out in 1979 as a fundraiser for the free-love movement spearheaded by the late Lou Abolafia (Nude Candidate for President in 1968; motto: "I have nothing to hide") quickly morphed into the public sexual spectacle it is today. Dennis Rodman once called the **Exotic Erotic Ball** the "Superbowl of parties," which explains why the people from the E! channel show up every year to shoot footage of the wackiness for their popular "Wild On" show.

There's no better city to host such a raucous event. After all, it's the diversity of the people and the range of its offerings that make San Francisco one of the world's great and most visited cities. Yet another reason why the **Exotic Erotic** experience will leave you shaking your head and making plans to return next year.

On the Calendar

Official Event Dates
October 31

Best 3 Days To Be There
10/29-31. Halloween and/or the Ball are on 10/31—you'll need two days to prepare.

Other Times To Go
See **Black and White Ball**, page 30.

☽ 52°/70° (11°/21°)

California

Exotic Erotic Ball/Halloween

(Note: The Exotic Erotic Ball event usually takes place the week before Halloween, but at press time the promoters were considering moving it to Halloween night, which is how the itinerary is set up. Call the Exotic Erotic Ball number for the latest news.)

DAY 1 October 29

9:30 am With walking shoes on—it's a four-mile day—pass through Chinatown to nearby North Beach, the Italian district, for some of the world's best espresso ❌ drinks. Among many choices, **The Steps of Rome** is a good place to chat up local coffee types. Former beatnik hangout **Caffè Trieste** roasts its own coffee. Another '50s icon is **City Lights Bookstore**, which carries many works rejected by the publishing establishment.

11:00 am Head north along Columbus, Grant and/or Stockton streets to Washington Square Park, the heart of Little Italy. Hike up Telegraph Hill to take in some of the city's most photographed views from **Coit Tower**.

12:30 pm Walk via Telegraph Hill/Lombard Street and head to Pacific Avenue to the ❌ **New Asia** restaurant in Chinatown. This is dim sum at its best, so the inevitable wait for a table—though they offer seating for 1,000—is well worth it.

3:00 pm It's only a few blocks to Chinatown, the largest Chinese community outside of Asia. **Tien Hou Temple** and **Jeng Sen Temple** are worthy stops amid this excessively commercial district.

7:00 pm Back in North Beach, enjoy a San Francisco institution, **Beach Blanket Babylon**, an outrageous cabaret show that helps confirm the city's offbeat reputation.

8:30 pm Hang out in North Beach, walking Columbus and Grant streets, but settle ❌ in for dinner at **Rose Pistola** for seafood and Italian dishes.

11:30 pm **Backflip** is fun both inside and poolside and provides a nice cap to your day.

DAY 2 October 30

10:00 am Breakfast at **Cafè de la Presse**, next ❌ to the Triton, which has an international newsstand and tables out front.

11:00 am Cab to Golden Gate Park and visit the **Japanese Tea Garden**, the oldest Japanese garden in the United States. Head east out of the park past bikers, skaters, runners and walkers to the Haight-Ashbury district.

1:30 pm In **Cha Cha Cha**'s tropical-fiesta ❌ atmosphere, piece together a *delicioso* lunch by sampling a variety of tapas.

3:00 pm Though decidedly retail-oriented, the Haight is still hip. **Wasteland, The Aardvark's Odd Ark** and **Piedmont Boutique** are sure bets for final touches on your costume. For Halloween, the fairly upscale clothing store **Jaxx** takes a turn for the raunchy and stocks see-through get-ups, French maid outfits and lots and lots of vinyl.

7:30 pm South of Market Area (SOMA) attracts hip bar-hoppers who often start ❌ their evening with dinner at **Dulcinea Café**. The food and music is good, but the atmosphere is great—like being at a party. Or catch a flick while eating well prepared American fare at **Foreign Cinema**, although the only sound you'll hear will be the room's buzz.

9:30 pm **Beauty Bar** is mostly a place for a trendy clientele to drink, but they can also get a manicure. **Butterfly** doesn't do nails, but this super-hip bar and restaurant doesn't need to.

11:00 pm Several blocks away, the **Power Exchange Substation**—claiming to be San Francisco's only hetero sex club—accommodates lascivious tastes. There are safety rules, but once inside, just about anything goes. Rooms are rigged with bondage gear. Peepholes allow voyeurs to watch the action. Although "women, transsexuals, transvestites and transgenders" are admitted free, only about a quarter of the patrons are hetero females.

35

Day-by-Day Plan

DAY 3 — October 31

9:30 am The **Buena Vista Cafe** at Fisherman's
Ⓧ Wharf claims to have introduced Irish
coffee to the United States. It's also a
fun place to have eggs and toast.

10:30 am Walk along Fisherman's Wharf to
the **Alcatraz** pier. Take in a wonderful
ride on the bay, an interesting self-
guided tour and spectacular views of the
city. (Tickets should be reserved a week
in advance.)

1:30 pm It's a short ride to **Greens** in Fort
Ⓧ Mason. The Buddhist community's Zen
Center operates this gourmet vegetarian
restaurant. After lunch, pay a quick visit
to the **Mexican Museum**'s changing
exhibits of art and culture.

4:00 pm Before returning to your hotel, relax
and watch the kites at the Marina Green
next door. An alternative plan is to go to
the **Asian Art Museum**, which recently
moved to its new, expanded location at
the Civic Center. It has the largest collection of Asian art in the Western world.

7:00 pm There are three great restaurants
located near the Halloween festivities.
Ⓧ **Mecca**'s mingle-friendly bar is popular and
its American-Mediterranean cuisine is
superb. **2223 Restaurant and Bar** has excellent food and a hopping crowd. **Zuni Cafe**
serves excellent nouveau Mediterranean-
inspired cuisine. One of the hottest restaurants in the city, it has a popular bar with
live piano music, and you won't feel out of
place in your costume.

8:30 pm *The Castro* is on fire for Halloween!
Especially from Market to 18th streets,
revelers in homemade or cabaret-quality
costumes dance, sing and create as
much mischief as possible. Beware the
forest of human trees—you could be
grabbed. Female impersonators dress as
Valley girls or truck-stop waitresses. The
ratio of voyeurs to participants varies,
but everyone is giddy and one person's
trick is another's treat at this All Hallow's
Eve blast that could take place only in
tolerant San Francisco.

11:00 pm For the **Exotic Erotic Ball**, leave
your inhibitions curbside and hop a cab
(or, if you've planned ahead, a limo),
since the ball takes place at the Cow
Palace, which is in a suburb south of the
city. If you've done your costume shopping right, you should blend into—or
stand out from—the sexual display while
experiencing the more adventurous side
of your libido.

3:00 am Head back to the city for the official *Exotic Erotic Ball* after-hours party,
which takes place at an upscale club
called NV located in the South of Market
entertainment area. The atmosphere is
more relaxed than the one you just came
from, but that's not saying much. Spend
time grooving on the dance floor with
your fellow freaks, or just hang out in
one of the lounges and reflect on all that
you have seen.

■

Accommodations

Hotel Triton is a perfect base for an unusual
weekend. It is cutting-edge clever, with
unique furnishings and amenities that will
add fun to your visit. The hip but funky
Phoenix Hotel (a motel, really) still attracts
rock stars to its seedy location; and you
won't have to worry about drawing attention
here dressed in your exotic get-up. **The W
San Francisco** brings the hotel chain to the
South of Market area of San Francisco.

Event & Ticket Info

Exotic Erotic Ball (Cow Palace at
Geneva Avenue and Santos Street):
Tickets ($49.50–$69) are usually available up to event time at the door. Call
the ball hotline (1-888-EXOTIC6) for
more information.

Castro Street Halloween Party
Event is free. For more information call
the *San Francisco Convention and
Visitors Bureau* (415-391-2000).

Hotels	Phone	Address	Price	Fax	Rooms/Best
Hotel Triton	415-394-0500 800-433-6611	42 Grant Ave.	$$	415-394-0555	140/Jr designer rms
Phoenix Hotel	415-776-1380 800-248-9466	601 Eddy St.	$	415-885-3109	44/Courtyard vw
W San Francisco	415-777-5300 800-877-9468	181 Third St.	$$	415-817-7823	423/Corner, 17-27th fl

Restaurants	Day	Phone	Address	Price	Rec	Food
2223 Restaurant and Bar	A	415-431-0692	2223 Market St.	$$	D	American
Buena Vista Cafe	3	415-474-5044	2765 Hyde St.	$	B/L	American breakfast
Café de la Presse	2	415-398-2680	352 Grant Ave.	$	B/LD	American breakfast
Caffè Trieste	1	415-392-6739	601 Vallejo St.	$	B	Pastries
Cha Cha Cha	2	415-386-5758	1801 Haight St.	$$	L/D	Spanish, Cajun, Caribbean
Dulcinea Café	1	415-552-5599	371 11th St.	$$	L/D	Modern America
Greens	3	415-771-6222	Fort Mason Center, Bldg. A	$$	L/D	Vegetarian
Mecca	3	415-621-7000	2029 Market St.	$$	D	Mediterranean
Rose Pistola	A	415-399-0499	532 Columbus Ave.	$$	LD	Seafood
The Steps of Rome	1	415-397-0435	348 Columbus Ave.	$$	B/LD	American breakfast
New Asia	1	415-391-6666	772 Pacific Ave.	$$	L	Dim sum
Zuni Cafe	2	415-552-2522	1658 Market St.	$$	D/L	Mediterranean, Southwest

Nightlife	Day	Phone	Address	Cover	Rec*	Music
Backflip	1	415-771-3547	601 Eddy St.	$	R(F)	
Beach Blanket Babylon	1	415-421-4222	678 Green St.	$$$	S	
Beauty Bar	2	415-285-0323	2299 Mission St.	None	R	
Butterfly	2	415-864-5570	1710 Mission St.	None	R(F)	
Power Exchange Substation	3	415-974-1460	86 Otis St.	$	S	

* M=Live music; P=Dancing (Party); R=Bar only; S=Show; (F)=Food served. For further explanation of codes, page 12.

Sights & Attractions	Day	Phone	Address	Entry Fee
Alcatraz	3	415-705-5555	Pier 41	$$
Asian Art Museum	3	415-379-8800	75 Tea Garden Dr.	$
Coit Tower	1	415-362-0808	1 Telegraph Hill Blvd.	$
Japanese Tea Garden	2	415-668-0909	9th Ave. & Lincoln Blvd.	$
Mexican Museum	3	415-441-0404	Laguna St. & Marina Blvd. at the Fort Mason Center	$

Other Sights, Shops & Services				
The Aardvark's Odd Ark	2	415-621-3141	1501 Haight St.	None
City Lights Bookstore	1	415-362-8193	261 Columbus Ave.	None
Jaxx	2	415-869-1070	1584 Haight St.	None
Jeng Sen Temple	1	415-397-2941	146 Waverly Pl.	None
Piedmont Boutique	2	415-864-8075	1452 Haight St.	None
Tien Hou Temple	1		125 Waverly Pl.	None
Wasteland	2	415-863-3150	1660 Haight St.	None

San Francisco CVB	415-391-2000	900 Market St.

California

 NYC -3 San Francisco, SFO <30 min./$30  Yes   Map Code: A05

Ski: Aspen

Key Month: n/a   Ratings: Event n/a City ★ ★ ★ ★ ☆   Origin: n/a   Attendance: n/a

A high-speed gondola whisks you to the top of a sun-glazed, 11,000-foot peak. You're surrounded by an endless palette of stunning, white summits. Skiers and snowboarders fan out in all directions, ready to carve another fresh batch of powder into ribbons. This could describe just about any major ski resort in the United States, if it weren't for that thumbnail-sized, twelve-block town nestled directly below called **Aspen**. Glide into this alpine mecca and you'll agree it's North America's most fun ski resort for skiers and non-skiers.

Aspen has come a long way in the past century. A former Rocky Mountain mining town set in the picturesque Roaring Fork Valley, it's now one of the world's most famous and chichi destinations—especially between November and April when the resort's four spectacular mountain sites (Ajax, **Aspen** Highlands, Buttermilk and Snowmass—all linked by free shuttle service) are open for schussing, mogul-mashing or trying out your first set of ski legs. Boasting humongous verticals and miles of varied alpine terrain, Aspen is still king of the hills for every sort of skier, boarder and fun-seeker.

Even without a lift ticket, visitors should brace themselves for an avalanche of non-ski-related excitement and good times. This tiny Victorian town has been accurately described as "Fifth Avenue at 8,000 feet"—and a few hours of browsing through **Aspen**'s myriad art galleries, bou-tiques, four-star hotels, gourmet restaurants and dreamy real estate offices requires no further explanation. Beyond the Picassos, cigar bars and Gucci gloves, you'll find a hopping après-ski scene, brimming with late-night live entertainment, cutting-edge cabaret, country-western dance halls and the famed **Aspen** Ballet. Head a bit further afield and some of the most sublime mountain backcountry can be explored by foot, horse, snowmobile or dogsled.

There's never a bad time to come to **Aspen**, and chances are your visit will coincide with some sort of world-class music, film, comedy or arts festival or even the annual Wintersköl bash. This four-day celebration in mid-January turns **Aspen** into a carnival of winter fun and looniness—canine beauty pageant and linked-arm slalom race included. But it's the aprés-ski atmosphere that keeps **Aspen** hot all winter long.

On the Calendar

Official Event Dates
Skiing is best from mid-January to mid-March.

Best 3 Days To Be There
Thursday-Saturday

Colorado

Accommodations

The **St. Regis Aspen** is a deluxe hotel steps away from Aspen Mountain's Silver Queen Gondola. Alpine amenities here include breathtaking mountain views from your room, marble bathrooms, spa facilities, two après-ski bars and an excellent restaurant on the premises. The **Little Nell Hotel** gets you even closer to the ski lifts—a lavish, five-star, ski-in, ski-out property with gas-burning fireplaces, down-filled sofas, Belgian wool carpeting and five-star prices. Next door, the **Aspen Club Lodge** offers comfort and convenience with a European flavor. Set in a handsomely restored Victorian building, the historic **Hotel Jerome** remains one of Aspen's great landmarks. **Hotel Lenado**, with its in-house library and rooftop hot tub, is a warm and intimate bed-and-breakfast. Rooms are furnished with four-poster hickory beds and come with a full gourmet breakfast.

Restaurants

You won't go hungry in Aspen. More than 100 restaurants offer a wider variety of dining experiences than one visit can stomach. **Piñons** continues to be Aspen's highest-rated restaurant, featuring American cuisine with a dash of Colorado in an elegant setting. **Montagna**, in the Little Nell Hotel, is another gorgeously set choice with an exquisite American-alpine menu. A night of dinner theater at the **Crystal Palace** is something completely different. Order prime rib or poached halibut and then watch your wait staff break into song and lampoon everything in sight. It's an Aspen institution. **Hickory House** is a longtime favorite for a hearty Colorado-style breakfast or, later in the day, the best barbequed babyback ribs in town. For great burgers, homemade soups and a lively local scene, check out **Little Annie's Eating House**.

Aspen's choice of phenomenal ethnic restaurants also runs the gamut. Sushi lovers should head for **Kenichi**, which offers a full pan-Asian menu. **Cache Cache** is a lively French bistro with light Provençal dishes, sharing the same charming patio with **Campo de Fiori**, a rustic, jam-packed trattoria with an exceptional wine list. The fun, Latin-influenced **Blue Maize** serves pleasing pitchers of sangria along with blue-corn trout and new-world fajitas. A fine dining and dogsled experience at **Krabloonik** is worth the twenty-minute shuttle to Snowmass Village. Dishes such as Escallope of Wild Boar and Noisettes of Caribou are served in a rustic log house—right next to a kennel of 200 sled dogs. Reserve a sled and take it for an evening run. Reserve a table at the small **Cloud Nine Bistro**, which serves up pastas, wild game and some of Aspen's most spectacular Alpine scenery.

Nightlife

Aspen has no shortage of spots for après-ski schmoozing, relaxing and (if your knees can handle it) dancing. Set in the comfortable Hotel Jerome, **The J-Bar** has been a favorite local watering hole since the 1890s—long before its satellite TV was installed. The **Greenhouse** is right at the base of mountain, serving cold drinks, appetizers and live jazz near a roaring fireplace in the hotel's luxurious lobby. **The Cigar Bar** is an elegantly furnished room, perfect for quiet socializing and smoking fine cigars—and under the same roof with pool tables (Aspen Billiards) and your choice of forty single malt Scotches (Eric's Bar).

One of Aspen's best late-night, live music venues is **Double Diamond**, featuring a spectrum of local and national music acts throughout the week. **Club Chelsea** provides a cool, subterranean setting with live entertainment in the jazz club, a disco and light, gourmet fare served until 1 a.m. **Whiskey Rocks** is from the makers of L.A.'s ultra-hip SkyBar—another beautiful-people spot accompanied by live rock and blues (on the Mill Street side of the St. Regis Hotel). Any extra energy can be expended at **Shooters Saloon and Dance Hall**, which has live music and a weekly disco night.

Ski Resorts

Aspen's family of four mountains satisfies experienced mogul hounds, first-time skiers and everyone in between. Overlooking the center of town, the 11,212-foot-tall **Aspen Mountain** (aka Ajax) caters to advanced and solid intermediate skiers—and, after holding out for several years, to snowboarders as well. An unforgettable alpine setting is furnished with a high-speed gondola and several restaurants—including two that share a 22,000-square-foot sundeck. A mile outside of town, **Aspen Highlands** (the local favorite) is the steepest, toughest and least crowded mountain of the bunch. **Buttermilk**, just a few miles out of town toward Snowmass, is the best choice for beginners and take-it-easy skiers. The mountain's gentle terrain makes the perfect learning site, but for this reason it tends to draw heavier crowds. About ten miles from Aspen, **Snowmass** is the largest mountain of the group and serves the widest range of ski levels. It's a favorite resort for families and has its own village of retail stores, twenty restaurants and by far the best ski-in, ski-out facilities.

Area Attractions
Aspen is as wild or as refined as you want it to be. A fun way to get oriented is with **Heritage Aspen**, whose costumed guides will introduce you to downtown Aspen and its historic West End. During summer months, "resident ghosts" can also tour you through the storied ghost town of nearby Ashcroft. Five minutes from Aspen is the **T Lazy 7 Ranch**, a secluded 400-acre property and outfitter that leads snowmobile tours, horseback riding and a bunch of other outdoor activities in Aspen's surrounding backcountry.

In town, the **Aspen Art Museum** is housed in a heritage brick building that was once the first hydroelectric plant west of the Mississippi. Now it's a place to enjoy world-class art exhibits, classes and other special art-related events. The **Wheeler Opera House** is an equally hallowed property, hosting more than 300 events annually, including concerts from the world's top musicians and actors.

Wintersköl
Aspen's annual **Wintersköl Celebration** is a favorite fifty-year tradition. Held in mid-January, the festival is a four-day tribute to anything revolving around fun in the snow—with some lunacy thrown in for good measure. Each of the four mountains gets its day in the sun during this long-long weekend, hosting ski competitions and non-ski events. It feels a little small-townish, but can be enjoyable if you go in for this sort of thing. Aspen Highlands Day hosts thought-provoking contests such as the Apple Strudel Downhill, the Linked-Arm Slalom Race and the Kidsculpt Snow Sculpture contest. On Aspen (Ajax) Day, animal lovers will enjoy the Canine Fashion Show, a catwalk of sorts for Aspen's most glamorous dogs. The Annual World's Fair in downtown Aspen is a recent addition, filled with clowns, face-painters and musical guests with names like The Flying Dog Bluegrass Band. Buttermilk hosts the annual Buttermilk Uphill and Pancake Breakfast, unleashing a horde of snowshoers, telemarkers and hikers on a race up to the summit. The most notorious event of all is held at Snowmass—Ski Splash, a rowdy competition where costumed (and barely clothed) entrants schuss downhill into a swimming pool. There's a torchlight descent down Aspen Mountain and a good display of evening fireworks.

The Top Five Fun Ski Destinations, North America

If your primary interest is skiing, you probably have a list of favorite places to go. But if you also care about après-ski culture, certain destinations stand out. Whether you read *Skiing* or *Travel and Leisure*, you'll find there's a general consensus regarding the five most fun ski resorts in North America.

The most significant challenger to Aspen's rank as the most fun place to ski is *Lake Tahoe*. Less exclusive than Aspen, Tahoe has as much scenery, charm, restaurants, nightlife and top-notch facilities and accommodations as any first-class ski resort. Straddling the California-Nevada border, it also offers something no other ski destination can: top-grade casino gambling. In March, it's the home of Snowfest—the biggest winter carnival in the West.

Killington is in Vermont and many of its visitors are high-intensity New Yorkers. *Park City* visitors compensate for being in anti-party Utah by being intensely dedicated to the late-night arts. *Whistler-Blackcomb*, in British Columbia, Canada, is now one of the world's largest and liveliest ski resorts.

General information numbers:
Aspen, Colo.: 800-525-6200
Killington, Vt.: 800-621-6867
Lake Tahoe, Nev.: 800-824-6348
Park City, Utah: 800-227-2754
Whistler-Blackcomb, Canada: 888-403-4727

The Hot Sheet

Hotels	Phone	Address	Price	Fax	Rooms/Best
Aspen Club Lodge	970-925-6760	709 E. Durant Ave.	$$$$	970-925-6778	93/Mtn vw
Hotel Jerome	970-920-1000	330 Main St.	$$$$+	970-925-2784	92/Mtn vw suite
Hotel Lenado	970-925-6246	200 S. Aspen St.	$$$	970-925-3840	19/Smuggler room
The Little Nell Hotel	970-920-4600	675 E. Durant Ave.	$$$$+	970-920-4670	92/Town suite
The St. Regis Aspen	970-920-3300	315 E. Dean St.	$$$$+	970-925-8998	257/Alpine suite

Restaurants	Phone	Address	Price	Rec	Food
Blue Maize	970-925-6698	308 S. Hunter St.	$$	D	Latin American, Southwestern
Cache Cache	970-925-3835	205 S. Mill St.	$$$	D	French
Campo de Fiori	970-920-7717	205 S. Mill St.	$$$	D	Italian
Cloud Nine Bistro	970-544-3063	Top of Cloud Nine Lift	$$$	D	American Continental
Crystal Palace Theatre & Restaurant	970-925-1455	300 E. Hyman Ave.	$$$$+	D	Continental/ dinner theatre
Hickory House	970-925-2313	730 W. Main St.	$$	BLD	American/ribs
Kenichi	970-920-2212	533 E. Hopkins Ave.	$$$	D	Pan-Asian/sushi
Krabloonik	970-923-3953	4250 Divide Rd. (Snowmass)	$$$$	LD	American
Little Annie's Eating House	970-925-1098	517 E. Hyman Ave.	$$	LD	American
Montagna	970-920-6330	675 E. Durant Ave.	$$$	BLD	American
Piñons	970-920-2021	105 S. Mill St.	$$$$	D	American

Nightlife	Phone	Address	Cover	Rec*	Music
The Cigar Bar	970-920-4244	315 E. Hyman Ave.	None	R	
Club Chelsea	970-920-0066	415 E. Hyman Ave.	$	MP(F)	Classic rock
Double Diamond	970-920-6905	450 S. Galena St.	$	MP	Funk, jazz, blues, hip hop
The Greenhouse	970-920-4600	675 E. Durant Ave.	None	R(F)	
The J-Bar	970-920-1000	330 E. Main St.	None	M(F)	
Shooters Saloon and Dance Hall	970-925-4567	Galena Street and Hyman Avenue	None	MP	Rock/Top 40
Whiskey Rocks	970-544-2485	515 S. Mill St.	None	MR	Rock, blues

* M=Live music; P=Dancing (Party); R=Bar only; S=Show; (F)=Food served. For further explanation of codes, page 12.

Sights & Attractions	Phone	Address	Entry Fee
Aspen Art Museum	970-925-8050	590 N. Mill St.	$
Heritage Aspen	970-925-3721	620 W. Bleeker St.	$
T Lazy 7 Ranch	970-925-4614	3129 Maroon Creek Rd.	$$$$+
Wheeler Opera House	970-920-5770	320 E. Hyman Ave.	$$

Other sites, shops & services	Phone	Address
Aspen Highlands	888-649-5984	Maroon Creek Road, 2 miles from town of Aspen
Aspen Mountain (Ajax)	800-525-6200	Hwy 82, 5 miles past Brush Creek Road
Buttermilk	888-649-5984	Hwy 82, 3 miles from town of Aspen
Snowmass	970-923-2000	Brush Creek Road, 5 miles west of Hwy 82

Aspen CVB   **970-925-2773**

 NYC -2   Aspen/Pitken County Airport (ASE) <10 min./$25   No   Map Code: A07

Colorado

Inauguration

Washington, D.C.

(Presidential Inauguration)

Key Month: Jan   Ratings: Event ★ ★ ★ ★ ☆   **P**   City ★ ★ ★ ★ ☆   Origin: 1809   Attendance: 15,000

It's been said that Washington, D.C. is considered the world's most important city—just not in the United States. That theory goes out the window at least once every four years when a new (or re-elected) American president is sworn into office—just in time for America's best party.

It doesn't come around every year, but *Inauguration* week overcomes often freezing weather to provide visitors with the most unforgettable visit to the nation's capital. For the network anchormen, noon on January 20th is the country's defining hour—when a peaceful transition of power symbolizes something far beyond the electoral mudslinging of months past. But for about 15,000 of the half-million people who show up in D.C., it is the slew of official and unofficial celebrations all week long that create the buzz. All of it is capped off by the *Inaugural Balls* (the first inaugural ball was thrown in 1809—there are now eight or nine of them each year) on the first night of the president's term.

Partying is interrupted for watching your new president and vice-president being sworn into office on the steps of the Capitol, hearing the president's inaugural address booming over the expansive National Mall and then mobbing storied Pennsylvania Avenue for the *Inaugural Parade*. Standing there, flanked by the country's most regal buildings, monuments and memorials, you're taking part in a tradition as old as George Washington's first oath of office (held in New York City) in 1789.

Every *Inauguration* week is different, a gigantic bash marked by the personality of the incoming commander in chief. Some presidents will walk across the Memorial Bridge with their family and pet (Clinton, 1993). Some will parade through town on horseback with thousands of cowboys, miners and Rough Riders (Roosevelt, 1905). Others will deliver a two-hour acceptance speech in an ice storm, contract pneumonia, and die a month later (Harrison, 1841). And others will throw a Black Tie 'n Boots Ball (Bush, 2001). New trends are paramount when the next American president comes to town.

Visitors will want to overdose on famous attractions such as the Smithsonian Institution, Arlington National Cemetery and the top of the restored Washington Monument. With its atmosphere of diplomacy, bevy of landmarks, ethnic diversity and refined nightlife, D.C. is one of the great world capitals—no doubt the greatest during *Inauguration* week.

On the Calendar

Official Event Dates

January 20 (if Sunday, then January 21), every four years beginning in 2005

Best 3 Days To Be There

January 18-20. The main event is the night of January 20, but pre-events are often as much fun.

☽ 27°/42° (-3°/6°)

District of Columbia

42   For links to most current web sites for cities and events, go to www.funrises.com

The itinerary includes a single Inaugural Ball on the 20th, but you will likely find yourself at other parties on the preceding two nights.

DAY 1 — January 18

9:30 am Stroll to the 115-year-old **Reeves ❌ Restaurant and Bakery** for a full breakfast. Grover Cleveland was president around the time this D.C. institution first opened its doors.

10:00 am Enjoy the varied collection of European and American art at the **National Gallery of Art**. Or visit the **National Air and Space Museum**, the world's most visited museum, with attractions ranging from the Wright brothers' 1903 Flyer to an exhibit that allows you to walk on a re-created moon surface. **Ford's Theatre**, the site of Lincoln's assassination, has a small museum as well.

Noon Walk to the beautifully restored Union ❌ Station and have lunch at **B. Smith's**. The stylish ambience suits the New American cuisine.

2:00 pm Head across the Memorial Bridge to the **Arlington National Cemetery**. Almost 275,000 veterans and their dependents are buried on the 612-acre grounds, which include John F. Kennedy's gravesite and the Tomb of the Unknown Soldier.

4:00 pm Explore one of Arlington's most recent attractions, the **Newseum**—an interactive museum solely devoted to journalism and the making of the news.

7:00 pm Pay your respects to the capital's most famous edifices on a Monuments by Moonlight Tour with **Old Town Trolley Tours**. This unique, after-hours excursion rolls you through the capital's illuminated highlights—including the White House, the Capitol, the Lincoln, Jefferson and Vietnam Veterans Memorials and other points of interest.

9:30 pm Dine at **Cities**, where the menu ❌ varies according to the featured city and the food is always well-prepared. At the swank **Prive**, a disco is located upstairs. You may not want to leave until its 3 a.m. closing, but ...

11:30 pm At **Zei Club**, you can toast this term's new executive team by boogying into the late hours to a state-of-the-art sound system with go-go dancers.

DAY 2 — January 19

10:00 am Have breakfast in the hotel and then brace yourself for the sobering **U.S. Holocaust Memorial Museum**. Artifacts, photos, films and interactive exhibits tell the story of Jewish persecution by the Nazis in one of the world's finest museums.

11:30 am The **Smithsonian Institution** is an incredible collection of fourteen separate, world-class museums. These include art museums, such as the Freer Gallery of Art and the Hirshhorn Museum and Sculpture Garden, as well as the National Museum of American History and the National Museum of Natural History.

1:30 pm Try the very fresh fish and atmos- ❌ phere at nearby **Kinkead's**. Downstairs is quick and casual; both levels serve full lunches.

3:00 pm Head to the Adams-Morgan district, Washington's most eclectic and multicul-tural neighborhood. You'll find sidewalk cafes, galleries and theaters here, as well as the city's best assortment of ethnic cuisine along 18th Street and Columbia Road. A worthwhile stop is the **D.C. Arts Center**, which displays work from emerging artists.

8:00 pm Enjoy dinner at **Cashion's Eat Place**, ❌ an Adams-Morgan spot where you'll be charmed by the atmosphere and the food. Or, in Georgetown, dine at **Café Milano**, where foreign diplomats often sit next to supermodels or basketball stars. Milano's phenomenal success comes from its jet-set atmosphere, as well as its light pastas and pizzas.

10:00 pm Cab to **Blues Alley**, the oldest jazz supper club in the United States. Its schedule often looks like a Who's Who of the jazz and blues world—all the legends have played the stage here at one time or another.

11:30 pm You'll find a fun crowd and good beer at **Nathan's**, **Clyde's** or a host of other Georgetown hangouts. A few blocks away, **Sequoia**'s patio-bar scene makes it a con-sistent local favorite.

1:30 am Good food after midnight? **Bistro Français** serves nightcaps until late, along with its famed chicken and *pommes frites*.

Day-by-Day Plan

DAY 3 — January 20

10:00 am Enjoy a hearty breakfast at the **Old** ✖ **Ebbitt Grill**, an institution serving politicos since 1856 in its wood-and-brass saloon.

11:00 am Make your way across the National Mall with hordes of other well-wishers (and the odd protester) to the west steps of the Capitol Building for the *Swearing-In Ceremony*. Don't worry if you don't have front row seats. There's always the Jumbo-tron.

Noon Ladies and gentleman, your president will now deliver the *Inaugural Address*. Maybe it'll be right up there with Lincoln's "With malice toward none" speech or JFK's "Ask not" opus. Or, better yet, as brief and to-the-point as George Washington's 135-word, second-term acceptance speech—still the shortest one in U.S. history.

2:00 pm You made it through all the solemn stuff. Now it's time to follow the festive swarm onto Constitution and Pennsylvania avenues for the *Inaugural Parade*—a regal pageant of marching and military bands, floats, tumblers, cheerleaders, a new American president and all walks of noisy American life.

6:00 pm After a hotel room break, have a coffee or pre-dinner drink downstairs in the Willard's acclaimed bar, **Round Robin**. The collection of wall portraits depicts famous hotel guests from Walt Whitman to Charles Dickens.

8:00 pm As is custom, there will be several *Inaugural Balls* tonight—with the commander in chief and his V.P. making guest appearances at all of them. You've had two days to prepare to get into whichever ball is designated the hippest based on the venue (first choice is either the Kennedy Center or Union Square station), or who is entertaining. The only other things that matter are: what the First Lady or First Gentleman wears, what the president sings or plays on stage, and ✖ what you have to eat.

1:00 am Close out the weekend driving past the Reflecting Pool, which is flanked by the Lincoln Memorial and the Washington Monument. The monuments, breathtakingly lit and mirrored on the water, will remind you of much of the drama and history that has placed Washington at the center of the modern world.

More Time, More Choices

For classy, elegant dining, try **Butterfield 9** for its contemporary American cuisine and seasonal menu. Other fun dining options include **Jaleo**, a chic spot for tapas, **Red Sage**, a Southwestern import and Congressional-staffer hangout, and **Bombay Club**, the city's best Indian restaurant. **Les Halles** is a D.C. institution, serving satisfying French-American cuisine. Make your own good time at **Café Atlantico**, a three-tiered dining room specializing in pan-Latin cuisine.

Drive downtown and catch **The Capitol Steps'** political-satire revue. Taking aim at similar targets, **The Gross National Product** is often just as funny. For a less-expensive alternative to Blues Alley, try **Bohemian Caverns** located in a historic landmark where every jazz great has played. Another good dancing scene is at the **Felix Restaurant & Lounge**. **Ozio's** and **Rumors** are two of downtown's best meeting places.

The **International Spy Museum** has a huge collection of memorabilia from your favorite government agencies—FBI, KGB, Interpol.

Accommodations

Check in at the historic and elegant beaux-arts **Willard Inter-Continental Hotel**, where Martin Luther King Jr. composed his "I Have a Dream" speech while a guest. Between Georgetown and Foggy Bottom, the **Four Seasons Hotel** is noted for its contemporary elegance. The dignified **Hay-Adams Hotel** is the capital's most prestigious temporary address, barring its neighbor, the White House.

Event & Ticket Info

Presidential Inauguration (West steps of the Capitol, Pennsylvania Avenue): Free.

Inaugural Parade (Pennsylvania Avenue): Bleacher seats are $15-$100.

Inaugural Balls (various venues): $125-$900. The committee handling tickets won't be determined until after the election. In the meantime, contact *D.C. Visitor Information Center* (202-328-4748) for information.

The Hot Sheet

Hotels	Phone	Address	Price	Fax	Rooms/Best
Four Seasons Hotel	202-342-0444 800-332-3442	2800 Pennsylvania Ave. NW	$$$$+	202-342-3442	257/Georgetown, garden vw
Hay-Adams Hotel	202-638-6600 800-424-5054	1 Lafayette Sq.	$$$$	202-638-2716	143/White House or St. John's Church vw
Willard Inter-Continental Hotel	202-628-9100 800-327-0200	1401 Pennsylvania Ave. NW	$$$$	202-637-7307	341/Capitol and Washington Monument vw

Restaurants	Day	Phone	Address	Price	Rec	Food
B. Smith's	1	202-289-6188	50 Massachusetts Ave. NE	$$	L/BD	Southern
Bistro Français	2	202-338-3830	3128 M St. NW	$$	D/L	French
Bombay Club	A	202-659-3727	815 Connecticut Ave. NW	$$	LD	Indian
Butterfield 9	A	202-289-8810	600 14th St. NW	$$$	LD	New American
Café Atlantico	A	202-393-0812	405 8th St. NW	$$$	D/L	Latin American
Café Milano	2	202-333-6183	3251 Prospect St. NW	$$$	D/L	Italian
Cashion's Eat Place	2	202-797-1819	1819 Columbia Rd. NW	$$	D	American
Cities	1	202-328-2100	2424 18th St. NW	$$$	D	Varies
Jaleo	A	202-628-7949	480 7th St. NW	$$	LD	Spanish
Kinkead's	2	202-296-7700	2000 Pennsylvania Ave. NW	$$	L/D	Seafood
Les Halles	A	202-347-6848	1201 Pennsylvania Ave. NW	$$	LD	French, American
Old Ebbitt Grill	3	202-347-4801	675 15th St. NW	$$	BLD	American
Red Sage	A	202-638-4444	605 14th St. NW	$$$	LD	American, Southwestern
Reeve's Restaurant and Bakery	1	202-628-6350	1306 G St. NW	$	B/L	American breakfast

Nightlife	Day	Phone	Address	Rec*	Cover	Music
Blues Alley	1	202-337-4141	1073 Wisconsin Ave. NW	M(F)	$$	Jazz
Bohemian Caverns	A	202-299-0801	2001 11th St.	M(F)	$	Jazz, blues
The Capitol Steps	A	202-312-1555	1300 Pennsylvania Ave. NW	S	$$$	
Clyde's	2	202-333-9180	3236 M St. NW	R(F)	None	
Felix Restaurant & Lounge	A	202-483-3549	2406 18th St. NW	MP	$	Funk
The Gross National Product	A	202-783-7212	701 Pennsylvania Ave. NW	S	$$$	
Nathan's	2	202-338-2000	3150 M St. NW	R(F)	None	
Ozio's	A	202-822-6000	1813 M St. NW	P(F)	$	International
Prive	1	202-328-2100	2424 18th St. NW	P(F)	None	Dance
Round Robin	3	202-628-9100	see the Willard hotel	R	None	
Rumors	A	202-466-7378	1900 M St. NW	P(F)	$	Top 40
Sequoia	3	202-944-4200	3000 K St. NW	R(F)	None	
Zei Club	2	202-842-2445	1415 Zei Alley NW	MP	$$	International

* M=Live music; P=Dancing (Party); R=Bar only; S=Show; (F)=Food served. For further explanation of codes, page 12.

Sights & Attractions	Day	Phone	Address	Entry Fee
Arlington National Cemetery	1	703-697-2131	Arlington, Va.	None
D.C. Arts Center	1	202-462-7833	2438 18th St. NW	None
Ford's Theatre	1	202-638-2367	511 10th St. NW	None
International Spy Museum	A	866-779-6873	800 F St. NW	$
National Air and Space Museum	1	202-357-1400	6th St. & Independence Ave. SW	None
National Gallery of Art	1	202-737-4215	4th St. & Constitution Ave. NW	None
Newseum	A	703-284-3544	1101 Wilson Blvd.	None
Old Town Trolley Tours	1	202-832-9800	2640 Reed St. NE	$$$
Smithsonian Institution	3	202-357-2700	1000 Jefferson Dr. SW	None
U.S. Holocaust Mem. Museum	3	202-488-0400	100 Raoul Wallenberg Pl. SW	None
White House	1	202-456-2200	1600 Pennsylvania Ave. NW	None

DC Visitor Center **202-328-4748** **1300 Pennsylvania Ave. NW**

 NYC   Dulles (IAD) <60 min./$45 Reagan National (DCA) <30 min./$15  No Map Code: A08

Bike Week

*Daytona Beach
(Orlando)*

Key Month: Feb/Mar Ratings: Event ★ ★ ★ ★ ☆ **V** City ★ ★ ★ ☆ ☆ Origin: 1937 Attendance: 500,000

Leave your Schwinns at home—we're talking Harleys! Unless you're already a tattooed hog-rider, **Bike Week** provides one of the most incredible scenes you're likely to encounter. Even if you weren't born to bike, herds of renegade wild ones in leather, constant roaring engines and high levels of biker camaraderie at Daytona **Bike Week** will make you feel like one of the gang.

Thousands of bikers thunder their iron horses into Daytona for this annual week of motorcycle worship amid a down-'n'-dirty schedule of events. The "Miss" contests are a big draw—Miss Jägermeister, Miss Florida Biker, Miss Jack Daniel's, etc.—as are the "ladies" arm-wrestling championships, tattoo contests and wet T-shirt contests. Some bars pit wrestlers in coleslaw or stage fashion shows featuring the latest in road-hog couture. You can always attend a motorcycle show or derby.

Even the meek can get a thrill watching the perpetual parade of Mad Max refugees cruising through town on motorcycle and foot. Especially toward the end of **Bike Week**, Daytona becomes Harley heaven (or hell, depending on your perspective) when hordes of windburned Hell's Angels and other moto-clubbers slowly rumble and belch their bikes along Main Street, reinventing traffic laws and triggering a chorus of car alarms.

On the Calendar

Official Event Dates

10 days (Friday-Sunday) beginning last Friday of February

Best 3 Days To Be There

Thursday-Saturday, before final Sunday. You'll miss the final races on Sunday, but none of the partying.

☾ 53°/75° (12°/24°)

Your bases for the weekend, Daytona Beach and Orlando, are separated by sixty miles of highway and light years of attitude. Daytona's free-wheeling spring-breaklike atmosphere features the world-famous Daytona International Speedway and a car-friendly, 500-foot-wide, twenty-mile-long beach. By comparison, Orlando is Type A, a planned city where people are more carefully groomed, and lodging and dining are available for even the most fastidious customer. You could spend more time in either place, but the contrast between the two cities over a three-day vacation heightens the fun.

For details on a visit to an entirely different world (a make-believe world) near Orlando, read the chapter on Walt Disney World (page 54). For the adventurous, however, **Bike Week** should prove that reality is often more incredible than fantasy.

DAY 1 — Thursday

10:00 am A short drive north, **Universal Studios Florida** is the country's second most popular theme park (Walt Disney World is first). In addition to rides and attractions, the 400-acre sprawl includes television and movie studios.

1:00 pm In Universal Studios' area reproducing San Francisco, grab an outdoor table with a view of the lagoon at ✖ **Lombard's Landing**. Lunch on specialties such as blackened-chicken sandwich or freshly caught fish.

2:30 pm Spend the rest of the afternoon completing your day's tour of the theme park. By the time you leave the park, you'll have survived a movie earthquake, zombie attack, robot shootout, extraterrestrial contact, a tornado, time travel and a cartoon chase.

7:30 pm *Orlando Weekly* picked **Timpano** ✖ **Italian Chop House** as the city's Best New Restaurant for 2001. It's got big portions of excellent seafood and great service in a romantic atmosphere.

9:00 pm Located in a 1928 building and illuminated by wall candles, **Sapphire** is the best jazz venue in town. Choose a drink from Sapphire's specialty list— maybe a Fris Super Dag Daddy or a Luscious Lushes.

10:30 pm Take a three-block walk south to the nineteenth-century-themed **Church Street Station**, where the Cheyenne Saloon and Opera House has a live Western show and dancing. It's touristy, but the period recreations are outstanding.

DAY 2 — Friday

8:30 am Have a traditional American breakfast beside a thirty-five-foot waterfall at ✖ **Cascade**, the Grand Cypress' restaurant.

10:00 am At leviathan theme park **SeaWorld of Florida**, visit Shamu, the splash-happy killer whale. Worth scheduling are the people-drenching mammals in the Dolphin Pool; a ride on the water coaster, Wild Atlantis; and the exhibit of endangered manatees.

1:30 pm **The Crab House** stands out among ✖ dozens of tourist restaurants on International Drive. Fresh fish is served in a casual atmosphere.

3:30 pm As you approach Daytona, an hour away, the spectacle of droves of motorcycles and choppers will inspire you to shift gears. You should be seeing part of the *Boardwalk Ride-in Bike Show*, which roars down the Main Street Boardwalk between 11 a.m. and 4 p.m., giving attendees the chance to proudly showcase their gleaming hogs. (You might want to skip Orlando activities today in order to get to Daytona Beach in time to see the whole Ride-in.)

5:00 pm In Daytona pick up a Bike Week schedule at the Official Bike Week Welcome Center. Have fun getting ready with biker-wear and tattoo decals at **Easyriders**.

7:30 pm There's a lot of cool biker memorabilia on the walls at **Cruisin' Cafe**. ✖ Tables are embossed with driver and racing trivia. It's a good place for a warm-up beer.

8:30 pm A couple miles north, **Billy's Tap Room** has been wetting whistles since 1922. At one time, it served mere pub food, but now the menu lists escargot, burgers and espresso.

10:00 pm A mile north, Ormond Beach's two main biker bars roll with Southern rock. Choppers are parked in rows out front of the **Iron Horse** and **Jackson Hole Saloon**— chances are you'll see an arm-wrestling match, a tattoo contest and at least one wet T-shirt contest. Be out front at midnight when one unfortunate motorcycle is exploded, just for fun.

Day-by-Day Plan

DAY 3 — Saturday

10:00 am After a hotel breakfast, make a pit stop at **Daytona U.S.A.** Added in 1996 to Daytona International Speedway—"the birthplace of speed"—it features interactive car-racing exhibits.

12:30 pm At the **Highlander Cafe**, savor a ❌ grilled steak on the shady deck while listening to local country or rock bands.

2:00 pm Hit every wet T-shirt, arm-wrestling and tattoo contest in Daytona. Stop by the Ocean Center to view Big Daddy Rat's **Rat's Hole Custom Chopper Show** and the **Harley-Davidson Motorcycle Expo**.

3:30 pm At any of Daytona's beach entrances, pay a small fee, then take your sport utility vehicle where it's supposed to go— off the road. Cruise the beach, park, and catch some final rays.

6:00 pm Join *Bike Week* partiers taking over Main Street. On Oceanfront Park a rock group will be playing. At the Adam's Mark beachside pool bar, **Splash Bar & Grill**, knock back tropical drinks.

8:00 pm Head to the airy **St. Regis** restaurant, ❌ four blocks away. Housed in an 1886 Victorian, it serves American-Continental cuisine on a garden patio.

9:30 pm Tonight it's "last chance" partying. The crowd is extra rowdy and pubs pump enough beer to threaten world reserves. Go to **Froggy's Saloon**, a *Bike Week* favorite, and **Boot Hill Saloon**, which has live music and a beer garden. Or retreat to the **Clocktower Lounge** at the Adam's Mark.

2:00 am With your leather lust stirred and wild side uncaged, vow to return to next year's *Bike Week* on the wings of an iron eagle.

After

On the last Sunday of *Bike Week*, a couple hundred motorcycles are blessed at 7 a.m. by a priest at St. Paul's Catholic Church in Daytona. At 9 a.m., fans gather to cheer 4,000 bikers parading from Bellair Plaza to Daytona International Speedway. At the **Daytona 200**, motorcycles buzz around extreme grades that make the racecourse arguably the fastest in the world.

More Time, More Choices

In Daytona, **Aunt Catfish's on the River** does down-home dishes such as fried catfish fingerlings. A linen-and-flowers retreat from Daytona's biker brouhaha, **Anna's Trattoria** is run by a Sicilian family who make Old Country specialties. There's also Ormond Beach's upscale **Frappes North**, which combines fresh and unusual ingredients in its dishes. On Highway 1, south from Ormond Beach, go east on Route 44 to **Gilly's Pub 44**, where live rock bands play until 2 a.m. Be sure to check out **Tabu,** which has seven bars on two levels.

Accommodations

In Orlando, the **Hyatt Regency Grand Cypress**, is set on 1,500 tropical acres. While many of Orlando's hotels are strictly cookie-cutter, the **Peabody Orlando** is distinguished by marble floors and fountains. Just outside the *Bike Week* action, the **Daytona Beach Hilton Oceanfront Resort** is a place to relax near the beach, whereas the **Adam's Mark Daytona Beach Resort** is party central.

Event & Ticket Info

Bike Week (Various sites in Daytona Beach): Most events are free. *Official Bike Week Welcome Center* (386-255-0981).

The Boardwalk Ride-in Show (Boardwalk at Main Street): Free. For more information, contact *Boardwalk Merchants Association* (386-253-0254).

Harley-Davidson Motorcycle Expo and **Rat's Hole Custom Chopper Show** (Ocean Center, 101 N. Atlantic Ave.): Free. For more information, contact *Ocean Center* (386-254-4500).

Daytona 200 (Daytona International Speedway): Call 386-253-7223 for dates and ticket information.

Daytona Beach (Orlando)

Hotels		Phone	Address	Price	Fax	Rooms/Best
Adam's Mark Daytona Beach Resort		386-254-8200 800-444-2326	100 N. Atlantic Ave.	$$$	386-253-0275	437/Ocean front
Daytona Beach Hilton Oceanfront Resort		386-767-7350 800-221-2424	2637 S. Atlantic Ave.	$$$	386-760-3651	214/Ocean front
Hyatt Regency Grand Cypress		407-239-1234 800-233-1234	1 Grand Cypress Blvd.	$$$$	407-239-3800	750/Pool or lake vw
Peabody Orlando		407-352-4000 800-732-2639	9801 International Dr.	$$$	407-351-9177	891/Poolside

Restaurants	Day	Phone	Address	Price	Rec	Food
Anna's Trattoria	A	386-239-9624	304 Seabreeze Blvd.	$$	D	Italian
Aunt Catfish's on the River	A	386-767-4768	4009 Halifax Dr.	$$	LD	Seafood
Billy's Tap Room	2	386-672-1910	58 E. Granada Blvd.	$$	D/L	American
Cascade	2	407-239-1234	see Hyatt Regency hotel	$$	B/LD	American
The Crab House	2	407-352-6140	8291 International Dr.	$$	L/D	Fish, seafood
Frappes North	A	386-615-4888	123 W. Granada Blvd.	$$	LD	New American
Highlander Cafe	3	386-322-0320	1821 S. Ridgewood Ave.	$	L/D	American
Lombard's Landing	1	407-363-8000	see Universal Studios Florida	$$	L/D	Seafood
St. Regis	3	386-252-8743	509 Seabreeze Blvd.	$$$	D	American, continental
Timpano Italian Chop House	1	407-248-0429	7488 W. Sand Lake Rd.	$$$	D/L	Italian, seafood

Nightlife	Day	Phone	Address	Cover	Rec*	Music
Boot Hill Saloon	3	386-258-9506	310 Main St.	None	MP	Blues, rock
Church Street Station	1	407-422-2434	129 W. Church St.	None	MPS(F)	Country
Clocktower Lounge	3	386-254-8200	see Adam's Mark Daytona Beach Resort	None	MP(F)	Jazz
Cruisin' Cafe	2	386-254-8200	2 S. Atlantic Ave.	None	F(R)	Classic rock
Froggy's Saloon	3	386-253-0330	800 Main St.	None	MP(F)	Blues, rock
Gilly's Pub 44	A	386-428-6523	1889 State Rd. 44	None	MP(F)	Rock
Iron Horse	2	386-677-1550	1068 N. US Hwy. 1	None	M	Southern rock
Jackson Hole Saloon	2	386-673-6996	1081 N. US Hwy. 1	None	M(F)	Southern rock
Sapphire	1	407-246-1419	54 N. Orange Ave.	$	MP	Varies
Splash Bar & Grill	3	386-254-8200	see Adam's Mark Daytona Beach Resort	None	M(F)	Reggae, rock
Tabu	A	407-648-8519	46 N. Orange Ave.	$	P(F)	Varies

* M=Live music; P=Dancing (Party); R=Bar only; S=Show; (F)=Food served. For further explanation of codes, page 12.

Sights & Attractions	Day	Phone	Address	Entry Fee
Daytona USA	3	386-947-6800	1801 International Speedway Dr.	$$
SeaWorld of Florida	1	407-363-2613	7007 SeaWorld Dr.	$$$
Universal Studios Florida	2	407-363-8000	1000 Universal Studios Plaza	$$$

Other Sights, Shops & Services		Phone	Address	Entry Fee
Easyriders	2	386-238-1645	605 Main St.	None

Daytona Beach Area CVB	800-854-1234	126 E. Orange Ave.
Orlando Orange County CVB	407-363-5871	8723 International Dr.

Daytona Beach area code: 386   Orlando area code: 407

 NYC   Orlando (MCO) <30 min./$15
Daytona Beach (DAB) <30 min./$10   Yes   Map Code: A09

Florida

Fantasy Fest

Key Month: Oct   Ratings: Event ★ ★ ★ ★ ☆   **V**   City ★ ★ ★ ☆ ☆   Origin: 1979   Attendance: 100,000

If your fantasies have ever included watching a gorgeous sunset on a sandy beach with daiquiri in hand, then dancing in the streets until morning with the world's friendliest and most imaginative extroverts, *Fantasy Fest* may be your dream come true. An international cast of revelers exhibit their own fantasies during this festival that's one of the country's wildest and most colorful. If party god Bacchus were to star in a Looney Tunes cartoon, the result might look like *Fantasy Fest*.

The festival's grand finale is a lunatic twilight parade down Duval Street, the city's main drag, that draws as many as 70,000 people—twice the population of the island. The giddy crowd mills around, gawking at one outrageous costume after another. Local saloons throw rambunctious parties that don't wind down until 4 a.m.

Key West's always been famous for its laissez-faire attitude, but during *Fantasy Fest*, the city's casual "no dress code" rule is, well, modified. Revelers roam the streets in costumes that range from amazing to absurd—the recent twenty-foot, spaghetti-spouting spaceship qualified as both. Annual themes— "BC," "Call of the Wild," "Lost in the '60s"—inspire costume ideas. And though nudity is not allowed, body paint usually squeaks by as a costume.

Special events generally include a faux Bahamian village celebration, royal coronation ball, Annual Headdress Ball, toga parties, costume contests, the ever-popular Epidermal Arts and Torso Tapestries contest and, of course, beach parties galore.

Fantasy Fest began in 1979 when local merchants threw a Halloween party hoping to entice a few out-of-towners to the town's empty off-season hotels and restaurants. Hundreds came in costume to watch a ragtag parade that included a Rolls-Royce whose famous naked-lady hood ornament was replaced by a real naked lady, painted gold. Wire-service photos intrigued revelers and got the festival rolling.

Now, the fantasy takes over this picturesque and friendly island. Most of Key West's many excellent restaurants and 150-plus bars encourage the craziness. There's something perversely fun about dining at a four-star restaurant when the table to your left is occupied by a family of coneheads and the one to your right includes a group of burly men in petticoats. Everyone gets into the spirit, so plan to be a participant, not just a spectator.

On the Calendar

Official Event Dates
Nine days, ending Sunday after last Saturday in October

Best 3 Days To Be There
Thursday-Saturday before final Sunday. Fun events on Thursday and Friday lead to a Saturday-night climax.

☽ 76°/84° (24°/29°)

Florida

Day-by-Day Plan

DAY 1 Thursday

10:00 am Walk along the historic waterfront ❌ to **Pepe's Cafe** and select from omelet and pancake specials. Established in 1909, it's Key West's oldest restaurant.

11:00 am Walk along Duval Street to get acquainted with the center of *Fantasy Fest* activity.

Noon At funky **B.O.'s Fish Wagon**, grab ❌ eats for your afternoon sailing trip. Proprietor Buddy Owen is a Conch (or Key West native, it's pronounced konk) who can box you up famous Grouper fish sandwiches.

1:00 pm Don't miss Key West's greatest attraction: North America's only living coral reef. The **Sebago Catamaran** will sail you comfortably to the reef for a three-and-a-half-hour snorkeling adventure with beer and wine on the trip back.

1:15 pm Or, if you prefer, check out Key West's second greatest attraction: Wander all the way up Duval Street to the clothing-optional **Atlantic Shores Resort Pool Bar** for a cold drink. No matter what you wear, you'll be overdressed.

6:00 pm Catch the world-famous, nightly **Mallory Square Sunset Celebration**. Jugglers, acrobats, and musicians perform, as oglers await the glorious, sometimes-applauded sunsets over the Gulf of Mexico.

6:30 pm Dine at the Pier House Resort's pop-❌ ular **One Duval Bar** where, tonight, your highly coveted table on the waterfront patio becomes a theater box seat for ...

8:00 pm ... the annual Pretenders in *Paradise International Costume Contest*. The biggest contest of the festival, it's set on a huge stage on the beach. Professional costume builders come from around the world to entertain the standing-room-only crowd. Amateur-division entries are often hysterical.

11:00 pm Head up Whitehead Street to the **Green Parrot Bar**, the oldest bar in Florida. This working-class rock-and-roll club holds a raucous costume contest open to all.

DAY 2 Friday

9:00 am Wait in line at **Camille's** on Duval for ❌ a satisfying breakfast. Try the French toast made with homemade bread.

10:30 am Stroll down Duval, the Historic District's main thoroughfare, to the **Shipwreck Historium**. It celebrates Key West's nautical history and the "wrecking" business that once made Key West the wealthiest city in America. Cross the street to The **Mel Fisher Maritime Museum** to see examples of $200 million in gold, silver and emeralds salvaged from the richest Spanish shipwreck ever.

Noon Stop into the European-style sidewalk ❌ cafe, **Mangoes**, for a gourmet pizza and views of the Duval bustle.

2:00 pm The **Street Fair** on Duval gets rolling with arts, crafts, food, beer, beer and more beer. Shop for costumes and accessories for tomorrow's big parade. Visit **Fast Buck Freddie's** to watch master mask-maker Michael Stark create fantastic masks and headdresses.

4:00 pm Stop at **Flamingo Crossing**, a home-made-ice-cream shop with unusual flavors, such as sour sop and key lime.

5:00 pm Walk to the Key West Cemetery, famous for headstones with epitaphs such as "I told you I was sick" and "At least I know where he's sleeping tonight." It's the staging area for the *Masquerade March*, a wacky procession of grown-ups that trick-or-treat their way through bars and guest houses en route to the Ocean Key Resort's Sunset Pier.

7:00 pm A block from the pier, **Bagatelle** ❌ serves very fresh and very good seafood. A table on the wraparound veranda is perfect for watching the growing chaos in the streets.

9:00 pm The *Masquerade Fantasies* costume contest on the Ocean Key House Pier is open to walk-ons as well as serious costumers who've labored long for big prizes. Early birds get the few convenient seats.

11:00 pm At nearby **Jimmy Buffet's Margaritaville**, chill with perfect margaritas and live entertainment. Jimmy might be there, but he'll be hard to spot among the masqueraders. (Hint: He's the guy who has lost his shaker of salt.)

DAY 3 — Saturday

10:30 am Once a bordello, **Blue Heaven** is ⊗ now a backyard patio restaurant famous for generous breakfasts and quirky ambience. Yes, that is a rooster under your table.

Noon The **Conch Tour Train** takes you around the island. You'll learn about local history and architecture.

2:30 pm Back in town, the *Duval Street Promenade* has begun. There's live entertainment as partyers in costume start arriving for the parade. At the Hilton Resort and Marina, get a temporary tattoo or have your body painted at the *Airbrush Artist Competition*.

3:30 pm At the **801 Bourbon Bar**, the *Tea Dance* gets you mingling with that segment of the *Fantasy Fest* crowd that just can't wait to be outrageous.

5:00 pm Put on your costume and get to ⊗ **Alice's at La-te-da** on Duval for a preparade dinner. Sample the New World Fusion Confusion Cuisine, typified by dishes such as Mexican pot-stickers and Florida yellowtail over curried couscous.

7:00 pm The **Fantasy Fest Parade** has begun! Don't worry if you're still dining—it'll take at least two more hours for the parade to travel the twelve blocks to the judge's reviewing stand near Alice's. After dinner, you'll encounter true oddities along some of the safest streets in the country. TV lights in the front of the Holiday Inn La Concha make it one of the best viewing locations.

10:00 pm If you're hungry, the **Lazy Gecko** is a local favorite for late-night sandwiches and beer.

11:00 pm Duval will be packed until 1 a.m. For a change of scenery, head to the historic seaport for an icy beer at the definitively funky **Schooner Wharf Bar**. With live blues and Motown, it's the locally elected favorite bar in Key West and the perfect place to shed your costume and maybe jump into the harbor to cool off.

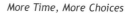

More Time, More Choices

On *Fantasy Fest* Thursday, **Sloppy Joe's** annual toga party makes the live-music bar even wilder than usual. Or try **Hog's Breath Saloon's** house beer and fresh seafood from the raw bar, then check out live entertainment on the patio, which includes a homemade-bikini contest (the schedule on this event varies, so call the bar ahead). Another place that gets crazy with costumes and revelers during Fantasy Fest is **Antonio's Italian** restaurant. Other dining options include **La Trattoria**, which offers fine Italian dining with a fabulous tiramisu; **P.T.'s** sports bar and restaurant, which serves tasty ribs and sandwiches until late; and **A&B Lobster House**, a good place to get a breather away from the madness.

Accommodations

Check into the **Ocean Key Resort**. With Jacuzzi suites at the edge of the harbor, it puts you in the center of the action. A short walk from Duval Street, the **Hyatt Key West** has a small beach along with first-class accommodations. The **Pier House Resort and Caribbean Spa** equips your stay with restaurants, bars, a spa and the only downtown beach.

Event & Ticket Info

Fantasy Fest (Various sites in Key West): Free admission. For a schedule of events, call *Fantasy Fest Headquarters* (305-296-1817).

Pretenders in Paradise (Pier House Resort): $25 at the door.

Hotels	Phone	Address	Price	Fax	Rooms/Best
Hyatt Key West	305-296-9900 800-233-1234	601 Front St.	$$$	305-292-1038	120/Gulf vw
Ocean Key Resort	305-296-7701 800-328-9815	0 Duval St.	$$$$	305-292-7685	104/All 900 sq ft suites, harbor front
Pier House Resort and Caribbean Spa	305-296-4600 800-327-8340	1 Duval St.	$$$	305-296-9085	142/Harbor front

Restaurants	Day	Phone	Address	Price	Rec	Food
A&B Lobster House	A	305-294-5880	700 Front St.	$$$	D	Seafood, lobster
Alice's at La-te-da	3	305-296-6701	1125 Duval St.	$$$	D/BL	Fusion
Antonio's	A	305-294-6565	615 Duval St.	$$$	D	Italian
B.O.'s Fish Wagon	1	305-294-9272	801 Caroline St.	$	L/D	Seafood
Bagatelle	2	305-296-6609	115 Duval St.	$$	D/L	Seafood
Blue Heaven	3	305-296-8666	729 Thomas St.	$	B/LD	American
Camille's	2	305-296-4811	703 1/2 Duval St.	$	B/LD	American
Flamingo Crossing	2	305-296-6124	1105 Duval St.	$	T	Ice cream
La Trattoria	A	305-296-1075	524 Duval St.	$$	D	Italian
Mangoes	2	305-292-4606	700 Duval St.	$	L/D	Continental
One Duval Bar	1	305-296-4600	see Pier House Resort	$$$	D/BL	American
P.T.'s	A	305-296-4245	920 Caroline St.	$$	LD	American
Pepe's Cafe	1	305-294-7192	806 Caroline St.	$	B/LD	American

Nightlife	Day	Phone	Address	Cover	Rec*	Music
801 Bourbon Bar	3	305-294-4737	801 Duval St.	None	S	
Atlantic Shores Resort	2	305-296-2491	510 South St.	None	R(F)	
Green Parrot Bar	1	305-294-6133	601 Whitehead St.	None	MP	Rock, salsa, blues, swing
Hog's Breath Saloon	A	305-292-2032	400 Front St.	None	MP(F)	Rock, pop
Jimmy Buffet's Margaritaville	2	305-292-1435	500 Duval St.	None	MP(F)	Rock, blues
Lazy Gecko	3	305-292-1903	203 Duval St.	None	P(F)	Varies
Schooner Wharf Bar	3	305-292-9520	202 William St.	None	MP(F)	Blues, jazz, Motown
Sloppy Joe's	A	305-294-5717	201 Duval St.	$	MP(F)	Rock, pop

* M=Live music; P=Dancing (Party); R=Bar only; S=Show; (F)=Food served. For further explanation of codes, page 12.

Sights & Attractions	Day	Phone	Address	Entry Fee
Conch Tour Train	3	305-294-5161	303 Front St.	$$
Fast Buck Freddie's	2	305-294-2007	500 Duval St.	None
Mallory Square Sunset Celebration	1		Mallory Sq.	None
The Mel Fisher Maritime Museum	2	305-294-2633	200 Greene St.	$
Sebago Catamaran	1	305-294-5687	200 William St.	$$$$+
Shipwreck Historium	2	305-292-8990	1 Whitehead St.	$

Chamber of Commerce	305-294-2587	402 Wall St.

 NYC Key West (EYW) <30 min./$5   No Map Code: A10

Florida

Do: Disney World

Walt Disney World

Key Month: n/a   Ratings: Event n/a   City ★ ★ ★ ★ ★   Origin: 1971   Attendance: n/a

Admit it. There's a kid in you that just loves the idea of wallowing in **Disney World**. Rides, attractions and even large, fuzzy cartoon characters never completely lose their appeal, but the park's often-overlooked emphasis on entertainment for grown-ups is a bigger draw than many fun seekers realize.

The Orlando offspring of the California original that invented the concept "theme park," **Disney World** has grown into a recreation district unrivaled perhaps anywhere on the globe. It covers forty-seven square miles—that's about twice the size of Manhattan Island—and in addition to the Magic Kingdom (more-or-less a facsimile of California's Disneyland) there are: Epcot Center, a world's-fair-cum-shopping-mall specializing in global iconography and corporate sponsorship; the Disney-MGM Studios, an ersatz production facility spiked with rides and shows; Disney's new 500-acre Animal Kingdom, an ostensibly cage-free salute to our relationship with animals; and two after-dusk entertainment zones, including a gated-admission nightclub island.

For much of the year, neophytes will find Walt's huge, shrewd machine defies concise touring plans. Tables for good restaurants are tied up weeks ahead, scampering moppets clog every artery and lines for the best attractions can top two hours (summer and holidays are the worst). Industry estimates point to **Disney World**'s theme parks posting an average of more than 100,000 admissions a day. So the perfect time to visit is when you'll encounter the shortest lines and the fewest families: early and mid-November, early December and mid-January are all quiet. Mid-October is the best time to find sublime weather and breathing room between the tourists.

What follows is a mere greatest-hits itinerary, rather than a top-to-bottom expedition strategy. You need a solid week to fully navigate it all, because **Disney World** also includes three lavishly themed water parks, five-and-a-half immaculately groomed golf courses, a Fantasia-inspired miniature-golf course and more. Today's **Disney World** adds up to a unique, 25,000-room resort/playground for everyone who refuses to stop being a kid, at least once in a while. (*For more on amusement parks, see page 207.*)

On the Calendar

Official Event Dates
Fall through spring is best time to avoid crowds/children (excluding Thanksgiving, Christmas and Easter holidays).

Best 3 Days To Be There
Thursday-Saturday

Florida

Day-by-Day Plan

DAY 1 — Thursday

8:30 am Drive or monorail to Epcot Center to be inside the gates before the "official" 9 a.m. opening. Ride Spaceship Earth, a fast-aging attraction about communication, inside the 180-foot-high silver golf ball. Make a beeline for Test Track, the ambitious speed ride simulating vehicle-performance testing, including a wildly-out-of-control brake test. Skip the GM car showroom and head for *Honey, I Shrunk the Audience*, an eighteen-minute, 3-D cinematic crowd-pleaser with surprising tactile effects. These three are Epcot's big kahunas—you'll want to knock them off first thing.

10:15 am Ride Journey into Your Imagination, an archetypal Disney *magnum opus* about creativity, then head to Living with the Land, a boat ride through dioramas and greenhouses that show how man can dominate Mother Nature through technology. Also tour The Living Seas.

11:45 am Leave Future World and enter World Showcase. Take a quick spin through the Mexico pavilion, but pass on the seductive-looking boat ride—it's a sorry infomercial for south-of-the-border tourism. Head to Norway and experience the cheery Maelstrom, the only real ride in World Showcase. The oft-missed Stave Church Gallery is a sanctuary from the throng.

12:30 pm Tender a hearty *koldtbord* at ✪ Norway's Restaurant **Akershus** (make reservations), one of Epcot's more successful eateries. Continue your tour of the World Showcase arena with China, Western Europe, Japan, Morocco, the United Kingdom and Canada. Of several promotional movies, *Impressions de France* is the best; the patriotic *American Adventure* is a large-scale, twenty-nine-minute production.

4:00 pm Return to Future World and Body Wars, a ride about a miniaturized voyage through the human body. Walk through Innoventions, a huge area exhibiting consumer products.

4:00 pm (cont.) If you stay late, have a snack and catch the incredible fireworks around the lake at 9 p.m.

9:30 pm Bus to Downtown Disney and ✪ **Bongo's Cuban Cafe** (no reservations; a wait is likely after 8 p.m.), a camp tribute to Ricky Ricardo's Havana, complete with Cuba libres and music.

11:00 pm After dinner, stop at Planet Hollywood, more a tourist attraction than a place to eat. Take in the music and scene at the **House of Blues**—it's modeled after an old-time Mississippi juke joint and showcases folk art from the Mississippi Delta (a Gospel brunch burns down the house on Sundays).

DAY 2 — Friday

8:30 am Enter the Magic Kingdom and head down Main Street to the Central Plaza in front of Cinderella Castle to get into position for the rope drop. At 9 a.m., bolt for Space Mountain and ride. Then quickly cross the park to Frontierland and experience Splash Mountain and Big Thunder Mountain Railroad. The three mountains are the park's biggest attractions and will grow long lines as the day wears on.

10:30 am Ride the Jungle Cruise, Pirates of the Caribbean and Haunted Mansion, a triumvirate of Disney classics. Head back ✪ to Tomorrowland—grab a snack at **Cosmic Ray's Starlight Cafe** (the veggie burgers are decent) before tackling the techno-horror of the ExtraTERRORestial Alien Encounter. Rinse that nasty aftertaste with Buzz Lightyear's Space Ranger Spin and the frisky Timekeeper. Wrap up at Fantasyland's It's a Small World, a saccharine rejoinder to your day at Epcot.

3:30 pm Monorail to the Grand Floridian for afternoon tea at the **Garden View Lounge**. Relax poolside or on the lakefront beach.

6:30 pm Take the bus to Disney's BoardWalk ✪ Resort. Dinner at the **Flying Fish Café** (make reservations two weeks ahead) is a seafood treat amid a frolicking carny/sealife ambience.

8:30 pm After dinner, explore Disney's wood-decked BoardWalk entertainment area, themed with an East Coast seaside leit-motif. **Jellyrolls Dueling Pianos** is pure fun. Try the **Atlantic Dance Hall** for martinis and occasional salsa dancing, or chill out in **The Belle Vue Room**, a 1930s sitting room adorned with antique radios playing nostalgic shows.

DAY 3 — Saturday

8:00 am Be at the front entrance to Animal Kingdom in time for opening. Head straight for Dinosaur, a rollicking thrill ride into the Cretaceous era. Do the Kilimanjaro Safaris, a twenty-minute adventure through the main wildlife enclosure (animals are most visible in the early morning). Walk the Gorilla Falls trail—note the detail of Harambe village.

10:00 am Travel to the ruins of Asia and ride Kali Rapids Run, a raft ride through a burning forest; walk the Maharajah Jungle Trek to see the Bengal tigers. Finish at the Tree of Life, a fabulous cement icon with more than 300 animals carved into its trunk. At its base is a theater where you'll find *It's Tough To Be a Bug*, a hilarious 3-D movie.

11:15 am Board a bus for the Disney-MGM Studios. Ride Star Tours, a motion simulator based on the *Star Wars* franchise, and see Jim Henson's *Muppet Vision* 3-D movie, starring the Muppets' cornball antics.

12:30 pm Lunch at the **Hollywood Brown ⊗ Derby** (make reservations), where drawings of legendary characters ornament the walls.

1:30 pm Note the start time for the afternoon parade (usually 1:30 or 3 p.m.) and time your visit to the Twilight Zone Tower of Terror to coincide with it. The studios' biggest hit, the Tower is a prodigious, special-effects-enhanced free fall that rates among Disney's best. Also see the Indiana Jones Epic Stunt Spectacular, the Great Movie Ride's history of Hollywood, and the Magic of Disney Animation (where *Mulan* was made).

1:30 pm (cont.) The Backlot Tour provides little filmmaking insight, but lots of crowd-pleasing explosions.

6:00 pm Finish at the studios with the first performance of *Fantasmic*, a fireworks-and-laser spectacular held after dusk.

8:00 pm Monorail to dinner at the **California ⊗ Grill**. A tribute to Wolfgang Puck-style cuisine, it's Disney's best restaurant. Located on the 15th floor of the Contemporary Resort, it has a great view of the Kingdom fireworks show (make reservations at least two weeks ahead).

10:00 pm Head downtown to **Pleasure Island**, a theme park for nightclubbing—country, jazz, rock and disco are housed in first-class venues. The quirky Adventurers Club is an improvisational all-night sketch set in a 1930s social club for world explorers. The nightly New Year's Eve street party starts at 11 p.m, providing a perfect way to close out one fun three-day chapter and ring in another.

■

More Time, More Choices

Get tickets for the famed Vegas show troupe, **Cirque du Soleil**, which puts on two shows daily at its permanent site in Downtown Disney West Side.

Disney's three water parks are a blast. The most thrilling is *Blizzard Beach*, a mock ski resort where the world's highest water slide (fashioned after a ski jump) towers over the Florida landscape.

Accommodations

Disney's **Grand Floridian Resort & Spa**, Mickey's premium digs, is themed after turn-of-the-century Florida resorts. From the hotel, you can easily drive or monorail to Epcot Center. The Michael Graves-designed **Walt Disney World Swan and Dolphin**, where over-the-top Floridian colors and themes meet postmodern whimsy, are two good alternative hotels. **Animal Kingdom Lodge** has 1,293 centrally located rooms where you can look out from your balcony and see zebras, giraffes and other exotic African animals.

Disney World

Hotels		Phone	Address	Price	Fax	Rooms/Best
Animal Kingdom Lodge		407-938-3000	Osceola Pkwy.	$$$	407-938-4799	1,293/Savannah vw
Grand Floridian Resort & Spa Lagoon		407-934-7639	4401 Grand Floridian Way	$$$$	407-824-3186	900/Lodge tower or vw of Seven Seas
Walt World Swan and Dolphin		407-934-3000 800-248-7926	1200-1500 Epcot Resorts Blvd.	$$$$	407-934-4710	2,267/Club rm w/ balc and resort vw

Restaurants	Day	Phone	Address	Price	Rec	Food
Bongo's Cuban Cafe	1	407-828-0999	Downtown Disney, West Side	$$	D/L	Cuban
California Grill	3	407-939-3463	4600 N. World Dr., Contemporary Resort, 15th flr.	$$$	D	American, seafood
Cosmic Ray's Starlight Cafe	2	407-939-3463	at the Magic Kingdom	$	L	American
Flying Fish Café	2	407-939-5100	on the BoardWalk	$$$	D	American, seafood
Garden View Lounge	2	407-824-3000	at the Grand Floridian Resort & Spa	$$	T	Afternoon tea
Hollywood Brown Derby	3	407-934-7639	at Disney-MGM Studios	$$$	L/D	American, seafood
Restaurant Akershus	1	407-939-3463	at Epcot Center	$$	L/D	Norwegian, seafood

Nightlife	Day	Phone	Address	Cover	Rec*	Music
Atlantic Dance Hall	2	407-939-5100	on the BoardWalk	$	P	Varies
The Belle Vue Room	2	407-939-5100	lobby of the BoardWalk Inn	None	R	
Cirque du Soleil	A	407-934-6110	1478 E. Buena Vista Dr.	$$$$+	S	
House of Blues	1	407-934-2583	Downtown Disney, West Side	$–$$$$+	M	Varies
Jellyrolls Dueling Pianos	2	407-939-5100	on the BoardWalk	$	M	Varies
Pleasure Island	3	407-934-7781	Downtown Disney	$$	MP	Wide variety

Event & Ticket Info

Walt Disney World offers a variety of ticket options. Most convenient is the length of stay pass which provides unlimited admission to all attractions (including Pleasure Island and water parks) from the morning of your arrival through the night of your departure. Prices vary based on the number of nights. Purchase tickets in advance through the *Walt Disney Travel Company* (800-828-0228).

Hot Tip: Disney resort guests (including Swan and Dolphin) may take advantage of an early-admission program called Surprise Mornings. Each of the main theme parks is open sixty to ninety minutes early two or three days each week—the result is minimal lines for big attractions at first, but higher-than-usual attendance by late morning. Either take advantage of the early-admission policy by arriving at 7:30 a.m., or skip the assigned Surprise Morning park for that day (the itinerary provided does not provide for the early-admission days).

Florida

 NYC Orlando (ORL) <30 min./$25 Yes/No Map Code: A11

Cruise: Carnival Victory

Port of Miami

Key Month: n/a   Ratings: Event n/a **V**   City ★ ★ ★ ★ ☆   Origin: 1996   Attendance: 2,700

The recipe is simple. Take 2,700 fun-loving people, put them in a first-class hotel where the scenery changes daily, provide warm weather, food, drink and music galore. Spice things up with a high-tech disco. Add water and you've got one hell of a party—and that's exactly what you'll find on the *Carnival Victory*.

The cruise industry is booming, with a surge prompted by the 1990s cinematic sinking of the *Titanic* (go figure). This is good news, because it means a wide range of choices among destinations, ship sizes, cruise lines and cabin prices.

While you can sail into any of the seven seas—it takes a harder-than-ice hull to navigate the Arctic and Antarctic—the most popular destinations include Mexico, Alaska, the Mediterranean and the most popular year-round cruise destination, the Caribbean. The combination of climate and island ambience—no heavy sightseeing here—also makes the Caribbean the most fun.

The cruise line to check out is *Carnival*, which takes fun so seriously they've registered the term *fun ship* for more than a dozen vessels decorated in what they call entertainment architecture. The quintessential fun ship, *Carnival Victory*, sails Sunday afternoons from Miami into the Caribbean and some of the fabled ports of paradise. You can sail eastward for San Juan, St. Maarten and St. Thomas, or as detailed here, head west toward Cozumel to tour the Maya ruins of the Yucatán, sunbathe on Grand Cayman's Seven Mile Beach and make a splashy climb up Dunn's River Falls in Ocho Rios.

One of the biggest cruise ships ever built, the 102,000-ton *Carnival Victory* carries not only 2,700 fun-seeking people, but also one of the largest water-slides ever built on a cruise ship (214 feet), two outdoor pools, a swim-up bar, an indoor pool, seven Jacuzzis, a high-tech disco with hundreds of video monitors, a 15,000-square-foot fitness facility and a 9,000-square-foot casino. But who's counting? The idea is just to kick back and have fun.

On the Calendar

Official Event Dates

Fall through spring is best time to avoid crowds/children (excluding Thanksgiving, Christmas and Easter holidays). Cruise is seven nights, eight days.

Florida

1 Sunday

12:30 pm When you arrive at the Port of Miami, the first thing you'll notice is how the **Victory** dwarfs the other ships docked in port. Take the obligatory boarding photo. You'll soon pass through the incredible nine-deck rotunda atrium on the way to your cabin.

1:15 pm Settle into your comfortable suite with a veranda. Other than the ship's library, this is about the only place to get away from it all. Head to ❌ *Mediterranean Restaurant* and get oriented with the extensive buffet and salad bar, complete with ice cream. Although plentiful, the food at all but dinner leaves much to be desired.

2:00 pm Report to the *Carnival Spa* for first dibs on booking a massage, manicure, haircut or beauty treatment—appointments fill up quickly. You'll get a tour of the giant coed hot tubs and his-and-hers saunas and steam rooms.

3:00 pm Partyers will already be on the Lido Deck dancing to calypso music, but you may want to use this time to explore the ship. You can watch videos about shore excursions, rent tuxedos or snorkeling equipment, or buy anything you may have forgotten.

4:30 pm Stay on deck after the mandatory (the only thing that is) lifeboat drill to watch the ship sail from port. You'll get good views of Miami Beach from the port (left) side of the upper decks. Explore *Neptune's Way*, the entertainment area that includes some of the ship's eight bars and lounges.

7:30 pm Drop by the casino for a complimentary rum swizzle and sit in the off-the-wall *Downbeat Lounge*, with its bigger-than-life musical instruments filling in as stools, tables, and wall decorations.

8:00 pm Late seating begins in the two ❌ attractive dining rooms. You'll be seated at the dinner table that will be yours for the rest of the cruise (although you can ask to be moved).

8:00 pm (cont.) A table for four is intimate, one for eight more fun. Every meal will have a version of pasta, fish, veal, pork and beef, along with appetizers, soup, salad, cheese and dessert. If you can't decide between two menu items, your waiter will cheerfully deliver both.

10:00 pm Singles over eighteen are invited to the singles party in the *Club Arctic Dance Club* for "getting to know you" games. With more than 200 people showing up, about a quarter of whom are over thirty, it's a great way to check out opportunities for the week.

10:30 pm You may want to check out the *Welcome Aboard* show in the 1,500-seat *Caribbean Lounge*. The audience-participation games are a bit goofy, but fun.

Midnight Each of the seven cruise nights offers a similar choice of activities. A band plays dance music each night in the *Adriatic Lounge*. You can sing along with a piano player in the *Irish Sea Bar*, with karaoke microphones at each table. The *Aegean Bar* has TVs for sporting events. The *Club Arctic Dance Club* will help you build an appetite for the midnight buffet. Below the disco is the attractive but under-utilized *Ionian Bar*. And, of course, there's always the casino.

DAYS 2,4,7 Monday, Wednesday, Saturday

These are "days at sea," which means the ship is cruising between ports and everything from deck games to the casino, shops and spa are running full blast. There's something to do every minute—check Carnival Capers, the daily program placed in your cabin.

10:00 am Have a leisurely breakfast in the ❌ dining room. You don't have to return to the table where you dined last night. Show up at either restaurant and you'll meet more fellow passengers.

11:00 am There will be a choice of shipboard activities, but your veranda is calling.

Day-by-Day Plan

Cruise:
Carnival Victory

Noon Choose from the ship's lunch venues— ✖ outdoor buffet, Asian, Italian and American restaurants. Eat outside in a lounge chair. A deck steward will fetch you a cold drink while you listen to a calypso band.

2:00 pm Check out the mens hairy-chest contest on Day Two; bring a partner to the massage demonstration on Day Four; take a line-dancing class on Day Seven.

7:15 pm This is the cocktail hour. Day Two is the formal *Captain's Welcome Aboard Party*. For a ship that attracts value-seeking travelers, passengers look mighty fine tonight.

8:00 pm If you're sitting with new acquain- ✖ tances at dinner, it will be much more enjoyable if you can master the art of cruise conversation—what you did today and what you plan to do tomorrow are stalwart topics.

10:30 pm Go to the *Caribbean Lounge* for the magic show. On Day Two there is the Las Vegas revue show, "Livin' in America."

DAY 3 Tuesday

7:00 am Head for the *Mediterranean* ✖ *Restaurant* for the express breakfast of scrambled eggs, bacon and toast.

7:40 am Meet at the *Caribbean Lounge* and get a boat to *Playa del Carmen*. A forty-minute drive along the Yucatán coast in an air-conditioned bus takes you to the Maya ruins of Tulum while the ship moves to Cozumel. You'll return to Cozumel by ferry around noon.

1:00 pm Have a delicious Mexican lunch at ✖ *Palmero's* on the main square across from the ferry pier.

2:00 pm Head for the beach or enjoy some of the best diving in the Caribbean at *Playa San Francisco*.

6:00 pm Don't expect an authentic Mexican experience—Cozumel exists for cruise-ship tourists. Nonetheless, rather than going back on ship, share stories and tequila shots with passengers from other ✖ ships at *Carlos 'n' Charlie's*. It's one of a chain of eating (pretty good) and drinking (great) joints, conveniently located near the pier.

Midnight Be on the Lido Deck for a balmy evening sail from Cozumel, with food, drink and games into the early hours. The casino and dance club open after the ship sails and you can sleep in tomorrow because it's a day at sea.

DAY 5 Thursday

7:30 am The ship arrives in Grand Cayman, but you can sleep through the early excursions. Later at dinner, you may hear stories about two of the more popular excursions here. *Atlantis Submarine* is an air-conditioned sub that dives to depths of 150 feet for looks at the incredible marine life on the reefs around Grand Cayman. The *Stingray City* tour allows you to snorkel beside divers feeding the stingray.

11:45 am Catch the party boat for drinking and dancing as you sail to *Seven Mile Beach*, or simply do the beach on your own.

4:00 pm Hang around the Lido Deck to watch the *Miss Carnival Victory* contest as the ship sails from Grand Cayman. The routine for the rest of the evening should be familiar by this time.

DAY 6 Friday

7:00 am Hit the breakfast buffet in the ✖ *Mediterranean Restaurant* and take your tray on deck to watch as the ship sails into Ocho Rios.

8:30 am Meet the *Cool Runnings* and Dunn's *River Falls tour on* the pier. With bathing suit, climbing shoes and waterproof camera, you'll experience one of the Caribbean's highlights as you climb alongside the 600-foot waterfall.

Cruise:
Carnival Victory

DAY 6 — Friday (cont.)

1:00 pm For genuine Jamaican jerk pork or chicken, walk a couple blocks from the pier to the *Jerk Center* (the ship's staff can direct you).

2:30 pm Join in the reggae at the *Jamaica Sailaway Party* on the Lido Deck. There'll be plenty of the island's Red Stripe Beer and live music.

6:00-8:30 pm Dressed in your fanciest get-up, make your way to the Farewell Happy Hour in various lounges. Then move on to your table for a gala dinner.

10:30 pm Head to the *Caribbean Lounge* for the Las Vegas-style musical show, "Vrooom!"

On night seven, remember you still have to pack—Miami comes at 8 a.m.—so take a final stroll on deck and, like the moon on the water, reflect on an extraordinary week.

Size matters
Any list of the largest cruise ships changes several times a year as new vessels come on-line.

Largest cruise ships	Tons (000)	Passengers
Voyager of the Seas (Royal Carribean)	136	3,114
Carnival Conquest (Carnival Cruise Lines)	110	2,974
Grand Princess (Princess Cruises)	109	2,600
Carnival Triumph (Carnival Cruise Lines)	101	2,758
Carnival Victory (Carnival Cruise Lines)	101	2,642
Disney Magic (Disney Cruise Lines)	85	2,400
Disney Wonder (Disney Cruise Lines)	85	2,400
Rhapsody of the Seas (Royal Caribbean)	78	2,435
Majesty of the Seas (Royal Caribbean)	74	2,744
Monarch of the Seas (Royal Caribbean)	74	2,744
Sovereign of the Seas (Royal Caribbean)	73	2,852
Fantasy (Carnival Cruise Lines)	70	2,600

Choosing a cruise ship
In the right situation small is beautiful, but partyers know that with size comes choice in on-board activities. Ship size is a good indicator of the kind of experience to expect. As a general rule, there's a direct relationship between the size of the ship (larger) and the cost of a cruise (cheaper), the quality of the food (poorer), and the average age of the passengers (younger). Unfortunately, there's also a direct relationship between the average age of the passengers and the let-your-hair-down partying on board. Here's a rough guide for what you can expect:

	Mega-ships (>1500 pass.) mass market	Midsize ships (500-1500 pass.) popular	Small ships (<500 pass.) deluxe
Price	$	$$	$$$$
Avg. age	35	45	55
Food	passable	acceptable	excellent
Range of activities	extraordinary	good	limited
Drink of choice	beer	Bahama mama	champagne
Excursions	party boats	sports activities	sightseeing

There are two notable exceptions to the size rule:

Crystal Cruises—although midsize (but pricier than most in the category), the *Crystal Harmony* and *Crystal Symphony* consistently rate among the top ships for food and service, and offer a surprisingly wide range of activities. They may be the best for combining sophistication with fun.

Windstar Cruises—these small, tall-sail ships, the *Wind Song*, *Wind Spirit* and *Wind Star*, attract an upscale but younger, sports-minded clientele looking for laid-back good times.

Florida

 NYC   Miami (MIA) <30 min./$15   No   Map Code: A12

Calle Ocho

Carnaval Miami

Key Month: Mar Ratings: Event ★ ★ ★ ☆ ☆   City ★ ★ ★ ★ ★ Origin: 1978 Attendance: 1,000,000

At the same time most of the world's great carnivals are moving into forty days of Lenten restraint, **Carnaval Miami** is cranking up two weekends filled with the flavors, sounds and exuberance of a Latin American fiesta. Dancing in the streets, raucous music, thinly clad revelers and high energy are its hallmarks, making it one of the world's best and friendliest parties.

What may be the world's largest street party, Calle Ocho (Eighth Street, the heart of Latin Miami), is filled with hordes of partiers dancing and singing while somehow simultaneously waving flags from their native Latin American and Caribbean countries. Bands, floats, street dancers and performers entertain while tens of thousands of **Carnaval**-goers are rallied in the annual attempt to break the world record for mass-dancing. One year, 119,000 dancers formed history's longest conga line. More recently, 65,000 joined in for the macarena. For those who need an excuse to spend ten days in Miami, **Carnaval** offers **Noche de Carnaval**, an impressive Latin music concert on the first Saturday night.

No other place in the United States can capture the spirit of a Latin carnival like South Beach (the hot spot of Miami Beach) and nearby Miami. With their well-deserved reputation for hedonism and beautiful people, they provide ready-made **Carnaval** allure. Sultry weather relaxes inhibitions and demands skimpy clothing. The region's ethnic populations infuse the event with authenticity.

A less intense party might get lost amid South Beach's art-deco chic, gorgeous people and white-sand beaches—you'll quickly see why the area attracts an international collection of jet-setters who display fame and affluence as conspicuously as models and wannabes flaunt their deep tans and gym-toned, silicone-shaped bodies. Outside of Hollywood, there's no bettter place than SoBe (that means South Beach, where doormen, chefs and club owners are royalty) to catch glimpses of just about any celebrity you've ever heard of. Any given weekend night of the November-to-March carnival season shows South Beach at its passionate and musical best.

On the Calendar

Official Event Dates
Nine days, ending second Sunday in March

Best 3 Days To Be There
Final three days of event (Friday-Sunday). Weekends in South Beach! And the main event is on Sunday.

☾ 63°/80° (17°/27°)

Florida

Day-by-Day Plan

DAY 1 — Friday

11:00 am In South Beach's Art Deco District, nearly a thousand buildings have been restored to their original elegance. Grab a map from the **Art Deco District Welcome Center** and walk through this zone of pastel beauty.

12:30 pm Madonna co-owns the **Blue Door** in the Delano Hotel, so you may have a celebrity sighting while lunching on a New World mélange of eclectic flavors. The Delano itself is a tourist attraction (staying there requires too much attitude).

2:30 pm Tote your megatowel to South Beach's ample white-sand beach and enjoy the Atlantic's warm waves. You might recognize this famed strip of sand from a number of movies and television shows.

5:00 pm With art deco map in hand, continue your walk of the district. During your stroll along Ocean Avenue, stop for a cold drink at any one of the sidewalk restaurant/bars. It is a great excuse for stopping to watch South Beach's incredible parade of beautiful people.

7:30 pm The buzz is deafening at **Rumi**, the new supper club that has spared no expense to attract the South Beach elite to its Latin and Caribbean cuisine. Competing for the "most beautiful people come here" title, **Joia** has a perfect mix of food and ambience, enhanced by a cozy bar. A somewhat more sedate scene can be found at **Mark's South Beach**, which is starting to corner the market on the sophisticated version of Florida cuisine.

9:30 pm Pedestrian-only Lincoln Road has become the Champs-Élysées of South Beach, with stores and cafes positioned to maximize the see-and-be-seen routine. One great stop for drinks or laid-back jazz is local favorite **Van Dyke Café**.

11:30 pm Later, drive ten minutes to plush **Jimmy'z**, where you can dance to modern music and select a bottle of wine from an $8 million cellar. Madonna and other upscale customers rent humidors here, where they stash their favorite smuggled stogies.

DAY 2 — Saturday

9:00 am There is no better way to get in the mood for tomorrow's big event than to breakfast at **Versailles**, a Cuban-American institution.

11:00 am Industrialist James Deering built **Vizcaya Museum and Gardens** in 1916 as his palatial winter residence, but you can stroll through its stately gardens, thirty-four rooms and displays of European antiques.

1:30 pm The lunch-only **Nikki Beach** is the only restaurant/club on the sand in South Beach, and, as a result, a happening spot on any afternoon. If you prefer, continue along Ocean Drive to the best restaurant with a view, **1220 at the Tides**. Even with your patio seat you'll be distracted by the outstanding food.

3:00 pm You might want to head back to Lincoln Road where the galleries are all open and the roller skaters look better in daylight. Browse the shops and art galleries on Lincoln Road, which is second only to Ocean Drive for people-watching. The **Bass Museum of Art** has fine examples of old European and new Latin-American art. Or browse the human artwork tanning around your hotel pool and on the beach.

6:00 pm Practice your Spanish by ordering from an array of appetizers on the authentic Cuban menu at Gloria Estefan's **Larios on the Beach**, in the middle of Ocean Drive's bustle. But save yourself for a late dinner.

8:30 pm Feeling tired and hungry? The perfect solution is the ultra-hip **B.E.D.**, where pajama-clad waiters serve you in bed. (Are they making it easy, or what?) Miami's latest must-get-in restaurant/club is **Tantra**, a sexy magnet for stars that serves Iranian caviar (the most expensive in the world), hosts fashion shows and promises a unique dining experience. Patrons enter on a carpet of fresh-cut grass, inhale jasmine-scented candles and let the staff take care of the rest. The food—Middle Eastern with Asian accents—is spectacular.

11:00 pm With eight bars and an integrated twenty-one-to-fortyish crowd, **crobar** is hotter than beach sand on a 100-degree day. The dance floor will be packed until 5 a.m. closing time. The enormous Asian theme club **Opium Garden** swings in every sexual direction. **Shadow Lounge** is usually crowded, as well.

DAY 3 Sunday

9:00 am Grab a curbside table at **News Cafe**. ✪ The food is passable, but this quintessential South Beach spot is the place to hang during the day. Along with great-looking models and wannabes sitting and passing by, you'll see the embodiment of the tourist board's statistics: About half of South Beach visitors are international, with nearly forty percent coming from South America, twenty percent from Central America and the Caribbean, and twenty-five percent from Europe.

1:00 pm *Calle Ocho* began at 11 a.m. (ending at 7 p.m.), so things should be warmed up by now. Make sure you have your combination walking/dancing shoes, and be prepared for sensory overload—people, music, food, half-naked bodies, dancing in the streets and glorious sunshine.

8:30 pm For "world modern" cuisine in a ✪ happening setting, try **Nemo**. Back on Lincoln Road, **Touch** competes for the best scene, and has some of the best food in South Beach.

Midnight Miami's latest nighttime phenom is **Club Space**. The revolutionary establishment is the first of its kind to promote the downtown area known as Park West. With a huge dance floor, video-worthy booty shaking and South Florida's only twenty-four-hour liquor license, this club is jammed with dancing souls from late night until, oh, noon or so.

4:00 am It is probably time to end your Latin-carnival weekend—and you didn't even need a visa.

More Time, More Choices

The communal spirit at **China Grill**, where diners are encouragaed to nibble together on Asian-inspired cuisine from several shared plates, helps make this restaurant quite a scene. You could do like the locals have done since 1913—wait in a long line to wield a mallet and clobber through stacks of clawed critters at **Joe's Stone Crab**. Too violent? Try **Yuca**'s superb Nouvelle Cuban cuisine—they have live salsa or Cuban music on weekends.

Another popular restaurant on Lincoln Road is **Pacific Time**. It serves excellent fusion-styled fish. Sushi and samba are served up at **Sushisamba dromo**, a New York concept that plays perfectly here. It is also great for satisfying late-night hunger.

Miami's club scene is ever-changing, but with its three dance floors and location, location, location, **Nikki Beach** looks to be a mainstay, particulary hot on Sunday nights. New to the scene is **Mynt Ultralounge**, with a unique plexiglass bar and lots of people waiting to get in.

Accommodations

Still the crème de la crème, the white and very chic **Delano** is a scene all unto itself. The nearby **Raleigh** is also away from the noise but within walking distance of just about everything in South Beach. You don't have to stay at The Raleigh to be stylish in South Beach. The art-deco-style **Tides** provides all the essentials right on Ocean Drive. The **Casa Grande Suite Hotel** is a classy, subdued spot in the center of the action.

Event & Ticket Info

Calle Ocho (Eighth Street, Miami): Free. For information contact *Kiwanis Club* (305-644-8888).

Miami (Miami Beach)

Hotels	Phone	Address	Price	Fax	Rooms/Best
Casa Grande Suite Hotel	305-672-7003 800-688-7678	834 Ocean Dr.	$$$$	305-673-3669	34/Ocean front
Delano	305-672-2000 800-555-5001	1685 Collins Ave.	$$$$	305-532-0099	185/Oceanfront above 8th
Raleigh	305-534-6300 800-848-1775	1775 Collins Ave.	$$$$	305-538-8140	107/Ocean vw
Tides	305-604-5000 800-688-7678	1220 Ocean Dr.	$$$$+	305-604-5180	45/Ocean vw

Restaurants	Day	Phone	Address	Price	Rec	Food
1220 at the Tides	2	305-604-5130	1220 Ocean Dr.	$$$	D/L	New American
B.E.D.	2	305-532-9070	929 Washington Ave	$$$	D	New French
Blue Door	1	305-674-6400	1685 Collins Ave.	$$$	L/BD	American, Brazilian
China Grill	A	305-534-2211	404 Washington Ave.	$$$$	D/L	Asian, World
Joe's Stone Crab	A	305-673-0365	227 Biscayne St.	$$	LD	Stone crab
Joia	1	305-674-8871	150 Ocean Dr.	$$$	D	Italian
Larios on the Beach	2	305-532-9577	820 Ocean Dr.	$$	D/L	Cuban
Mark's South Beach	1	305-604-9050	1120 Collins Ave.	$$$	D	New American
Nemo	3	305-532-4550	100 Collins Ave.	$$$	LD	New American
News Cafe	3	305-538-6397	800 Ocean Dr.	$	B/LD	American
Nikki Beach	2	305-538-1111	1 Ocean Dr.	$$	L	Beach food
Pacific Time	A	305-534-5979	915 Lincoln Rd.	$$$	D	New Asian
Rumi	1	305-672-4353	330 Lincoln Rd.	$$$	D	Latin
Sushisamba dromo	A	305 673 5337	600 Lincoln Road	$$	LD	Sushi
Tantra	2	305-672-4765	1445 Pennsylvania Ave.	$$$$+	D	Middle Eastern
Touch	3	305-532-8003	910 Lincoln Rd.	$$$	D	New American
Versailles	2	305-445-7614	3555 SW Eighth St.	$	B/L	Cuban
Yuca	A	305-532-9822	501 Lincoln Rd.	$$$	LD	Cuban

Nightlife	Day	Phone	Address	Cover	Rec*	Music
Club Space	3	305-372-9378	142 N.E. 11th St.	$$$	P	House
crobar	2	305-531-5027	1445 Washington Ave.	$$$	P	House
Jimmy'z	1	305-604-9798	432 41st St.	$$	P(F)	Dance
Mynt Ultralounge	A	786-276-6132	1921 Collins Ave	P	$$	Hip hop
Nikki Beach	A	305-538-1231	1 Ocean Drive	P	$$	Various
Opium Garden	2	305-531-5535	136 Collins Ave.	$$	P	Hip hop, house
Shadow Lounge	2	305-531-9411	1532 Washington Ave.	$$$	P	House
Van Dyke Café	1	305-534-3600	846 Lincoln Rd.	$	M(F)	Jazz

* M=Live music; P=Dancing (Party); R=Bar only; S=Show; (F)=Food served. For further explanation of codes, page 12.

Sights & Attractions	Day	Phone	Address	Entry Fee
Art Deco District Welcome Center	1	305-672-2014	1001 Ocean Dr.	None
Bass Museum of Art	2	305-673-7530	2121 Park Ave.	$
Vizcaya Museum and Gardens	2	305-250-9133	3251 S. Miami Ave.	$

Miami CVB		305-539-3000	701 Brickell Ave.

Florida

 NYC  Miami (MIA) <60 min./$40 Yes/No   Map Code: A12

Gasparilla

Tampa

Gasparilla Pirate Festival

Key Month: Jan/Feb Ratings: Event ★★★☆☆ **V** City ★★☆☆☆ Origin: 1904 Attendance: 400,000

Disney's *Pirates of the Carribean* comes to life in Tampa. Be in town on the first weekend of February, and you're smack in the middle of **Gasparilla**—an outrageous and flamboyant all-out street party on Florida's side of the Gulf Coast.

The century-old festival gets its colorful name from Jose Gaspar (aka "Gasparilla"), a notorious eighteenth-century pirate who ravaged the Florida waters like no other nautical outlaw of his day. In 1904, a lively band of Tampa civic leaders adopted him as their patron rogue, forming their own secret union called "Ye Mystic Krewe of Gasparilla" and staging a mock, fully-costumed pirate attack on the city of Tampa.

Ever since, this handsome city on the water has been annually barraged by a huge local cast of cutlass-waving buccaneers who storm into Tampa Bay via, what else, the world's only fully-rigged pirate vessel. After a quick mayoral-surrender and three-mile triumphant pirate parade along the waterfront, the city erupts in a spectacular two-day street celebration that Señor Gaspar would surely have been proud of.

From the Spanish explorers who founded it, to the pirates who preyed upon ships in its bay, to the hundreds of Cuban *tabaqueros* (cigar rollers) who once built an empire here, Tampa's vibrant legacy lives on. In Spanish, *tampa* means "sticks of fire"—a fitting title for a place once hailed the Cigar Capital of the World. About three miles northeast of Tampa's revitalized downtown, Ybor City is the city's oldest neighborhood, a former Latin quarter and cigar-rolling barrio. Its enduring red-brick streets and aged cigar factories have been converted into Tampa's most happening nightspot, lined with clubs, bars, galleries and top dining.

When you're not living it up in Ybor City or partying with pirates at the two-day **Gasparilla** street festival downtown, Tampa's myriad attractions are hard to exhaust and will draw you in every direction. They include the world-class roller coasters and savannas of Busch Gardens, excellent art galleries and museums, and some of the state's top restaurants and hotels. Not to mention a full year of the kind of weather they splash all over travel brochures.

A short drive across the bay delivers you to the beaches and bars at the end of The Pier in St. Petersburg. Sure, Walt Disney World is a mere ninety minutes away in the other direction—but don't plan on making it there when **Gasparilla** drops anchor.

On the Calendar

Official Event Dates
Two days, ending first Sunday in March

Best 3 Days To Be There
Friday-Sunday. Enjoy Friday night in a party town, then Gasparilla for the weekend.

Other Times To Go
Guavaween (813-621-7121), held the Saturday of or before Halloween (October 31) in the Ybor district, gives Tampa another great way to party in costume.

☼ 52°/70° (11°/21°)

Day-by-Day Plan

DAY 1 Friday

9:00 am Get your bearings in downtown Tampa before the festival takes over. Fuel up with a bacado omelet (bacon, avocado, jack cheese) and other hearty ✖ brunch fare at the institutional **First Watch Restaurant** on Tampa Street.

10:30 am To pet your first shark, visit the "touch tank" at **The Florida Aquarium**. The huge four-gallery facility features more than 10,000 marine animals and plants. Art buffs can opt for the **Tampa Museum of Art**, which showcases the city's local talent (in the Florida Gallery) and a prominent collection of antiquities. Just across the Hillsborough River, The **Henry B. Plant Museum** specializes in architecture and opulent furniture exhibits.

1:00 pm Cruise over the Gandy Bridge into St. Petersburg for an afternoon of culture and calm amid quaint streets, many good art galleries and lovely bay ✖ views. At the **Stone Soup Cafe**, join locals lunching on homemade soups, salads and hearty sandwiches.

2:30 pm Drive to the **Salvador Dali Museum** for a look at the world's largest private collection of the surrealist's work. On the forty-five-minute tour, pay attention to the similarities between the seascape images of Dali's native northern Spain and the pale-blue waters of Tampa Bay.

4:30 pm Cha Cha Coconuts, on the St. Petersburg Pier, is part of a chain of tropical-themed bars. You can order an afternoon cocktail or iced tea—it doesn't really matter since you're mostly here for the terrific views of the bay and its gentle, sandy shores.

5:30 pm When the sun merges with the water to the west, grab a spot on the Lower Gandy Bridge to take in St. Pete's best sunset views. The stunning light show might convince you to stay ✖ for dinner at **The Hurricane**, a typical beach-town seafood restaurant. If you do, there's also a disco and rooftop bar that make for a nice ending to the evening. But …

7:30 pm Ybor City is the place to be on *Gasparilla* eve, or on any other Friday night in Tampa for that matter. Make advance reservations at the **Columbia Restaurant**, Florida's oldest and "the world's largest" Spanish restaurant. There's a very colorful flamenco show here (in one of the eleven dining rooms) as well as excellent, heaping plates of paella. (Ybor parking tip: Use the city parking garage at Sixth Avenue and 15th Street).

10:00 pm Seventh Avenue and its brick-paved tributaries east of 13th Street in Ybor City is Tampa's best late-night bar-hopping scene. Get an aerial view of it all from the balcony at the recently opened hotspot, **Fun**. Next door is the granddaddy of Tampa alternative clubs, **The Masquerade**, with its huge dance floor and intimate Aqua Lounge. **Harpo's** features multiple stages in a squeezing-room-only club and out on airy patios. **Castle** is a Gothic-themed bar serving Black Forest martinis. Stop at **Centro Ybor**, the area's brand new entertainment complex, filled with restaurants, bars, a comedy club and Steven Spielberg's Sega GameWorks center.

DAY 2 Saturday

10:00 am Enjoy a full buffet breakfast and one of the city's best harbor views at ✖ your hotel's **Luna di Mare** restaurant. Watch the marine traffic pick up as pirate invasion-hour approaches.

Noon Find your place in the crowds gathering on Bayshore Boulevard for the *Gasparilla* Parade. Or have a light lunch ✖ at **Jackson's** on Harbour Island and enjoy the most comfortable front-row seats in town. Keep an eye out for the Jose Gaspar, a fully-rigged pirate ship, making her way north across Hillsborough Bay into downtown Tampa. She'll be hard to miss, sailing amidst a flotilla of small pleasure craft attempting (in vain) to defend the city. At one o'clock the mayor will officially present the captain of Ye Mystic Krewe of Gasparilla with the key to the city.

1:30 pm Make way for a cannon-blasting parade of 700 marauding buccaneers showing off all their treasures and vowing to turn Tampa on its head for the next few days. You'll find them and a procession of more than fifty floats rolling up along Bayshore Boulevard (the parade starts at Howard Avenue) and into downtown.

3:00 pm Follow the parade and immerse yourself in *Gasparilla*'s rowdy downtown street festival. Pace yourself. This hearty celebration carries on into the late hours, featuring endless sets of top-name entertainment on several stages. There's also a pirate-themed arts show and, on Ashley Street between Cass Street and Twiggs Street, a *Gasparilla* midway with blocks of games and amusement rides.

7:00 pm **Mise en Place** is a superb New ✗ American-style bistro serving culinary creations such as duck salad with raspberry vinaigrette and chocolate-pecan-toffee mousse. On top of the Hyatt Regency Westshore, **Armani's** specializes in elegant northern Italian dining with the city's best panoramic view.

9:30 pm The downtown street party is now in full swing.

DAY 3 — Sunday

11:00 am After a room-service breakfast, take a thirty-minute drive to **Busch Gardens**, where you can experience the United States' closest thing to a genuine African safari. The extensive 355-acre theme park includes a world-class zoo of 2,800 animals. Your expedition starts at the Edge of Africa, which includes seven separate habitats for African animals.

1:00 pm Wander to the Timbuktu section of ✗ the park for lunch at **Das Festhaus**, where you can get a decent cafeteria meal while listening to the oompah band in a cavernous hall.

2:30 pm From the Sky Ride gondola, watch rhinos, gazelles and zebras romp in the African Veldt below, or hand-feed a giraffe on a tour through the refurbished Serengeti Plain. Move on to dolphin, bird and ice shows before braving sixty mph cruising speeds on Montu, which the park says is the world's tallest and longest inverted roller coaster.

5:00 pm After a rugged day of rides and safaris, close the afternoon with a relaxing swim in your hotel's heated pool.

7:30 pm At **Bern's Steakhouse**, the 85,000-✗ bottle wine cellar is the world's largest, and the steaks are nearly as impressive. You could also try the **8th Avenue Grille**, an elegant spot for martinis and continental American cuisine in a heritage building in Ybor City.

10:00 pm Cap it off in Ybor City with a late-night round of Ybor Gold (the very local home brew) at the ever-popular **Green Iguana Bar and Grill**.

■

Accommodations

Wyndham Harbour Island Hotel makes a perfect three-night, four-star home for *Gasparilla* weekend. Situated on its own island in the heart of Tampa Bay, the luxury hotel offers front row views of all invading pirates and is a two-minute monorail ride from downtown. The **Hyatt Regency Tampa** is a convenient choice in downtown Tampa. In Ybor City, the **Hilton Garden Inn**'s charming, four-story brick structure blends right into the historic neighborhood. Further afield, the '20s-era **Don CeSar Beach Resort and Spa** is a luxurious and quiet alternative on the St. Pete side of the bay.

Event & Ticket Info

Gasparilla Pirate Fest (Parade: Bayshore Boulevard; Street Fest: downtown Tampa): Free admission. For more information contact *Event Makers* (813-353-8070).

Hotels	Phone	Address	Town*	Price	Fax	Rooms/Best
Don CeSar Beach Resort and Spa	813-360-1881 800-282-1116	3400 Gulf Blvd.	SP	$$$	813-367-7597	275/Bayside city vw
Hilton Garden Inn	813-626-6700 800-774-1500	10309 Highland Garden Dr.		$$	813-626-6755	152
Hyatt Regency Tampa	813-225-1234 800-233-1234	2 Tampa Center		$$	813-273-0234	518/Regency club rm
Wyndham Harbour Island Hotel	813-229-5000 800-996-3426	1725 S. Harbour Island Blvd.		$$	813-229-5022	300/Harbour vw, even #s, close to 30

Restaurants	Day	Phone	Address	Town*	Price	Rec	Food
8th Avenue Grille	2	813-242-6616	1811 15th St.		$$	D/L	Continental, American
Armani's	2	813-281-9165	6200 Courtney Campbell Causeway		$$$	D	Northern Italian
Bern's Steakhouse	3	813-251-2421	1208 S. Howard Ave.		$$	D	American
Columbia Restaurant	1	813-248-4961	2117 E. 7th Ave.		$$	D/DL	Spanish, Cuban
First Watch Restaurant	1	813-307-9006	520 Tampa St.		$	B/L	American
The Hurricane	1	727-360-9558	Golf Way at 9th Ave.	SP	$$	D	Seafood
Jackson's	2	813-277-0112	601 S. Harbour Island Blvd		$	L/D	Bistro
Luna di Mare	2	813-229-5038	1725 S. Harbour		$$	B/LD	American, seafood
Mise en Place	2	813-254-5373	442 W. Kennedy Blvd.		$$	D/DL	New American
Stone Soup Cafe	1	727-526-2975	4122 16th St.	SP	$	L	American

Nightlife	Day	Phone	Address	Town*	Cover	Rec	Music
Castle	1	813-247-7547	2004 N. 16th St.		$	MP	Industrial, electro
Cha Cha Coconuts	1	727-822-6655	800 2nd Ave. NE	SP	None	M(F)	Acoustic '70s rock
Fun	1	813-247-4225	1507 E. 7th Ave.		$	MP	Rock, house, hip hop
Green Iguana Bar and Grill	3	813-248-9555	1708 E. Seventh Ave.		None	M(F)	Cover rock
Harpo's	1	813-248-4814	7th Ave. at 18th Ave.		None	P	Top 40
The Masquerade	1	813-247-3319	1503 E. 7th Ave.		$	P	Hip hop, alternative

* M=Live music; P=Dancing (Party); R=Bar only; S=Show; (F)=Food served. For further explanation of codes, page 12.

Sights & Attractions	Day	Phone	Address	Town*	Entry Fee
Busch Gardens	3	813-987-5082	3000 E. Busch Blvd.		$$$
Centro Ybor	1	813-242-4660	1600 E. 8th Ave.		
The Florida Aquarium	1	813-273-4020	701 Channelside Dr.		$$
The Henry B. Plant Museum	1	813-254-1891	401 W. Kennedy Blvd.		$
Salvador Dali Museum	1	727-823-3767	1000 3rd St. S	SP	$
Tampa Museum of Art	1	813-274-8130	600 N. Ashley Dr.		$

Tampa/Hillsborough CVA 813-223-1111 400 N. Tampa St.

*SP=St. Petersburg

 NYC   Tampa (TPA) <30 min./$15   Yes Map Code: A14

Florida

St. Patrick's Day Celebration

Savannah

Key Month: Mar   Ratings: Event ★ ★ ★ ★ ☆   **V**   City ★ ★ ☆ ☆ ☆   Origin: 1813   Attendance: 300,000

St. **Patrick's Day** in Georgia? Other cities may have more Irish blood than Savannah, but for nearly two centuries this city has hosted one of the country's biggest **St. Patrick's Day** celebrations. If the South's proud Irish legacy (ever heard of Scarlett O'Hara?) doesn't convince you this is the best place to celebrate the day, then a few hundred-thousand indefatigable partiers probably will. The improbable mix of Southern hospitality and Irish moxie make this a party like no other in the world.

As many as one-third of Southern settlers immigrated from Ireland. By the nineteenth century, Savannah had built a reputation for hospitality, welcoming many different groups of new Americans. Now, "Irish" revelers from across the nation—largely college age up to mid-thirties—descend on moss-draped Savannah each year, swelling its population from 140,000 to about 450,000. The Savannah Waterfront Association sponsors the weeklong event that creates an infectious party atmosphere and, in the best of American tradition, allows everyone to be Irish, at least for a day or two.

Although most days the celebratory siege officially lasts until 11 p.m., many inspired partiers cram local streets and pubs until at least 3 a.m. Crowds are so thick along the 100 block of East River Street that movement is often restricted to slow shuffling and desperate guarding of filled beer cups. Bands, dancing, souvenir stands, food tents and beer stands attract so many people that some are nearly forced into the Savannah River. Few seem to mind.

Prepare yourself by being one of the few partiers who actually knows what *Erin go bragh* means (Ireland forever), and that drinking outside the designated festival zone without the required $5 wristband (buy them at ramps all along River Street) can get you a $90 fine.

Just a few blocks from the riverfront's wild party, Savannah remains incredibly calm and lush, providing an appropriately green backdrop for a more relaxed **St. Patrick's Day** that is rich with sights and history. Take time for some old-fashioned touring and find out why *Walking* magazine called Savannah one of the country's top-ten walking cities. Savannah's seasonally hospitable weather enhances the on-foot experience and adds the return of spring to your excuses for either remembering or pretending you're Irish.

On the Calendar

Official Event Dates

Four days surrounding St. Patrick's Day (March 17)

Best 3 Days To Be There

March 16-17 plus a weekend day, if possible. One of the wildest parties in America is wildest on the night before the holiday and the closest weekend days.

☽ 47°/70° (8°/21°)

St. Patrick's Day Celebration

DAY 1 — March 15

10:30 am It's a pleasant walk to the **Telfair Mansion and Art Museum**. Its collection includes works by American impressionists and European artists.

12:15 pm Nearby, you can lunch on **The Lady** ❌ **& Sons'** Southern buffet. It's known for bargain prices, crab burgers and asparagus sandwiches.

1:30 pm If you'd prefer to ride through the historic district, reserve a trip with **Carriage Tours of Savannah**. Otherwise, walking is the best way to get acquainted with Savannah's charm. Mosey four blocks west to the **Owens-Thomas House Museum**—designed by famed English architect William Jay—considered the finest example of English Regency architecture in the United States.

3:00 pm Five blocks south is the **Juliette Gordon Low Birthplace**, a gorgeous Regency-style house that was home to the founder of the Girl Scouts of America. At the **Green-Meldrim Mansion**, General Sherman set up headquarters during the Civil War. To see the interior, go on Tuesday, Thursday or Saturday.

5:00 pm Gear up for your evening with a glass of sherry. Savannahians always have what they call a get-ready drink.

7:00 pm Take a cab or trolley for a classic ❌ Southern dinner at the **Olde Pink House**, which occupies an eighteenth-century mansion that was once used as a bank. The cast-iron vaults with their dungeon-like doors are still used today—not to hold gold bullion, but to shelter a selection of fine wines.

> Taste a local tradition—Chatham Artillery Punch—a favorite at large celebrations. This powerful stuff—concocted with wine, rum, gin, brandy, Benedictine and rye, plus some sweet ingredients—packs a big punch.

9:00 pm The riverfront party is raging on, but a short walk away you can cap off the night with drinks or dessert at **Hannah's East** (another *Midnight* landmark), the premier place to hear live jazz.

DAY 2 — March 16

9:30 am Walk to a late breakfast at **Clary's**. ❌ You may recognize the modest diner from John Berendt's bestseller, *Midnight in the Garden of Good and Evil*. There will be a line, but the food is fresh, and the staff is friendly. Afterward, head over to River Street.

10:30 am Catch up with anything you missed on your tour of historic Savannah.

12:15 pm In the midst of party central, **River** ❌ **House Seafood** is an oasis of calm, providing views of the chaos outside. Its lengthy menu features local fish, crab and shrimp.

2:00 pm Reflect on the craziness you see taking place on the waterfront as you relax on the **River Street Riverboat Company**'s one-hour cruise.

3:30 pm Meander around City Market, a four-block area of shops, galleries and restaurants that provides live music throughout the afternoon and evening during this holiday. The crowd is a little calmer and older than on River Street.

7:00 pm Try the sautéed shrimp or crisp ❌ pecan chicken at **Bistro Savannah**.

9:30 pm On the 100 block of East River Street, various parties have been underway for hours. Near the Hyatt Regency, there's a makeshift sidewalk disco where you can rub shoulders with the usual thousands. You'll notice the attempt to introduce beads, à la Mardi Gras, but shamrocks-en-face remain the fashion of choice. **Kevin Barry's** is a great spot for Irish music and a view of the party and river. Or pop into **Huey's**, which has a New Orleans-style porch providing views of the action below.

March 17

8:30 am Start your day with Southern ❌ cooking at **Mrs. Wilkes Dining Room**. The set-menu monster breakfasts are served family style at big tables.

10:00 am "The beauty of the city means you don't have to have great floats," one tourist-board offical has explained. Savannah's mostly homespun (i.e., occasionally dull for visitors) *parade* features a lot of local dignitaries waving from automobiles. Clear paths and not-too-deep crowds allow for walking the parade route in reverse to see the whole show in less than half the time it would take if you sat still. It's also a great way to see the city. Begin at the parade terminus, Madison Square. A good place to stop for a look at parade spectators is on the 600 block of Abercorn Street, or along Bay Street. This also puts you within easy reach of River Street's food booths, restaurants and tireless party people.

1:30 pm Grab an outside table at **Belford's**, a ❌ good place to watch the parade roll by. Steaks and seafood are prepared with hints of Mediterranean and Asian influences.

3:00 pm Postparade, stop by and have drinks at the waterfront party. Much of the crowd will have been at it since morning, but pace yourself for the finale.

7:00 pm Cab to midtown to dine at **Elizabeth** ❌ **on 37th**, the finest restaurant in Savannah. Almost single-handedly, Elizabeth Terry invented Savannahian cuisine by blending classic Southern ingredients, such as fried grits and black-eyed peas, with contemporary dishes.

9:00 pm After dinner you may want to stop back at the hotel to dress down for the festivities in the waterfront area.

9:00 pm (cont.) The drinking, dancing and socializing achieve critical mass on the street and in the bars. The Irish may not have invented partying, but they have added an important personality to the concept. River Street flows with green beer and people as Savannah reaffirms its heritage with a type of cheer that few other cities in the world can muster.

■

More Time, More Choices

Wet Willie's and **Spanky's River Street** are popular nightspots on the riverfront. Both serve food. Another is the **Cotton Exchange**, a longtime local favorite for meaty meals, bar snacks, stiff drinks and socializing. Various publications have voted **Churchill's** Best Pub in Savannah for several years running. They have good pub food and the usual Irish and Brit beers on tap. **Garibaldi's** is a highly respected South Carolina transplant with Old-World-meets-New-World dishes such as flounder with apricot-shallot glaze.

Accommodations

Check into the **Magnolia Place Inn**. It was built in 1878, but Jacuzzis and gas fireplaces in selected rooms lend a modern touch. Not that you'll need a fire—you'll be enjoying the warmest climate of all major *St. Patrick's Day* celebrations. **The Ballastone Inn** (1838) and The **Gastonian** (1868) are two more of the city's best-known inns. Each features period-style furnishings, tea time and Southern breakfasts. Because of its central riverfront location, **Hyatt Regency Savannah** is probably the best of Savannah's chain hotels.

Event & Ticket Info

St. Patrick's Day Celebration
(Various sites, especially the Waterfront): Free admission. *The Savannah Waterfront Association* (912-234-0295).

Who has the biggest parade?						
	Irish Pop.	Spectators*	In Parade	Date Held	Hrs.	Miles
New York	7%	2,000,000	150,000	17th	4	1.5
Boston	22%	1,000,000	10,000	Sun. before 17th	2	3.2
Dublin	95%	500,000	5,000	17th	1	1.0
Chicago	8%	400,000	15,000	Sat. before 17th	2	1.0
Savannah	10%	300,000	10,000	17th	3	3.2
*Approximate, dependent on weather						

Hotels	Phone	Address	Price	Fax	Rooms/Best
The Ballastone Inn	912-236-1484 800-822-4553	14 E. Oglethorpe Ave.	$$$$	912-236-4626	17/Scarborough Fair w/access to balc
The Gastonian	912-232-2869 800-322-6603	220 E. Gaston St.	$$$$	912-232-0710	17/Scarborough w/access to whirlpool, balc
Hyatt Regency Savannah	912-238-1234 800-233-1234	2 W. Bay St.	$$$$	912-944-3678	346/River vw
Magnolia Place Inn	912-236-7674 800-238-7674	503 Whitaker St.	$$$	912-236-1145	13/3rd fl rms w/vw and veranda

Restaurants	Day	Phone	Address	Price	Rec	Food
Belford's	3	912-233-2626	315 W. St. Julian St.	$$	L/D	Steak, seafood
Bistro Savannah	2	912-233-6266	309 W. Congress St.	$$	D	Southern
Clary's	2	912-233-0402	404 Abercorn St.	$	B	Diner
Elizabeth on 37th	3	912-236-5547	105 E. 37th St.	$$$	D	Nuvo Southern
Garibaldi's	A	912-232-7118	315 W. Congress St.	$$	D	Northern Italian
The Lady & Sons	1	912-233-2600	311 W. Congress St.	$$	L/D	Southern
Mrs. Wilkes Dining Room	3	912-232-5997	107 W. Jones St.	$	B/L	Southern
Olde Pink House	1	912-232-4286	23 Abercorn St.	$$	D	Classic
River House Seafood	2	912-234-1900	125 W. River St.	$$$	L/D	Seafood

Nightlife	Day	Phone	Address	Cover	Rec*	Music
Churchill's	A	912-232-8501	9 Drayton St.	None	R(F)	Varies
Cotton Exchange	A	912-232-7088	201 E. River St.	None	R(F)	
Hannah's East	1	912-233-2225	20 E. Broad St.	$	M(F)	Jazz
Huey's	2	912-234-7385	115 E. River St.	None	M(F)	Guitar mix
Kevin Barry's	2	912-233-9626	117 W. River St.	$	M(F)	Irish
Spanky's River Street	A	912-236-3009	317 E. River St.	None	R(F)	
Wet Willie's	A	912-233-5650	101 E. River St.	None	P(F)	Lite rock

* M=Live music; P=Dancing (Party); R=Bar only; S=Show; (F)=Food served. For further explanation of codes, page 12.

Sights & Attractions	Day	Phone	Address	Entry Fee
Carriage Tours of Savannah	1	912-236-6756	St Julian & Jefferson Sts.	$$
Green-Meldrim Mansion	1	912-232-1251	1 W. Macon St., Bull St. at Madison Sq.	$
Juliette Gordon Low Birthplace	1	912-233-4501	10 E. Oglethorpe Ave.	$
Owens-Thomas House Museum	1	912-233-9743	124 Abercorn St.	$
River Street Riverboat Company	2	912-232-6404	9 E. River St.	$$
Telfair Mansion and Art Museum	1	912-232-1177	121 Barnard St.	$

Savannah Visitor Information	877-728-2662	101 Bay St.

 NYC　　　　 Savannah (SAV) <30 min./$20　　　　 No　　　Map Code: A15

Georgia

Aloha Festival

Honolulu

| Key Month: Sep | Ratings: Event ★ ★ ☆ ☆ ☆ | ⓟ | City ★ ★ ★ ☆ ☆ | Origin: 1947 | Attendance: 300,000 |

Hula girls and sunsets. Mai tais on a catamaran at dusk. Plumeria-scented trade winds that cool sun-kissed skin. If these are clichés, bring on a Hawaiian paradise full of them. Any time's fine to ease into the aloha spirit, but Hawaii's *Aloha Festivals*, held each autumn, provide a great excuse to visit one of earth's perfect places.

The festivals encompass more than 300 events on all six major Hawaiian Islands, including the most visited island of Oahu, site of the state's capital, Honolulu. Oahu's *Aloha Festival* is anchored by two *ho'olaule'a* celebrations—with lei and food booths, music from metal to rap to Hawaiian, and entertainment including traditional hula—that draw residents and visitors by the thousands.

Aloha Week was created in 1947 as a cultural celebration of Hawaii's music, dance and history. After the tragic toll World War II took on the islands, it quickly became a welcome peacetime ritual. *Aloha Festivals*, as the events were renamed in 1991, were scheduled in the fall for two reasons: to honor the *makahiki*, the ancient Hawaiian season of music, dance and feasting, when war was not a permissible activity; and to attract visitors to the islands after the summer season.

Today, the festivals—the only such statewide celebration in the United States—revolve around a series of free street parties and are still centered mostly on music and food. The Oahu festival opens in front of the Iolani Palace with a presentation of the annual Royal Court, young people who have gone through a yearlong process of selection and training. Once the playground of King Kamehameha, Honolulu boasts having the only royal palace in the United States.

It might be argued that no other state occupies such a unique and exotic place in American history. The full breadth of Hawaii's legacy will be on display throughout the festivals—and, of course, history is a lot easier to appreciate when you're learning about it in the midst of some of the world's greatest beaches and bathwater warm ocean surf.

Upon arrival at Honolulu International Airport, you'll definitely want to lose yourself for a few days, get out your SPF-15, "rubba slippas" (beach sandals, also known as flip-flops) and just hang loose. Sure, for great resorts, seasoned travelers probably think of the outer islands when they think of Hawaii. But Oahu, especially during the **Aloha Festivals**, is the place to be for both natural beauty and three days of exciting restaurants, night life and attractions.

On the Calendar

Official Event Dates
Ten days beginning on Friday of the second weekend in September

Best 3 Days To Be There
Friday-Sunday, first or second weekend. Either weekend is fun, but the first weekend gives you a better taste of Honolulu.

☾ 73°/87° (23°/31°)

Hawaii

For links to most current web sites for cities and events, go to www.funrises.com

Aloha Festival

This itinerary is for the first weekend of the festival.

DAY 1 — Friday

10:00 am Start your trip by hiking forty-five minutes into **Manoa Falls**. You'll pass through a soothing, green rainforest before arriving at the cool freshwater pool at the top of the trail.

12:15 pm Drive downtown and tour **Iolani Palace**. Make reservations in advance. In the Blue Room, Queen Liliuokalani was dethroned, marking the beginning of United States annexation maneuvers.

1:30 pm Take a long walk down King Street to the Chinatown Historic District at the end of town farthest from Diamond Head. If you're hungry, stop for dim ✪ sum at **Legend Seafood Restaurant**. Or near the Chinatown Cultural Plaza, snack on *manapua* (meat- and curry-filled buns) at the downscale but beloved **Royal Kitchen**.

5:30 pm A small crowd gathers for the festival's opening ceremony, including music and a hula performance, which takes place in a gorgeous setting in front of the palace.

6:30 pm Follow the Royal Court in procession to the *Ho'olaule'a* fun. You won't have ✪ trouble locating food booths and music stages. Alcohol isn't served on the streets, so most party-goers pop in and out of downtown's many pubs between mingling, eating, dancing and people-watching sessions on the crowded, closed-off streets.

10:00 pm After the festivities end, head to Aloha Tower Marketplace on the harbor. At the **Gordon Biersch Brewery**, kick back with local music and microbrews.

11:30 pm If you watch the E! channel you might know that **Ocean Club** has been picked as one of the better nightclubs in Hawaii. With three bars and one dance floor, it's a bit more upscale than most Hawaii nightclubs.

DAY 2 — Saturday

8:30 am Start early on just another day in paradise. Beginning at the entrance to the crater on Diamond Head Road, hike up hills and stairs for a spectacular view of the Waikiki sprawl from **Diamond Head**.

10:00 am You've earned a treat—breakfast ✪ at the **Hau Tree Lanai** in the New Otani Kaimana Beach Hotel. The fried rice and eggs is a local favorite and you can watch Kaimana Beach begin to hum with local and tourist activity.

11:00 am Third in attendance for rose parades, behind the Rose Bowl Parade and the Portland Rose Festival's parade, the *Aloha Festivals Floral Parade* draws thousands to the streets and millions via television. Each island sends its own pa'u princess and escorts, decorated with their island's special flowers. These ladies and their costumes are beautiful sights to see. The beginning of the parade will just be reaching the end of the parade route at the corner of Kalakaua and Kapahulu avenues in Waikiki. It lasts two hours, but you can walk the route in reverse (forty-five minutes).

1:00 pm "Eh, bruddah, try one chicken katsu ✪ plate lunch from **Grace's**. Two scoops rice with shoyu on top. Broke da mouth." Translation: The chicken plate at Grace's, a true local legend, will knock your socks off. So will the rest of Hawaii's "local food," a calorie-laden melting pot of cultural influences that include teriyaki from Japan, fried rice and dim sum from China, sweet bread from Portugal and lau laus and poi from the South Pacific.

2:00 pm Nearby, the **Honolulu Academy of Arts**, housed in beautiful seventy-five-year-old building, has one of the world's finest collections of Asian and Pacific art, along with American and European works. Okay, afterward you can go to the beach.

6:30 pm Relax at the Halekulani's **House without a Key** with a drink, a sunset and possibly a slack-key guitar.

Day-by-Day Plan

8:30 pm Drive downtown to the Harbor Court Building and its dramatic ❌ entrance to **Palomino**. The crowd, having drinks and contemporary European fare at tables or the white-marble bar, is as chic as the décor.

10:30 pm Atop of Ala Moana hotel, the sedate and jazzy longtime favorite Aaron's has late-night dining and live music. Off the lobby, **Rumours** has disco into the early hours with high-tech lighting and two dance cages for customer use. This place is loaded with tourists cutting loose.

DAY 3 Sunday

8:30 am The buffet breakfast at the **Rainbow Lanai** ❌ at the Hilton Hawaiian Village hotel is worth a detour. It offers the island's greatest variety of foods in bright, pleasant surroundings.

9:30 am Drive the Pali Highway to Kailua. About halfway (twenty minutes), stop for a magnificent view of the island at the Pali Lookout.

10:30 am Kailua Beach is windsurfing heaven (the Kailua end of the beach is used primarily by singles and couples) and a good place to walk.

1:30 pm If you haven't eaten, stop for ❌ lunch at **Haleiwa Joe's** (formerly the Chart House). Check out the view of the sprawling gardens below in Haiku Plantation while enjoying coconut-encrusted shrimp.

4:00 pm **Duke's Canoe Club** gets hopping Sunday afternoons. Great music and a fun mix of locals and tourists ensure lots of mai tais and people-watching, both in the bar and on the beach.

7:00 pm Enjoy unique, innovative dishes of ❌ Hawaiian regional cuisine at **Alan Wong's**, probably the best restaurant in Honolulu.

10:00 pm Make a final circuit of dance spots, including the **Esprit Lounge** in the Sheraton Waikiki for a live show band that keeps a tanned and happy crowd dancing all night. If you can manage, stay late enough to "accidentally" miss tomorrow's flight back to earth.

After

The second weekend's party moves to Waikiki for a block party drawing a quarter-million people.

More Time, More Choices

Try brunch at the Kahala Mandarin's **Plumeria Beach Cafe**. The Japanese dishes, in particular, are outstanding. Be sure to check out the dolphin feedings at 11 a.m. For a French taste with local ingredients, try **Bali By The Sea**, which was voted Best in Hawaii by *Honolulu* magazine. **Chef Mavro**, which consistently rates among the islands' top restaurants has a delectable French-Hawaiian menu, which includes incredible dishes such as coriander crisp beef entrecôte. Drive to **Roy's** in Hawaii-Kai for a fine meal, complete with interesting interior and exterior views. Chef Roy Yamaguchi put Hawaii's version of Pacific Rim cuisine on the culinary map. Or you could dine at romantic **La Mer** (reservations required). The cuisine is local-inspired French—this is dining at a spiritual level. Ask for a table with a Diamond Head view.

After dinner head to **Blue Tropix**, open till 2 a.m. It's a fun place with live monkeys behind the bar.

To explore more of the island, drive to the North Shore. Stop at the **Polynesian Cultural Center** and sample its many eating options (including an evening luau) amid seven model villages representing Hawaii, Samoa, Tonga, Fiji, New Zealand, Tahiti and the Marquesas.

Accommodations

You could probably spend your whole trip hanging at the **Halekulani**, the "House without a Key," which offers 456 elegant rooms built around an eighty-year-old beach house in the middle of Waikiki. The size of the **Hilton Hawaiian Village** may put off some people, but you can get one of the best view rooms on Oahu at a reasonable price, along with an outstanding beachfront. Or stay at the more secluded **Kahala Mandarin Oriental** hotel.

Event & Ticket Info

Aloha Festivals (Throughout the Hawaiian Islands): Many events are free, including the *Floral Parade* and *Ho'olaule'a*, but some performances and activities require admission fees. *Aloha Festivals* (800-852-7690) can send you a brochure with a complete schedule of activities.

The Hot Sheet

Hotels		Phone	Address	Price	Fax	Rooms/Best
Halekulani		808-923-2311 800-367-2343	2199 Kalia Rd.	$$$$+	808-926-8004	456/Diamond Head vw
Hilton Hawaiian Village		808-949-4321 800-445-8667	2005 Kalia Rd.	$$$	808-951-5458	2,998/ "01" rms w/2 balc
Kahala Mandarin Oriental		808-739-8888 800-367-2525	5000 Kahala Ave.	$$$$	808-739-8800	371/Beachfront vw

Restaurants	Day	Phone	Address	Price	Rec	Food
Alan Wong's	3	808-949-2526	1857 S. King St.	$$$	D	Local cuisine
Bali By The Sea	A	808-941-2254	see Hilton Hawaiian Village	$$$	D	French
Chef Mavro	A	808-944-4714	1969 S. King St.	$$$$	D	French-Hawaiian
Grace's	2	808-593-2202	1296 S. Beretania St.	$	L/BD	Local cuisine
Haleiwa Joe's	3	808-247-6671	46336 Haiku Rd.	$$	D	American, seafood
Hau Tree Lanai	2	808-921-7066	2863 Kalakaua Ave.	$$	B/LD	American, Japanese
La Mer	A	808-923-2311	see Halekulani hotel	$$$$+	D	French, local influences
Legend Seafood Restaurant	1	808-532-1868	100 N. Beretania St.	$$	L/BD	Chinese
Palomino	2	808-528-2400	66 Queen St.	$$$	D/L	Continental
Plumeria Beach Cafe	A	808-739-8888	see Kahala Mandarin Oriental hotel	$$$	BLD	Local cuisine
Rainbow Lanai	3	808-949-4321	see Hilton Hawaiian Village	$$	B/LD	Continental
Royal Kitchen	1	808-524-4461	Kukui and River sts.	$	L/B	Chinese
Roy's	A	808-396-7697	6600 Kalanianaole Hwy.	$$$	D	Pacific Rim

Nightlife	Day	Phone	Address	Cover	Rec*	Music
Aaron's	2	808-955-4466	410 Atkinson Dr. at the Ala Moana hotel	None	MP(F)	Top 40
Blue Tropix	A	808-944-0001	1700 Kapiolani Blvd.	$	P(F)	Varies
Duke's Canoe Club	3	808-922-2268	2335 Kalakaua Ave.	None	M(F)	Hawaiian
Esprit Lounge	3	808-922-4422	2255 Kalakaua Ave. at the Sheraton Waikiki	$	MP(F)	Contemporary
Gordon Biersch Brewery	1	808-599-4877	1 Aloha Tower Dr.	None	MP(F)	Contemporary, Hawaiian, rock
House without a Key	2	808-923-2311	see Halekulani hotel	None	M(F)	Hawaiian
Ocean Club	1	808-526-9888	500 Ala Moana Blvd.	$	P(F)	Dance
Rumours	2	808-955-4811	410 Atkinson Dr. at the Ala Moana hotel	$	MP(F)	Top 40, '60s, '70s

* M=Live music; P=Dancing (Party); R=Bar only; S=Show; (F)=Food served. For further explanation of codes, page 12.

Sights & Attractions	Day	Phone	Address	Entry Fee
Diamond Head	2	808-971-2525	Monsarrat Ave. at 18th St.	None
Honolulu Academy of Arts	2	808-532-8701	900 S. Beretania St.	$
Iolani Palace	1	808-522-0832	King and Richards sts.	$$
Manoa Falls	1		North end of Manoa Rd.	None
Pali Lookout	3		Pali Hwy. to Kailua	None
Polynesian Cultural Center	A	808-293-3333	55370 Kamehameha Hwy.	$$$

Hawaii CVB	808-924-0266	2270 Kalakaua Ave.

 NYC -5   Honolulu (HNL) <30 min./$25   Yes   Map Code: A16

Hawaii

Taste of Chicago

Key Month: Jun/Jul   Ratings: Event ★ ★ ★ ☆ ☆   **ⓟ**   City ★ ★ ★ ★ ★   Origin: 1980   Attendance: 3,500,000

Calling this ten-day feeding frenzy in Chicago's Grant Park "the nation's largest outdoor food festival" is an understatement. A few years ago, more than 3.5 million visitors managed to consume 220,000 scoops of ice cream, 197,060 cobs of corn and 120,000 pounds of turkey legs right here—all between several main courses.

Just like its music and pork-belly futures, Chicago loves its food—all kinds, and lots of it. **Taste of Chicago**, the city's annual gastronomic summit, is one of the world's great tributes to eating. Every summer, more than seventy restaurants set up shop along Grant Park's Columbus Drive, turning the whole attractive lakeside area into a music- and fun-filled food court that features rows of cheap, worldwide delicacies. Eat your way through famous Chicago staples here (Sweet Baby Ray ribs, Billy Goat cheezborgah-cheezborgahs) and forge into a smorgasbord of Korean, African, Swedish and Vietnamese specialties, along with every other exotic cuisine now at home in Chicago.

Between comestibles, savor everything else Grant Park is serving up during this healthy week of gluttony. Lift some new recipes and cooking techniques from celebrity chefs in the Cooking Corner's demo kitchens. In the Living Pavilion, learn how to improve your home and garden or how to interpret dreams. Take a morning yoga or pilates class or an afternoon-swing dance lesson. Have a seat in a ninety-foot Ferris wheel or a white-water flume ride.

Or just sit back on the grass, digest your samosas and enjoy hours of big-name musical and comedy entertainment by the lake. Then get up and eat some more. If country music is your thing, consider attending the opening weekend of **Taste**, which coincides with the annual _Country Music Festival_.

Exploring the rest of Chicago by foot, cab, boat and elevator will quickly burn off any excess calories. The Midwest's cultural and financial mecca is still right here where it's always been, spread beneath a towering skyline that (almost) rivals New York City's. It'll take more than one visit to appreciate Chicago's world-class museums and galleries, its famous jazz, blues and comedy clubs, its old-style ball parks and countless ethnic neighborhoods. Between helpings of great food, you'll get a fine taste of it all. (_For more on food festivals, see page 213._)

On the Calendar

Official Event Dates
Ten days beginning the last Friday in June

Best 3 Days To Be There
First or second weekend

Other Times To Go
The smaller scale **Chicago Blues Festival** (312-744-3370) takes place in the same venue as **Taste** on the first weekend in June.

☼ 57°/79° (14°/26°)

Illinois

Day-by-Day Plan

DAY 1 — Friday

9:00 am Start your weekend Chicago-style by grabbing a beige booth on the other end ❌ of The Loop at **Lou Mitchell's**. This popular breakfast spot serves great pancakes, coffee and Chicago attitude.

10:30 am Head to the **Chicago Mercantile Exchange** for a lesson in commodities madness. From the observation level, the trading floor of the "Merc" seems to be a pit of madness—crowded insanity unleashed beneath a board of symbols and numbers. You don't want to miss the trading of pork-belly futures and options—your lunch might some day depend on the exchanges between the savvy traders below.

Noon Across the street, Chicago's highest point is atop the 110-story (quarter-of-a-mile-high) **Sears Tower Skydeck**. The observation deck is a minute's elevator ride up to the 103rd floor. Once the world's tallest building, the Sears Tower took a controversial second place to a skyscraper in Malaysia (by the length of an antenna).

1:00 pm Hope you're hungry. It's time to ❌ take a *Taste of Chicago*—several tastes, actually. Purchase your food tickets at the nearest booth and dive into a food city of colorful tent kitchens lined up along Columbus Drive. All the standard Chicago specialties are here, plus turtle soup, pad thai and everything else. You can pace yourself with mini-portions (by ordering "a taste of a taste") or enjoy a fine sit-down meal at the Gourmet Dining Pavilion. Enjoy hours of entertainment at several performance stages.

6:00 pm Order some cheap beers and watch the Cubs blow it in the ninth at **Harry Caray's**, a classic brick-warehouse Chicago sports bar founded by the famous former Cubs and White Sox baseball announcer.

7:30 pm Chicago has no shortage of phenomenal restaurants. For an unforgettable gourmet meal in a cozy town house set- ❌ ting, try **Charlie Trotter's**, named for the owner, one of America's top chefs.

10:00 pm Take in a night of live jazz at **Green Dolphin Street**. The best performers appear at this classic, '40s-style club, which has two bars, dining room and cool outside porch.

Midnight Yet another nightspot not to be missed is **The Redhead Piano Bar**, an upscale place with a fun and talented pianist who keeps the joint jumping.

DAY 2 — Saturday

9:30 am Fuel up at the **West Egg Café**, a ❌ favorite eggs-and-bacon joint near the Fairmont hotel.

11:00 am From its colossal skyscrapers to its heritage Frank Lloyd Wright homes, Chicago is famous for cutting-edge architecture. A great way to see it while getting to know the city is with a **Chicago Architecture Foundation** walking tour.

Noon Escape to Chicago's revived Navy Pier, a public activity center filled with shops, entertainment attractions. From here it's an easy walk north to the trendy Oak St. Beach. Yes, there's big-time sunbathing in Chicago, too.

1:00 pm Cross the bridge over the Chicago River to the Tribune Tower and you're at the south end of the Magnificent Mile. This fashionable strip of Michigan Avenue is loaded with restaurants, art museums and enough shopping to work your credit card into a sweat. Nearby lunch options include the upscale Mexican-influenced ❌ **Topolobampo** and its less formal, adjoining neighbor, **Frontera Grill**.

3:00 pm Cab to **The Art Institute of Chicago**. Flanked by giant bronze lions, the museum houses more than 250,000 pieces dating from 3000 BC to the present, including many outstanding impressionist and post-impressionist paintings.

7:30 pm Before dinner, go to the John Hancock Building and head to the **Signature Lounge** on the ninety-sixth floor for panoramic views of Chicago's illuminated skyline.

Day-by-Day Plan

8:30 pm Chicago is cooking with Nouveau American cuisine. The best and liveliest options include **Harvest on Huron**, with dishes such as macadamia-nut-crusted halibut with papaya-butter sauce. For less fancy Chicago-style dining, try either **Ben Pao Chinese Restaurant** or the original **Pizzeria Uno** for local deep-dish pies.

10:30 pm Cab to **The Second City**, the improvisational-comedy theater that helped catapult the careers of John Belushi, Bill Murray, Julia Louis-Dreyfus and Chris Farley. If you want good seats, arrive at least thirty minutes early.

12:30 am In the yuppie-friendly Lincoln Park neighborhood, the high-energy **Kingston Mines** encourages guests to "hear blues, drink booze, talk loud" until 4 a.m.

DAY 3 Sunday

9:30 am Have a light room-service breakfast. Keep in mind you'll be surrounded by food for most of the afternoon.

11:00 am Celebrate the opening hour of *Taste of Chicago* with an "early morning" yoga, pilates or feng shui class in the Living Pavilion. Sample your way through several early and late lunches and take in a concert or two at the Petrillo Music Shell. Be sure to reserve some time to enjoy the lake view from Buckingham Fountain.

4:00 pm Head to the **Museum of Science and Industry** to experience one of the nation's largest touch-and-feel exhibits. It includes a walk along Yesterday's Main Street and one through a giant heart.

6:00 pm **Wendella Sightseeing Boats** offers a sunset cruise on Lake Michigan and under the bridges of the Chicago River, which flows "backwards" (the river was redirected to prevent sewage from running into Lake Michigan).

8:00 pm At **Gibsons** you'll be served the exact same flawlessly-prepared, enormous steaks that Michael Jordan, Jack Nicholson and Tony Bennett order—with gargantuan dessert chasers.

10:00 pm Get some more Chicago blues at classic venues like **Blue Chicago**, featuring mainly female performers, and the slightly less touristy and always happening **Buddy Guy's Legends**.

11:30 pm Rush Street is well-known for fun in Chicago. The best place to go is **Jilly's Retro Club**, an upscale disco. To cap off your night they have a piano bar next door playing mostly Sinatra. What better way to end your weekend than with a chorus of "My kinda town, Chicago is ... "

More Time, More Choices

Enjoy excellent food with a piano bar at **Palette's**. At **Dick's Last Resort** you'll find classic rock blaring into the late hours and a large, outdoor floating patio. **Narcisse** is another intense bar scene in a very sophisticated setting. **Brasserie Jo** is a fine French restaurant with a lively Parisian-style atmosphere.

Accommodations

The Fairmont is considered one of the city's top three hotels. Steps from Michigan Avenue, its spacious, elegant rooms overlook Grant Park and the *Taste of Chicago* festival. Another excellent choice is **The Drake**, a grand 1920s building set on the northern tip of the Magnificent Mile. The nearby **Raphael Hotel** offers Old World charm on a quiet tree-lined street in the heart of the city. An ultra-chic option is the **Sutton Place Hotel**, decked out in modern accents of granite, glass and metal.

Event & Ticket Info

Taste of Chicago (Grant Park): Free admission (tickets sold for food and beverages). For information contact *Chicago Mayor's Office of Special Events* (312-744-3315).

The Hot Sheet

Hotels		Phone	Address	Price	Fax	Room/Best
The Drake		312-787-2200 800-553-7253	140 E. Walton Pl..	$$$	312-787-1431	535/Lake Michigan vw
The Fairmont		312-565-8000 800-527-4727	200 N. Columbus Dr.	$$$	312-856-1032	758/Grant Park vw
The Raphael Hotel		312-943-5000 800-983-7870	201 E. Delaware Pl.	$$	312-943-9483	172/Quiet #02 rms
Sutton Place Hotel		312-266-2100 800-810-6888	21 E. Bellevue Pl.	$$$$	312-266-2103	246/Superior rms

Restaurants	Day	Phone	Address	Price	Rec	Food
Ben Pao Chinese Restaurant	2	312-222-1888	52 W. Illinois St.	$$	LD	Chinese
Brasserie Jo	A	312-595-0800	59 W. Hubbard St.	$$	D	French
Charlie Trotter's	1	773-248-6228	816 W. Armitage Ave.	$$$$$+	D	New American
Gibsons	3	312-266-8999	1028 N. Rush St.	$$$	D	Steakhouse
Harry Caray's	1	312-828-0966	33 W. Kinzie St	$	LD	Sports Bar and Grill
Harvest on Huron	2	312-587-9600	217 W. Huron St.	$$$	LD	New American
Lou Mitchell's	1	312-939-3111	565 W. Jackson Blvd	$	B/L	American
Palette's	A	312-440-5200	1030 N. State St.	$$	D	New American
Pizzeria Uno	2	312-321-1000	29 E. Ohio St.	$$	LD	Pizza
Topolobampo/Frontera Grill	2	312-661-1434	445 N. Clark St.	$$	L/D	Mexican
West Egg Café	2	312-280-8366	620 N. Fairbanks Ct.	$	B/LD	American breakfast

Nightlife	Day	Phone	Address	Cover	Rec*	Music
Blue Chicago	3	312-642-6261	736 N. Clark St.	$	MP	Blues
Buddy Guy's Legends	3	312-427-0333	754 S. Wabash Ave.	$	M(F)	Blues
Dick's Last Resort	2	312-836-7870	435 E. Illinois St.	None	M(F)	Rock
Green Dolphin Street	1	773-395-0066	2200 N. Ashland Ave.	$	M	Jazz
Jilly's Retro Club	3	312-664-1001	1009 N. Rush St.	$	P	Disco
Kingston Mines	2	773-477-4646	2548 N. Halsted St.	$$	M(F)	Blues
Narcisse	A	312-787-2675	710 N. Clark St.	None	R(F)	
The Redhead Piano Bar	1	312-640-1000	16 W. Ontario St.	None	M	Jazz, pop, blues
The Second City	2	312-337-3992	1616 N. Wells St.	$$	S	Improv comedy
Signature Lounge	2	312-787-9596	875 N. Michigan Ave.	None	M(F)	Jazz

* M=Live music; P=Dancing (Party); R=Bar only; S=Show; (F)=Food served. For further explanation of codes, page 12.

Sights & Attractions	Day	Phone	Address	Entry Fee
The Art Institute of Chicago	2	312-443-3600	111 S. Michigan Ave.	$
Chicago Architecture Foundation	2	312-922-8687	224 S. Michigan Ave.	$
Chicago Mercantile Exchange	1	312-930-1000	30 S. Wacker Dr.	None
Museum of Science and Industry	3	773-684-1414	57th St. at Lake Shore Dr.	$
Sears Tower Skydeck	1	312-875-9449	233 S. Wacker Dr.	$
Wendella Sightseeing Boats	3	312-337-1446	400 N. Michigan Ave.	$$

Chicago CVB		**312-744-2400**	**77 E. Randolph St.**

Illinois

 NYC -1   O'Hare (ORD) <60 min./$35
Midway (MDW) <30 min./$25   No   Map Code: A17

Indy 500

The 500 Festival

Key Month: May Ratings: Event ★ ★ ★ ☆ ☆ **P** City ★ ★ ☆ ☆ ☆ Origin: 1911 Attendance: 400,000

Noise, speed, sun, danger and courage are the hallmarks of the **Indianapolis 500**, but the days leading up to the big race are filled with the kind of go-for-broke excitement that turns the whole **Indy** package into the "greatest spectacle in racing." Two types of zealots are attracted to **Indy**—racing fans and party fans—and there's more than enough going on to keep everybody's motor running.

The actual race—a few hours around a 2.5-mile oval that circles part of a golf course and accommodates up to 500,000 spectators—is the biggest single sporting event in the world. Cars whiz by at 235 mph, fans debate timeless racing questions, such as the merits of Firestone vs. Goodyear and Bud vs. Miller, and the auto world's latest hero is crowned.

Fans longing for bawdy partying and topless women at the track's infield Snake Pit should be aware that the **Indy 500** recently has become kinder and gentler. Speedway officials have gone out of their way to make the **Indy 500** a more family-oriented event. Organized activities have replaced Snake Pit debauchery. Some of the prerace events draw big crowds—on Pole Day, drivers and teams compete for the most coveted qualifying award in motorsports, the MBNA Pole Award and its $100,000 bonus. For the most part, however, unless you're a racing fan, the three days before the race are actually more fun than the race itself.

> ### On the Calendar
>
> #### Official Event Dates
> Festival runs from first Saturday in May until the race on the Sunday before Memorial Day (last Monday of May)
>
> #### Best 3 Days To Be There
> Thursday-Saturday before the race. Race day (Sunday) is no longer as revved up as the fun beginning on Thursday.
>
> ☾ 52°/73° (11°/23°)

Most higher-end partying is underwritten by sponsors. With a few strategic phone calls, you could bag a sponsorship connection through a local business back home. You could spend an afternoon at a swanky hospitality suite, at a banquet in the garage of restaurateur and team owner Jonathan Byrd, or at former 500-driver Stefan Johansson's Karting Center. Even if you don't hook into a private party, your days and nights will be filled.

Indianapolis is the state's capital, with a population of more than 800,000 that spends half a year getting ready for the Indy 500, another few months preparing for NASCAR's Brickyard 400, and the rest of the year recuperating. As most locals already know, a few days at The 500 Festival are generally enough to teach even the most staunch partier the value of a pit stop. So, plan for a restful week after leaving this heartland hell raiser. (*For more on car racing, see page 210.*)

Day-by-Day Plan

DAY 1 — Thursday

9:30 am After a hotel breakfast, drive to the City of Speedway. You can't miss the track, it's like approaching Stonehenge—a monument of mythic proportions. Today is *Carburetion Day*, the last chance for drivers to practice.

10:00 am Stop at the **Indianapolis Motor Speedway Hall of Fame Museum**. Worship displays of thirty Indy 500 winners as well as a variety of classic and antique cars.

11:00 am Final practice runs start at 11 a.m. Two to three cars at a time take a few turns and their crews make last-minute adjustments.

12:30 pm Next to the Hall of Fame Museum, ✖ grab lunch at the Gasoline Alley Cafe or the Pepsi Pit Stop.

1:30 pm Teams compete to fuel and change tires at breakneck speed during the annual *Pit Stop Competition*. Speed here is just as important as on the track. Races have been won and lost in the pits.

3:30 pm A live concert (until 6 p.m.), entertains the crowds with rock music.

6:00 pm From the track, head to Union **Jack Pub**, a favorite local hangout for race-team members and drivers. Knock back beer with traditional American fare, surrounded by great race memorabilia.

8:00 pm **Palomino** is a good example of a hip ✖ chain of restaurants. The Continental-influenced American menu is almost as good as the people-watching scene.

10:00 pm Help 5,000 others consume 150 barrels and 200 cases of beer at the *Rally in the Alley* (4 p.m.-midnight), an outdoor dance party sponsored by **Ike and Jonesy's**. The party starts in front of the club, then moves inside after midnight.

DAY 2 — Friday

9:00 am Stroll to **Acapulco Joe's**, a funky ✖ restaurant that serves Mexican food as well as a traditional Hoosier breakfast of biscuits and gravy.

10:00 am Make a quick visit to the **Saturday Evening Post Museum**, which houses a collection of *Post* covers from the '50s and '60s.

Noon Head to the Westin hotel for the *Championship Auto Racing Auxiliary's (CARA)* luncheon fashion show, which started at 11 a.m. Drivers and their wives and children strut in the latest ✖ fashions. Or drive to **P.F. Chang's Bistro**, which opened in Indianapolis in late 2000. It's part of the very good casual Chinese chain and has quickly become a fixture on the local dining scene.

2:30 pm At downtown's pleasant White River State Park is the **Eiteljorg Museum of American Indians and Western Art**, which has one of the nation's best collections of crafts, sculpture and painting. Check out the **Canal Walk**, which has paddle boats for rent and a riverside outdoor cafe.

4:30 pm Take a reserved table for high tea at the **Canterbury Hotel**. Tea and piano music make for a welcome contrast to all the hubbub soon to follow.

7:00 pm Party around numerous floats at *Flotatious*, a festival event held at the state fairgrounds. Live music, wild cos-✖ tumes, food and a Mardi Gras-like atmosphere kick off at 6:30 p.m. and end at 11 p.m.

11:00 pm A fun late-night destination is the **Slippery Noodle Inn**, a historic blues joint that announces to everyone, "dis is it." Apparently that's true. It's been a road-house, a way station for the underground railroad, a bordello, a slaughterhouse and the scene of a murder.

DAY 3 — Saturday

10:00 am After breakfast in your hotel, visit the **Indianapolis Museum of Art**. A collection of J.M.W. Turner work is highlighted along with Asian and African art.

Noon *The 500 Festival Parade* marches down Pennsylvania Street, around Monument Circle and north on Meridian toward 14th Street. About 250,000 spectators show up and many break out the noise-makers, masks, crowns and red noses that come with each reserved seat.

Day-by-Day Plan

DAY 3 — Saturday (cont.)

2:00 pm Have lunch at **The Claddagh** ❌ (Irish everything, including the staff and furniture).

4:00 pm Hire a **Yellow Rose Carriage** and ride around downtown's hub, Monument Circle. Or take in the 360-degree city view with a drink in the revolving **Eagle's Nest** restaurant atop the Hyatt hotel.

7:00 pm **Tiki Bob's** has a good beach-party atmosphere to get you warmed up—and a specialty, sixty-four-ounce drink called Tiki Nuts, served in giant, clear plastic coconuts. It's always busy around Indy time.

9:00 pm Head to Indianapolis' most famous ❌ steakhouse, the elegant **St. Elmo Steakhouse Restaurant**, which is lauded for its shrimp cocktail as well as its filets and prime rib. Tuxedoed waiters serve you in the Hulman Room, named for the Speedway's patriarch, the late Tony Hulman.

11:30 pm You can hang around at 16th Street and Georgetown Road for the infamous Indy 500-eve party, but a more lively crowd preps for race day at Broad Ripple Village. Especially after midnight, it's a popular nightspot for young adults and professionals looking for music and bar-hopping in a casual atmosphere. While shopping around for your choice of live-music clubs, stop into **The Vogue**—one of the area's top spots—to put a fast finish on this weekend of classic American partying.

After ■

If you stay Sunday for the *Indy 500*, you can show up for the track opening at 5 a.m., even though the gentlemen don't actually start their engines until nearly 11 a.m. There's an early buffet breakfast at the Speedway American Legion. Getting to the track isn't hard, it's leaving along with hundreds of thousands of others that's a pain. The city's Metro bus is efficient, but still no picnic. If you drive, buy a front-yard parking space from a local, or join veteran fans who park a few miles away and walk in to ensure a faster getaway. Rent a scanner at the track to hear drivers talking to their crews. Radio frequencies are listed in the newspaper.

More Time, More Choices

Rick's Cafe Boatyard serves great food and has live jazz and a quiet elegance. A casual downtown restaurant is **Buca di Beppo**, which does solid Italian.

Accommodations

In the heart of downtown Indianapolis, the four-star accommodations at **The Westin Hotel Indianapolis** are connected by sky bridge to the Indiana Convention Center and Circle Centre Mall. Not as stylish as the Westin, The **Hyatt Regency Indianapolis** does offer modern accommodations and a downtown location. Another is the **Omni Severin Hotel**. The best spot in town, the **Canterbury Hotel**, will likely be booked with *Indy* patrons.

Event & Ticket Info

Indy 500—The 500 Festival (Indianapolis Motor Speedway at 4790 W. 16th St., and sites around Indianapolis): Admission tickets for the **Indy 500** ($35 for terrace seats to $140 for penthouse box) generally sell out one year in advance. Requests for reserved seats are accepted only in writing. Order forms are available thirteen months prior to the race. Orders are filled after the previous year's race. Contact *Indianapolis Motor Speedway* (PO Box 24152, Speedway, IN 46224). Since scalping is legal in Indianapolis, scalpers are plentiful around the Speedway. *Indianapolis Motor Speedway* (317-484-6700); *The 500 Festival* (800-638-4296).

The 500 Festival Parade (Pennsylvania Street, Monument Circle, then north up Meridian to 14th Street): The 35,000 reserved seats ($12-$25) sell out months in advance (this is the largest ticketed parade in North America). Though there's no charge to stand, the crowd makes it difficult to see. For tickets, contact *The 500 Festival* (800-638-4296).

Carburetion Day (Indianapolis Motor Speedway, 4790 W. 16th St.): Tickets ($10) never sell out and are available at the gate. Admission includes all events inside the Motor Speedway. For more information, contact *Indianapolis Motor Speedway* (317-484-6700).

CARA's Annual Luncheon Fashion Show (Westin Hotel, 50 S. Capitol Ave.): Tickets ($60 CD) can be purchased from *Championship Auto Racing Auxiliary* (317-299-2277).

Hotels	Phone	Address	Price	Fax	Rooms/Best
Canterbury Hotel	317-634-3000 800-538-8186	123 S. Illinois St.	$$$$	317-685-2519	99/City vw
The Hyatt Regency Indianapolis	317-632-1234 800-233-1234	1 S. Capitol Ave.	$$$$	317-616-6299	497/City vw
Omni Severin Hotel	317-634-6664 800-843-6664	40 W. Jackson Pl.	$$$$	317-687-3612	424/City vw
The Westin Hotel Indianapolis	317-262-8100 800-937-8461	50 S. Capitol Ave.	$$$$+	317-231-3928	573/Dlx rms

Restaurants	Day	Phone	Address	Price	Rec	Food
Acapulco Joe's	2	317-637-5160	365 N. Illinois St.	$	BLD	Mexican
Buca di Beppo	A	317-632-2822	35 N. Illinois St.	$$	D	Italian
Canterbury Hotel	3	317-634-3000	see Canterbury Hotel	$$	T	Tea, sandwiches
The Claddagh	3	317-488-8686	Circle Center Mall, 3rd level	$$	L/D	Irish
Eagle's Nest	3	317-231-7566	see The Hyatt Regency	$$$$	D	American
Palomino	1	317-974-0400	Washington and Illinois sts.	$$$	D/L	Regional American
P.F. Chang's Bistro	2	317-974-5747	49 W. Maryland St.	$$	DL	Chinese
Rick's Cafe Boatyard	A	317-290-9300	4050 Dandy Trail	$$$	LD	American
St. Elmo Steakhouse	3	317-635-0636	127 S. Illinois St.	$$$$	D	Steakhouse

Nightlife	Day	Phone	Address	Cover	Rec*	Music
Ike and Jonesy's	1	317-632-4553	12 Jackson Pl.	$	P(F)	Rock, blues
Slippery Noodle Inn	2	317-631-6974	372 S. Meridian St.	$	MP(F)	Blues
Tiki Bob's	3	317-974-0954	231 S. Meridien St.	$	MP	Varies
Union Jack Pub	1	317-243-3300	6225 W. 25th St.	$$	D	American
The Vogue	3	317-259-7029	6259 N. College Ave.	$	MP(F)	Techno, Top 40

* M=Live music; P=Dancing (Party); R=Bar only; S=Show; (F)=Food served. For further explanation of codes, page 12.

Sights & Attractions	Day	Phone	Address	Entry Fee
Canal Walk	2		White River State Park	None
Eiteljorg Museum of American Indians and Western Art	2	317-636-9378	500 W. Washington St.	$
Indianapolis Motor Speedway Hall of Fame Museum	1	317-484-6747	4790 W. 16th St.	$
Indianapolis Museum of Art	3	317-923-1331	1200 W. 38th St.	None
Saturday Evening Post Museum	2	317-636-8881	1100 Waterway Blvd.	None
Yellow Rose Carriage	3	317-634-3400	Outside The Hyatt Regency	$$$

Indianapolis CVB	**317-639-4282**	**1 RCA Dome, Ste. 100**	

 NYC   Indianapolis (IND) <30 min./$25    Yes/No   Map Code: A18

Indiana

Kentucky Derby

Kentucky Derby Festival

Key Month: Apr/May   Ratings: Event ★ ★ ★ ★ ☆   **ⓟ**   City ★ ★ ★ ☆ ☆   Origin: 1875   Attendance: 140,000

Twenty horses, 600 roses, 80,000 mint juleps. On the first Saturday in May, America's best three-year-old thoroughbreds race for glory (and lots of money) in the **Kentucky Derby**. With steel in their teeth and mud in their eyes, horses with legs become horses with wings in the first jewel of the Triple Crown, held each year in Louisville. The odds on owning the winner are 30,000 to 1. The odds on getting a reserved seat under the famed Twin Spires of Churchill Downs are slightly better, but box seats are generally handed down with the family silver.

At one of the oldest sporting facilities in the United States still in use, a $2 bet buys a million thrills. It's tough to ignore the pressure to wager at this next-largest sporting event for betting after the Super Bowl ($10 million is wagered at the track, five times that, nationally). A bugler plays the "Call to Post" and everyone sings "My Old Kentucky Home." Red-coated outriders escort horses to the starting gate, binoculars go up, the bell sounds and the gate flies open.

The **Derby** is called the most exciting two minutes in sports, but the days leading up to the race might be the most exhausting two weeks in sports. The **Kentucky Derby Festival** hosts more than seventy events. "Thunder over Louisville," the nation's largest fireworks show, ignites two weeks of revelry. The **Pegasus Parade** and **Kentucky Oaks** race mark the final approach to **Derby**

On the Calendar

Official Event Dates
Race is first Saturday in May; festival runs three weeks prior

Best 3 Days To Be There
Final three days of festival (Thursday-Saturday). Race day is a must, as are the parties Thursday and Friday.

☽ 54°/76° (12°/24°)

Day. Celebrities descend on Louisville for elaborate balls, and everyone, it seems, has a house full of guests. Think Mardi Gras, Super Bowl and New Year's Eve mixed with the Great Balloon Race, Great Steamboat Race (both are **Derby Festival** events) and great local bourbon.

Although Louisville's metro-area population is about a million, for visiting urbanites the pace may feel like syrup coursing through a julep's crushed ice. When you arrive at the airport you'll be handed bourbon bon-bons by gracious Derby Belles. The visitor's biggest challenge is pronouncing the name correctly: *Loo ah vull*. Come spring, though, the pace quickens as more than a million people arrive for the **Derby Festival**, the **Run for the Roses** (arguably the world's greatest race) and an unforgettable three-day trifecta.

Kentucky

Day-by-Day Plan

DAY 1 Thursday

10:00 am Trot over to the **Louisville Slugger Museum and Bat Factory** for highlights of the great game and a tour of the bat factory.

1:00 pm Walk toward the river to ❷ Waterfront Park and the **Derby Festival Downtown Chow Wagon**. There should be live music, cheap eats from food stands, and an opportunity to be ridiculed for your mispronunciation of the city's name.

2:30 pm Drive to the **Speed Art Museum** and its collection of Rembrandt, Monet and contemporary works.

5:30 pm Head to Broadway for the **Pegasus Parade** (6–7:15 p.m.), the granddaddy of all *Derby Festival* events. You can easily walk the thirteen-block parade route in reverse for a quick review of the spectacle.

8:00 pm Retrieve the car and proceed to ❷ **Azalea** for trendy blends of New American cuisine.

10:00 pm Sip a martini and hear jazz at **Bobby J's**, a bistro and nightclub with a balcony and separate bar for the cigar set. If you prefer the blues, **Stevie Ray's** is the place. It has warm brick walls and a hot dance floor.

Midnight Change the pace with a visit to **O'Malley's Corner**, one of Louisville's two popular multiclub venues. This one has four clubs within its building: disco, rock, country (the dancing here is not for amateurs) and techno.

DAY 2 Friday

8:00 am Slip on the feed bag at **Lynn's** ❷ **Paradise Cafe**. It's a short drive to this kitschy, '40s-style diner that serves country ham, biscuits and comfort food. Go early to beat the herd.

10:30 am Follow your concierge-assisted transportation plan to the **Kentucky Derby Museum**. The displays and exhibits celebrate every Derby, every day. Lay off the pace and grab a bite in ❷ its **Derby Cafe**, a local institution.

When you arrive at the airport, you'll be handed bourbon bon-bons by gracious Derby Belles to set the mood for three glorious days of Southern tradition.

2:00 pm Walk to Churchill Downs for the **Kentucky Oaks** (11:30 a.m.–6:30 p.m.) race. Locals say the "Run for the Lilies" is a good bet for avoiding Derby crowds. Head to the infield where a band starts playing after the fifth race. You can see the whole track from there.

7:30 pm Attend one of the legendary Derby's-eve parties. First choice is the wild **Madden Derby Eve** party for 2,500 close friends. It's an hour's drive away in Lexington, but everything you'd want a party to be: A star-studded charity event—dress is black-tie—with cocktails, ❷ dinner, dancing and entertainment.

Midnight Savor the bourbon and jazz at the **Old Seelbach Bar**, one of the South's jewels among watering holes. Or go to local favorite **Zena's**, which also has jazz and is open until at least 4 a.m.

DAY 3 Saturday

9:00 am Hit the **Derby Day Breakfast** ❷ (9 a.m.–noon, location TBA). It's a great way to meet people—about 700, including the Derby Queen and her court—listen to jazz and have a traditional Derby breakfast.

Noon A limo is the preferred way to arrive at Churchill Downs for the **Kentucky Derby** (11:30 a.m.–7 p.m.). Once inside, go to the infield where, weather permitting—the weather can be as fickle as the outcome of the race; temperatures range from the 40s to the 90s and rain is not unusual—a party atmos- ❷ phere prevails. Snack on excellent bar-becue beef, pork or turkey sandwiches. Try a Bones of Beer—eighteen inches and twenty-eight ounces of beer in a green glass with a bulbous bottom. It's slightly less traditional but, for many, slightly more tasty than the bourbon, water, sugar and mint leaves that go into the ubiquitous mint julep.

Saturday (cont.)

5:45 pm High-tail it after the *Derby* race (the eighth of ten races) to beat the crowd. Return to your stall and collapse, briefly.

7:30 pm Drive to **Brasserie Dietrich** for a ✪ classic meal in a stunning dining room, a restored movie theater.

11:00 pm Louisville's second multiclub venue is **Jim Porter's**, where you can choose between blues, '70s disco, '90s rock and a swingin' (literally, above the bar) singer. If you feel the need for food or quiet, stop in at the **Bristol Bar & Grille** for a good late-night snack. You may need the down time, because, whether you've won or lost this weekend, the smart money says it was the wildest time you've ever had hanging around a bunch of three-year-olds.

■

More Time, More Choices

Louisville has three major restaurant strips: Bardstown Road, Frankfort Avenue and Hurstbourne Parkway. For ethnic influences, **Asiatique** offers Pacific Rim fare. Or, go to critic's fave, **Lilly's**. Chef/owner Kathy Cary— you might have seen her on the *Today Show*—changes her menu with the seasons. **Club Grotto** and **Zephyr Cove** are two other popular spots in town. Or consider a dining cruise on the ***Star of Louisville***, a yacht-style cruiser with dancing and live music.

Accommodations

The hotel situation this weekend is bleak— you may not know where you're staying until a waiting list clears, and you'll be paying two to three times the normal rate for a room you won't spend much time in. There's little hope of getting a room at **The Camberly Brown Hotel**, a restored 1923 jewel. You may clear a wait list at **The Seelbach Hilton Hotel**, another downtown gem. Another option is **The Galt House** and **Galt House East** complex with 1,300 rooms. The best bet for getting a downtown room is the **Club Hotel by Doubletree Louisville Downtown**.

Event & Ticket Info

Kentucky Derby–Kentucky Derby Festival (Churchill Downs, 700 Central Ave. and various sites around Lexington): Churchill Downs requires written requests (beginning the day after the Derby) for the few available reserved seats to the Derby and Oaks (combined tickets): clubhouse ($175-$550), grandstand ($42-$160) or infield bleachers ($70). General admission tickets ($40 for Derby/$25 for Oaks) are sold on race day for standing only, including the infield. Send request to Special Events, Churchill Downs, 700 Central Ave., Louisville, KY 40208. For race information contact *Churchill Downs* (502-636-4400). For festival information, contact *Kentucky Derby Festival* (502-584-6383).

Derby Festival Downtown Chow Wagon (Waterfront Park): $5

Pegasus Parade (Broadway, from Campbell to Ninth streets): Bleacher and chair tickets ($9-$11) are available (although standing is preferred) at *Kentucky Center for the Arts* ticket service outlets (502-584-7777).

Derby Day Breakfast (Location TBA): For information and tickets ($95 CD), which sell out a few weeks before the event, contact (starting in January) *Historic Homes Foundation* (502-899-5079).

Madden Derby Eve Party (Hamburg Place Farm, Lexington): $300 CD. Request an invitation (in January) in writing from Anita Madden, P.O. Box 12128, Lexington, KY 40580.

Hotels	Phone	Address	Price	Fax	Rooms/Best
The Camberly Brown Hotel	502-583-1234 800-555-8000	335 Broadway	$$$$+	502-587-7006	293/North vw
Club Hotel by Doubletree Louisville Downtown	502-585-2200 888-444-2582	101 E. Jefferson St.	$$$$	502-584-5657	182
The Galt House and Galt House East	502-589-5200 800-626-1814	Riverfront at 4th Ave.	$$$	502-585-9029	1,300/River vw
The Seelbach Hilton Hotel	502-585-3200 800-333-3399	500 4th St.	$$$$+	502-585-9240	321/Dlx (larger)

Restaurants	Day	Phone	Address	Price	Rec	Food
Asiatique	A	502-899-3578	106 Sears Ave.	$$	D	Seafood
Azalea	1	502- 895-5493	3612 Brownsboro Rd.	$$$	D/L	New American
Brasserie Dietrich	3	502-897-6076	2862 Frankfort Ave.	$$	D	American bistro
Bristol Bar & Grille	3	502-456-1702	1321 Bardstown Rd.	$$	T/LD	New American
Club Grotto	A	502-459-5275	2116 Bardstown Rd.	$$$	D	American bistro
Derby Cafe	2	502-637-7097	see Kentucky Derby Museum	$$	L	American
Lilly's	A	502-451-0447	1147 Bardstown Rd.	$$$	D/L	International
Lynn's Paradise Cafe	2	502-583-3447	984 Barret Ave.	$	B/LD	American
Zephyr Cove	A	502-897-1030	2330 Frankfort Ave.	$$$	D	American bistro

Nightlife	Day	Phone	Address	Cover	Rec*	Music
Bobby J's	1	502-452-2665	1314 Bardstown Rd.	None	MP(F)	Jazz
Jim Porter's	3	502-452-9531	2345 Lexington Rd.	$	MP	Rock, blues
Old Seelbach Bar	2	502-585-3200	500 4th St.	None	MP(F)	Jazz, R&B
O'Malley's Corner	1	502-589-3866	133 W. Liberty St.	$	MP	New rock, alternative
Stevie Ray's	1	502-582-9945	230 E. Main St.	$$	M	Blues
Zena's	2	502-584-3074	122 W. Main St.	$	M(F)	Jazz

* M=Live music; P=Dancing (Party); R=Bar only; S=Show; (F)=Food served. For further explanation of codes, page 12.

Sights & Attractions	Day	Phone	Address	Entry Fee	
Kentucky Derby Museum	2	502-637-7097	704 Central Ave.	$	
Louisville Slugger Museum and Bat Factory	1	502-588-7228	800 W. Main St.	$	
Speed Art Museum	1	502-634-2700	2035 S. 3rd St.	None	
Star of Louisville	A	502-589-7827	151 W. River Rd.	$$$$+	

Greater Louisville CVB	502-584-2121	400 S. 1st St.

Kentucky

 NYC   Louisville/Standiford Field (SDF) <30 min./$15   Yes   Map Code: A19

Mardi Gras

New Orleans

Key Month: Feb/Mar   Ratings: Event ★★★★★   ⓥ   City ★★★★★   Origin: 1837   Attendance: 3,500,000

There are parties, and then there are—PARTIES! During the days leading to Ash Wednesday and Lenten abstentions, New Orleans blasts off beyond our humble universe and enters an entirely superior galaxy, a world where parties transport you into a kind of unrestrained bliss you never knew you were capable of.

A citywide, unabashed bash of epic proportions, *Mardi Gras* (don't be fooled by hometown imitations that criminally borrow the name) is by far North America's most raging party and, by many accounts, the best annual event in the world. Day and night, crowds of exhibitionists and masked revelers pack Bourbon Street, taking full advantage of the city's liberal alcohol policies.

A more select audience spends its evenings at a series of fancy-dress balls thrown by legendary "krewes"—social clubs dedicated to *Mardi Gras* week festivities. Stately mansions are draped with purple, green and gold—official colors of *Mardi Gras*—and extravagant floats take over the streets, catapulting millions of beads into huge crowds during a series of musical parades. The explosion of colors—and beautiful people wearing them—makes Mardi Gras a photographer's dream.

The city's unofficial motto—*laissez les bons temps rouler*—means "Let the good times roll." Mostly, they roll out of control during *Mardi Gras*. Highlights include Sunday's spirited *Bacchus Parade and Ball*; the classy *Orpheus Parade and Ball* held on Fat Monday (Lundi Gras); and Fat Tuesday's (Mardi Gras) street partying and parades, starring the *Zulu* and *Rex* parades.

New Orleans' combination of French, African, Spanish and Caribbean cultures has lent *Mardi Gras* celebrations a distinctive flair in a city that often seems like an exotic, foreign place, even to visiting Americans. You could easily occupy all your time partying and recovering from *Mardi Gras* festivities, but make a point of exploring the city's French Quarter, with its French-Creole buildings and flower-laden iron balconies. And don't miss the Garden District, known for rambling mansions and turn-of-the-century streetcars.

The music, food and spirit of the people—locals and visitors—make New Orleans one of the world's favorite destinations. The wild days of *Mardi Gras* are when the city is at its most alive, colorful and joyful.

On the Calendar

Official Event Dates
Runs from beginning of January until Tuesday before Ash Wednesday

Best 3 Days To Be There
Final three days of festival (Sunday-Tuesday). They save the best for last.

Other Times To Go
See *New Orleans Jazz Festival*, page 94.

☾ 46°/75° (8°/24°)

Louisiana

DAY 1 Sunday

9:30 am Head to the nearby Windsor Court ❌ Hotel's classy **Grill Room**, which serves a wide selection of first-rate breakfasts in a clubby, English-style dining room.

10:30 am Cab to the **New Orleans Museum of Art** on the grounds of City Park. One of the top museums in the South, it showcases European, African, pre-Columbian and local arts. This time of year, some exhibits focus on Mardi Gras and New Orleans culture.

12:30 pm Return to the French Quarter by ❌ taxi. In the thick of things is the **Desire Oyster Bar**, where you can have great oysters and jambalaya while watching the festivities outside on Bourbon Street.

2:00 pm Get up to speed with one of the smaller parades this afternoon. Your hotel will have schedules.

5:00 pm Get some rest before partaking in the night's high-intensity revelry. You might want to have a light meal at the hotel, but save room for street foods and drinks.

7:30 pm *Bacchus Parade* floats along Canal Street, carrying celebrities and masqueraders, who toss doubloons, coasters, medallions and beads to wall-to-wall crowds. The parade ends at the Ernest N. Morial Convention Center (often called the New Orleans Convention Center), where the Bacchus Krewe holds the night's biggest ball. The Roman god of wine and partying would be proud to lend his name to this wild party.

8:30 pm Make a quick stop in your room to dress formally for the night, but don't forget to bring your beads.

9:00 pm With luck, you can get a cab (the walk isn't too bad, if you don't mind hiking in formal wear) to the enormous Morial Convention Center, where the **Bacchus Ball** moves into high gear. The cream of New Orleans society, plus a smattering of Hollywood types, turn out ❌ for a night of dance, drink (food is available, but useful only to allow you to continue drinking) and music by top-name performers.

Midnight Head to the French Quarter, where you'll experience a scene like nowhere else. Costume-clad crowds cram the streets and clubs and hoot themselves hoarse. Both ladies and gentlemen expose every bit of their anatomy. Bare breasts abound. New Orleans has no last call, so most of these people are used to staying out until all hours. For many, this evening/morning is the high point of *Mardi Gras*.

DAY 2 Monday

9:30 am For action with your cup o' joe, try ❌ **Poppy's Grill**, a '50s-style diner and the most popular brunch place in town.

10:30 am Explore the charming French Quarter, where wisteria hangs gracefully from iron balconies. Begin at the magnolia-filled epicenter, Jackson Square. Aristocratic nineteenth-century town houses line three sides of the square. Standing guard at the northern end is the eighteenth-century St. Louis Cathedral. A few blocks east of Jackson Square, tour the Old Ursuline Convent, an elegant French-Colonial structure from the 1730s. Across the street, look inside the antebellum Beauregard-Keyes House.

1:30 pm In a historic French Quarter town ❌ house, chef Emeril Lagasse's festive **NOLA Restaurant** serves updates of classic Creole recipes to a trend-conscious crowd.

2:30 pm Walk to the nearby French Market. A former Indian trading post, it's been a lively social and commercial center since the eighteenth century. Today, this covered market is famous for fruit and vegetable merchants, fishmongers, oyster shuckers, butchers and knickknack sellers, as well as a number of popular cafes. Jazz bands serenade the crowds.

3:00 pm Meander toward New Orleans' largest shopping district, Riverwalk, at the foot of Canal Street. Take in views of the New Orleans skyline and Mississippi during the fifteen-minute **Canal Street Ferry** ride to Algiers Point, across the Mississippi River. There, a shuttle whisks you to **Mardi Gras World**, which includes *Mardi Gras* float workshops and exhibits detailing *Mardi Gras*' history.

5:30 pm Back at Riverwalk, more than 200 shops and food stalls are housed in a series of refurbished warehouses. Enjoy the riverfront promenade and permanent New Orleans exhibits.

6:00 pm At Riverwalk, Rex the King proclaims the beginning of *Mardi Gras* and asks the mayor to make the day an official holiday so that people can take off work. The mock ceremony is followed by fireworks and rock music.

7:00 pm By now, the *Orpheus Parade* will be rolling along Canal Street, hailing doubloons, medallions, beads, cups and sports bottles onto the crowds. Founded by local boy Harry Connick Jr., the Orpheus Krewe's ball and parade emphasize music. The floats take Canal Street to the Morial Convention Center for Monday's grandest gala, which you'll join later.

8:00 pm It's dress-up time again. Don fancy duds and weave your way from the hotel ❌ to ultratrendy **Emeril's Restaurant**. Another Emeril Lagasse venture, this up-market, Nouveau Creole restaurant occupies a refurbished warehouse and serves a heavenly crawfish over jambalaya cakes.

10:00 pm One of *Mardi Gras*' major balls, the ***Orpheuscapade*** attracts local and national celebrities for the music, dancing and carefree schmoozing that are the hallmarks of New Orleans social events. *Mardi Gras* partying will reach a fever pitch tonight.

1:30 am New Orleans always comes alive after dark, but during *Mardi Gras*, the fun approaches frenzy. Head to the French Quarter, where the bars and clubs fuel wild times on Bourbon Street until dawn—at least. Duck into the **House of Blues** for a dose of live music at one of New Orleans' premier venues.

4:00 am Stop at the city's party-people pit-stop, twenty-four-hour **Café du Monde**. Find a seat on the covered patio, facing Jackson Square and order the house specialties: beignets coated with powdered sugar and chickory-flavored coffee.

DAY 3 Tuesday

10:00 am Sure, you didn't get much sleep, but nobody said this would be easy. The ***Zulu Parade*** passes on enormous, tree-lined St. Charles Avenue, the Garden District's main drag. In addition to showering street celebrants with the usual *Mardi Gras* swag, the roughly 1,500 parade members toss hand-decorated coconut shells. The regally themed *Rex Parade* follows a similar path.

1:00 pm Go to **Commander's Palace** in the ❌ Garden District. In an upstairs room with a courtyard view, enjoy outstanding Creole cuisine.

2:30 pm Venture into the surrounding Garden District, which still serves as home to the New Orleans elite. The neighborhood is packed with graceful old mansions that are distinctly New Orleans.

4:30 pm Return to the French Quarter madness, then head back to your hotel for a nap. Then throw on your most outrageous get-up for the final throes of *Mardi Gras.*

6:30 pm Build an appetite by searching the French Quarter for a krewe, perhaps the Krewe of Mystic Debris, who lead a march that you can join.

8:30 pm You're not too far from where Paul Prud'homme has set up his famous ❌ restaurant, **K-Paul's Louisiana Kitchen.** The place is always bustling and the classic-to-contemporary Louisiana fare gives overindulgence a good name.

10:30 pm The French-run **Le Jazz** allows for a relatively calm after-dinner drink where talented jazz bands perform for a fashionable clientele.

Midnight Just as Le Jazz winds down, Bourbon Street moves into overdrive. Don't pass up the party at the trendy **Cat's Meow**, which sports the street's liveliest balcony. A New Orleans classic, **Pat O'Brien's Bar** has an old-fashioned bar, attractive patio and piano lounge that gets very rowdy. The young, preppy crowd knocks back enough drinks to make Pat O'Brien's legendary for reputedly selling more liquor than any other bar in the world.

DAY 3 Tuesday (cont.)

Midnight (cont.) The house specialty, Skylab, has vodka, peach brandy, pineapple juice and grenadine. Stumbling around Bourbon Street is the appropriate way to wrap up *Mardi Gras* in the city that takes fun more seriously than any other on the continent.

Before

If you're in New Orleans on the Saturday before Fat Tuesday, you'll get high from the gigantic love fest known as the **Endymion Parade and Ball**. Deriving its name from a racehorse named after the Greek god of youth and fertility, Endymion's forty bands and twenty-eight double-decker floats (each carries up to 3,000 people) travel down Canal Street. They end up at the Louisiana Superdome for *Mardi Gras*' single biggest party (15,000 people), which features top-name entertainers, celebrity guests and fireworks. The fact that women are required to wear long gowns at this black-tie affair doesn't stop them from climbing on tables and jumping for beads.

More Time, More Choices

For a century, one of New Orleans' favorites has been **Galatoire's**. Its brass fittings, ornate chandeliers and beveled mirrors recall *fin-de-siècle* Paris, and its classic Creole dishes have been refined to perfection. The chic bar and cafe at **Napoleon House Bar and Café** cater to the colorful and affluent. Local dishes are elegantly prepared and served in an 1814 town house allegedly built for Napoleon. The more hip version of Commander's Palace is **Palace Cafe**, which serves New Creole cuisine in a grand cafe setting. **Bayona** does up Mediterranean recipes in a charming French Quarter cottage, and the busy **Acme Oyster House** specializes in shellfish straight from the Gulf waters.

In the Garden District, venerable **Tipitina's** nightclub, home base for the Neville Brothers, will draw a mixed crowd for live jazz. **Snug Harbor Jazz Bistro** features top jazz musicians—maybe even regular Ellis Marsalis, father of Wynton and Branford. **Le Bon Temps Roule** is another great music venue.

Accommodations

The glamorous **Le Meridien New Orleans** situates you by the French Quarter in the midst of the *Mardi Gras* hubbub. An international clientele prefers the luxurious hotel for its contemporary design and rooms with views of Canal Street (the parade route) and downtown skyscrapers. The elegant **Windsor Court Hotel**'s canopy beds, plush carpets and marble bathrooms envelope you in luxury. The **Royal Sonesta Hotel** could not be any closer to the madness. A few blocks off the French Quarter, **The Lafayette Hotel** is a charming and comfortable alternative.

Event & Ticket Info

Bacchus Ball (Ernest N. Morial Convention Center, 900 Convention Center Blvd.): Arrange tickets (generally $100) through area hotels or travel agents. For more information, contact your hotel concierge.

Orpheuscapade (Ernest N. Morial Convention Center, 900 Convention center Blvd.): For tickets ($100) contact *Krewe of Orpheus* (504-822-7200).

Endymion Ball (The Superdome): Tickets ($110) go on sale after November 1. For more information, contact *Mardi Gras Guide* (504-838-6111).

 NYC-1 New Orleans (MSY) <30 min./$25 No   Map Code: A20

New Orleans Jazz Festival

New Orleans Jazz & Heritage Festival

Key Month: Apr/May   Ratings: Event ★ ★ ★ ☆ ☆   **P**   City ★ ★ ★ ★ ★ Origin: 1970   Attendance: 480,000

Born in the "clubs" of New Orleans' red-light district, the fame of jazz and ragtime are inseparable from the city. New Orleans celebrates its musical heritage 365 days a year, but without doubt, the party is best during the last weekend in April, when the **New Orleans Jazz & Heritage Festival** brings in hundreds of top musicians for ten days of music, food and Nawlins fun.

Jazz Fest is more like three giant festivals in one. First and foremost, it highlights music. The largest music festival in the United States, it books top names in jazz, ragtime, funk, R&B, zydeco, gospel, Latin, Caribbean, blues, rock and country music. After music, New Orleans' passion is food, and you can relish savory local cuisine—from crawfish to andouille gumbo to alligator pie—at the festival grounds. Finally, the festival acts as a giant crafts show, with special emphasis on the folk art of old Louisiana. Some artisans craft their wares on the spot.

The music stages, tents, food stands and crafts stalls dress up the otherwise drab Fairgrounds Race Course setting. But the combination of top-flight talent and the New Orleans backdrop makes this one of America's top events.

The **Jazz Fest** is the more quiet and sophisticated of New Orleans' two world-class events, but, really, what event isn't quieter than Mardi Gras? The festival runs 11 a.m.-7 p.m. each day. The typical daily routine is brunch or lunch, festival, "disco nap," dinner and nightclubbing until 3 or 4 a.m. Regulars say that the last weekend is best, when the partying is most intense. Closing Sunday starts with a stirring gospel concert and ends with hometown favorites, The Neville Brothers. For all that's best to do in the city, refer to the itinerary (page 91-92) and New Orleans Hot Sheet (page 95). (*For more on jazz festivals, see page 218.*)

On the Calendar

Official Event Dates
Two, four-day weekends, including last Sunday in April and first Sunday in May

Best 3 Days To Be There
Thursday-Saturday, either weekend. Anticipation-Thursday is better than exhausted-Sunday.

Other Times To Go
See **Mardi Gras**, page 90.

☽ 65°/85° (18°/29°)

Event & Ticket Info

New Orleans Jazz Festival
(Fairgrounds Race Course, 1751 Gentilly Blvd.): Tickets ($20) are available at the gate. The Jazz Festival never sells out, except in the late evening. Advance tickets ($15) are available from *Ticketmaster* (800-488-5252). For more information, contact *New Orleans Jazz & Heritage Foundation* (504-522-4786).

Louisiana

94   For links to most current web sites for cities and events, go to www.funrises.com

The Hot Sheet

Hotels		Phone	Address	Price	Fax	Rooms/Best
The Lafayette Hotel		504-524-4441 800-733-4754	600 St. Charles Ave.	$$$	504-523-7327	44/2nd fl balc
Le Meridien New Orleans		504-525-6500 800-543-4300	614 Canal St.	$$$$	504-525-8068	496/Dlx corner rm w/city vw
Royal Sonesta Hotel		504-586-0300 800-766-3782	300 Bourbon St.	$$$$	504-586-0335	484/Balc on Bourbon
Windsor Court Hotel (Orient Express Hotel)		504-523-6000 800-262-2662	300 Gravier St.	$$$$	504-596-4513	324/River city vw

Restaurants	Day	Phone	Address	Price	Rec	Food
Acme Oyster House	A	504-522-5973	724 Iberville St.	$$	LD	Seafood
Bayona	A	504-525-4455	430 Dauphine St.	$$$	LD	Mediterranean
Café du Monde	2	504-525-4544	800 Decatur St.	$	T/B	French doughnut
Commander's Palace	3	504-899-8221	1403 Washington Ave.	$$$$	L/D	Creole
Desire Oyster Bar	1	504-586-0300	see Royal Sonesta Hotel	$$	L/D	Oysters, Creole
Emeril's Restaurant	2	504-528-9393	800 Tchoupitoulas St.	$$$	D/L	Creole
Galatoire's	A	504-525-2021	209 Bourbon St.	$$$$	LD	French, Creole
The Grill Room	1	504-522-1992	see Windsor Court Hotel	$$$	B/LD	Continental
K-Paul's Louisiana Kitchen	3	504-524-7394	416 Chartres St.	$$	D/L	Cajun, Creole
Napoleon House Bar and Café	A	504-524-9752	500 Chartres St.	$	LD	Mediterranean
NOLA Restaurant	2	504-522-6652	534 St. Louis St.	$$	L/D	New American, Creole
Palace Cafe	A	504-523-1661	605 Canal St.	$$	LD	Seafood, Creole
Poppy's Grill	2	504-524-3287	717 St. Peter St.	$	BLD	American

Nightlife	Day	Phone	Address	Cover	Rec*	Music
Cat's Meow	3	504-523-1157	701 Bourbon St.	$	P	Karaoke
House of Blues	2	504-529-2583	225 Decatur St.	$	M(F)	Blues, rock, reggae
Le Bon Temps Roule	A	504-895-8117	4801 Magazine St.	None	M(F)	Zydeco, blues, rock
Le Jazz	3	504-525-6500	see Le Meridien hotel	$	M(F)	Jazz
Pat O'Brien's Bar	3	504-525-4823	718 St. Peter St.	None	M	Jazz, R&B
Snug Harbor Jazz Bistro	A	504-949-0696	626 Frenchmen St.	$$	M(F)	Modern jazz, blues
Tipitina's	A	504-895-8477	501 Napoleon Ave.	$$	M	Blues, zydeco, rock

* M=Live music; P=Dancing (Party); R=Bar only; S=Show; (F)=Food served. For further explanation of codes, page 12.

Sights & Attractions	Day	Phone	Address	Entry Fee		
Mardi Gras World	2	504-361-7821	233 Newton St.	$$		
New Orleans Museum of Art	1	504-488-2631	1 Collins Diboll Circle	$		

Other Sights, Shops & Services						
Canal Street Ferry	2	504-364-8100	Canal Street Wharf	$		

| New Orleans CVB | | 504-566-5005 | 1520 Sugar Bowl Dr. | | | |

 NYC-1 New Orleans (MSY) <30 min./$25 No   Map Code: A20

Preakness

Preakness Celebration

Key Month: May   Ratings: Event ★ ★ ☆ ☆ ☆   **P**   City ★ ★ ★ ☆ ☆   Origin: 1873   Attendance: 90,000

For the hard-core horse-racing crowd, the world-renowned **Preakness** is the high-stakes follow-up to the Kentucky Derby. But for the 150,000 partyers in Baltimore, the second jewel in horse racing's Triple Crown is really just an excuse for partying on race day and a black-tie ball to kick off the event. You can be part of the pomp that surrounds the sport of kings in the Pimlico Race Course's grandstand, which rivals Ascot's Royal Enclosure for fancy dress and refined manners.

Or cruise the infield, where wet T-shirts and cheap beer carry the day. If your breeding wasn't good enough to get you an invitation to the former, or too good for the latter, there's always a great party in the corporate-hospitality Preakness village.

Race fever is at a critical level by the Thursday night before the race, when the black-tie **Triple Crown Ball** attracts a Who's Who of Baltimore—from politicians and corporate bigwigs to the region's horse-happy gentry. Other events include a parade, crab race and week-long block party. All this is mere warm-up, however, for a raucous day at the races on the third Saturday of May, which combines a series of quaint traditions with let-it-all-hang-out revelry.

On the Calendar

Official Event Dates
Nine days, ending with the race on third Saturday in May

Best 3 Days To Be There
Thursday-Saturday, including race day. The party is at the races on Saturday, but Baltimore warms up on Thursday and Friday.

☾ 53°/75° (12°/24°)

Baltimore, with a population of more than 700,000, was once the butt of unkind jokes. In the last twenty years, though, what was once an ugly duckling of a city has grown into a savvy swan. Downtown has gotten a makeover, especially the revitalized harbor. Once-decaying factories and warehouses are now occupied by chic restaurants and boutiques. The city's cuisine is built on the Chesapeake's shellfish, an object of local love and obsession. Eating, clubbing and sightseeing for three days and nights among the world's equestrian elite in one of America's best "new" cities will erase any doubts you may have had about Baltimore's resurgence.

Maryland

Day-by-Day Plan

DAY 1 — Thursday

10:00 am Drive or cab up the Charles Street corridor. A former neighborhood of railroad barons, it's now filled with restaurants and boutiques. Stop at the 1806 neoclassical masterpiece, the **Basilica of the Assumption**. Continue past mansion-lined Mount Vernon Square to the **Baltimore Museum of Art**, which holds one of the world's largest Andy Warhol collections.

12:30 pm A short drive back to Lexington Market allows you to enjoy the oldest continuously operating market in the United States and the **Preakness Crab Derby**.

1:30 pm Head back to the harbor and the American Visionary Art Museum for lunch at **Joy America Cafe**. The food is just what you'd expect—Latin-Caribbean-fusion with a touch of American thrown in.

3:00 pm The **American Visionary Art Museum** is the only one in the country restricted to works by self-taught "artists" drawn from various walks of life.

5:00 pm Stroll the promenade along Inner Harbor. Stop for oysters on the half shell or steamed shrimp at one of Harborplace's seafood stands.

7:30 pm Although the venue and date often changes (call to confirm), the **Triple Crown Ball** is always the highlight of Baltimore's social season. This black-tie tradition-bound event has a definite Southern charm, with hostesses clad in jockey satins. Afterward, a big-name pop band plays, and the tony crowd breaks stuffy tradition by packing the dance floor.

8:30 pm If you don't attend the ball, enjoy one of Baltimore's two new hot restaurants. **Ixia** brings a hip, zen-like attitude to the presentation of its fusion cuisine. And in a similar mode, **Red Maple** serves its Asian food tapas-style.

Midnight There's still time (till 2 a.m.) for a drink and salsa dancing at the nearby **Havana Club**.

DAY 2 — Friday

9:00 am Have a room-service breakfast. Then get an early start to beat the long lines at the **National Aquarium**. A self-guided tour takes you past four floors of extraordinary exhibits up to the rooftop rainforest.

11:00 am Get a higher perspective on Baltimore from **The Top of the World**, a twenty-seventh-floor observatory atop the World Trade Center, the world's tallest pentagonal building.

Noon At ground level in the Harborplace Amphitheater, watch well-known locals compete in the **Celebrity Crab-Picking Contest**. Then follow the Harborside promenade to **Phillips Harborplace**, a favorite stop for the city's seafood lovers. The famed blue crabs are prepared in a variety of ways—crab cakes, soft-shell crab sandwiches, crab imperial and steamed crabs.

3:00 pm Take a two-hour jaunt on **Clipper City**'s replica of an 1854 clipper ship. Major waterfront sites include Fort McHenry, home of the original star-spangled banner that inspired the national anthem.

5:00 pm Water Street is the usual venue (call 410-837-3030 to confirm) for **Miller Lite Nites**, a week-long block party with rock bands and copious amounts of anything you want to drink as long as it's Miller. Or head to the **Preakness Pub** (5–8 p.m.) where celebrity jockeys tend bar and tell suprisingly tall tales.

8:30 pm Take a short drive to **Charleston**, one of Baltimore's newer restaurants featuring Southern style and cuisine.

10:00 pm There's live jazz nightly at **Buddies Pub and Jazz Club**. The clientele ranges from bohemian to professional. You can also go to Pisces for dancing to Top 40 music, or for a younger, louder scene, the **Baja Beach Club**. The elegant **Owl Bar** is a former haunt of F. Scott Fitzgerald and H.L. Mencken.

The spirit of Baltimore and the Preakness may best be represented by Joe Kelly, the bugler brought in annually from Chicago just for the race. He plays the jazziest "Call to Post" you'll ever hear. "I took a very boring, traditional post call and made it a lot of fun," Joe says. "The audiences love it. They can be losing money, they hear the music, they perk up, they start bopping." Joe's attitude also fittingly represents the spirit of this book. "No matter what your job is or what you're doing," he says, "you can find a way to have fun with it."

Day-by-Day Plan

DAY 3 — *Saturday*

9:00 am **Donna's** is good for a quick break- ✕ fast of bagles and pastries.

11:30 am Pimlico Race Course, twenty minutes' drive—with reasonable parking options—offers four ways to enjoy the **Preakness Stakes**, the eleventh race of the day. (Gates open at 8:30 a.m., first race is at 10:45 a.m.) You can join Baltimore's elite in the reserved grandstand (invitation only), sit in the grandstand (ordinary), cruise the infield with the shorts-and-T-shirt crowd (wild), or finesse an invite to sip champagne at the corporate tents clustered around the finish line (fun). Unfortunately, Pimlico's design and large crowds make it difficult to move from one area to another.

4:50 pm In the infield, a local radio station's T-shirt giveaway—which consists of women giving away their own T-shirts—is over. In the corporate tents, you've consulted psychics to help you pick the winners and downed your final "black-eyed Susan" (a good one has bourbon, Kahlua, triple sec and orange juice). Joe Kelly sounds the "Call to Post" and prepares you for the singing of "Maryland, My Maryland."

5:00 pm Jockey for position to see the big race. In two minutes, the winner will be blanketed with black-eyed Susans (just like the crowd) and paraded into the Winner's Circle. Leave before the twelfth race—after collecting your winnings—to get out of the racecourse within a reasonable amount of time.

7:30 pm Take a water taxi from the Inner Harbor to the Fell's Point area, where the younger Preakness crowd congregates. ✕ **Bertha's**, an eccentric and inexpensive restaurant known for its mussels, attracts professionals, locals and artsy types.

10:00 pm A few blocks away, **Bohager's** bar and grill has music and dancing. Spending what's left of your winnings at the **Cat's Eye Pub** (Irish music); or the appropriately named **Horse You Came In On** (rock) might be just the thing to get you racing back to Baltimore for next year's **Preakness**.

More Time, More Choices

The New York-style steakhouse **The Prime Rib** has leopardskin carpet, a cigar bar and, naturally, great prime rib and steaks.

Time permitting, check out the Mount Vernon area. Its **Walters Art Museum** houses European paintings and medieval arms and armor. Nearby, the 1826 **Washington Monument**'s winding stairway leads to full-city views, and the **George Peabody Library** has a five-stories-high reading room lined with brass and leather.

Accommodations

The red-brick **Harbor Court Hotel** overlooks the water and puts you in prime location for the best of Baltimore. Other hotels with great views of the harbor are the **Hyatt Regency Baltimore** and the **Renaissance Harborplace Hotel**.

Event & Ticket Info

The Preakness (Pimlico Race Course, 5201 Park Heights Ave.): Tickets for seats ($55–$100) or standing-only ($15–$18) go on sale the Monday after Thanksgiving. Seats often sell out by February, but scalped tickets are available on the day of the race. For tickets and information, contact *Pimlico Race Course* (410-542-9400).

Hot Tip: Exactly two weeks before the race, returned Horseman's Box seats go on sale ($165–$200), but these great seats sell out within hours.

Triple Crown Ball (Venue TBA): Tickets ($275 CD) should be purchased well in advance from the Maryland Jockey Club (410-452-9400).

Celebrity Crab-Picking Contest (Harborplace Ampitheater) and **Preakness Pub** (Mother's Federal Hill Grill, 1113 S. Charles St.): Free. **Miller Lite Nites** (venue TBA): Get tickets ($5) at the gate. For more information, contact the *Preakness Celebration* (410-837-3030).

Preakness Crab Derby (Lexington Market, 400 W. Lexington St.): Free. For more information, contact *Lexington Market* (410-685-6169).

Baltimore

Hotels	Phone	Address	Price	Fax	Rooms/Best
Harbor Court Hotel	410-234-0550 800-824-0076	550 Light St.	$$$$	410-659-5925	200/Harbor vw
Hyatt Regency Baltimore	410-528-1234 800-233-1234	300 Light St.	$$$	410-685-3362	486/12th fl harbor vw
Renaissance Harborplace Hotel	410-547-1200 800-468-3571	202 E. Pratt St.	$$$	410-539-5780	622/12th fl harbor vw

Restaurants	Day	Phone	Address	Price	Rec	Food
Bertha's	3	410-327-5795	734 S. Broadway	$$$	D/L	Seafood
Charleston	2	410-332-7373	1000 Lancaster St.	$$$	D	Southern
Donna's	3	410-385-0180	2 W. Madison St.	$	B/LD	Pastries
Ixia	1	410-727-1800	518 N. Charles St.	$$	D	Fusion
Joy America Cafe	1	410-244-6500	800 Key Hwy.	$$	L/D	Latin American, Caribbean, American fusion
Phillips Harborplace	2	410-685-6600	301 Light St.	$$	L/D	Seafood
Red Maple	1	410-547-0149	930 N. Charles St.	$$	D	Asian
The Prime Rib	A	410-539-1804	1100 Calvert St.	$$$	D	Steakhouse

Nightlife	Day	Phone	Address	Cover	Rec*	Music
Baja Beach Club	2	410-727-0468	55 Market Pl.	$	P	Rock
Bohager's	3	410-563-7220	515 S. Eden St.	$	M(F)	Jazz, rock
Buddies Pub and Jazz Club	2	410-332-4200	313 N. Charles St.	None	M(F)	Jazz
Cat's Eye Pub	3	410-276-9085	1730 Thames St.	None	M	Jazz, blues, rock, Irish
Havana Club	1	410-468-0022	600 Water St.	None	P	Salsa
Horse You Came In On	3	410-327-8111	1626 Thames St.	$	M	Rock
Owl Bar	2	410-347-0888	1 E. Chase St.	None	R(F)	Varies

* M=Live music; P=Dancing (Party); R=Bar only; S=Show; (F)=Food served. For further explanation of codes, page 12.

Sights & Attractions	Day	Phone	Address	Entry Fee
American Visionary Art Museum	1	410-244-1900	800 Key Hwy.	$
Baltimore Museum of Art	1	410-396-7100	10 Art Museum Dr.	$
Basilica of the Assumption	1	410-727-3564	408 N. Charles St.	None
Clipper City	2	410-539-6277	301 Light St.	$$
George Peabody Library	A	410-659-8179	17 E. Mt. Vernon	None
National Aquarium	2	410-576-3800	501 E. Pratt St.	$$
The Top of the World	2	410-837-8439	401 E. Pratt St.	$
Walters Art Museum	A	410-547-9000	600 N. Charles St.	$
Washington Monument	A	410-396-0929	Mt. Vernon Pl.	$

Baltimore CVB	410-659-7300	100 Light St.

Maryland

 NYC   Baltimore-Washington (BWI) <30 min./$20  No   Map Code: A22

Boston Harborfest

Boston

Key Month: Jul   Ratings: Event ★ ★ ☆ ☆ ☆   Ⓗ   City ★ ★ ★ ★ ☆   Origin: 1982   Attendance: 2,500,000

Big-time partying in America began in Boston on December 16, 1773. That's the date some 7,000 citizens came to the Old South Meeting House, spilled into the streets protesting imperial oppression and just maybe exceeded modern DMV standards for legal blood-alcohol content.

Close to midnight on that fateful day when British officials refused for the final time to take their tea back home, almost a hundred men disguised as Mohawk Indians suddenly appeared outside Old South's doors, and the cry "To the wharves!" rang out. When the night was over, nearly sixty tons of tea leaves were floating in the harbor and America had enjoyed its first raging party, the Boston Tea Party.

These days, the town's big shindig, **Harborfest**, gives thanks to Samuel Adams, Paul Revere, John Hancock and all the other colonists who gave us the freedom to hear the Boston Pops perform Tchaikovsky's *1812 Overture* while watching an awesome fireworks display overhead. The weeklong festival features more than 170 events that not only celebrate Boston's role in the American Revolution, but its rich maritime history. More than two million visitors come to **Harborfest** to view the U.S.S. *Constitution*, go on whale-watching cruises, see free jazz and rock concerts and watch the Independence Day Parade. The highlight of the weekend is the Boston Pops concert on the Esplanade. The Pops play patriotic favorites while three tons of pyrotechnic showers burst overhead in a deafening crescendo.

Even with all the **Harborfest** happenings, try to visit as many of Boston's other top attractions as you can. The Museum of Fine Arts, Boston has an excellent collection of early-American paintings. The Freedom Trail brings you historic sites of the American Revolution, including one of the country's oldest pubs, the Green Dragon Tavern. During the Revolutionary period, Sam Adams held many meetings in the bar's secret back room. Venture inside, give a toast to this incendiary speaker and do your duty as an American (or sympathetic ally) by downing a beer with his name on it.

On the Calendar

Official Event Dates
Usually six days surrounding July 4

Best 3 Days To Be There
July 4 plus a weekend day, if possible. The Fourth of July fireworks and concert are a must, but Boston is at its best on Thursdays and Fridays.

☀ 65°/81° (18°/28°)

Massachusetts

For links to most current web sites for cities and events, go to www.funrises.com

DAY 1 — July 2

10:00 am Head to Beacon Street and start along the Freedom Trail. Toss away your map and follow the red line that takes you past sixteen monumental sites and into the city's cherished neighborhoods— Beacon Hill, with century-old brick brownstones, North End, with winding streets and lively Italian community, and Charlestown, home to the Battle of Bunker Hill and now resting spot for America's most celebrated ship, the U.S.S. *Constitution*. Stop at the graves of Paul Revere, Samuel Adams and John Hancock; the Old South Meeting-House; and Boston's number-one attraction, Quincy Market, a renovated historic district now filled with shops and restaurants.

1:00 pm Lunch at **Ye Olde Union Oyster House**, the oldest restaurant in continuous service in America. Opened in 1826, this is where Daniel Webster had his daily breakfast of three dozen oysters with several tumblers of brandy, and where John F. Kennedy often dined on lobster stew.

2:30 pm Part Two of the Freedom Trail brings you to Boston's oldest building, the home of Paul Revere, then across the Charlestown Bridge to reach Old Ironsides and Bunker Hill. Return via $1 ferry ride from the Charleston Navy Yard.

7:00 pm Head to the sixtieth-floor observation deck of the **John Hancock Building**. A terrific light display traces the history of Boston.

8:30 pm Dine at one of Boston's hottest restaurants, **Clio**, in the swank Eliot Suite Hotel. Chef Ken Oringer gets rave reviews for his continental fare, served at intimate tables.

10:30 pm Cab to **Aria** and plop down in an overstuffed sofa for an after-dinner drink. Afterward, salsa and tango the night away at **Europa's** Latin night.

12:30 am If you have energy for more, try **Trattoria Il Panino**—the restaurant and dance floors are split among five levels.

DAY 2 — July 3

9:00 am Say hello to the swans in the Public Garden as you walk to Beacon Hill for breakfast at **Panificio.** The waffles with fresh fruit are sublime.

10:30 am Cab to the **Museum of Fine Arts**, Boston to view the excellent permanent collection. Gilbert Stuart's well-known portrait of George Washington is here along with works by Winslow Homer, Fitz Hugh Lane and French Impressionists.

12:30 pm Stroll to the **Isabella Stewart Gardner Museum** where the cafe serves lobster bisque, along with a wide selection of salads and sandwiches. The courtyard is filled year-round with flowers.

3:00 pm Cab to the corner of Newbury and Fairfield Streets. Walk down Newbury Street, Boston's low-key version of New York's Fifth Avenue, back toward the Ritz. Here, you'll find the finest boutiques in Beantown. Stop for a drink at an outdoor cafe such as **Armani Café** or the very hip **Sonsei**.

6:00 pm Walk twenty minutes to City Hall Plaza to see a popular band perform at the *Party on the Plaza*.

8:30 pm Eat at **Southend Galleria**, where the food is worth the wait. Reservations are highly recommended.

10:30 pm On your way back to the hotel you could try **The Big Easy Bar**, a large but comfortable dance hall. **Mercury Bar**, a bit more mellow, is another good choice for an upscale scene and great snack food.

DAY 3 — July 4

8:00 am **Charlie's Sandwich Shoppe** is an old-time urban diner with famous banana and blueberry pancakes. This is strictly a local joint so be prepared to talk about the Red Sox and Celtics.

9:00 am Take the **Beantown Whale Watch** cruise. Lasting about four hours, it will also reward you with the best views of Boston's skyline.

Day-by-Day Plan

DAY 3

July 4 (cont.)

1:30 pm Lunch at hip **Biba**, where tables ✖ overlook the Boston Public Garden.

2:30 pm Tour America's most celebrated campus, then head to Harvard Square to people-watch. Ecuadorian musicians, mimes, heavy-metal guitarists, beggars and jugglers all entertain the bespectacled Harvard intellectuals.

5:00 pm Cab to downtown Boston before the crowds get too thick. Head to the Four Seasons' **Bristol Lounge**. Year after year, its martini is voted the best in town by *Boston Magazine*.

8:00 pm The main event (even though it is not offically part of Harborfest)! You can try to squeeze into the Esplanade or you can walk across Longfellow Bridge to Cambridge and see the same fireworks with far less people. You won't be able to see Keith Lockhart leading the Pops from there, but you can certainly hear them.

10:30 pm There's no better late-night dining ✖ scene than **Mistral**. Owned by famed nightclub impresario Seth Greenberg, Mistral is known for excellent French food in a stylish Provençal setting.

12:30 pm Insomniacs head to **Wally's Cafe** for late-night jazz and blues. It's the kind of place where you can get some help bringing your Fourth to an end with a fifth.

After

Usually the Sunday after the Fourth is *Chowderfest*, a chowder-cooking contest where the public is invited to sample.

More Time, More Choices

Hamersley's Bistro has been awarded four stars (the highest ranking) by the *Boston Globe*. **Grill 23 & Bar** is one of the city's best steakhouses. **Legal Sea Foods** is a chain, but worth a visit. **Les Zygomates** (French for the muscles that make us smile), is a buzzing bistro.

Terrific outdoor tables at **29 Newbury** allow you to enjoy new-American cuisine while people-watching.

Regattabar in the Charles Hotel features high-caliber jazz acts such as Sonny Rollins and Herbie Hancock. **Lizard Lounge** is known for its eclectic mix of acid-jazz and rock. One of few remaining seventeenth-century taverns is the **Green Dragon Tavern**, which has live music on weekends.

The **John F. Kennedy Library and Museum** will bring back memories of the president and his era.

Accommodations

Located on the edge of the Public Garden, **The Four Seasons Hotel**, Boston has the same views as the **Ritz**. One of Boston's finest boutique hotels, **The Eliot Suite Hotel** has undergone an elegant renovation.

Event & Ticket Info

Boston Harborfest: Most events are free. For more information, contact *Boston Harborfest* (617-227-1528).

Party on the Plaza (City Hall Plaza on Cambridge Street): Free.

Chowderfest (City Hall Plaza on Cambridge Street): Tickets ($5) can be purchased at the event.

The Hot Sheet

Hotels		Phone	Address	Price	Fax	Rooms/Best
The Eliot Suite Hotel		617-267-1607 800-443-5468	370 Commonwealth Ave.	$$$$	617-536-9114	95
The Four Seasons Hotel Boston		617-338-4400 800-332-3442	200 Boylston St.	$$$$	617-426-7199	274/Garden vw
The Ritz-Carlton Boston Common		617-574-7100 800-241-3333	10 Avery St.	$$$$	617-574-7200	193/Boston Common vw

Restaurants	Day	Phone	Address	Price	Rec	Food
29 Newbury	A	617-536-0290	29 Newbury St.	$$	LD	American eclectic
Armani Café	2	617-437-0909	214 Newbury St.	$$$	T/LD	Italian
Biba	3	617-426-7878	272 Boylston St.	$$$$	LD	American eclectic
Charlie's Sandwich Shoppe	3	617-536-7669	429 Columbus Ave.	$	B/L	American
Clio	1	617-536-7200	370 Commonwealth Ave. In The Eliot Hotel	$$$$	D	New French
Grill 23 & Bar	A	617-542-2255	161 Berkeley St.	$$$	D	Grill house
Hamersley's Bistro	A	617-423-2700	553 Tremont St.	$$$	D	Country French
Legal Sea Foods	A	617-426-4444	26 Park Square Park Plaza Hotel	$$	LD	Seafood
Les Zygomates	A	617-542-5108	129 South St.	$$$	LD	French
Mistral	3	617-867-9300	223 Columbus Ave.	$$$	D	French, Mediterranean
Panificio	2	617-227-4340	144 Charles St.	$	B/LD	American
Sonsie	2	617-351-2500	327 Newbury St.	$	T/LD	Bistro
Southend Galleria	2	617-236-5252	480A Columbus Ave.	$$$	D	Italian, Asian
Ye Olde Union Oyster House	1	617-227-2750	41 Union St.	$$	L/D	Seafood

Nightlife	Day	Phone	Address	Cover	Rec*	Music
Aria	1	617-330-7080	246 Tremont St.	$$	P	Techno, house
The Big Easy Bar	2	617-351-7000	1 Boylston Pl.	$	M	Top 40, dance, house, hip hop
Bristol Lounge	3	617-338-4400	see Four Seasons Hotel	None	M	Jazz
Europa	1	617-482-3939	51 Stuart St.	$	P	Latin, disco
Green Dragon Tavern	A	617-367-0055	11 Marshall St.	$	M	Rock
Lizard Lounge	A	617-547-1228	1667 Massachusetts Ave.	$	M	Jazz, alternative, funk
Mercury Bar	2	617-482-7799	116 Bolyston St.	$	P(F)	Top 40
Regattabar	A	617-864-1200	1 Bennett St., Cambridge in the Charles Hotel	$$	M	Jazz
Trattoria Il Panino	1	617-338-1000	295 Franklin St.	None	P(F)	Top 40, '70s, '80s
Wally's Cafe	3	617-424-1408	427 Massachusetts Ave.	None	M	Blues, jazz, Latin jazz

* M=Live music; P=Dancing (Party); R=Bar only; S=Show; (F)=Food served. For further explanation of codes, page 12.

Sights & Attractions	Day	Address	Phone	Entry Fee
Beantown Whale Watch	3	617-542-8000	60 Rowes Wharf	$$$
Isabella Stewart Gardner Museum	2	617-566-1401	280 Defend Way	$$
John F. Kennedy Library and Museum	A	617-929-4523	Columbia Pt.	$
John Hancock Observatory	1	617-572-6429	200 Clarendon St.	$
Museum of Fine Arts, Boston	2	617-267-9300	465 Huntington Ave.	$$
Boston CVB		617-536-4100	147 Tremont St.	

 NYC   Logan (BOS) <30 min./$20   No   Map Code: A23

Detroit Auto Show

North American International Auto Show, NAIAS

Key Month: Jan   Ratings: Event ★ ★ ☆ ☆ ☆   🅗   City ★ ★ ★ ☆ ☆   Origin: 1907   Attendance: 790,000

Detroit in the dead of winter may not sound like an inviting proposition for fun-seeking travelers. Hearty souls, however, can spend a stellar weekend during the first three days of the **North American International Auto Show**—the United States' most prestigious event for auto lovers. It's the only event in North America that features the finest international exhibits, and it commands the worldwide acclaim necessary to place it among the top five international auto shows, along with shows in Frankfurt, Geneva, Paris and Tokyo.

The action kicks off Friday night with the black-tie **Charity Preview**. Raising nearly $4 million, it's the most profitable, annual, single-night fund-raising event in the world, and its 15,000 well-dressed VIPs and schmoozing make it the social highlight of the city's season. All the following week, a more casual crowd of car enthusiasts will step through the doors of the Cobo Center to ogle hundreds of cars and trucks that international automakers unveil throughout 700,000 square feet of floor space. Not surprisingly, 5,900 media representatives come from across the globe to cover this ten-day event.

Detroit's history makes it a natural choice for **NAIAS** host city. Founded in 1701 by a French trader named Cadillac, Detroit was the first site of the mass-production car industry, earning the nickname "Motortown" on the way to launching a worldwide auto boom of unforeseen proportions. Since the 1960s, oil crises and foreign competition have forced industry closures in the region. Still, the auto industry's legacy endures in the city's site and street names, industrial zones and industry-related attractions.

Detroit also has been consistently on the point of America's musical cutting edge. Motown has remained a worldwide phenomenon, but white rappers such as Eminem and Kid Rock have kept the Detroit scene vibrant. Its blues clubs are grittier, but every bit as legit as Chicago's.

Motortown comes through for **NAIAS** attendees, topping off this tanked-up weekend with high-octane night life, great dining options, famous blues venues and plenty else to do and see. New businesses and more than $1 billion have gone into reviving Detroit's downtown area and the city's entertainment offerings draw increasing numbers of out-of-towners. Especially in the heart of winter, Motown offers mo' than most visitors expect.

On the Calendar

Official Event Dates

Ten days, from Friday after the first weekend in January

Best 3 Days To Be There

Thursday-Saturday, beginning day before official opening. The highlight is the pre-opening Gala, followed by a weekend in Detroit. Yes, Detroit!

☾ 19°/32° (-7°/0°)

Day-by-Day Plan

DAY 1 — Thursday

Noon After the obligatory walk through
❷ Greektown, stop for lunch at **Fishbone's Rhythm Kitchen Café**. Connected to the Atheneum, it's a fun spot for cocktails, oyster-slurping and Cajun cuisine, including smoked whiskey ribs and crispy fried catfish. Check out the world's tallest indoor waterfall.

1:30 pm Take a cab up the nation's fifth-longest thoroughfare, Woodward Avenue, to visit the **Detroit Institute of Arts**. Sample some of more than 100 galleries that bring together famous and obscure works of the past five millennia. Especially significant to **NAIAS** pilgrims are Diego Rivera's *The Detroit Industry* frescoes that cover all four walls of the institute's colorful courtyard.

3:30 pm Walk to the nearby **Detroit Historical Museum**. Stroll through displays, city-scene reproductions and an automotive exhibit that relates the century-long story of our four-wheeled friends.

6:00 pm Touch base back at the hotel, then take its shuttle to **The Summit Lounge** to toast a stunning seventy-third-floor view from the crown of the Marriott—the world's tallest hotel.

8:00 pm Shuttle back to the tremendously
❷ popular **Rattlesnake Club**. Enjoy Detroit River views and the creative menu of world-renowned chef Jimmy Schmidt.

10:00 pm Near the Rattlesnake Club, Rivertown, the surrounding four-block area, is rich with nightlife. The brick-lined **Rhinoceros** has funky, live music.

DAY 2 — Friday

10:30 am Have room-service breakfast before taking a short drive to the handsome new **Charles H. Wright Museum of African American History**. Local African-American artists designed the museum's building and contributed the mosaics, sculptures and detailing that adorn the structure and its grounds. The museum includes exhibits created by Ralph Applebaum, known for his poignant displays at the Holocaust Museum in Washington, D.C.

1:00 pm By now you ought to have built an
❷ appetite worthy of the **Majestic Cafe**'s Middle Eastern favorites and other more inventive dishes, such as bleu-cheese encrusted beef tenderloin.

2:30 pm Visit the **Motown Historical Museum**, where Barry Gordy Jr. set up the original Motown studios using guts, gumption and $800 in 1959. Now a bit rundown, the former site of "Hitsville, U.S.A." is still a twentieth-century-music mecca.

5:30 pm Cab to the Cobo Center for the *Charity Preview* or avoid traffic by taking Detroit's clean, elevated monorail, the **People Mover**. Arrive at Cobo's concourse in time to see industry executives launch the event with a ribbon-cutting ceremony, a spectacle of music, indoor fireworks and fuel-injected fanfare.

6:00 pm (to 9:00 pm) About 15,000 attendees get an auto-show sneak peak on the carpeted show floor. You can talk catalytic converters and design over champagne and hors d'oeuvres with other dapper show-goers, from moto-zealots to celebrities to pleasure-seekers who mourn the passing of the days when 6' 2" blonde babes decorated displays. (The ladies were gone once research revealed that women make the final decision on eighty percent of all new-car purchases.)

9:00 pm **The Whitney**'s exquisitely prepared
❷ American cuisine is served in a nineteenth-century mansion that once belonged to lumber baron David Whitney. The experience is well worth the planning and effort required to secure a table for *Charity Preview* night.

11:00 pm Move into The Whitney's lounge for after-dinner drinks and live music until past midnight. The crowd will be dominated by others who have come from the *Charity Preview*.

Midnight Cab to the **Pure Bar Room**, a "New York-style" bar that's become one of Detroit's hip nightclubs.

9:30 am Stop at **The Clique**, where word-of-mouth and the *Detroit Free Press* have made their breakfasts famous.

10:30 am A short drive southwest takes you to the **Henry Ford Museum & Greenfield Village**, which claims to be the world's largest indoor-outdoor museum. The Henry Ford Museum displays more than a century's worth of cars, along with exhibits on just about everything made in America. Work spaces of innovative Americans have been relocated to Greenfield Village, where you can see (only exteriors during winter season) the Wright brothers' workshop, portions of Thomas Edison's laboratory and much more.

1:30 pm Back in Detroit's Greektown, **Pegasus Taverna** serves Greek food in a bustling atmosphere. Start with a fiery *saganaki*—Greek *kasseri* cheese with flaming brandy.

3:00 pm Head back to Cobo, where you'll see last night's cars and displays, but without the fanfare. Don't miss presentations of new and experimental vehicles, as well as special exhibitions from automakers and ad-campaign debuts.

7:30 pm In a wide-open space of brick and bare wood, **Intermezzo** is an appropriately boisterous setting for a hearty Italian meal. The place sometimes gets as loud as the abstract art hung on its walls.

10:00 pm Laugh off your lasagna at **The Second City**, the first copy of the Chicago original, where live comedy sketches mix down-home humor with timely political and social satire.

Midnight Stop back at **Intermezzo** for a goodbye drink in the lounge, with live music, an upscale crowd and a year's worth of car fantasies.

■

More Time, More Choices

Try **Sweet Lorraine's**, a critically respected, sophisticated bistro that nonetheless has a relaxed atmosphere. Tom's Oyster Bar has nice views of downtown Detroit and a nautical theme, which goes well with the great seafood. They usually have live bands on the weekends.

The **Bleu Room Experience** claims to have the number-one sound and lighting system in the Midwest—it just might—and lures Detroit's best-looking crowd.

If you stay over Saturday night, find a cozy nook for Sunday brunch at **Limerick's**, which features homemade soups and shepherd's pie.

Head for Detroit's newest attraction—big-time casino gambling. High rollers have traditionally gone south into Canada—yes, due south—to get lucky at the **Casino Windsor**. But Detroit now boasts three casinos: **MGM Grand, Motor City Casino** and **Greektown Casino**. Each features all the usual tricky ways of separating you from your money.

Accommodations

Occupying a converted nineteenth-century warehouse, **The Omni River Place** offers luxury accommodations and proximity to nightlife. It sits on the river away from the downtown hub. Detroit's preferred hotel is the **Atheneum Suite Hotel**, but it's reserved this week for Auto Show bigwigs. You can still check out its grand lobby, with Greek-style murals, and for this week only, a gleaming car parked in the middle of the lobby's marble-and-granite floor. At **The Marriot Renaissance Center**, views, amenities and a convenient location compensate for the blah rooms.

Event & Ticket Info

The North American International Auto Show (Cobo Center and Exhibition Hall, 1 Washington Blvd.): Tickets ($8) are available in advance from *Ticketmaster* (248-645-6666) or from the *Cobo Center* (313-877-8111) during the show. For more information, contact the *Detroit Auto Dealers Association* (248-643-0250).

Charity Preview (Cobo Center and Exhibition Hall): The 15,000 tickets ($250 CD) usually sell out two months in advance. To request an invitation, contact *Detroit Institute for Children* (313-832-1100 ext. 202).

Hotels		Phone	Address	Price	Fax	Best/Rooms
Atheneum Suite Hotel		313-962-2323 800-772-2323	1000 Brush St.	$$$	313-962-2424	174/Suite w/bedside whirlpool bath
The Marriott Renaissance Center		313-568-8000 800-228-9290	Renaissance Ctr.	$$	313-568-8146	1,200/Upper flrs w/city vw
The Omni River Place		313-259-9500 800-890-9505	1000 River Pl.	$$	313-259-0657	108/Deluxe rms w/full river vw

Restaurants	Day	Phone	Address	Price	Rec	Food
The Clique	3	313-259-0922	1326 E. Jefferson St.	$	B/LD	American
Fishbone's Rhythm Kitchen Café	1	313-965-4600	400 Monroe St.	$$	L/BD	Cajun
Intermezzo	3	313-961-0707	1435 Randolph Ave.	$$$	D/L	Italian
Limerick's	A	313-964-0936	1411 Brooklyn Ave.	$$	B/LD	Comfort food
Majestic Cafe	2	313-833-0120	4124 Woodward Ave.	$	L/D	Middle Eastern
Pegasus Taverna	3	313-964-6800	558 Monroe St.	$	L/D	Greek
Rattlesnake Club	1	313-567-4400	300 River Pl.	$$$	D/L	Contemporary American
Sweet Lorraine's	A	248-559-5985	29101 Greenfield Rd.	$$	LD	Contemporary American
The Whitney	2	313-832-5700	4421 Woodward Ave.	$$$	D/L	Contemporary American

Nightlife	Day	Phone	Address	Cover*	Rec	Music
Bleu Room Experience	A	313-222-1900	1540 Woodward Ave.	$$	P	Dance
Pure Bar Room	2	313-471-7873	1500 Woodward Ave.	$$	R	Electronic
Rhinoceros	1	313-259-2208	265 Riopelle St.	$	M	Jazz, Top 40
The Second City	3	313-965-2222	2301 Woodward Ave.	$$	S	
The Summit Lounge	1	313-832-5700	see The Marriott hotel	$$	R	

* M=Live music; P=Dancing (Party); R=Bar only; S=Show; (F)=Food served. For further explanation of codes, page 12.

Sights & Attractions	Day	Phone	Address	Entry Fee
Casino Windsor	A	519-258-7878	337 Riverside Dr. E	None
Charles H. Wright Museum of African American History	2	313-494-5800	315 E. Warren Ave.	$
Detroit Historical Museum	1	313-833-1805	5401 Woodward Ave.	$
Detroit Institute of Arts	1	313-833-7900	5200 Woodward Ave.	$
Greektown Casino	A	313-223-2999	555 E. Lafayette St.	None
Henry Ford Museum & Greenfield Village	3	313-271-1620	20900 Oakwood Blvd.	$$
MGM Grand	A	877-888-2121	1300 John C. Lodge	None
Motor City Casino	A	877-777-0711	2901 Grand River Ave.	None
Motown Historical Museum	2	313-875-2264	2648 W. Grand Blvd.	$
People Mover	2	313-961-6446		$

Detroit CVB	800-338-7648	211 W. Fort St.

 NYC Detroit Metropolitan Wayne County (DTW) <60 min./$30 Yes/No Map Code: A24

Michigan

Burning Man

Black Rock City

Key Month: Aug/Sep Ratings: Event ★★★★★ **ⓥ** City n/a Origin: 1986 Attendance: 20,000

It's the fourth-largest metropolitan area in Nevada, but don't bother looking for it on the map. It appears for a single week each year, then sinks without a trace into the miles-deep dust of an ancient lake bed. It's Black Rock City, home to the **Burning Man** festival, an eclectic mix of offbeat art, impromptu performance and cultural experimentation that draws 10,000 or so free spirits to the middle of nowhere each Labor Day weekend.

Tall as a five-story building, trimmed with neon and stuffed with fireworks, the Man is an impressive piece of work, but the real story is in the culture that has sprung up around it. **Burning Man** has become a magnet for many strange and unexpected offerings. Surrealist sculptors and solar-powered multimedia auteurs share the stage with musicians, painters, dancers, poets and gearheads. People labor all year to construct elaborate theme camps ranging from potluck barter bars to full-tilt circus sideshows. Costumes abound, including the ever-popular birthday suit. There are two daily newspapers in operation along with a dozen or so pirate radio stations. There's even an opera.

Burning **Man**'s motto—"No spectators"—means no matter how hard you try, you can't avoid becoming part of the show. It's an intensely participatory event, with no proscenium to separate the players from the crowd. Be prepared to interact with people.

There's no on-site vending and little for sale in nearby towns, so you'll need to bring all your own gear and supplies. Likewise, you'll need to take everything with you when you leave. **Burning Man** provides sanitation and basic safety services, but no dumpsters. One of the few rules is that the desert has to be restored to its natural state of pristine emptiness when this counter-culture Eden disappears for another year.

It's hot, it's dusty and it's a lot of work to get there. But once you've made it to Black Rock City, you'll understand why so many people call it home, if only for a few days each year.

On the Calendar

Official Event Dates
Eight days ending on Labor Day (first Monday in September)

Best 3 Days To Be There
Friday party and Saturday night climax. Sunday is the post-party bonding.

☀ 39°/82°(4°/28°)

Nevada

      For links to most current web sites for cities and events, go to www.funrises.com

Day-by-Day Plan

DAY 1 Friday

10:00 am From the Reno airport, skip the slot machines and make a beeline for your rental RV. Try to reserve one with a roll-out side-awning, and see if you can get a few folding chairs thrown in along with the standard "housekeeping package" of linens and kitchenware. You'll appreciate having a shady place to relax, have a drink and people-watch during the day. Remember, there are no RV hookups in Black Rock City. You'll need to be self-contained or carry generator fuel.

11:30 am Reno is your last chance to really shop, so make the most of it: ice chest, cold drinks, sun block, trash bags, earplugs, food, lip balm, ice and more cold drinks. You won't be that hungry—the desert is a natural appetite suppressant—but you will be thirsty. Make sure you have at least a gallon of water per person per day in addition to all the beer, wine, juice and soft drinks you can carry. Hats and sunglasses are survival essentials in the desert.

1:00 pm Drive the 120 miles north from Reno to the **Burning Man** site. The solitude and beauty of this terrain makes the desert a paradise for many people.

3:00 pm If nowhere does in fact have a middle, you can hear it talking to itself in Gerlach, Nevada, population 300. One gas station, no stores, five bars, and the **Burning Man** ticket office, located in what was once a jailhouse. If you're hungry, stop by Bruno's Country Club for a plate of Bruno's famous ravioli. Be sure to stop in the bar and check out Bruno's fine collection of memorabilia from land-speed-record teams, including Richard Noble's Thrust SSC, the first vehicle to break the sound barrier on land.

5:00 pm Roll into Black Rock City and set up camp. If you've got questions, stop one of the khaki-clad Danger Rangers, the festival's well-trained volunteer force.

5:00 pm (cont.) Have a drink and introduce yourself to your neighbors. Like any town, Black Rock City has different neighborhoods with different flavors. Get to know yours—its citizenry and major landmarks—before it gets dark. Interacting with folks is the essence of **Burning Man**.

8:30 pm Raise a glass to the spectacular desert sunset, slip into (or out of) your hottest outfit, then set out for an evening of surreal entertainment. A full schedule of Saturday-night performances culminates in the opera, an allegorical fantasy with spectacular costumes, original music and (no kidding) a burning stage. Kind of like the Met, but with a looser dress code and bigger explosions.

Midnight Put a little distance between yourself and the bright lights by relaxing under a gorgeous desert sky and spending quality time with billions of burning stars. Afterward, you can dance or head back to the RV for late-night socializing with a set of neighbors straight out of *The Twilight Zone*.

DAY 2 Saturday

Dawn If you're a morning person, head out to the **Burning Man** at sunrise and look for Java Cow, a bizarre creature known to dispense coffee to the early-rising faithful.

10:00 am Better yet, sleep in, then shuffle over to center camp when you're good and ready and order a latte at the coffee bar, **Burning Man**'s sole concession to commerce and its de facto social hub. Sit in the shade of many parachutes and read the *Black Rock Gazette*, the town's leading daily. Along with several pirate radio stations, it's part of **Burning Man**'s always-entertaining media.

11:00 am If you feel energetic, take a stroll around camp before it gets too hot. Soak up the ambience of the theme camps and try your hand at some of the arts workshops, such as casting molten aluminum at Recycling Camp or assembling your own burnable offering from scrap lumber.

Midday Take a tip from the desert wildlife and lay low during the hottest part of the day. Drink water *constantly*. Don't resist the urge to nap—it's your body's way of telling you there's a huge party tonight. There's a lot to see, but don't worry, it'll all still be there when you wake up.

Late afternoon In the spectacular golden light of the late-day desert, check out some of the theme camps you've missed or pay return visits to the ones where you've made friends. Don't forget to get your **Burning Man** passport stamped at all your theme-camp stops—it'll make a great souvenir when you get home.

Dusk Showtime! Put on your finest regalia and head to center camp for the Cacophonists' Cocktail Party, a **Burning Man** tradition started by the San Francisco Cacophony Society, the loose network of pranksters and urban adventurers who nurtured this event through its formative years. Formal attire is always appropriate, but if you have an idea for a crazy costume, you should please the crowd by wearing it. After a few rounds (BYOB, of course), follow the sound of drums to the burning of the Man, the festival's climactic spectacle. Skyrockets scream from its upraised arms, tracing bright arcs across the sky, until at last it collapses into the biggest bonfire you've ever seen.

Night Shake all night at the big community dance. Remember those earplugs you bought back in Reno? This is where they'll come in handy. Share all your remaining beverages and treats with your new friends. At some point, you'll probably be treated to a speech or appearance by Larry Harvey, the event's originator, who is known by the trademark Stetson he's almost never seen without. (He wears the hat as a tribute to his late father.) Harvey is an eccentric idealist who began this event in San Francisco in 1985 by burning an eight-foot structure on the beach as a reaction to a severe romantic breakup.

Night (cont.) Now, his community of friends has grown, graduate thesis papers have been written about him and his event, and he's been invited to speak at Harvard University about this idyllic community that comes together in the desert each year. Because of the way he speaks in fits and stutters, many of his friends believe Harvey is possessed—by friendly spirits.

DAY 3 Sunday

Morning Donate at least an hour to the group clean-up effort, more if you can spare it. **Burning Man** has a strong environmental aesthetic and the citizens of Black Rock City take great pride in "leaving no trace" when they pack up and leave. Don't be surprised if you make some friends in the process. Now that you're a veteran, inquire about becoming a Danger Ranger volunteer at next year's gathering.

Noon Head back to Reno—coming from **Burning Man**, prepare for massive culture shock as you approach the neon-lit gambling oasis with an empty ice chest and a chapped smile on your face. Start making your list of things to bring next year.

Event & Ticket Info

Burning Man (Black Rock City, Nevada): Tickets ($250 on site, $200 before August 15) can be purchased at the event, but it's best to get them ahead of time from *The Burning Man Project* (415-863-5263) so that you can receive the official Survival Guide and other helpful planning tools.

Black Rock City

Your hotel is an RV, you bring your own food and there are no phone numbers for the nightlife and attractions. But what is essential for a great and comfortable Burning Man experince is a well-packed bag. Here's a checklist:

Clothes

- ❏ Warm clothes (don't be fooled by the "desert" venue)
- ❏ 1-2 pair socks for each day
- ❏ Underwear
- ❏ T-shirts
- ❏ Bandana
- ❏ Sunglasses (two pair—lose one and you're finished)
- ❏ Goggles
- ❏ Rain gear (include an umbrella)
- ❏ Jeans
- ❏ Shorts
- ❏ Sleeveless T's
- ❏ 2 pair sneakers
- ❏ Backpack

Electronics

- ❏ Flashlights
- ❏ Batteries
- ❏ Two-way radios
- ❏ Battery powered radio with CD player
- ❏ Cameras
- ❏ Film
- ❏ Video camera
- ❏ Video cleaners
- ❏ Video tapes
- ❏ Protective coverings for all camera equipment

Transportation

- ❏ RV (definitely beats sleeping in a tent, car or truck)
- ❏ Bikes (leave your valuable ones at home)
- ❏ Bike lights
- ❏ Golf cart and art car/bus (if you want to be among the elite)

Dress

- ❏ Anything you like
- ❏ Light-making sticks
- ❏ Glow in the dark paint
- ❏ Body paint
- ❏ Makeup (and don't forget suntan lotion)

Food (only coffee and ice are available)

- ❏ Water, water and more water
- ❏ Ice
- ❏ Coffee, tea, juice, etc.
- ❏ Milk
- ❏ Sandwich material
- ❏ Grill
- ❏ Charcoal
- ❏ Chips (anything salty)
- ❏ Any special foods make for good barter

Sleeping gear

- ❏ Sleeping bags
- ❏ Blankets with covers
- ❏ Pillows

Nevada

 NYC -3   Reno/Tahoe Cannon (RNO) <30 min./$10    RV   Map Code: A25

Las Vegas Rodeo

National Finals Rodeo

Key Month: Dec   Ratings: Event ★ ★ ★ ☆ ☆   **P**   City ★ ★ ★ ★ ★   Origin: 1985   Attendance: 140,000

What's riskier than wrestling a one-armed bandit in Glitter Gulch? If you're cinching up atop one of the world's meanest 2,000-pound bulls, high steaks takes on a whole new meaning. To an outsider, Las Vegas might seem incongruous with the down-and-dirty sport of rodeo, but this is big business Vegas style: The purse at the **National Finals Rodeo (NFR)** has grown from $500,500 in 1980 to around $5 million.

The **NFR** features the cream of the crop from each year's Professional Rodeo Cowboys Association regular-season competitions. The top fifteen in each of the rodeo's seven main events—saddle-bronc riding, bull riding, bareback riding, calf roping, team roping, steer wrestling and barrel racing—compete for prize money, sponsors and glory.

The best cowboys and cowgirls travel thousands of miles to as many as 125 rodeos each year with the dream of driving their pickups down the Strip, past the lights, noise and other hopefuls to the Thomas and Mack Center on the University of Nevada, Las Vegas campus. But the contestants aren't the only ones who find it a tough row to hoe to get to the **Finals**. More than 170,000 tickets to the ten-performance event are sold each year, but the **NFR** is still one of the toughest tickets to come by in the sporting world. Thousands of fans travel to Las Vegas each December in the often-vain attempt to pick up scalped tickets.

Rodeo events are must-sees every night, but what goes on before and after is vintage Las Vegas, albeit with a kind of twang that speaks to the city's frontier roots. Las Vegas doesn't see this many cowboy hats in a year (for Vegas with a more Rat Pack feel, come for Super Bowl weekend, page 116), and Western entertainment is found at almost every casino lounge and showroom. This weekend's standouts—Gold Coast, Sam's Town and the ever-present Ricky and the Red Streaks at the Stardust—provide a look at an edgy, Western side of Vegas most people don't expect.

On the Calendar

Official Event Dates
Nine days beginning first Friday in December

Best 3 Days To Be There
Final weekend (Friday-Sunday). The excitement of the Finals carries over into everything Las Vegas.

Other Times To Go
See **Super Bowl Weekend**, page 116.

☾ 34°/57° (1°/14°)

Nevada

The day-by-day plan for this chapter is abandoned in favor of a more general overview of options built around the rodeo.

Accommodations

If you're not dressed in Western attire, you might feel out of place at the **Gold Coast Hotel & Casino**, which caters to bull riders and buckle bunnies—as in most other casinos, the **NFR** is broadcast live and free on closed-circuit television. Other hotel favorites are the **Binion's Horseshoe** hotel and **Sam's Town Hotel and Gambling Hall**. The only classy resort on the Strip that draws a large country contingent is the **MGM Grand**. The place is so big they could hold the rodeo in the center of the casino and no one would even notice. In the late '90s, the refurbished **New Frontier Hotel** added a sixteen-story, all-suite tower where many of the rooms have great mountain views.

Breakfast and lunch

Cheap eats are synonymous with Vegas. You won't have much farther to look for a bountiful breakfast than your hotel or casino's coffee shop. If you prefer your meals with all the excess this town is known for, line up for one of the huge buffets around town.

Area attractions

Las Vegas' main attraction is, of course, gambling. But this is the only week of the year when you can experience gambling as it might have been in the Old West, with lots of cowboy hats seated around blackjack tables waiting for the chance to cash in a winning hand with a big ol' "Yahoo!"

The **Fremont Street Experience** is a five-block electric canopy of twinkling Christmas lights suspended ninety feet above downtown Las Vegas. Live entertainment and more than two million light bulbs dazzle viewers. If you're craving a man-made wonder of a different type, make the short trip to the impressive **Hoover Dam**.

If you don't have the duds to do up the weekend right, do a little Western shopping at the NFR Cowboy Christmas Gift Show at Cashman Field Center. Remember this inviolable rodeo rule: No Gap jeans! Wranglers jeans and Justin boots are what you want.

Many Vegas hotels offer modern "visual attractions." At Sam's Town, it's the **Sunset Stampede**, an entertaining laser-and-water show.

Dinner

It's easy to eat cheap and big in Vegas—casinos don't mind losing money on food as long as customers walk across gaming floors to eat it. For down-home barbecue, many hotels feature cook-offs. **Mortoni's** in the Hard Rock Hotel offers high-quality Italian. New York, New York is worth a visit, not only for its awe-inspiring construction, but for the upscale **Gallagher's Steakhouse** and Italian restaurant, **Il Fornaio**, on its lower level. Other fine choices are **Mark Miller's Coyote Cafe** for Southwestern-influenced food; **Commander's Palace** serves up Creole classics such as turtle soup, gumbo and pecan-crusted trout.

Late-night entertainment

Lookin' for your next ex? **Dylan's Dance Hall & Saloon** is the place you might meet him or her. Big beers and lots of music act as aphrodisiacs during the **NFR**, or so the tall tale goes. Many of country music's biggest stars make a point to play to their fans during the **NFR**, so check local papers. Test your skills on the mechanical bull at **Gilley's** if you think you got what it takes to be a bull rider. If not, steer your way to the dance floor surrounded by a corral.

Other hot spots are **Sam's Town Live** and the hideaway with the postage-stamp-size dance floor at **Roxy's Saloon**. Nonstop action at **Rockabilly's** and the **Gold Coast Showroom**, converted during Rodeo to a huge Western dance hall, compete with the popular Ricky and the Red Streaks at the **Stardust Ballroom**. Ricky's raucous show, great dance music and no dance floor make for quite a scene as hundreds of people end up dancing on the tables.

Rodeo rules

In addition to music, Las Vegas also hosts other rodeo events (see Event & Ticket info). For **NFR** action itself, don't plan any activities from about 6:45–9 p.m. nightly and for the final Sunday-afternoon competition. Here's a quick primer: Rodeos consist of two types of events. Bareback riding, saddle-bronc riding and bull riding are the roughstock events. To qualify, cowboys have to stay on the bucking horse or bull for eight seconds. There are also timed events: calf roping, steer wrestling (also called the big-man's sport) and team roping. Ladies compete in barrel racing, where the line between human and animal blurs in a colorful display of teamwork and tight pants.

Hotels	Phone	Address	Price	Fax	Room/Best
Binion's Horseshoe	702-382-1600 800-237-6537	128 E. Fremont St.	$	702-384-1574	360/Mtn vw
Gold Coast Hotel & Casino	702-367-7111 888-402-6278	4000 W. Flamingo Rd.	$	702-365-7505	750/Mtn vw
MGM Grand	702-891-1111 800-929-1111	3799 Las Vegas Blvd.	$$	702-891-1030	5,005/Grand Tower
New Frontier Hotel	702-794-8200 800-634-6966	3120 Las Vegas Blvd. S	$	702-794-8445	984/Atrium Tower
Sam's Town Hotel and Gambling Hall	702-456-7777 800-634-6371	5111 Boulder Hwy.	$	702-454-8014	650/Park vw

Restaurants	Phone	Address	Price	Rec	Food
Commander's Palace	702-892-8272	3663 Las Vegas Blvd. S	$$$$	LD	Creole
Gallagher's Steakhouse	702-740-6450	3790 Las Vegas Blvd. S, New York New York hotel	$$$	D	Steakhouse
Il Fornaio	702-650-6500	3790 Las Vegas Blvd. S, New York New York hotel	$$$	D/BL	Italian
Mark Miller's Coyote Cafe	702-891-7349	3799 Las Vegas Blvd. S, in MGM Grand	$$	BLD	Southwestern
Mortoni's	702-693-5047	4455 S. Paradise Rd., Hard Rock Hotel	$$$	D	Northern Italian

Nightlife	Phone	Address	Cover	Rec*	Music
Dylan's Dance Hall & Saloon	702-451-4006	4660 Boulder Hwy.	None	MP	Country
Gilley's	702-794-8200	see New Frontier Hotel	$	MP(F)	Country
Gold Coast Showroom	702-367-7111	see Gold Coast Hotel	None	MP	Country
Rockabilly's	702-641-5800	3785 Boulder Hwy.	None	MP(F)	Country
Roxy's Saloon	702-456-7777	see Sam's Town Hotel	None	MP	Country, Top 40
Sam's Town Live	702-456-7777	see Sam's Town Hotel	$	M	Country, Top 40
Stardust Ballroom	702-732-6111	3000 Las Vegas Blvd. S	$	MP	Country

* M=Live music; P=Dancing (Party); R=Bar only; S=Show; (F)=Food served. For further explanation of codes, page 12.

Sights & Attractions	Phone	Address	Entry Fee
Fremont Street Experience	702-678-5600	downtown, Fremont Street	None
Hoover Dam	702-294-3523	Hwy. 93, 36 miles SE of Las Vegas	$
Sunset Stampede	702-456-7777	see Sam's Town Hotel	None

Las Vegas CVB	**800-332-5333**	**3150 Paradise Rd.**	

Event & Ticket Info

National Finals Rodeo (Thomas and Mack Center, UNLV, Tropicana Avenue at Swenson): Tickets ($27-$40) always sell out and are available only by lottery. About 200-500 SRO tickets are released the day of each rodeo. For ticket-lottery applications and information, contact *Las Vegas Events* (702-260-8605).

Downtown Hoedown & Downtown Rodeo Stampede: Contact *Fremont Street Experience* (702-678-5600).

Benny Binion's NFR Bucking Horse and Bull Sale: Contact *Las Vegas Events* (702-260-8605).

Wrangler Tight Fittin' Jeans: (Holiday Inn Boardwalk Hotel & Casino, 3750 Las Vegas Blvd. S.): Free. Contact *Inventive Incentives* (888-321-7238).

Miss Rodeo America Pageant: Contact *Miss Rodeo America, Inc.* (719-948-9206).

 NYC -3   McCarran (LAS) <30 min./$15   Yes/No   Map Code: A26

Nevada

A Whale Of A Good Time

About Gambling

Whales are beloved creatures, but nowhere more beloved than in Las Vegas. Las Vegas? Yep, in Las Vegas, a whale is someone who gambles more than $1 million per visit, with lines of credit up to $20 million. Casinos love them.

If you don't happen to be one of the world's 250 or so players in this league, perhaps you're one of the thousands who wager more than $100,000 per visit. These are the people you see filling casinos during Super Bowl weekend, betting green ($25), black ($100) and pink ($500) chips on the turn of every card or the toss of the dice. These players help create a buzz in casinos and attract the attention of other gamblers, dealers, good-looking "escorts" and chip hustlers.

Apparently, there's something enjoyable about losing money. More than thirty million people come to Las Vegas each year to drop money on a variety of games—slot machines, Keno, roulette, baccarat, blackjack, poker and pai gow are a few favorites. But for most aficionados of fun, the only worthwhile thrill is craps. When conditions are right, craps evolves beyond being a simple game and becomes a party. Anyone who can get near the table is invited.

Craps, whether played in the garages of the Runyonesque Guys and Dolls, or in billion-dollar resorts, is the fastest and liveliest casino game. Money moves quickly—it's fun for novices to simply watch dealers move the chips around—and it takes a fair amount of familiarity and comfort to play it well. Many books have been written about playing and winning at craps. To have fun, however, you only need to understand the language of the game. Start by learning how to count in crapsese:

Two: aces or low
Three: ace-deuce
Four: little Joe
Five: fever
Six: sex
Seven: seven, seven out or lucky seven
Eight: eighter from Decatur
Nine: Nina from Pasadena
Ten: ten on the end or Big Ben
Eleven: yo or yo-lev
Twelve: boxcars or high

Get the counting down and you'll soon understand terms such as Two rolls, no coffee! Hands high, they fly! Too tall to call! and Pause is the cause! Pretty soon you'll be kissing the dice (or letting the good-looking gamer next to you kiss them) and shouting "C'mon, dice, baby needs a new pair of shoes!" or the ever-popular "Rent money!" as you throw the bones across the felt. After that, you're just a slippery slope away from calling out bets such as "Section eight press and a high/low with the cheese!" When you want to roll an eight, you'll call out "How do you spell relief?" and get the response "Roll eight!" When you win, you'll hear the stickman say, "Winner, winner, chicken dinner" and get high-fives all around. This sure beats pushing buttons and waiting for a bunch of cherries.

TERMINOLOGY

Whatever game you play, start with a rudimentary understanding of casino terminology and you can swim with the sharks, if not the whales.

Boxman: a craps dealer who sits over the drop box and supervises bets and payoffs

Casino boss: a person who oversees the entire casino

Comp: short for complimentary or free

Drop box: a locked box on tables where dealers deposit paper money

Eye in the sky: surveillance equipment, usually ceiling mirrors that conceal people assigned to watch the action to prevent cheating by players or dealers

Limit: the minimum or maximum bet accepted at a gambling table

Marker: an IOU owed the casino by a gambler allowed by the hotel to play on credit

Pit boss: a person who oversees table dealers

RFB comp: free room, food and beverage

Shooter: a gambler who is rolling the dice on a craps table

Stickman (Stick chick): a dealer who moves the dice around on a craps table with a hooked stick

Super Bowl Weekend

Las Vegas

Key Month: Jan   Ratings: Event ★ ★ ★ ☆ ☆   City ★ ★ ★ ★ ★   Origin: 1967   Attendance: 200,000

On the last Sunday in January, everyone wants to be in the town that hosts the **Super Bowl**, right? Well, not really. That's because the best **Super Bowl** action takes place in Las Vegas, where casinos unfurl red carpets for high rollers and party veterans who know that the football game is just a sidelight during the most exciting gambling weekend of the year.

More people head to Las Vegas for **Super Bowl Weekend** than to the site of the game. By the tens of thousands, they hit the sports books, pick a team, place a bet, then cruise the inescapable array of football parties and gatherings.

Just arriving in Las Vegas by plane is a unique experience. Slot machines jam the terminal. Screens in the baggage area tout shows, hotels and anything else good-looking showgirls can sell. Outside, a battalion of limousines await privileged guests.

This is the showiest weekend of the year in a town that defines America's obsession with big-time glitz. (For another side of Las Vegas, see page 112.) In years past, the famous lights of the Strip simply amazed out-of-towners. Now, coming into Vegas is like entering a neon dreamscape. In recent years, Las Vegas has attempted to rebuild itself as a family destination, but this twenty-four-hour city still caters mostly to adults. Even museums have made entry onto the Las Vegas strip. But world-class attractions offered by most casinos remain mere diversions from the serious business at hand—gambling.

The combination of gaming and entertainment has paid off. The $1.7 billion Bellagio hotel, for example, can afford to transport northern Italy to the middle of the desert. The Sistine Chapel, Eiffel Tower and Empire State Building have also been recreated in Las Vegas.

The macho allusion isn't out of place during this weekend that celebrates the most watched annual sporting event in the world. **Super Sunday** can almost be considered America's first holiday after New Year's Day and no place rings it in like Vegas.

On the Calendar

Official Event Dates
Super Bowl is played on the last Sunday in January, except 2004 when it will be played the first Sunday in February.

Best 3 Days To Be There
Friday-Sunday. The intensity of this weekend begins Friday, and continues through the post-game second-guessing on Sunday night.

Other Times To Go
See *Las Vegas Rodeo*, page 112.

☀ 33°/56° (1°/13°)

Nevada

The itinerary for this chapter is abandoned in favor of a more general overview of options built around the Super Bowl weekend.

Hotels

For the **Super Bowl**, pick a hotel that has top-end accommodations and caters to high rollers. **Caesars Palace** holds the heavyweight title as the first top-class theme hotel and casino in Las Vegas. At the heart of the Strip, Caesars was completed in 1966 in ageless Greco-Roman style. The four-acre Garden of the Gods outdoor area was completed in 1998. With a ninety-foot atrium filled with exotic palms and tropical foliage, **The Mirage** evokes a Polynesian paradise. The erupting volcano and Siegfried and Roy's rare white tigers complete the set. **Bellagio** is the Strip's deluxe hotel, catering to upper-crust patrons with gardens, waterfalls and the world-renowned Cirque du Soleil performing above and below the surface of a large fresh-water pool. For something different, the avant-garde suites at **The Rio Suite Hotel & Casino**—close to the Strip—cater to a somewhat hipper crowd. Operators of the **Mandalay Bay Resort and Casino** wanted a place that was "cool for fifty-year-olds." The result is an opulent, South Seas-themed resort that stands out as one of the Strip's best places to stay and have fun. You can take a gondolier ride through the simulated Grand Canal of Venice at the **Venetian Resort Hotel Casino**, one of the city's most ambitious architectural projects—and that's saying something here. Attracting young hipsters, the **Palms Casino Resort** has fewer rooms than most places (thus, more attentive service), but amenities include a fourteen-screen movie theater and hopping rooftop nightclub.

Casinos

Each recommended hotel has a terrific casino, but part of the fun in Vegas is making the rounds. Although the games of chance are all the same, each casino has a different ambience and attracts a different crowd. Despite the fact that minimum betting amounts are higher all over town this weekend, you'll find an unusual number of people crowding around tables, waiting for an opening to play. Get close enough and you'll see more people betting more money than you thought possible.

Breakfast and lunch

Assigning names like breakfast and lunch to meal times will have no meaning to you or your body this weekend. The casinos and their coffee shops operate twenty-four hours. All major hotels have coffee shops that are particularly useful from midnight until dinner time. Many casinos also serve elaborate buffet breakfasts.

Area attractions

Daytime attractions in Glitter Gulch run the gamut. Arrive early for a good vantage point of **Treasure Island Buccaneer Bay Show** to watch pirates battle the British Navy every ninety minutes starting at 4 p.m. Spend your winnings at **The Forum Shops at Caesars**; take a break with the fountain show when Roman statues come to life for eight splashy minutes on the hour. Visit the Mirage shark tank and dolphin exhibit; return at night for the **Mirage Volcano** eruption every fifteen minutes. **New York, New York** has the Statue of Liberty West outside and more Big Apple nostalgia inside, including a Coney Island roller coaster and Manhattan Express. Billing itself as the Gen X Casino, the **Hard Rock Hotel & Casino** doubles as a museum of popular culture, with a $3 million collection of rock-and-roll memorabilia.

The Super Bowl

The major hotels fill their rooms with "invited" guests who attend private parties on **Super Bowl Sunday**. However, "party" is just a hook used to gather a lot of people into a room to watch a big-screen television. If you don't go to a party, just watch the game on giant screens along with a crowd of people in any of the major casinos. It's fun and usually easy to pick out the white-knuckled gamblers who have backed the team that is winning or losing.

Wherever you go, you can be sure there'll be plenty of **Super Bowl** paraphernalia, hot dogs and beer. In between tackles, cheers and drinks, several casinos will have ex-NFL stars and current-day cheerleaders on hand to keep things interesting in case the score of the game gets (typically) out of hand. The game itself may sometimes be called the Super Bore, but nobody ever accused Las Vegas of falling asleep while there was still a player on the field or a bet to be made.

Super Bowl betting

The gigantic electronic display boards at The Race and Sports Book at Caesars Palace offer continuous computer wagering information, including odds changes and player-injury reports. Funky bets are *de rigueur*. Will the quarterback fumble the ball in the third quarter? How many times will the fullback run up the middle? Will the towel boy accidentally spill the Gatorade bucket, thereby ruining the traditional postgame Gatorade celebration? Okay, you can't bet on that last one, but you can wager money on just about any other game situation you can think of.

Dinner

In the old days, major casino hotels used a standard formula—offer guests a choice of a gourmet restaurant, a steakhouse and Italian and Asian eateries. Results were often bland. But resorts have been busy in recent years, plucking the nation's most famous restaurateurs from hometown nests, transplanting them to the desert and turning Vegas into a great eating town.

California cuisine has invaded Las Vegas, with honors for best restaurant going to **Nob Hill**. For another nouvelle eatery done à la West Coast, including an extraordinary wine list, check out **Napa**. Try the crab cakes or tuna sashimi, followed by a creamy risotto. Los Angeles moves east with **Spago**, where cuisines from around the world combine seamlessly; try the fried catfish with ginger-miso aioli and spicy bok choy. Other fine choices are Wolfgang Puck's **Chinois** for fusion; and **Emeril's New Orleans Fish House**. Another New Orleans transplant is **Commander's Palace**, which turns out spicy Creole classics such as gumbo and turtle soup. Enjoy real Picasso paintings while dining on French cuisine with a Spanish influence at **Picasso**. From the wine selection (bottles are kept in an enormous glass tower) to the dining room, it's all huge at **Aureole**. The progressive American cuisine includes tequila-cured salmon gravlax with shrimp toast, but the clean, open architecture and dramatic surroundings get most of the attention. Along with "a return to simple French food," the only real outdoor seating on the Strip evokes a classic continental feel to **Mon Amí Gabi** at the Paris hotel.

Entertainment

Major casinos have enough entertainment to keep you busy for weeks. Lounge shows are typically free, allowing you to drop in for a drink and listen to top-notch club entertainers. Picking a show is a matter of personal taste, but the must-see for everyone is Cirque du Soleil's "**O**" (or any other show by this amazing French Canadian troupe), which is housed in a theater at Bellagio especially for this show.

Late Night

While there's no such thing as being too late in this city, there are post-dinner hot spots where the action makes the *Super Bowl* look like training camp. The Rio has two top-shelf choices: **Club Rio**, a raging disco with a very long line to get in, and **VooDoo Cafe & Lounge**, where you can check out Top 40, Motown and jazz acts from the comfort of an animal-print booth. Luxor's **Club Ra**, with an Egyptian motif, is another popular disco. **Studio 54** may be the most striking disco, with a backstage film-lot décor. If you're into leather-clad waitresses and translucent walls, **Baby's** at the Hard Rock is also worth a stop, though more for the energetic crowd than the ambience. Try **Cleopatra's Barge** at Caesars for live music.

For clubs not in a hotel, **The Beach** is lower-tech and generally has less attitude. **Club Utopia**, on the other hand, is high-tech with a rave atmosphere and a younger crowd. **Rum Jungle** is one of the latest hot spots in town. And remember, if you've had too much dancing and need to sit down, the slot machines have been known to sing a few tunes.

With a stylized interior, no-hats-no-tennies policy, $20 weekend cover ($10 Thursday and Sunday, free Monday-Wednesday) and a 360-degree-view from the top of the fifty-five story Palms resort, the Chicago-transplant **Ghost Bar** has become one of the city's hippest spots for cocktails and pretty people.

Las Vegas

Hotels	Phone	Address	Price	Fax	Rooms/Best
Bellagio	702-693-7111 888-987-6667	3600 Las Vegas Blvd. S	$$$$+	702-693-8546	3,005/Strip vw
Caesars Palace	702-731-7110 800-634-6001	3570 Las Vegas Blvd. S	$$$$+	702-731-6636	2,454/Palace tower
Mandalay Bay Resort and Casino	702-632-7777 877-632-7000	3950 Las Vegas Blvd. S	$$$$	702-632-7234	3,646/Strip vw
The Mirage	702-791-7111 800-627-6667	3400 Las Vegas Blvd. S	$$$	702-791-7446	3,049/Strip vw
Palms Casino Resort	702-942-7777 866-942-7777	4321 W. Flamingo Rd.	$$	702-942-6999	455/Playpen suite
The Rio Suite Hotel & Casino	702-777-7777 800-752-9746	3700 W. Flamingo Rd.	$$	702-252-7611	2,500/Las Vegas valley vw
Venetian Resort Hotel Casino	702-414-1000 877-875-1861	3355 Las Vegas Blvd. S	$$$$	702-414-1100	3,036/Strip vw

Restaurants	Phone	Address	Price	Rec	Food
Aureole	702-632-7777 877-632-7401	3950 Las Vegas Blvd. S	$$$	D/L	Progressive American
Chinois	702-737-9700	see The Forum Shops at Caesars	$$	LD	Chinese, fusion
Commander's Palace	702-892-8272	at Aladdin resort, 3667 Las Vegas Blvd. S	$$$	D	Creole
Emeril's New Orleans Fish House	702-891-7374	3799 Las Vegas Blvd. S, in MGM Grand	$$$$	LD	Creole, Cajun
Mon Amí Gabi	702-944-4224	at Paris hotel, 3655 Las Vegas Blvd. S	$$	D/L	French
Napa	702-252-7777	see The Rio Suite Hotel	$$$$	D	Country French
Nob Hill	702-891-1111	3799 Las Vegas Blvd. S	$$$$	D	California
Picasso	702-693-7223	3600 Las Vegas Blvd. S	$$$$+	D	French w/ Spanish influence
Spago	702-369-6300	see The Forum Shops at Caesars	$$$$	LD	California

Nightlife	Phone	Address	Cover	Rec*	Music
Baby's	702-693-5000	4455 Paradise Rd. Hard Rock Hotel	$$	MP	Techno, hip hop
The Beach	702-731-1925	365 Convention Center Dr.	$	P(F)	Top 40
Cleopatra's Barge	702-731-7110	see Caesars Palace hotel	None	MP(F)	Top 40
Club Ra	702-262-4000	3900 Las Vegas Blvd. S	$	P(F)	Disco
Club Rio	702-252-7777	see The Rio Suite Hotel	$	P	Top 40
Club Utopia	702-593-5935	3765 Las Vegas Blvd. S	$	P	House
Ghost Bar	702-938-2666	See Palms resort	$$	R	Varies
"O" (Cirque du Soleil)	702-693-7111	see Bellagio	$$$$+	S	Nuvo circus
Rum Jungle	702-632-7408	3950 Las Vegas Blvd. S	$$	MP(F)	House, hip hop, reggae
Studio 54	702-891-7915	3799 Las Vegas Blvd. S	$$	P	House
VooDoo Cafe & Lounge	702-252-7777	see The Rio Suite Hotel	$	M	Jazz, Top 40

* M=Live music; P=Dancing (Party); R=Bar only; S=Show; (F)=Food served. For further explanation of codes, page 12.

Sights & Attractions	Phone	Address	Entry Fee
The Forum Shops at Caesars	702-893-4800	see Caesars Palace hotel	None
Hard Rock Hotel & Casino	702-693-5000	4455 Paradise Rd.	None
Mirage Volcano	702-791-7111	see The Mirage hotel	None
New York, New York	702-740-6969	3790 Las Vegas Blvd. S	None
Treasure Island Buccaneer Bay Show	702-894-7111	3300 Las Vegas Blvd. S, Treasure Island Hotel	None
Las Vegas CVB	800-332-5333	3150 Paradise Rd.	

Nevada

 NYC -3   McCarran (LAS) <30 min./$15   No   Map Code: A27

Balloon Fiesta

Kodak Albuquerque International Balloon Fiesta

Key Month: Oct   Ratings: Event ★★★☆☆   **Ⓗ**   City ★★★☆☆   Origin: 1972   Attendance: 1,500,000

With nearly 1,000 multicolored balloons ascending at dawn into the clear Southwestern sky, nearly all of them framed by the dusky Sandia mountains, it's no wonder Albuquerque's **Balloon Fiesta** is the most photographed event in the world. Official sources claim twenty-five million pictures are snapped during the event's nine days, which are highlighted by mass ascensions, target and precision competitions, and as much color as a roll of film can handle.

Albuquerque's unique "box" geography—mountain formations hold in mostly glorious weather patterns—makes for perfect ballooning conditions. But it's not just the professionals who get high here. Visitors can take rides along the majestic Sandia Mountains or make graceful circuits over the Rio Grande.

While most events in this book pulsate into the early hours, in Albuquerque you get up in the dark hours for spectacular daybreak events. Dusk is the other time to be outside, as hundreds of brilliantly lit, tethered balloons sway against sunset skies, creating a surreal skyscape of colors.

The **Balloon Fiesta** takes over and transforms Albuquerque, but the city still offers lively nightlife along with award-winning restaurants. Though its population is about 500,000, Albuquerque has a small-town feel consistent with its history as a frontier crossroads and trading center.

On the Calendar

Official Event Dates
First two weekends in October

Best 3 Days To Be There
Second weekend (Thursday-Saturday). Allows you to catch all the main events and an Albuquerque weekend.

☽ 44°/71° (7°/22°)

Old Town, the four-block "village" at the heart of the city since 1706, is a charming adobe area lined with galleries, cafes and winding brick walkways.

Within an hour's drive of Albuquerque are awe-inspiring natural areas such as Petroglyph National Monument, with 17,000 ancient Indian writings carved into black rock from five extinct volcanoes. Native Americans carry on the centuries-old traditions of their ancestors with ceremonial dances and skillful artisanship. The big skies and muted-color desert vistas that seem to go on forever continue to inspire great art, much of which is showcased in museums and art galleries throughout the city. In October, visitors come to Albuquerque for the brilliant balloons, but most leave equally colored with a new appreciation of the artistry and grace of New Mexico's ancient and modern cultures.

New Mexico

For links to most current web sites for cities and events, go to www.funrises.com

<table>
</table>

DAY **1**	*Thursday*

10:00 am Start your day with a visit to the **Albuquerque Museum of Art and History**. It combines an interesting sculpture garden with Native American art and historical displays.

11:00 am Explore Old Town's sheltered walkways, winding brick paths and quaint patios on the museum's walking tour.

12:30 pm Across the street from the museum is a wonderful spot for a light lunch. ❌ **Seasons Rotisserie & Grill** serves pastas, sandwiches and American cuisine in an upscale, casual setting.

2:30 pm Visit the **National Atomic Museum**. It features models of the first atomic bombs, aircraft, rockets, missiles and nuclear weapons.

5:30 pm Leave radioactivity for a more benign kind of glow. Head for Balloon Fiesta Park and the *Special Shapes Rodeo Glow*. Sailing ships, cows, tennis shoes and pink dragons are lit up with a host of other character balloons to create a fascinating menagerie against the sky. Balloons start inflating—and parking lots fill up—at 5:30 p.m. Pilots set off "burns" synchronized to music at dusk, about 7 p.m.

8:00 pm Stay for the *fireworks show*, which, against the brilliant stars of the desert sky, is one of the most beautiful in the world.

9:00 pm Get pampered in a turn-of-the-century brick building at the **Artichoke Cafe**, an Italian-French-American bistro with exquisite dinners.

11:00 pm Relax at the seductive **Martini Grille**, the perfect finish to a perfect day. The nearby **Club Rhythm and Blues** has good music.

DAY **2**	*Friday*

5:30 am Don't worry, your 4 a.m. wake-up call will be worth the pain. Hurry to Balloon Fiesta Park for the *Dawn Patrol*, a haunting ceremony that sends one luminous, solitary balloon into the dawn sky to greet the sun as it climbs over the Sandias.

7:00 am Remember all those crazy-shaped balloons you saw glowing in last night's sky? Now watch them all rise together in the dramatic *Special Shapes Ascension*.

9:00 am You may want to finish your night's sleep, or just warm up with a hotel ❌ breakfast. If not ...

9:30 am Visit one of the many Native American pueblos within an hour's drive of Albuquerque. Fall is the perfect time to catch harvest ceremonies, which are heralded by hypnotic drumming and gorgeously feathered and beaded dancers. Try the Indian fry bread, hot and honey-drizzled, straight from the pan.

Noon Not long ago, Route 66 ran through three time zones and eight states, from Chicago to Los Angeles. Today it has all ❌ but vanished, but the **66 Diner** still serves a mean lunch while paying homage to this special part of American history.

1:30 pm Head east out of Albuquerque on I-40, then north on New Mexico Highway 14, and pick up the road to the Sandia Crest and the Turquoise Trail. Wind through the Cibola National Forest for breathtaking views at 10,000 feet and above. Continue through old mining towns (gold, silver, turquoise and coal), stopping at artists' shops between the views.

6:15 pm Take in an incredible sunset on the **Sandia Peak Tramway**, the world's longest aerial tramway. You'll be lifted from the desert floor, above canyons and lush forests, to the top of Sandia Peak, where panoramic views take in more than 11,000 square miles.

7:00 pm High-class takes on new meaning at ❌ the **High Finance** restaurant atop Sandia Peak. The steaks, seafood and pastas are superb (if you can tear yourself away from the awesome panoramic views long enough to order). If you're craving downtime, head back to the hotel and **Conrad's Downtown**, La Posada's excellent restaurant. Featuring award-winning recipes from Jane Butel, a celebrated cookbook author synonymous with Southwestern cuisine (her Southwestern Cooking School is just off the lobby),

7:00 pm (cont.) Conrad's is great for feasting and people-watching. Try one of three versions of traditional Spanish paella while flamenco-guitar music plays in the background.

9:00 pm Stop by **The Lobby Bar** at La Posada for blues and jazz in one of the city's popular meeting spots.

11:00 pm The night's still young (unless you got up for the Dawn Patrol this morning). Check out **Burt's Tiki Lounge** for late-night drinking and a party atmosphere.

DAY 3 — *Saturday*

5:00 am If you missed the Dawn Patrol yesterday, go today, but don't miss the *Mass Ascension* at 7 a.m. Nearly a thousand balloons take off together for an unforgettable dawn. You could be in one of them by splurging on a *Rainbow Riders* ride.

9:00 am Head back to La Posada de Albuquerque for a leisurely breakfast at ✖ **Conrad's Downtown**.

10:30 am New Mexico boasts the art, history and culture of nineteen Pueblo tribes. Learn how climate and geography made each one unique at the **Indian Pueblo Cultural Center**, where traditional dance performances and art demonstrations are held on weekends.

12:30 pm Savor culinary history with lunch ✖ at **La Placita Restaurant**, Albuquerque's oldest restored hacienda. It serves New Mexican and American cuisine in a Spanish atmosphere.

2:30 pm See Native American art at **Petroglyph National Monument** on the city's west side. Several walking trails, ranging from easy to moderately difficult, wind around 17,000 petroglyphs carved into volcanic rock.

5:30 pm The *Night Magic Glow* is one of the most anticipated events of the week. Balloons are slowly inflated until the sky is filled with the fantastic sight of hundreds of luminous balloons pulsating with light.

8:00 pm Stay for the *fireworks*, a spectacular end to a fiesta day.

9:30 pm **Cafe Bodega** boasts an extensive, international wine list, receiving an award of excellence from *Wine Spectator*. Enjoy the seasonal menu of New American cuisine in its simple yet elegant décor.

11:30 pm Two-step to country music at the **Midnight Rodeo** or settle in next door at its Gotham Room and shake your booty to dance music.

◼

More Time, More Choices

McGrath's Bar & Grill is a good eating choice, serving well-prepared American fare in an attractive room. **Kanome** serves Asian fusion cuisine and is vegetarian-friendly. **Terra, an American Bistro** is a good stop for dishes made with familiar ingredients.

Two small unusual museums are the **American International Rattlesnake Museum** and the **Turquoise Museum**.

Accommodations

Accented with antique frescoes, beamed ceilings and Spanish-tile floors in the lobby, **La Posada de Albuquerque** is native son Conrad Hilton's first hotel. At the **Sheraton Old Town**, you can wake up each morning to 300 years of history and culture. The **Crowne Plaza Pyramid** hotel has the dramatic, ten-story Aztec Pyramid Atrium. The **Hyatt Regency Albuquerque** has an attractive lobby and standard Hyatt rooms.

Event & Ticket Info

Albuquerque International Balloon Fiesta (Balloon Fiesta State Park, Interstate 25 at Tramway): Daily tickets ($4) are purchased at the gate. Five-day tickets ($15), which eliminate the need to wait in lines, can be ordered from *Albuquerque International Balloon Fiesta* (800-725-2477 or 505-823-1111).

Rainbow Riders, the official ride concession for Balloon Fiesta, arranges rides for $225 per person. For more information, contact *Rainbow Riders* (505-293-6800).

The Hot Sheet

Hotels	Phone	Address	Price	Fax	Rooms/Best
Crowne Plaza Pyramid	505-821-3333 / 800-227-6963	5151 San Francisco Rd. NE	$$	505-828-0230	311/Mtn vw
Hyatt Regency Albuquerque	505-842-1234 / 800-233-1234	330 Tijeras NW	$$$	505-766-6710	395/Mtn vw
La Posada de Albuquerque	505-242-9090 / 800-777-5732	125 2nd St. NW	$$	505-242-8664	114/Mtn vw
Sheraton Old Town	505-843-6300 / 800-237-2133	800 Rio Grande NW	$$	505-842-8426	187/City vw

Restaurants	Day	Phone	Address	Price	Rec	Food
66 Diner	2	505-247-1421	1405 Central Ave. NE	$	B/LD	American
Artichoke Cafe	1	505-243-0200	424 Central SE	$$	D/L	French, American
Cafe Bodega	3	505-872-1710	4243 Montgomery NE	$$	LD	New American
Conrad's Downtown	2,3	505-242-9090	see La Posada hotel	$$$	D/BL	Southwestern
High Finance	2	505-243-9742	40 Tramway Rd. NE	$$$	D/L	American
Kanome	A	505-265-7773	3128 Central Ave. SE	$$	D	Asian fusion
La Placita Restaurant	3	505-247-2204	208 San Felipe	$$	L/D	New Mexican
McGrath's Bar & Grill	A	505-766-6700	see Hyatt Regency Albuquerque hotel	$$	BLD	American, continental
Seasons Rotisserie & Grill	1	505-766-5100	2031 Mountain Rd. NW	$$	L/D	American
Terra, an American Bistro	A	505-792-1700	1119 Alameda NW	$$	LD	American

Nightlife	Day	Phone	Address	Cover	Rec*	Music
Burt's Tiki Lounge	2	505-243-2878	313 Gold Ave.	None	P(F)	Party
Club Rhythm and Blues	1	505-256-0849	3523 Central Ave. NE	$	M	Jazz, blues
The Lobby Bar	2	505-242-9090	see La Posada hotel	None	M(F)	Flamenco, jazz, blues
The Martini Grille	1	505-255-4111	4200 Central SE	None	M(F)	Piano bar
Midnight Rodeo	3	505-888-0100	4901 McLeod NE	$	P(F)	Country, rock

* M=Live music; P=Dancing (Party); R=Bar only; S=Show; (F)=Food served. For further explanation of codes, page 12.

Sights & Attractions	Day	Phone	Address	Entry Fee
Albuquerque Museum of Art and History	1	505-242-4600	2000 Mountain Rd. NW	$
American International Rattlesnake Museum	A	505-242-6569	202 San Felipe NW	$
Indian Pueblo Cultural Center	3	505-843-7270	2401 12th St. NW	$
National Atomic Museum	1	505-284-3243	Wyoming Blvd. SE	$
Petroglyph National Monument	3	505-899-0205	4735 Unser Blvd. NE	None
Sandia Peak Tramway	2	505-856-7325	Tramway Rd. at Tramway Blvd.	$$
Turquoise Museum	A	505-247-8650	2107 Central NW	$

Albuquerque CVB	**800-733-9918**	**20 1st Plaza Bldg. NW**	

 NYC -2   Albuquerque (ABQ) <30 min./$15   Yes   Map Code: A28

Fiesta de Santa Fe

Key Month: Sep   Ratings: Event ★ ★ ☆ ☆ ☆   Ⓗ   City ★ ★ ★ ☆ ☆   Origin: 1712   Attendance: 75,000

Santa Fe's wild side ignites during the riotous *Fiesta de Santa Fe*, a fiery (literally) party that makes September the best time of year to visit one of the most scenic capital cities in the United States. Held on the weekend after Labor Day, the event unofficially begins Thursday night when *Zozobra*, a forty-foot-tall puppet, is torched near the central plaza as 50,000 spectators cheer. Accompanied by dancers, fireworks and heart-rending groans representing the bizarre puppet's death cries, it's all done in a joyous effort to banish gloom from the lives of the onlookers.

Once *Zozobra* has disappeared in a dark cloud of flames and smoke, a party unfolds around Santa Fe's historic Plaza. The rest of the weekend is a combination of 300 years of tradition and Santa Fe-style fun. The *Gran Baile de la Fiesta* (Fiesta Ball), the *Historical, Hysterical Parade* and the *Desfile de los Niños* (Children's Pet Parade) are all part of the entertainment.

Santa Fe's reputation for world-class art, opera and cuisine is really nothing new. Founded by order of the Spanish Crown in 1609—thirteen years before the Pilgrims landed at Plymouth Rock— the city was a center of art, culture and religion from the start. Its population is only 65,000, but Santa Fe's rich mix of museums and more than 150 art galleries makes it the third-largest art market in the country. With more than 200 restaurants, Santa Fe is also considered the gastronomic center of the Southwest.

St. Francis Cathedral, built by papal decree in 1851 to tame the "unruly and godless" local inhabitants, presides over Santa Fe. Getting around town on foot is easy, allowing you to enjoy the Santa Fe-style architecture which, like the food, reflects a combination of Anglo, Native American and Spanish cultures. You may want a car for day trips into the high desert of northern New Mexico, the mythic source of the pure air and magical atmosphere that inspire the *Fiesta de Santa Fe*.

On the Calendar

Official Event Dates
Begins Friday after Labor Day
(first Monday in September)

Best 3 Days To Be There
Thursday-Saturday. Fiesta eve Zozobra really kicks off the event.

☾ 50°/81° (10°/27°)

New Mexico

DAY 1 — Thursday

9:30 am Definitely worth the wait in line, **Cafe Pasqual's** is always packed with diners in search of great Southwestern breakfasts (think huevos rancheros).

11:00 am The **Museum of International Folk Art** houses a truly amazing collection—probably the largest of its kind—that's both fun and enriching.

1:00 pm Go to Canyon Road for a casual lunch at **El Farol**. Have tapas on the front patio. After lunch, take a walk along Canyon Road. It's filled with arts-and-crafts galleries.

3:30 pm Cab to Fort Marcy Park, where you'll be part of the singing, dancing and giddy atmosphere surrounding the dusk burning of *Zozobra*. Created from chicken wire, muslin and shredded paper, the giant puppet requires 600 hours of work to complete. Constructed at a secret location by volunteers of the local Kiwanis Club, the giant image has a different look every year.

7:30 pm The **Anasazi** serves food that combines New Mexican and Native American influences in an elegant Southwestern setting.

9:30 pm The **Paramount Nightclub** with its sprawling dance floor is an alternative night spot to check out. Or try the chic **Bar B** for martinis and live music.

11:00 am (cont.) In between museum visits, stop at one of the many food booths set up in the Plaza for *Fiesta*. Sample roast mutton on fried bread, fajitas and ice-cold watermelon juice.

Noon At the Plaza bandstand, you'll see the *Fiesta*'s opening ceremonies, followed by entertainment all afternoon. Don't miss the *Entrada de Don Diego de Vargas* in the Plaza. It's an interesting reenactment—complete with costumes—of the conqueror's entrance into the city.

3:00 pm Continue your exploration with a tour of the **Palace of the Governors** that includes a history museum. Built in 1610, it's the oldest public building in continuous use in the United States. Outside, Native American craftspeople sell exquisite silver, turquoise jewelry and pottery in one of the oldest open-air markets in the country.

7:00 pm Have dinner at one of Santa Fe's hottest restaurants, **Geronimo**, on gallery-lined Canyon Road. Guests are welcomed with a glowing fire and sophisticated yet relaxed Southwestern décor. A menu standout is the peppery elk tenderloin.

9:00 pm The Plaza is alive with the traditional music and dancing of the *Baile de la Gente* (9 p.m.–midnight). Put on your most outgoing persona and get invited to one of the many private *Fiesta* parties in town.

DAY 2 — Friday

10:00 am Stroll to **Santa Fe Baking Co**. and stake out an outdoor table. Enjoy gourmet coffee and home-baked pastries. Reading material includes international newspapers and a good selection of magazines.

11:00 am Explore the compact heart of Santa Fe. The **Georgia O'Keeffe Museum**, located just west of the Plaza, houses the most extensive collection of O'Keeffe paintings in the world. Two blocks east of the Plaza, the **Institute of American Indian Arts Museum** features a mix of 7,000 works by Native American artists, the widest range of contemporary Native American art in the United States.

DAY 3 — Saturday

10:00 am After a relaxed breakfast at the hotel, it's time for the *Desfile de los Niños* (Children's Pet Parade). Kids and their pets produce laughs and smiles as they wind from Cathedral Park down Paseo de Peralta, Palace Avenue, Sandoval Street and San Francisco Street back to the park. The *Fiesta* is now in full swing. Food, traditional entertainment and an arts-and-crafts market filled with authentic Southwestern creations are the major attractions until midnight.

2:00 pm Be sure to attend the wacky *Historical, Hysterical Parade*.

5:30 pm For great margaritas and a sunset, head to the **Belltower** bar on the fifth-floor terrace of the La Fonda Hotel.

7:30 pm Walk to Water Street and the **Coyote ✖ Cafe**. Known to food lovers all over the world, this star of the Santa Fe culinary scene has a modern ambience, but the food is pure Southwest. The New Mexican Black Angus rib chop is a must.

9:00 pm *For* more than 100 years, the *Gran Baile de la Fiesta* has been one of the most eagerly awaited annual events in Santa Fe. A public homage to Don Diego de Vargas and La Reina, it's noteworthy for magnificent costumes. The splendidly dressed De Vargas and La Reina, with entourage in tow, sweep through the ballroom accompanied by mariachis and a big band playing traditional Spanish tunes. If you don't know the *ranchera*, *cumbria* or *valtes*, don't worry, there's contemporary dance music as well.

11:00 pm For a lively scene and more dancing, you could go back to **El Farol**. At **Vanessie of Santa Fe**, pianist Doug Montgomery is a local favorite. This nightspot is also a great place to reflect on the mix of dancing in the street, history and natural beauty that makes *Fiesta de Santa Fe* so spectacular.

■

More Time, More Choices

Another restaurant high on everyone's list is **Santacafe**, where fusion cuisine is served in a romantic setting. **Pranzo Italian Grill** features northern Italian dishes in an elegant, contemporary setting. Ask for a table on the open-air roof garden. Elegant, peaceful **Wall Street West** offers continental contemporary dishes such as lemongrass and molasses roast chicken breast and beef tenderloin in merlot sauce. **Tulips'** Grand Marnier chocolate mousse tulip won Taste of Santa Fe's best dessert. The rest of the menu is enticing as well.

For an amazing day trip, wander through the ancient cliff dwellings and kivas at **Bandelier National Monument** on the Jemez Mountain Trail. You can climb ladders into these nearly 1,000-year-old Anasazi pueblos and get an insider's view of life in this ancient civilization.

In striking contrast is the nearby Los Alamos National Laboratory, the home of the Manhattan Project, where the atomic bomb was developed. Today, you can visit its **Bradbury Science Museum** for exhibits describing the history of the laboratory, as well as demonstrations of its research activities.

Farther north, past Abiquiu on Highway 84, you can get a close-up look at the majestic, otherworldly natural beauty of northern New Mexico. Take a forty-five-minute hike from Ghost Ranch, where Georgia O'Keeffe spent much of her painting life, to the top of Chimney Rock.

Accommodations

The **Inn of the Anasazi** is a gem in the heart of Santa Fe. It's attractive, environmentally sensitive and comfortable, and it provides a contemporary Santa Fe feel. For a taste of Old Santa Fe with modern amenities, **La Fonda Hotel** is the place to hang your hat. Located on the Plaza, this classic hostelry features adobe architecture, hand-carved furniture, fireplaces and balconies. With its award-winning Pueblo architecture and wonderful views, the **Inn at Loretto** is another excellent choice. The **Inn of the Governors** is a small and intimate hotel with kiva fireplaces in the garden patio.

Event & Ticket Info

Fiesta de Santa Fe: Most activities are free. For information, contact the *Santa Fe CVB* (800-777-2489).

Grand Baile de Fiesta (Sweeney Convention Center, 201 W. Marcy St.): Order tickets ($15) well in advance from *the Santa Fe Fiesta Council* (505-988-7575).

Hotels	Phone	Address	Price	Fax	Rooms/Best
Inn at Loretto	505-988-5531 800-727-5531	211 Old Santa Fe Trail	$$$	505-984-7988	141/Mountain, river vw
Inn of the Anasazi	505-988-3030 800-688-8100	113 Washington Ave.	$$$	505-988-3277	59/Deluxe
Inn of the Governors	505-982-4333 800-234-4534	101 W. Alameda St.	$$$	505-989-9149	100/City vw
La Fonda Hotel	505-982-5511 800-523-5002	100 E. San Francisco	$$$	505-988-2952	163/Loretto Chapel vw

Restaurants	Day	Phone	Address	Price	Rec	Food
Anasazi	1	505-988-3030	see Inn of the Anasazi	$$$	DBL	Asian-influenced Southwestern
Cafe Pasqual's	1	505-983-9340	121 Don Gaspar	$$	B/LD	Southwestern
Coyote Cafe	3	505-983-1615	132 W. Water St.	$$$$	D	Modern Southwestern
El Farol	1	505-983-9912	808 Canyon Rd.	$	L/D	Spanish, Southwestern
Geronimo	2	505-982-1500	724 Canyon Rd.	$$$	D/L	New American
Pranzo Italian Grill	A	505-984-2645	540 Montezuma Ave.	$$	LD	Italian
Santa Fe Baking Co.	2	505-988-4292	54 W. Cordova Rd.	$	B/L	American
Santacafe	A	505-984-1788	231 Washington St.	$$$	LD	New American
Tulips	A	505-989-7340	222 N. Guadalupe	$$$	D	Southwestern
Wall Street West	A	505-988-2933	919 W. Alameda	$$$	LD	Continental contemporary

Nightlife	Day	Phone	Address	Cover	Rec*	Music
Bar B	1	505-982-8999	331 Sandoval St.	$	MP	Jazz, rock, hip hop
Belltower	3	505-982-5511	see La Fonda Hotel	None	R	
El Farol	3	505-983-9912	see El Farol Restaurant	$	MP(F)	Salsa, flamenco, R&B, rock
Paramount Nightclub	1	505-982-8999	331 Sandoval St.	$	MP(F)	Varies
Vanessie of Santa Fe	3	505-982-9966	434 W. San Francisco St.	None	M(F)	Jazz, pop, classical

* M=Live music; P=Dancing (Party); R=Bar only; S=Show; (F)=Food served. For further explanation of codes, page 12.

Sights & Attractions	Day	Phone	Address	Entry Fee
Bandelier National Monument	A	505-672-0343	Hwy. 4, 8 miles west of White Ranch	$
Bradbury Science Museum	A	505-667-4444	Central and 15th sts.	None
Georgia O'Keeffe Museum	2	505-995-0785	217 Johnson St.	$
Institute of American Indian Arts Museum	2	505-983-8900	108 Cathedral Pl.	$
Museum of International Folk Art	1	505-476-1200	706 Camino Lejo	$
Palace of the Governors	2	505-476-5060	100 W. Palace St.	$

Santa Fe CVB	800-777-2489	201 W. Marcy St.

 NYC -2   Santa Fe (SAF) <30 min./$20
Albuquerque (ABQ) <60 min./$30   Yes   Map Code: A29

New Mexico

New Year's Eve New York

Key Month: Dec   Ratings: Event ★ ★ ★ ☆ ☆   City ★ ★ ★ ★ ★   Origin: 1904   Attendance: 500,000

Year-round party warriors may say that New Year's Eve is for amateurs. Not in New York. And definitely not in Times Square. With the best of almost everything, anywhere, it's not surprising that New York hosts the biggest and most extravagant December 31 celebration on the planet.

If you're ready to give up your seat on the couch come the end of the year, head for Times Square for the dropping of the famous ball (300 million will view the annual ritual on television). Don't want to stand in the cold with 500,000 of your closest and newest friends? Reserve a spot offering glamour, comfort and a view at one of several hotels and restaurants overlooking Times Square. Watch as the famous rhinestone ball begins its descent at 11:59 p.m., accompanied by one-and-a-half tons of fluffy, floating confetti.

Ever since *The New York Times*, namesake of the square, sponsored the first ball lowering in 1907, the celebration has been a worldwide symbol of **New Year's Eve**. Now organized by the Times Square Business Improvement District, the festival includes strobe lights, pyrotechnics and speeches, as well as the famous countdown to the new year and the booming of fireworks going off in nearby Central Park. While the Times Square festivities are revving up, several other parties are already in full swing around the city, including **First Night**, a spinoff of the party that originated in Boston featuring various events throughout the day and evening.

Gear up for the big night by exploring Manhattan Island, which stretches a narrow 22.7 miles between the East River and Hudson Bay, provides the backdrop for countless Hollywood movies and is one of the most popular travel destinations in the world. Contrary to popular opinion, New York City sometimes does sleep, but it does so only grudgingly, and never before popping a few corks to toast the new year.

On the Calendar

Official Event Dates
December 31

Best 3 Days To Be There
New Year's Eve day plus two days before. January 1 is for resting in preparation for another year of fun.

☾ 30°/41° (-1°/5°)

128   For links to most current web sites for cities and events, go to www.funrises.com

Day-by-Day Plan

DAY 1 — December 29th

9:00 am Start your visit to New York the way the ancestors of one out of four living Americans did—at **Ellis Island Museum**. Cab to Battery Park at the tip of Manhattan and take the ferry. First stop is the **Statue of Liberty**. Unless you plan to climb the 354 steps for the twenty-two-story view, it'll be a short visit to the ground-level museum before catching the ferry to Ellis Island. In ninety minutes the museum tour presents not only the history, but the fear, exhilaration and hope associated with immigrating to the United States.

1:00 pm Hail one of the 12,000 new and rejuvenated cabs that fill the city streets, and head to Union Square. Check out Green Market days (Monday, Wednesday, Friday and Saturday) before settling in for lunch at the **Union Square Cafe**, one of the most popular restaurants in New York.

3:00 pm Go to the **United Nations Headquarters** for a glimpse of the inner workings of the Security Council and General Assembly.

7:30 pm A new and happening **Jimmy's Downtown** provides Latin cuisine to accompany its buzz. Hang out and enjoy the bar scene before or after dinner. Both the bar and restaurant of **44** are still hot.

11:00 pm Make a foray to **5757 Bar**, the classiest bar in New York. Across the street is a longtime hot spot **Au Bar**, a semiprivate club with a "guest list."

Midnight Kick your heels over to **China Club** for house music and dancing. It's a loud, crowded place with lots of good-looking players. Proceed to **The Supper Club** for swing until your feet hurt—or 4 a.m., whichever comes first.

DAY 2 — December 30th

10:00 am Head for the **American Museum of Natural History**, which displays more than 500,000 artifacts. Must-sees include the History of Man exhibit.

12:30 pm In the middle of the winter wonderland at Rockefeller Center is an eight-story-high Christmas tree that stands alongside an ice rink with skaters of all ages happily gliding around. The **Sea Grill** sits next to the ice and gives diners a fabulous view of the action. After lunch—the fresh fish is great—rent a pair of skates.

2:30 pm Stroll down Fifth Avenue—'tis the season for decorations in the shop windows. Explore St. Patrick's Cathedral along the way.

4:30 pm Stop for full-service tea at the elegant **New York Palace**.

7:15 pm For nighttime entertainment, pick a Broadway play or choose from offerings at Lincoln Center, including **New York City Ballet**'s *The Nutcracker* (for more on *The Nutcracker*, see page 225). Going to New York and not seeing a live performance is like going to Alaska and not seeing snow.

10:00 pm Have a post-theater dinner at **Asia de Cuba**. This hot restaurant elevates unique Cuban-Chinese cuisine to a sophisticated level. Make a drink foray to the ultrachic **Morgans Bar**, also in the Morgans hotel.

12:30 am Head to the **Tunnel** disco for dancing before calling it a night.

DAY 3 — December 31st

9:30 am Head to Greenwich Village or farther south to SoHo. Both neighborhoods provide wonderful walking opportunities. Or go to the **Empire State Building**, the tallest building in the world when King Kong scaled it in 1933. The eighty-sixth floor observation deck has an unobstructed view of Central Park.

11:30 am Visit the **Carnegie Deli** for scrambled eggs with lox and an onion bagel, or mile-high corned-beef sandwiches.

1:00 pm Get on your high horse—with a buggy attached. Pick from the lineup of horse-and-buggy duos at the south end of Central Park.

2:00 pm The **Metropolitan Museum of Art** is practically a city in itself. Choose from ancient Egypt, the twentieth-century sculpture court or one of many other fascinating exhibit areas.

Day-by-Day Plan

DAY 3 — December 31st (cont.)

4:30 pm ✖ Buy a knish or a pretzel with mustard from one of the street carts in front of the museum. Walk down Madison Avenue, which in recent years has begun rivaling Fifth Avenue for shopping.

7:00 pm It's *New Year's Eve*! The party begins at Times Square. Maneuver past the crowds that started assembling in the late afternoon.

7:30 pm Head to the Renaissance Hotel for a spectacular party at *Foley's Fish House*, the upscale place to be. It's high above the crowds and has an awesome, unobstructed view of the *New Year's Eve* ball drop. Hang out at the bar before dining on very fresh fish. With room for only eighty folks, this classy, exclusive party is the gala of a lifetime. Dance to a jazz band and wait for the ball to drop. If you'd rather feel closer to the street-party atmosphere, trade the perfect view for more excitement at the nearby *Marriott Marquis*. It offers a bigger and rowdier party in two areas of the hotel. The views of Times Square are not as good, but you still get great city views and a feel of the energy circulating below.

11:45 pm Watch as the excitement mounts in the square, and the mayor gets ready to drop the ball with practice count-downs and cheering from the parka-covered crowd. At 11:59 p.m., the ball begins its descent.

Midnight The glittering ball falls toward the heart of Times Square, 3,000 pounds of confetti float down on the heads of the party-goers below, the crowd erupts in cheers and fireworks fill the skies.

12:30 am The square clears out soon after the year commences, but there's no reason you have to go home yet. Unless, of course, you're planning to catch a quick flight to the Bahamas for Junkanoo, an event that begins the year with a 2 a.m. party. Whenever you do get to bed, dream about all the fun the new year will bring!

■

More Time, More Choices

The distinction between restaurant and club is never so blurred as it is in New York. *Blue Water Grill* on Union Square prepares fish as well as anyone in New York. And you can enjoy it while listening to jazz in their down-stairs club. *Guastavino's Downstairs* is a Terrance Conran creation—new American fare in beautiful wide-open restaurant. The Hudson Cafeteria, with communal seating and a comfort food menu, is just the warm-up for the hotel's bar scene. Buddha-dominated *Tao* attracts a stylishly dressed younger crowd to share Chinese dishes while watching multi-bar scenes unfold. *Orsay's* re-creation of a brasserie has *très* chic people traveling north of city center. *Ferrier Bistro* has a small bar and restaurant, but it has the best recorded music in the city, along with good French-bistro fare. For rooftop dining with a retractable glass roof, try *AZ* for Asian-influenced American cuisine.

Le Zinc has a lively bar scene along with a very good restaurant. In SoHo, the place to be is *Boom*, a restaurant with an active bar scene. Or try the *Mercer Kitchen*. Or, party with the stars at *Suite 16*. The *Frick Collection* houses world-class European masterpiece portraits, antique furniture and other valuable items.

The *Solomon R. Guggenheim Museum* offers fantastic shows and art collections in a six-story spiral rotunda.

Accommodations

A stroll through the *Royalton* hotel's block-long luxury-liner lobby prepares you for a three-day cruise through the greatest city on earth. The location is perfect, as is the service. *Morgans* hotel delivers modern comfort. Called the handsomest hotel in New York, it's located in Midtown Manhattan. The *Four Seasons Hotel* is about as expensive as you can get, but it's elegant, chic and the hotel of choice for many celebrities. The *W New York* is classic W— small rooms, well appointed. But few hotels in the world have such an active lobby bar scene.

Event & Ticket Info

New Year's Eve Times Square (Times Square, Broadway at 47th Street): For information, contact *Times Square Business Improvement District* (212-768-1560).

Foley's Fish House (Renaissance New York Hotel, 714 Seventh Ave.): Most recent information lists tickets at $575 per person. *Foley's Fish House* (212-765-5027).

New York Marriot Marquis (1535 Broadway): Most recent information lists *The View Lounge Party* at $799 per couple and *The Party Within the Party* at $699 per couple. Contact the *New York Marriot Marquis* (212-704-8747).

First Night: First Night Hotline (212-922-9393).

Hotels	Phone	Address	Price	Fax	Rooms/Best
The Four Seasons Hotel	212-758-5700 800-332-3442	E. 57th St.	$$$$+	212-758-5711	368/Central Park vw
Morgans	212-686-0300 800-334-3408	237 Madison Ave.	$$$$	212-779-8352	113/Madison Ave. vw
Royalton	212-869-4400 800-635-9013	44 W. 44th St.	$$$$	212-575-0012	168/Suites w/Japanese circular tubs
W New York	212-755-1200 877-946-8357	541 Lexington Avenue	$$	212-319-8344	Spectacular rm w/city vw

Restaurants	Day	Phone	Address	Price	Rec	Food
44	1	212-944-8844	44 W. 44th St.	$$$$	D/BL	American, continental
Asia de Cuba	2	212-726-7755	237 Madison Ave.	$$$	D/L	Latin, Asian fusion
AZ	A	212-691-8888	21 W. 17th St.	$$$	LD	Asian-American
Blue Water Grill	A	212-675-9500	31 Union Sq. W.	$$$	D/L	Seafood
Boom	A	212-431-3663	152 Spring St.	$$	LD	Italian
Carnegie Deli	3	212-757-2245	854 Seventh Ave.	$$	B/LD	Deli
Ferrier Bistro	A	212-772-9000	29 E. 65th St.	$$$	LD	French
Guastavino's Downstairs	A	212-980-2455	409 E. 59th St.	$$$	D/L	New American
Hudson Cafeteria	A	212-554-6000	356 W. 58th St.	$$$	D/L	American
Jimmy's Downtown	1	212-486-6400	400 E. 57th St.	$$$	D	Latin
Le Zinc	A	212-513-0001	139 Duane St.	$$	BLD	French
Mercer Kitchen	A	212-966-5454	99 Prince St.	$$$	BLD	American
New York Palace	2	212-888-7000	455 Madison Ave.	$$	T	Finger sandwiches
Orsay	A	212-517-6400	1057 Lexington Ave.	$$$	D	French
Sea Grill	2	212-332-7610	19 W. 49th St.	$$$	L/D	Seafood
Tao	A	212-888-2288	42 E. 58th St.	$$	D	Asian
Union Square Cafe	1	212-243-4020	21 E. 16th St.	$$$$+	L/D	American

Nightlife	Day	Phone	Address	Cover	Rec*	Music
5757 Bar	1	212-754-9494	57 E. 57th St.	None	R(F)	
Au Bar	1	212-308-9455	41 E. 58th St.	$	P(F)	Varies
China Club	1	212-398-3800	268 W. 47th St.	$$	MP	Rock
Morgans Bar	2	212-726-7600	see Morgans hotel	None	R(F)	
New York City Ballet	2	212-870-5570	20 Lincoln Center	$$$$+	S	
Suite 16	A	212-627-1680	127 8th Ave.	$	P	Varies
The Supper Club	1	212-921-1940	240 W. 47th St.	$$$	MP(F)	Swing
Tunnel	2	212-695-4682	220 Twelfth Ave.	$$$	P	Contemporary

* M=Live music; P=Dancing (Party); R=Bar only; S=Show; (F)=Food served. For further explanation of codes, page 12.

Sights & Attractions	Day	Phone	Address	Entry Fee
American Museum of Natural History	2	212-769-5100	Central Park W at W. 79th St.	$
Ellis Island Museum	1	212-363-3200	Ellis Island	$
Empire State Building	3	212-736-3100	350 Sixth Ave.	$
Frick Collection	A	212-288-0700	1 E. 70th St.	$
Metropolitan Museum of Art	3	212-535-7710	Fifth Ave. at 82nd St.	$
Solomon R. Guggenheim Museum	A	212-423-3500	1071 Fifth Ave.	$$
Statue of Liberty	1	212-363-3200	Liberty Island	$
United Nations Headquarters	1	212-963-7713	First Ave. betwn 42nd and 48th sts.	$

New York City CVB	212-484-1222	810 Seventh Ave.

 NYC   John F. Kennedy (JFK) <60 min./$40
LaGuardia(LGA) <30 min./$30   No   Map Code: A30

New York

Oktoberfest-Zinzinnati

Cincinnati

Key Month: Sep   Ratings: Event ★★☆☆☆   ⓟ   City ★★★☆☆   Origin: 1976   Attendance: 500,000

Okay, so the original Oktoberfest celebration in Munich, Germany, is a few million liters of beer and a couple thousand roasted pork knuckles larger than the United States' largest Oktoberfest in, that's right, Cincinnati, Ohio. But you can bet that Munich's has never featured 30,000 revelers blowing on free, neon-colored kazoos. No doubt there will be more world records to be had and many more beer steins to be emptied at next year's pinnacle of Bavarian-American civic pride—***Oktoberfest-Zinzinnati***.

This weekend-long, free-admission blitzkrieg has hit Cincinnati every September since 1976. Originally a small block party honoring the city's proud German heritage, the festival has expanded to several blocks of Fifth Street (from Race Street to Broadway) and attracts about half a million people annually. Highlights include hours of entertainment from ensembles with names such as The Pete Wagner Schnapps Band and the Donauschwaben Youth Dancers. There's also the world's largest kazoo band and chicken dance to partake in. Enjoy all the ale, accordion and good times you can stomach in forty-eight hours—and stretch it out by attending Cincinnati's famous Gemuetlichkeit Games the week before Oktoberfest (with big-league contests such as "Sprint for the Stein" and "Beer Barrel Rolling"). Two weekends before that is Cincinnati's pyrotechnic Riverfest.

Cincinnati is a very pretty and friendly place, with its gorgeous skyline and scenic Ohio River border. It claims to offer more award-winning restaurants per capita than any other U.S. city, with abundant ethnic cuisine and local specialties such as hearty German fare and the ubiquitous Cincinnati-style chili. Downtown entertainment districts such as Backstage, Over-the-Rhine and nearby Mount Adams provide ample entertainment options, as does the city's armada of nightclubs right on the river and nearby floating casinos (in Indiana).

You may be surprised when you fly to Cincinnati—and land in Kentucky. The Ohio city shares plenty with its southern neighbor, including an airport. It's also headquarters to Proctor & Gamble, and a reputedly conservative place most of the year. But that just means the locals really let their hair down when the kazoos come out to play in September.

On the Calendar

Official Event Dates
Third full weekend in September

Best 3 Days To Be There
Friday-Sunday

Other Times To Go
Riverfest (513-352-4000), a more family-oriented event, is great for fireworks and picnic gathering, usually held the day before Labor Day (first Monday in September).

�☽ 57°/80° (14°/27°)

Ohio

DAY 1 Friday

9:00 am Walk through town to **Aroma** for ❌ freshly baked pastries, coffees, espressos and cold drinks.

10:00 am Around the corner from the hotel stands the Tyler-Davidson Fountain. Its splendor and starring role in the opening credits of *WKRP in Cincinnati* have made it one of the most photographed spots in the city. Take a few steps and grab an elevator forty-eight floors to the observation deck of **Carew Tower**, downtown's tallest building. You'll get panoramic views of the Ohio River and surrounding valleys in Ohio, Indiana and Kentucky.

11:30 am Wander east along Fifth Street and get acquainted with the five blocks between Fountain Square and P&G's twin towers that will soon be blooming with five *Oktoberfest* stages and more than forty food vendors.

Noon You'll want to be at Fountain Square for the official "Tapping of the Keg," *Oktoberfest*'s opening ceremony performed by the Cincinnati mayor. Then head around the corner to The Atrium Building, take the Skywalk over the highway, past Cinergy Field, and down to the cobbled wharf at Public Landing—about a fifteen-minute walk. There's a great view of the Roebling Suspension Bridge, a prototype of its world-famous descendent in Brooklyn built over a century ago. Follow the Riverwalk east, along the Serpentine Wall, and into Bicentennial Commons at Sawyer Point for excellent people watching with a view.

1:00 pm At the end of the park, the ❌ **Montgomery Inn Boathouse** overlooks the river. Roll up your sleeves and dig into some of the best ribs in the world (according to experts such as Bob Hope and Johnny Bench).

3:00 pm A scenic plan for Friday afternoon is a trip to Eden Park. It's filled with lakes, fountains, walkways and gardens, and is home to the renowned **Cincinnati Art Museum**, which displays masterpieces and art objects spanning thousands of years.

6:00 pm Close by is the so-called Greenwich Village of Cincinnati, Mount Adams. Stop by the Immaculata Church for a terrific view of the Ohio river, before having dinner at a view table at the first-class ❌ **Celestial Restaurant**.

9:00 pm For after-dinner drinks and live music each weekend night, there's **Havana Martini Club** across the street from Maisonette.

DAY 2 Saturday

9:00 am Enjoy exceptional service and cui-❌ sine with Victorian ambience at **The Palace** in the Cincinnatian Hotel.

10:00 am Tour the old German neighborhood, Over-the-Rhine. It's said to have the country's largest collection of nineteenth-century Italianate buildings. They're now filled with antique and art galleries, coffeehouses and clubs.

11:30 am Drive to the **Taft Museum of Art** for a look at its fantastic collection of European and American art. It's housed in a mansion once occupied by relatives of Cincinnati native William Howard Taft.

1:30 pm At **Skyline Chili**, try a Cincinnati ❌ favorite, a three-way. No, it has nothing to do with massage oils and velvet robes: It's spaghetti topped with chili and cheese.

2:30 pm Head back to Fifth Street, grab a free kazoo and prepare to shake your tailfeathers at the one *Oktoberfest* event you'll definitely be telling your grandchildren about. The world's largest chicken dance and kazoo band begins at 4 p.m. at Fountain Square, led by the celebrity du jour. If there's one thing you don't want to miss, it's this.

6:00 pm **Jeff Ruby's** steakhouse is a 1940s-❌ style fixture with reputedly the best steak between New York and Chicago.

8:00 pm Grab your polka shoes and beer cozy, *Oktoberfest*'s now in high gear. Wander up and down Fifth Street's temporary Little Bavaria, sample the goods and absorb all the music, dance and guzzling. The headline act takes center stage at Fountain Square at eight o'clock.

11:30 pm End up at The Waterfront, the hippest upscale restaurant-and-nightclub complex in the area. Have drinks at **Las Brisas** and dance at **Rumba**. Or cap it off at **Neon's on 12th**, a favorite blues-cigar bar in the Over-the-Rhine district with an outdoor garden, live entertainment and shuffleboard.

DAY 3 Sunday

11:00 am Have Sunday brunch in the Westin
❌ Hotel's gorgeous **Albee**, overlooking Fountain Square. Stroll over to the riverfront which should be hopping with the usual Sunday activities—boats filling the docks, people hanging out on picnic blankets, tossing Frisbees, playing volleyball and noshing on strudel from just up the street.

1:30 pm Walk over the 352-yard Roebling Suspension Bridge at the bottom of Walnut Street. On the Kentucky side, continue about ten minutes southwest to the charming, tree- and antique shop-lined nineteenth-century German village of MainStrasse in Covington. Start at the **Cathedral Basilica of the Assumption**, an example of Gothic design, with trappings that include the world's largest stained-glass window. Once you've had your fill of flying buttresses, explore the area's streets, which buzz with art and entertainment for the weekend.

4:00 pm Take a taxi or fifty-cent shuttle ride back to Cincinnati and visit **Graeter's Confectionery**, the oldest surviving ice-cream manufacturer in America. Try to divine the "secret, Old World creaming methods" that make their scoops so rich and smooth.

6:00 pm If you aren't yet *Oktoberfest*ed out, there's still a bratwurst or two with your name on it, plus the Sunday headliner takes the stage at 6:30 p.m. Otherwise,
❌ catch a **BB Riverboat** cruise (boards in Covington) on an authentic Mark Twain-era stern-wheeler. Enjoy dinner as the big paddle wheel turns and the sun sets.

10:00 pm Try not to leave Cincinnati without having a drink (preferably served by veteran bartender Walter Brown) at **Blind Lemon**. The tiny, stone-walled bar in Mount Adams is an institution (as is Walter). It remains one of the city's most colorful, intimate spots with great music.

More Time, More Choices

Take in some jazz at Celestial's **Incline Lounge**, or settle into the outdoor patio at **Mount Adams Pavilion** for river views and local bands.

Cincinnati prides itself on its dining options. For the best potato pancakes in town and other hearty breakfast/deli fare, head up Main Street to **Izzy's**. Trendy downtown restaurants include **Redfish Looziana Roadhouse and Seafood Kitchen** for seafood and Cajun specialties. Or splurge at **Maisonette**, the only restaurant in America to retain a top-star rating for more than thirty-five years. For surf and turf, try **South Beach Grill at the Waterfront**, a hot spot for sports stars and other celebrities.

■

Accommodations

The Cincinnatian Hotel is the lodging of choice for visiting dignitaries, celebrities and presidents. Luxurious amenities give this landmark regal splendor—from the French second-empire exterior to the eight-story atrium rising above a magnificent walnut-and-marble staircase. Another option is the **Omni Netherland Plaza**, an art-deco masterpiece with pierced nickel-silver wall sconces and a spectacular sea-horse fountain. **The Westin Hotel** offers deluxe rooms overlooking *Oktoberfest* and Fountain Square.

Event & Ticket Info

Oktoberfest-Zinzinnati (Five blocks of Fifth Street, downtown): Free admission. For more information contact *Cincinnati Visitors Bureau* (800-246-2987).

The Hot Sheet

Hotels	Phone	Address	Price	Fax	Rooms/Best
The Cincinnatian Hotel	513-381-3000 800-942-9000	601 Vine St.	$$$	513-651-0256	148/Atrium vw
Omni Netherland Plaza	513-421-9100 800-843-6664	35 W. 5th St.	$$	513-421-4291	619/Carew Tower vw
The Westin Hotel	513-621-7700 800-937-8461	21 E. 5th St.	$$$	513-852-5670	448/Fountain Sq vw

Restaurants	Day	Phone	Address	Price	Rec	Food
Aroma	1	513-352-0555	39 E. 7th. St.	$	BT	Pastries
The Albee	3	513-852-2740	see the Westin Hotel	$$	BLD	American
BB Riverboat	3	859-261-8500	1 Madison Ave.	$$$$	DL	American
Celestial Restaurant	1	513-241-4455	1071 Celestial St.	$$$$	D	French, continental
Graeter's Confectionery	3	513-381-0653	41 E. 4th St.	$	T/BL	Ice cream
Izzy's	A	513-241-6246	610 Main St.	$	B/LD	American/Deli
Jeff Ruby's	2	513-784-1200	700 Walnut St.	$$$	D	American/Steak
Maisonette	A	513-721-2260	114 E. 6th St.	$$$$	LD	French
Montgomery Inn Boathouse	1	513-721-7427	925 Eastern Ave.	$$$	L/D	Ribs
The Palace	2	513-381-3000	see The Cincinnatian Hotel	$$	BLD	American
Redfish Looziana Roadhouse and Seafood Kitchen	A	513-929-4700	700 Race St.	$$	LD	Cajun, creole
Skyline Chili	2	513-241-4848	254 E. 4th St.	$	LD	Chili
South Beach Grill at the Waterfront	A	859-581-1414	14 Pete Rose Pier	$$$	D	American

Nightlife	Day	Phone	Address	Cover	Rec*	Music
Blind Lemon	3	513-241-3885	936 Hatch St.	None	M	Acoustic folk, jazz
Havana Martini Club	1	513-651-2800	580 Walnut St.	$	M	Jazz, blues
Incline Lounge	A	513-241-4455	1071 Celestial St.	None	MP	Jazz, swing
Las Brisas	2	859-581-1414	14 Pete Rose Pier	$	MP	Top 40
Mount Adams Pavilion	A	513-744-9200	949 Pavilion St.	$	MP	Rock, alternative
Neon's on 12th	2	513-721-2919	208 E. 12th St.	$	M	Blues, R&B
Rumba	2	859-581-1414	14 Pete Rose Pier	$	P	Rock, hip hop, Top 40

*M=Live music; P=Dancing (Party); R=Bar only; S=Show; (F)=Food served. For further explanation of codes, page 12.

Sights & Attractions	Day	Phone	Address	Entry Fee
Carew Tower	1	513-241-3888	441 Vine St.	$
Cathedral Basilica of the Assumption	3	859-431-2060	1140 Madison Ave.	None
Cincinnati Art Museum	1	513-721-5204	953 Eden Park Dr.	$
Taft Museum of Art	2	513-241-0343	316 Pike St.	$

Greater Cincinnati CVB	513-621-2142	300 W. 6th St.

Cincinnati area code: 513　　Northern Kentucky area code: 859

Ohio

 NYC　 Cincinnati/Northern Kentucky (CVG) <30 min./$25　 Yes　Map Code: A31

Fourth of July

Sunoco Welcome America

Key Month: Jul   Ratings: Event ★ ★ ★ ☆ ☆   **P**   City ★ ★ ★ ★ ☆   Origin: 1993   Attendance: 1,000,000

Ever since the Founding Fathers converged on Philadelphia in 1776 to put their John Hancocks on the Declaration of Independence, Philadelphians have made certain their *Fourth of July* soiree is the best in the country. Celebrating America's birthday in America's birthplace, more than two million revelers flock to Philly's green lawns and riverside parks for a series of food fests, parades, outdoor concert and fireworks shows that paint the city's summer nights in red, white and blue.

Philly's well-preserved historic setting makes it the perfect place for celebrating the nation's birth. About forty free events are scheduled between the end of June and the *Fourth of July*. Top names in popular music give free outdoor concerts and, on opening night, fireworks light the sky over Penn's Landing on the Delaware River. Not bad for opening acts, but the main event comes on *Independence Day*, when the Benjamin Franklin Parkway is invaded by an army of all-American floats. Another outdoor concert warms up the crowd for the grand fireworks display above the Philadelphia Museum of Art and Schuylkill River. The spectacular pyrotechnics are accompanied by patriotic songs performed by the Philly Pops.

America's fifth-largest city is best-known for cheese steaks and hoagies, but there's much more to the city than unforgettable sandwiches. In 1994, Philadelphia was voted by readers of *Condé Naste Traveler* as America's best restaurant city. The Philadelphia Orchestra enjoys a reputation that places it among the best in the world. The vast Philadelphia Museum of Art houses 2,000 years' worth of art.

And when the sun goes down, hedonists can partake of the chic new night-club scene along the banks of the Delaware River. The City of Brotherly Love has been dubbed "America's Friendliest City." Helpful natives and a treasure-trove of historic sites make Philadelphia an easy city for first-timers to explore.

Sure, taxation without representation was a good spin, but America has always been about the pursuit of happiness and the right to peaceable assembly. Find out what really fueled the American Revolution during the week when all of Philly transforms into one big historic block party.

On the Calendar

Official Event Dates:
Ten-day festival precedes or overlaps the Fourth of July

Best 3 Days To Be There
July 2-4 or July 3-5, depending on event schedule.
July 3 and 4 are a must.

☾ 67°/87° (19°/31°)

Pennsylvania

Day-by-Day Plan

DAY 1 — July 2

10:30 am A walk through Philadelphia's city center will take you to **Reading Terminal Market**, housed in the old Reading Railroad (do not pass go, do not collect $200) station. Restaurants and food stalls serve everything from Chinese to soul food to Pennsylvania Dutch specialties.

Noon Have **Rick's Philly Steaks** grill you a ❌ cheese steak. Before leaving the market try one of the city's famous soft pretzels.

1:00 pm Walk to the **Rodin Museum**, which houses the largest collection of the master's sculptures outside France. The nearby **Philadelphia Museum of Art** follows with one of America's largest art collections. European masters are featured alongside a Hindu temple, twelfth-century French cloister and Japanese teahouse.

7:30 pm You've had time to rest up for a night on the town. Start with a drink at the forty-foot mahogany bar inside ❌ **Circa**—located in an impressive 100-year-old building—then enjoy creative versions of classic American cuisine. After dinner hours, Circa turns into a dance club frequented by attractive young professionals.

10:00 pm If you'd prefer live music, cab to **Warmdaddy's for Blues**, a New Orleans-style blues club that draws a prosperous clientele for big-name performers.

12:30 am For some late-night dancing, try the hip **Soma**, which attracts an urban crowd.

DAY 2 — July 3

10:00 am After breakfast at the **Down Home** ❌ **Diner** in the Reading Terminal Market, walk to the **Franklin Institute Science Museum**. It's crammed with interactive science exhibits, highlighted by the famed Franklin Institute heart. Wander into blood vessels large enough to accommodate a tall man and hear the deafening thud of a beating heart.

Noon Try the crab cakes at nearby **Bridgid's**, ❌ a sophisticated eatery serving international cuisine. Or order to-go at **Ben's Garden Cafe**, the institute's cafeteria, and picnic on the lawns of nearby Fairmount Park.

1:30 pm Stroll through the Philadelphia Museum's azalea gardens to picturesque **Boat House Row**, a series of Victorian mansions along the Schuylkill River. Then walk through **Fairmount Park**, the world's largest landscaped city park, measuring some 8,900 acres. Begin at Lemon Hill, an elegant mansion noted for its oval-shaped rooms.

4:30 pm Fortify yourself (it will be a while before dinner) amid Old World elegance at the **Rittenhouse Hotel**. This charming establishment is Philly's premier spot for high tea.

7:30 pm From your hotel, walk or cab to **Penn's Landing** for the free, outdoor pop *concert*. You can probably snag an open spot along the retaining wall to the left of the stage, which beats showing up at 5 p.m. to ensure a seat. The concert is followed by fantastic *fireworks* over the Delaware River.

10:15 pm When the pyrotechnics are over, ❌ head to the trendy **Rock Lobster**. This lively outdoor riverside restaurant serves steak and shellfish dishes amid a festive but casual atmosphere.

Midnight Nearby, **Katmandu**, Philly's best summertime outdoor nightclub, is already jammed with partiers dancing to live and recorded music. If you prefer an indoor club, try **Egypt** or **The Eighth Floor**, or squeeze in all three on your way to bed.

DAY 3 — July 4

9:00 am Have breakfast in the **Azalea Room** ❌ of the Omni Hotel as you look out onto the Second Bank of the United States, a beautiful Greek Revival building.

DAY 3 — July 4 (cont.)

10:00 am Stroll along with performers in eighteenth-century costumes who set the stage for a memorable birthday. In front of Independence Hall, the Liberty Medal ceremony includes stirring speeches by award recipients. Past winners have included Nelson Mandela, Yitzak Rabin and Ted Turner.

11:00 am If you don't choose to rub elbows with Philadelphia's political and business elite at the Philadelphia Liberty Medal Luncheon, stick around for "Ben Franklin's Greatest Hits," a musical-comedy skit that recounts the major events in Franklin's life. The show is followed by a mass exodus to the Liberty Bell, where descendants of signers of the Declaration of Independence get to ring the revered artifact.

12:30 pm Nearby, **City Tavern**, an eighteenth-century eatery with restored Revolutionary charms, has a quaint dining room decorated with period furniture. The costumed staff serves delicious American culinary classics and unusual ales.

2:00 pm Explore the historic district and Society Hill from a horse-drawn carriage—while a local at the reins gives his salty take on Revolutionary history. Don't miss **Independence Hall**, where the Declaration of Independence was signed; Christ Church, where many of the Founding Fathers prayed for liberty; the elegant First Bank of the United States, America's first major building in the Greek Revival style; and Carpenters' Hall, where the First Continental Congress convened in 1774. Another interesting stop is Franklin Court, an open-air, skeletal version of Ben's home that leads to an unusual post office and museum.

6:00 pm An evening of red-white-and-blue festivities begins with a *parade* that turns onto Ben Franklin Parkway at 16th Street. The parade proceeds to the Philadelphia Museum of Art, which serves as the backdrop for a *concert* by pop superstars, along with patriotic music by the Philly Pops. Food stands are plentiful and make the most sense for dinner.

10:00 pm A spectacular *fireworks* show above the museum caps the evening. As crowds disperse, vie for space at the **Swan Lounge** in the nearby Four Seasons hotel. According to historian Benson Bobrick, most of the secret planning for the revolution took place in taverns and inns, so before taking your leave, hoist a final grog for patriotism's sake and toast every Tom, George and Benjamin in the bar.

■

More Time, More Choices

Brasserie Perrier is the more hip and lively sister of the famous **Le Bec-Fin**, which is often ranked as Philadelphia's, if not the nation's, best restaurant. **Striped Bass**, a beautiful all-seafood restaurant, is a strong challenger to the title. *Zagat* considers **Fountain Restaurant** as top-ten worldwide. It offers contemporary French-American cuisine in a setting that's simply elegant.

On bar-hopping South Street, **The Monte Carlo Living Room** encourages you to put your dancing shoes on for Top 40. For some other late-night options, **Zanzibar Blue** and **T. Rodgers** feature recorded dance music and live jazz.

Accommodations

The perfectly appointed **Omni Hotel** is located in the center of the Independence National Historical Park. The **Park Hyatt Philadelphia** is another excellent choice for a hotel. Like the Omni, it's located on Independence Park. Although its location is less appropriate for this occasion, the **Four Seasons Philadelphia** is generally recognized as the city's top hotel.

Event & Ticket Info

Fourth of July: Most activities, including the recommended concerts, are free. For more information, call *Philadelphia Visitors Center* (800-770-5883).

Philadelphia Liberty Medal Luncheon (Philadelphia Marriott, 1201 Market St.): For tickets ($150 CD) and information, contact *Greater Philadelphia First* (215-575-2200).

Hotels		Phone	Address	Price	Fax	Rooms/Best
Four Seasons Philadelphia		215-963-1500 800-332-3442	1 Logan Sq.	$$$$	215-963-9506	365/Logan Circle vw
Omni Hotel		215-925-0000 800-843-6664	401 Chestnut St.	$$$	215-925-1263	150/Vw of Independence Park
Park Hyatt Philadelphia		215-893-1776 800-233-1234	1415 Chancellor Ct.	$$$	215-732-8518	172/Stratford rms have bdrm and lr with city vw

Restaurants	Day	Phone	Address	Price	Rec	Food
Azalea Room	3	215-925-0000	see Omni Hotel	$$	B/LD	New American
Ben's Garden Cafe	2	215-448-1200	20th St. and Ben Franklin, see the Franklin Institute	$	L/B	Salad, pasta, cheese steaks
Brasserie Perrier	A	215-568-3000	1619 Walnut St.	$$$$	LD	Italian, French, w/Asian influence
Bridgid's	2	215-232-3232	726 N. 24th St.	$	L/D	International
Circa	1	215-545-6800	1518 Walnut St.	$$	D/L	New American
City Tavern	3	215-413-1443	138 S. 2nd St.	$$	L/D	Traditional fare
Down Home Diner	2	215-627-1955	12th and Arch sts., inside Reading Terminal Mkt.	$	B/LD	American, Southern
Fountain Restaurant	A	215-963-1500	Ben Franklin Pkwy and 18th St.	$$$$+	LD	Seafood
Le Bec-Fin	A	215-567-1000	1523 Walnut St.	$$$$+	D/L	Haute French
Rick's Philly Steaks	1	215-925-4320	12th and Arch sts., inside Reading Terminal Mkt.	$	L	Cheese steaks
Rittenhouse Hotel	2	215-546-9000	210 W. Rittenhouse Sq.	$$	T	High tea
Rock Lobster	2	215-627-7625	Pier 13-15, near Columbus Blvd.	$$	D/L	Steak and shellfish
Striped Bass	A	215-732-4444	1500 Walnut St.	$$$$	LD	Seafood

Nightlife	Day	Phone	Address	Cover	Rec*	Music
Egypt	2	215-922-6500	520 N. Delaware Ave.	$	P	House, hip hop, dance, disco
The Eighth Floor	2	215-922-1000	800 N. Delaware Ave.	$$	P	'70s, progressive
Katmandu	2	215-629-7400	417 N. Columbus Blvd. at Pier 25	$	MP(F)	Reggae, Top 40
The Monte Carlo Living Room	A	215-925-2220	150 South St.	$	P(F)	Top 40
Soma	1	215-873-0222	33 S. 3rd St.	None	P	Varies
Swan Lounge	3	215-963-1500	see Four Seasons hotel	None	R	
T. Rodgers	A	215-568-4406	122 S. 18th St.	None	M(F)	Blues, jazz
Warmdaddy's for Blues	1	215-627-2500	4 S. Front St.	$	M(F)	Blues
Zanzibar Blue	A	215-732-4500	200 S. Broad St.	$$	M	Jazz

* M=Live music; P=Dancing (Party); R=Bar only; S=Show; (F)=Food served. For further explanation of codes, page 12.

Sights & Attractions	Day	Phone	Address	Entry Fee
Boat House Row	2		on Schuylkill River	None
Fairmount Park	2	215-685-0000	River Dr., Belmont Ave., or Kelly Dr.	None
Franklin Institute Science Museum	2	215-448-1200	2222 N. 20th St.	$$
Independence Hall	3	215-597-8974	5th and Chestnut sts.	None
Liberty Bell	3	215-597-8974	Market St. betw. 5th and 6th Sts.	None
Penn's Landing	2	215-922-2386	Delaware River, Spring Garden St. to Pier 40	None
Philadelphia Museum of Art	1	215-763-8100	26th St. and Ben Franklin Pkwy.	$
Reading Terminal Market	1	215-922-2317	12th and Arch Sts.	None
Rodin Museum	1	215-763-8100	22nd St. and Ben Franklin Pkwy.	None

| **Philadelphia CVB** | | **800-321-9563** | **16th and John F. Kennedy Blvd.** | |

 NYC Philadelphia (PHL) <30 min./$20 No   Map Code: A32

Pennsylvania

Spoleto

Spoleto Festival USA/Piccolo Spoleto

Key Month: May/Jun Ratings: Event ★ ★ ★ ☆ ☆ **ℙ** City ★ ★ ★ ☆ ☆ Origin: 1977 Attendance: 72,000

By and large, artists are not associated with frivolity—tortured souls and unappreciated genius are the shopworn clichés—but Charleston's **Spoleto** festival explodes the notion that fine art can't be fun. The giant performing-arts festival's secret weapon is diversity. Mix poets, painters, dancers, musicians and actors in one place and everyone's creative energy tends to shine in its most brilliant light.

The result is one of the world's best interdisciplinary arts parties—neither drunken bacchanal nor hoity-toity gathering—a congenial affair where you can take in as much culture as you like against the backdrop of one of the nation's most beautiful cities. Because it's especially dedicated to young artists and contemporary effort, there's always a cutting-edge aura surrounding **Spoleto**. Established artists and critics from around the world show up to catch glimpses of new stars—more than 100 operas, concerts, plays and other performances are staged during the festival's seventeen-day run—and hobnob around town with tens of thousands of visitors sampling everything from chardonnay to sushi. Filling in the gaps around the parent gathering, **Piccolo Spoleto**, founded in 1979, is an auxiliary event showcasing the brightest talent of America's Southeast region with more than 400 performing-arts events.

On the Calendar

Official Event Dates
Begins Friday before Memorial Day (last Monday in May) and runs through two following weekends

Best 3 Days To Be There
Last weekend (Friday-Sunday). The high point of 17 days comes on the last Saturday night and Sunday finale.

☀ 61°/83° (16°/28°)

Spoleto's party scene takes its cues from the rarefied world of the city's high society, which is largely private and requires skill to penetrate. But the great thing about **Spoleto** is that you can attend a morning chamber concert, have brunch, take a nap, then move on to the next performance and meal.

When you aren't catching a show, you can soak up sunny Charleston's lush gardens, fantastic architecture, distinctive regional cuisine and irrepressible Southern charm. The city is a walker's paradise, so you're better off ditching the car and strolling through **Spoleto** venues or exploring the area's fabulous beaches. Charleston makes it easy to hop from cafe to cabaret, from performance to pool, from wet swim suit to dry martini, and most important of all, from high art to high fun.

South Carolina

Spoleto performances are generally held in mid-afternoon and evening. Piccolo Spoleto events are scattered throughout the day. The itinerary assumes you'll be attending performances each afternoon and evening.

DAY 1 — Friday

10:00 am Walk to the Visitor Information Center to catch the video **Forever Charleston**, a great introduction to the city. Narrated by locals, it's accurate, affectionate, lively and fun.

11:00 am Walk fifteen minutes to your first *Spoleto* performance. Built in 1736, The Dock Street Theatre—which is actually on Church Street— is where Charles Wadsworth, known as the festival ham, conducts an entertaining chamber-music concert. Take note of performers' names—some years ago, a young singer by the name of Jessye Norman got her stardom-bound start here.

12:30 pm On to lunch at **Slightly North of Broad**, a short walk away. The casually elegant restaurant serves contemporary low-country cuisine—examples include shrimp and grits, and grilled tuna topped with fried oysters. Head up Church Street and take note of St. Philip's Episcopal Church. Built in 1847 with its landmark steeple, it was hit hard by Union Army fire. St. Philip's is Charleston's most beautiful church, but on nearby Meeting Street, St. Michael's is the oldest. It was built in 1761.

3:00 pm Take your pick of a *Spoleto* performance: music, theater or dance.

6:30 pm Have dinner at **Carolina's**, where the Vietnamese chef mixes Asian and regional ingredients and gets terrific results. Savor excellent seafood in an attractive, shrimp-colored room.

10:30 pm After the evening performance, head to **Meritage** to listen to some jazz and blues while hitting the tapas bar.

Midnight Have a nightcap at **Club Habana**. Located above a cigar store, this bordello-style place has an excellent selection of novelty martinis, wines and after-dinner drinks, including thirteen ports, eleven Scotches, and assorted sherries, cognacs, Armagnacs and Madeiras.

1:00 am All those clichés you've heard are true: It's the hour of moonlight, magnolias and magic. Saunter down Meeting Street to the sepulchral garden of the Circular Congregational Church, across from Hibernian Hall. Established in 1696, the cemetery is the city's oldest, with sequestered nooks and crannies where lovers sneak kisses.

DAY 2 — Saturday

8:30 am Order scones, muffins and coffee at the **Bakers Cafe**.

10:00 am Walk thirty minutes to the new **South Carolina Aquarium** featuring the state's indigenous water life such as river otters, sea turtles and alligators. A site to behold is the Great Ocean tank, which holds 330,000 gallons of saltwater and a twenty-eight-foot-tall aquarium window, one of the tallest in the world.

12:30 pm At **Vickery's Bar & Grill**, indulge in big plates of food, big cocktails and the sort of low-stress atmosphere that makes GenXers and yuppies all feel at home. Make a note to come back later—the place is lively until its 2 a.m. closing.

3:00 pm Again, your afternoon should be taken up by the *Spoleto* performance of your (difficult) choice.

6:00 pm One of Charleston's popular spots, known for its lively atmosphere and great food, is **Magnolia's**. It serves New Southern cooking at its best.

8:00 pm The new *Spoleto Soirée* continues a tradition of highlighting a night to get people's juices flowing with a lively performance followed by Rose Garden dancing.

10:30 pm Have a drink at the **Roof Top at the Vendue Inn**. There's a wonderful view of the waterfront and the city's church spires.

11:30 pm Although **Club Tango's** name is a bit misleading—the music inside actually covers a range of dance genres—this new hot spot tops the list for sophisticated dancing venues in town.

Day-by-Day Plan

DAY 3 Sunday

8:30 am Take advantage of the hotel's room service for a light breakfast.

9:30 am Take a boat (located next to the aquarium) across Charleston Harbor to **Fort Sumter**, where the first shots of the Civil War were fired in 1861. Boats leave at 9:30 a.m. (also noon and 2:30 p.m.) to make the two-hour tour.

12:30 pm Back in town, have brunch at ❌ **Hominy Grill**. The chef's a Southern boy with New York credentials and an Alice Waters philosophy. Try the grilled veggie plate with a cool avocado-and-exotic-rice salad, followed by a comforting slice of buttermilk pie.

3:00 pm There's still plenty to choose from at *Spoleto*, but consider taking off the afternoon to rest up for the big evening to come.

5:30 pm Dine early at **McCrady's Tavern** for ❌ contemporary American food with a French influence. Local artists create the paintings hanging on the walls.

7:00 pm Drive or cab fourteen miles northwest on Ashley River Road (Highway 61) and spend the morning at the eighteenth-century **Middleton Place** plantation. The sixty-five acres of landscaped gardens— punctuated with butterfly lakes and gnarly oaks—are the oldest in America. Take a house tour and watch artisans demonstrating colonial crafts-making.

8:30 pm The *Spoleto Festival Finale*, with an orchestra concert and fireworks, is held on the rambling grounds of the Middleton Place plantation.

11:30 pm Sip champagne at **Club Trio**. Offer a "we shall meet again" toast to *Spoleto*. Like the best performers, Charleston and its top event always leave you wanting a little more.

■

Before

The *Spoleto Opening Weekend Celebration* includes an elegant black-tie dinner dance, brunch and a dinner in a historic home.

More Time, More Choices

For contemporary-style cooking in a happening atmosphere, try **Blossom Cafe**. If you prefer refined dining, try **Circa 1886**, which is located in a carriage house. Another choice is the **Peninsula Grill** at the Planter's Inn. Voted one of the United States' best new restaurants by *Esquire* magazine, it's a fine place for romance, juicy steaks, fresh fish and an aphrodisiac champagne-and-oyster menu. One of the city's best soul-food restaurants is **Alice's Fine Foods**.

Head to **Indigo** for some dancing to tunes ranging from '70s to contemporary. For a nightlife alternative, the **Mandalay** is a microbrewery that has live music six nights a week. The **82 Queen** is a lively meeting spot, especially around the bar.

Accommodations

For an unbeatable combination of ambience, location and comfort, check into the **Planter's Inn. Charleston Place**, a deluxe hotel, shows the city at its finest. **Mills House Hotel** is a beautifully updated historic hotel. **Westin Francis Marion** is a renovated hotel where many *Spoleto* performers stay. All four hotels are conveniently located close to the action.

Event & Ticket Info

Spoleto Festival U.S.A.: To order tickets, call *South Carolina Automated Ticketing/ SCAT* (843-216-6705). For more information, contact *Spoleto Festival U.S.A.* (843-722-2764).

Piccolo Spoleto Festival: To order tickets, call *South Carolina Automated Ticketing/SCAT* (843-216-6705). For more information, contact *Office of Cultural Affairs* (843-724-7305).

Spoleto Opening Weekend Celebration and *Spoleto Festival Finale:* For more information, contact *Spoleto Festival U.S.A. Events* (843-724-1192).

The Hot Sheet

Hotels	Phone	Address	Price	Fax	Rooms/Best
Charleston Place Orient-Express	843-722-4900 800-611-5545	205 Meeting St.	$$$$	843-722-0728	440/Garden and courtyard vw
Mills House Hotel	843-577-2400 800-874-9600	115 Meeting St.	$$	843-722-0623	214/Downtown vw
Planter's Inn	843-722-2345 800-845-7082	112 N. Market St.	$$$	843-577-2125	62/Courtyard vw
Westin Francis Marion	843-722-0600 877-756-2121	387 King St.	$$	843-723-4633	226/Downtown vw

Restaurants	Day	Phone	Address	Price	Rec	Food
Alice's Fine Foods	A	843-853-9366	468 King St.	$	LD	Soul food
Baker's Cafe	2	843-577-2694	214 King St.	$	B/L	Pastries
Blossom Cafe	A	843-722-9200	171 E. Bay St.	$$$	LD	Mediterranean
Carolina's	1	843-724-3800	10 Exchange St.	$$	D	Contemporary, Asian-influence
Circa 1886	A	843-853-7828	149 Wentworth	$$$	D	Southern
Hominy Grill	3	843-937-0930	207 Rutledge Ave.	$	L/BD	Southern
Magnolia's	2	843-577-7771	185 E. Bay St.	$$$	D/L	Southern
McCrady's Tavern	3	843-577-0025	2 Unity Alley	$$$	D	American, French influence
Peninsula Grill	A	843-723-0700	see Planter's Inn	$$$	D	Southern seafood
Slightly North of Broad	1	843-723-3424	192 E. Bay St.	$$	L/D	Regional Southern
Vickery's Bar & Grill	2	843-577-5300	15 Beaufain St.	$$	L/D	American, Cuban influence

Nightlife	Day	Phone	Address	Cover	Rec*	Music
82 Queen	A	843-723-7591	82 Queen St.	None	R(F)	
Club Habana	1	843-853-5008	177 Meeting St.	None	R	
Club Tango	2	843-577-2822	39 Hutson St.	$	SP(F)	Dance
Club Trio	3	843-965-5333	139 Calhoun St.	$	M(F)	Jazz, Latin, Funk
Indigo	A	843-577-7383	5 Faber St.	$	P	'70s, '80s, '90s
Mandalay	A	843-722-8507	275 King St.	$	MP(F)	Varies
Meritage	1	843-723-8181	235 East Bay St.	None	M(F)	Jazz, blues
Roof Top at the Vendue Inn	2	843-577-7970	23 Vendue Range	None	R(F)	

* M=Live music; P=Dancing (Party); R=Bar only; S=Show; (F)=Food served. For further explanation of codes, page 12.

Sights & Attractions	Day	Phone	Address	Entry Fee
Forever Charleston	1	843-853-8000	375 Meeting St.	$
Fort Sumter	3	843-722-1691	171 Lockwood Blvd.	$$
Middleton Place	3	843-556-6020	4300 Ashley River Rd.	$$
South Carolina Aquarium	2	843-577-3474 800-722-6455	360 Concorde St.	$$

Charleston Area CVB	**800-868-8118**	**375 Meeting St.**

South Carolina

 NYC Charleston (CHS) <30 min./$20 No   Map Code: A33

Memphis in May Barbeque

Memphis in May World Championship Barbecue Cooking Contest

Key Month: May   Ratings: Event ★ ★ ★ ☆ ☆   (H)   City ★ ★ ★ ☆ ☆   Origin: 1976   Attendance: 80,000

Memphis is smokin'! One million disciples of blues, beer and barbecue descend on this city by the Mississippi during the month-long **Memphis in May** festival, highlighted by the world's largest and most prestigious barbecue contest. Although this cookin' of pork grabs the spotlight, the aura of American originals such as Elvis and B.B. King ensure that a trip to the River City means much more than that.

Tom Lee Park, bordering the mighty river, is party central for the **Memphis in May World Championship Barbecue Cooking Contest**. Held the third weekend of the month, more than 240 invited international teams, sporting names like Aporkalypse Now and Swinefeld, compete for pride and prize money. Thirty-three acres of distinctively decorated booths set the stage for wild, noisy and informal parties, as teams prepare a variety of whole pigs, ribs, shoulders and both dry and wet spices.

Health codes demand that you be a "guest" of a team in order to sample its barbecue. This simply entails chatting up a team member and getting invited into their area. Don't be shy—arranging "invites" is common and the only way to sample much of what this event offers.

Eating, however, is only part of the action. The Hog Calling, Ms. Piggie and Showmanship contests will redefine your notion of hams (the human kind). Live music and dancing add fuel to the party fires as afternoon fades into night.

Ever since vaudeville days, when Beale Street was crammed with theaters, musicians have been drawn to Memphis—"I've got a fifth of whiskey and a case of the blues," reads one T-shirt—and it's no accident Elvis turned up here to make famous his blend of blues, gospel and country sounds. So what if Beale is only four blocks long? The historic stretch of blacktop is packed with clubs and music and can rock until 6 a.m., thanks to its special licensing law.

Tennessee's largest city and home to half a million people, Memphis is easy to get around. The weather, river, Elvis, blues and barbecue team up for one of the South's spiciest weekends of the year. (*For more on barbecue, see page 208.*)

On the Calendar

Official Event Dates
Third Thursday-Saturday in May

Best 3 Days To Be There
Thursday-Saturday. You've got to be there for the whole hog thing, especially since it's a weekend in Memphis.

Other Times To Go
The Beale Street Music Festival (901-525-4611 ext.105) kicks off Memphis in May (first weekend). Then there's *Elvis Week*, (901-332-3322) with all-things-Elvis on the anniversary of his death, August 16.

☾ 61°/81° (16°/27°)

Tennessee

Memphis in May
Barbecue

DAY 1 — Thursday

10:30 am **Smithsonian's Rock 'N Soul Museum** is the first permanent Smithsonian partnership outside of Washington, D.C. The audio-guided tour covers music history from the '30s through the '70s, including greats such as B.B. King, Otis Redding and Jerry Lee Lewis. A few blocks away, continue your musical sojourn with a one-hour tour of **Sun Studio**, where Elvis first recorded.

1:00 pm Drive to nearby Overton Square and ✖ the hip **Café Au Lait** for some tasty Mexican food before eating all-things-barbeque at the festival.

2:30 pm The **Memphis Brooks Museum of Art** in Overton Park is a short drive and pleasant afternoon respite. The park and museum building provide an attractive setting for a small but wide-ranging collection.

4:30 pm Have a drink at the Peabody's lobby bar, then join visitors who come to see the famous **Peabody Ducks**. At 11 a.m. and 5 p.m. daily, five well-cared-for ducks traverse a red carpet from the elevator to the travertine fountain in the middle of the hotel's elegant lobby. You can follow the ducks home—they live on the roof—for a Thursdays-in-May Sunset Serenade on **The Peabody Rooftop**. If there's a "scene" in Memphis, this is it.

7:00 pm Walk a few blocks to Tom Lee Park for the outrageous *Hog Calling Contest*, followed by a performance of the *Ms. Piggy Contest* winners. Allow time to make the one-mile walk from the festival entrance, past the spectacle of barbecue booths/homes, to the main stage. The festival runs 3–11 p.m.

9:00 pm Take a different path back through the park, exit at Beale Street and walk ✖ to **Elvis Presley's Memphis**. The restaurant serves American cuisine, including many of Elvis' favorites such as meatloaf and grilled peanut-butter-and-banana sandwiches. There's a stage for live '50s-'70s music, a dance floor and video monitors throughout.

11:00 pm If you're a night owl, drive an hour to gamble in Tunica, Mississippi—which boasts the country's third-largest collection of casinos after Las Vegas and Atlantic City. Or check out Beale Street before the weekend crowds arrive.

DAY 2 — Friday

9:00 am Drive to **The Arcade** for a tradi-✖ tional Southern breakfast of grits, eggs and smoked bacon in a '50s setting. Elvis used to hang out here with friends. His booth is the last one on the left.

10:00 am **Graceland**, a twenty-minute drive, is more interesting than most people expect. You'll need at least two hours to take the fascinating tape-guided tour of Elvis Presley's far-from-humble abode and final resting place and to view other exhibits across the street. When you leave Graceland, you'll feel as if you knew the King.

1:00 pm Near the Peabody, have lunch at ✖ **Cafe Samovar**. Russian food, such as blinis and borscht, makes for a nifty switch from barbecue and Elvis.

3:00 pm Head back to Tom Lee Park for the entertainment highlight—the *Showmanship* competition. Teams lip-sync to popular songs with lyrics irreverently changed to pay homage to pigs and more.

4:00 pm Get down to the serious business of barbecue and the high points of the festival. Tension and excitement fill the air as competitors prepare for judging on Saturday. Despite a competitive seriousness, family, friends and business associates taste, schmooze and party heavily. Get yourself invited to do the ✖ same by becoming a barbecue team's "guest," or buy dinner from the vendors and simply enjoy the sunset and scene.

11:00 pm Your nightcap possibilities include Beale Street and the lobby bar at the Peabody.

Day-by-Day Plan

DAY 3 — Saturday

9:00 am Before walking to the festival, have ✖ breakfast in **Cafe Expresso**, the Peabody's pastry-shop-cum-deli.

11:00 am Tom Lee Park has undergone a transformation. The music has stopped, trash has disappeared and barbecue areas have been carefully decorated. Team members don clean aprons or T-shirts with their logos. Tables are sometimes set with crystal, candelabras, flowers and wine. The judging team arrives (ushered in by a team member who then "guards" the gate), gets a tour and introduction to all team members, and is served the team's cuisine, accompanied by an entertaining verbal description. If the team makes the finals, they will be revisited by different judges a few hours later.

1:00 pm Break for lunch at the Peabody's ✖ casual **Dux** restaurant.

2:30 pm Then drive to the **National Civil Rights Museum**, which has converted the site of Martin Luther King, Jr.'s assassination into an emotional exhibit.

6:30 pm Find out if your favorite barbecued ribs are, in fact, the world's greatest as the festival culminates with the *awards ceremony*. With a last taste of 'cue and a beer, bid farewell to the friends you've made.

8:30 pm If you're hungry, walk to **Automatic** ✖ **Slim's Tonga Club** for a dinner featuring Caribbean, Southwestern and New York-style cuisine. Admire the zebra skins and modern furnishings of this top rendezvous spot.

10:30 pm Nighttime on Beale Street! This lively strip pulsates with jazz, Delta blues, rock, rhythm and blues and a smattering of gospel. The street will be packed with drinking-age kids, the clubs with adults. A good place to start is **B.B. King's Club & Restaurant**. Down the street is the **Rum Boogie Cafe**, where you can check out guitars that once belonged to the legends who have performed on this grand boulevard of blues.

2:00 am After all this living high on the hog, beat the sun back to the hotel. Then sing the blues about tomorrow's departure before hunkering down to a sleep befitting a king.

■

More Time, More Choices

Sleep Out Louie's is a popular oyster bar with live music on weekends. For a party atmosphere, try **Club 152**. The blues clubs on Beale Street are not known for their food (which is mostly 'cue), but a good late-night dive for food and music is **Blues City Cafe**. A couple more dining options are **McEwen's**, which serves contemporary southern cuisine, and **Melange**, which won a *Wine Spectator* award of excellence. When you go to the Brooks Museum, a good alternative for lunch is their **Brushmark Restaurant**, which serves an adequate selection of Nouvelle American cuisine.

The unusual **Mud Island** includes a scale model of the Mississippi River and a museum devoted to the river, its history and the people who have lived alongside it.

Accommodations

Check out the landmark, perfectly located **Peabody Hotel**, the address of choice in Memphis. Antique luxury and attentive service will make you feel like a Southern aristocrat. Memphis' downtown lacks a choice of top-class hotels. For a good location near Beale Street, the **Radisson Hotel Memphis** has a pool, sauna and exercise room, and the **Holiday Inn Select Downtown** is somewhat better than standard.

Event & Ticket Info

Memphis in May World Championship Barbecue Cooking Contest (Tom Lee Park): Tickets ($6) are available at the park. For more information, contact *Memphis in May* (901-525-4611 ext. 105).

Hotels		Phone	Address	Price	Fax	Rooms/Best
Holiday Inn Select Downtown		901-525-5491 888-300-5491	160 Union Ave.	$$$	901-529-8950	192/King executive
Peabody Hotel		901-529-4000 800-732-2639	149 Union Ave.	$$$	901-529-3600	468/W. side 10th/11th flrs w/vw of river
Radisson Hotel Memphis		901-528-1800 800-333-3333	185 Union Ave.	$$	901-526-3226	280/King resort rms face Beale or Union sts

Restaurants	Day	Phone	Address	Price	Rec	Food
The Arcade	2	901-526-5757	540 S. Main St.	$	B/L	Southern
Automatic Slim's Tonga Club	3	901-525-7948	83 S. 2nd St.	$$$	D/L	Caribbean fusion
Blues City Cafe	A	901-526-3637	138 Beale St.	$$	LD	Southern
Brushmark Restaurant	A	901-544-6223	1934 Poplar in the Brooks Museum	$	L	American
Café Au Lait	1	901-274-1504	959 Cooper St.	LD	$$	Mexican
Cafe Expresso	3	901-529-4000	see the Peabody Hotel	BLD	$	Pastries, deli
Cafe Samovar	2	901-529-9607	83 Union Ave.	LD	$	Russian
Dux	3	901-529-4000	see the Peabody Hotel	L/BD	$$	Southern
Elvis Presley's Memphis	1	901-527-6900	126 Beale St.	D/L	$$	American
McEwen's	A	901-527-7085	122 Monroe	LD	$$$	Contemporary Southern
Melange	A	901-276-0002	948 South Cooper	D	$$$	American-French fusion

Nightlife	Day	Phone	Address	Cover	Rec*	Music
B.B. King's Club & Restaurant	3	901-524-5464	143 Beale St.	$$	MPF	Blues, R&B
Blues City Cafe	A	901-526-3637	see restaurants	$	MF	Blues
Club 152	A	901-544-7011	152 Beale St.	$	MP	Jazz
Elvis Presley's Memphis	1	901-527-6900	see restaurants	$	MPF	Oldies, rockabilly
The Peabody Rooftop	1	901-529-4000	see the Peabody Hotel	$	MP	Rock
Rum Boogie Cafe	3	901-528-0150	182 Beale St.	$	MP	Blues
Sleep Out Louie's	A	901-527-5337	88 Union Ave.	None	M	Acoustic, '70s, '80s, '90s

* M=Live music; P=Dancing (Party); R=Bar only; S=Show; (F)=Food served. For further explanation of codes, page 12.

Sights & Attractions	Day	Phone	Address	Entry Fee
Graceland	2	901-332-3322	3764 Elvis Presley Blvd.	$$
Memphis Brooks Museum of Art	1	901-722-3500	1934 Poplar Ave. in Overton Park	$
Mud Island	A	901-576-7241	125 N. Front St.	$
National Civil Rights Museum	3	901-521-9699	450 Mulberry St.	$
Peabody Ducks	1	901-529-4000	see the Peabody Hotel	None
Smithsonian's Rock 'N Soul Museum	1	901-543-0800	145 Lieutenant George W. Lee Ave.	$
Sun Studio	1	901-521-0664	706 Union Ave.	$

| **Memphis CVB** | | **901-543-5333** | **119 N. Riverside Dr.** | |

 NYC -1   Memphis (MEM) <30 min./$20   Yes/No   Map Code: A34

Country Music Fan Fair

International Country Music Fan Fair

Key Month: Jun   Ratings: Event ★ ★ ★ ☆ ☆   **P**   City ★ ★ ☆ ☆ ☆   Origin: 1972   Attendance: 125,000

The only thing more sacred than a country star's relationship with God and Momma is his bond with The Fans. Wives come and go, but The Fans stick by, for better or worse—during the arrest for waving a gun on the highway, when he gets caught in the back of a Ford with pants at the ankles or his failure to get another hit song onto the charts.

For country-music singers and their fans, **Fan Fair** is like Christmas, Independence Day and Woodstock wrapped into one package. Sponsored by the Country Music Association and the *Grand Ole Opry*, this annual four-day orgy of appreciation pays homage to the ties that bind in country music. Every June, 24,000 die-hard fans from all corners of the United States and the world head south for thirty-five hours of performances and face time with their beloved stars. And the stars are happy to indulge the fans who pay their bills: One year Garth Brooks signed autographs for twenty-three straight hours without a break.

For four days, the faithful line up at booths packed into Nashville's convention center downtown, patiently waiting hour after hour for a photograph with Alan Jackson, Brooks and Dunn or Toby Keith. At Adelphia Stadium, record labels showcase their best acts and rising stars.

Nashville, which has earned the title of Music City, U.S.A., is the state's capital and home to one of the nation's finest universities, Vanderbilt. The past decade has seen Nashville approach its goal of becoming an A-list city. The downtown area, boarded up and depressing in 1990, has been transformed into a thriving tourist destination, while regaining most of its former charm.

Around town there are historic attractions such as The Hermitage (President Andrew Jackson's estate) and the Parthenon, a full-size replica of the original in Athens. With a three-day jaunt to Music City, you can take it all in with a sampling of fan mania, the vaunted Grand Ole Opry and a crash course in America's music: country. Yahoo!

On the Calendar

Official Event Dates
Thursday-Sunday, ending second Sunday in June

Best 3 Days To Be There
Thursday-Saturday

☽ 66°/88° (19°/31°)

Tennessee

Country Music Fan Fair

You could spend all three days at Fan Fair, but the itinerary suggests you take in all that Nashville offers.

DAY 1 Thursday

10:00 am Drive downtown for the *Fan Fair* (the Convention Center is open 10 a.m.-4 p.m. each day). Wear comfortable shoes and casual clothes. The daily routine consists of morning, afternoon and evening shows. Each is a showcase for a different label. The convention center is filled with booths where you can buy memorabilia or sing a voice-over. If you want a star's autograph, hop in line.

1:00 pm It won't be much to sing about but have lunch at the convention center.

3:30 pm Head to Riverfront Park for one of the afternoon concerts.

7:30 pm One of Nashville's finer restaurants, **Cafe One Two Three** serves eclectic, Southern-accented cuisine.

9:30 pm Downtown Nashville should be swinging by now. Start on Second Avenue and Broadway. It's touristy—Hard Rock Cafe, NASCAR Cafe, Planet Hollywood and Hooters have all moved in—but still a good block for walking, with funky bars, upscale junk shops, cheesy souvenir stands and the terrific **Wildhorse Saloon**. This high-tech country emporium has free dance lessons, a huge dance floor and live entertainment.

11:30 pm Slide into **Tootsie's Orchid Lounge**, one of the world's greatest dives. Despite its popularity, the joint hasn't had a significant renovation in at least fifty years. During the Grand Ole Opry's heyday, the legendary Hank Williams used to slip out the back door of the Ryman Auditorium to tie one on at Tootsie's. Live performers croon for tips in the front and bands play in the back. Tootsie's looks intimidating from the outside, but walk right in and you'll feel welcome.

DAY 2 Friday

9:00 am Drive fifteen country miles for breakfast at the **Loveless Restaurant**. Fried chicken, ham, hot biscuits and hospitality are the specialties.

10:30 am Drive a few miles to **The Hermitage**, home of Andrew Jackson. The seventh American president, Old Hickory lived here until his death in 1845. The Greek Revival mansion and 650-acre grounds are splendid.

12:30 pm Back in town, lunch at the **Blue Moon Waterfront Cafe**, the one restaurant locals don't want you to know about. Nestled on the Cumberland River, it serves upscale, eclectic seafood.

2:00 pm Head back to *Fan Fair* in time for the afternoon show or to finish collecting those autographs.

6:45 pm Get an outdoor table at **Sunset Grill** and enjoy New American cuisine at this highly rated restaurant. Try one of more than sixty wines served by the glass.

9:30 pm Enjoy a *Fan Fair* main event performance by some of country music's best at the Coliseum.

DAY 3 Saturday

9:00 am Celebrities are often spotted at the **Pancake Pantry**, a local institution. Plow through heaping plates of pancakes, served in every possible style.

10:30 am The **Country Music Hall of Fame and Museum** is especially good for people who don't know much about country music or think they don't like it. The museum displays thousands of fascinating items and tributes to country-music legends.

Noon Drive to **Centennial Park** for Nashville's most eccentric attraction, a full-size replica of the Parthenon. The city art museum and the Western world's tallest indoor sculpture, Athena Parthenos, are inside.

DAY 3 **Saturday (cont.)**

1:30 pm Adjacent to the park, Nashville's ❌ best barbecue is served at **Hog Heaven**. The pulled-chicken sandwich, with an unusual spicy white sauce, is especially good. Or you could get a burger and malt at **Elliston Place Soda Shop**, a 1939 soda fountain adjacent to the park.

3:00 pm Head downtown to the Cumberland River for the two-mile **Nashville City Walk**. The self-guided tour begins at Fort Nashborough in Riverfront Park, where you can ride the whimsical Tennessee Fox Trot Carousel. Follow the green line on the sidewalk to Printer's Alley, the Men's Quarter, Nashville's Historic Black Business District, the State Capitol and the Tennessee State Museum. Take the tour at the **Ryman Auditorium**, a red-brick 1892 revivalist hall which was home to the Grand Ole Opry from 1943 to 1974.

5:30 pm Have an early dinner at **Capitol Grille** ❌ **and Oak Bar**. Choose from a menu of varied, regional American cuisine.

7:00 pm Drive to **Opryland Hotel**. A hotel like no other in the world, it has a colossal, nine-acre indoor complex of lush gardens, murals, waterfalls, lakes, rivers and covered bridges. Walk or shuttle to Opry Plaza. The **Grand Ole Opry Museum** is open late when the Opry's on.

9:00 pm Nashville's main attraction since 1925, the *Grand Ole Opry* (the show starts at 7:30 p.m.) is also the longest-running radio show in history. The set is pure corn pone—a red-barn backdrop and a microphone—but the pace is fast, and the performances are great. About twenty cast members take the stage, from newcomers to old-timers such as Porter Wagoner. Be sure to pick up some Goo Goo (Grand Ole Opry, according to myth) clusters at the snack bar.

11:00 pm You probably have some boot-scootin' left in you, so try **Robert's Western World**, a smoky honky-tonk that old Hank would've loved. Hipsters two-step around the small dance floor. Line dancing is not encouraged, but after a visit here, you'll impress your friends back home with all you've learned in Nashville.

More Time, More Choices

If the Grand Ole Opry's not your style, call for the lineup at the **Bluebird Cafe**, where Nashville's finest singer/songwriters practice their craft in an intimate room. It has the best folk, country and blues in town, even on open-mic nights. The **Bound'ry** serves upscale global cuisine. The **Stockyard Restaurant** in the historic stockyard building is elegant and romantic. For dinner and dancing under one roof, try **Atlantis**, which serves seafood in a casual setting. If you're in the mood for contemporary French food, head to **Wild Boar**. It's considered one of the world's top forty wine cellars—with 15,000 bottles and 3,000 different selections.

Another Nashville diversion is a stroll at **Cheekwood Botanical Garden and Museum of Art** amid fifty-five acres of botanical gardens and an art museum.

Accommodations

In the heart of Nashville, the **Westin Hermitage Hotel** is the only commercial beaux-arts structure in Tennessee. Built in 1910, the Grecian and Tennessee marble in the lobby, and the French doors at the original "ladies entrance," make a grand setting. Downtown, **Union Station Hotel** is a beautifully restored Victorian train depot with a breathtaking, sixty-five-foot barrel-vaulted ceiling in the lobby. **Opryland Hotel**, about fifteen minutes from downtown, is more of an event hotel, with lots of hubbub. Ask for a room overlooking the gardens, with a private terrace.

Event & Ticket Info

Fan Fair (Convention Center, The Coliseum and Riverfront stages downtown): Your ticket (about $125-$145) covers admission all four days to all events. Tickets should be purchased by February from *Fan Fair Ticket Office* (866-326-3247).

The Hot Sheet

Hotels	Phone	Address	Price	Fax	Rooms/Best
Opryland Hotel	615-889-1000 888-976-1998	2800 Opryland Dr.	$$$	615-871-5728	2,884/Garden and waterway vw
Union Station Hotel	615-726-1001 800-996-3426	1001 Broadway	$$	615-248-3554	124/Gallery vw
Westin Hermitage Hotel	615-244-3121 888-888-9414	231 6th Ave. N	$$	615-254-6909	120/Capitol vw

Restaurants	Day	Phone	Address	Price	Rec	Food
Atlantis	A	615-327-8001	1911 Broadway	$$$	D	Seafood
Blue Moon Waterfront Cafe	2	615-352-5892	525 Basswood Ave.	$$	D	Seafood
Bound'ry	A	615-321-3043	911 20th Ave. S	$$$	D	New Southern, continental
Cafe One Two Three	1	615-255-2233	123 12th Ave. N	$$$	D	New Southern, continental
Capitol Grille and Oak Bar	3	615-244-3121	see Hermitage Hotel	$$$	D/BL	Southern fusion
Elliston Place Soda Shop	3	615-327-1090	2111 Elliston Pl.	$	L/BD	American
Hog Heaven	3	615-329-1234	115 27th Ave. N	$	L/D	Barbecue
Loveless Restaurant	2	615-646-0067	8400 Hwy. 100	$	B/LD	Southern
Pancake Pantry	3	615-383-9333	1796 21st Ave. S	$	B/L	American
Stockyard Restaurant	A	615-255-6464	901 2nd Ave. N	$$$$	D	American
Sunset Grill	2	615-386-3663	2001A Belcourt Ave.	$$$	D/L	Nuvo American
Wild Boar	A	615-329-1313	2014 Broadway	$$$	D	Contemporary French

Nightlife	Day	Phone	Address	Cover	Rec*	Music
Bluebird Cafe	A	615-383-1461	4104 Hillsboro Rd.	$	M(F)	Original country, blues, folk
Grand Ole Opry	3	615-889-6600	2802 Opryland Dr.	$$	S	Country
Robert's Western World	3	615-256-7937	416 Broadway	None	MP(F)	Country
Tootsie's Orchid Lounge	1	615-726-0463	422 Broadway	None	MP(F)	Country
Wildhorse Saloon	1	615-251-1000	120 2nd Ave. N	$	MP(F)	Country

* M=Live music; P=Dancing (Party); R=Bar only; S=Show; (F)=Food served. For further explanation of codes, page 12.

Sights & Attractions	Day	Phone	Address	Entry Fee
Centennial Park	3	615-862-8431	West End and 25th Ave.	$
Cheekwood Botanical Garden and Museum of Art	A	615-353-2162	1200 Forrest Park Dr.	$
Country Music Hall of Fame and Museum	3	615-416-2001	222 5th Ave. S.	$
Grand Ole Opry Musuem	3	615-889-7070	2804 Opryland Dr.	None
The Hermitage	2	615-889-2941	4580 Rachel's Lane	$
Nashville City Walk	3		Riverfront Park	None
Opryland Hotel	3	615-889-1000	see hotel listing	None
Ryman Auditorium	3	615-254-1445	116 5th Ave. N	$

Nashville CVB	**615-259-4700**	**501 Broadway**

 NYC -1   Nahville (BNA) <30 min./$20    Yes   Map Code: A35

Tennessee

South by Southwest

South by Southwest Music and Media Conference, SXSW

Key Month: Mar   Ratings: Event ★★★☆☆   ℗   City ★★★☆☆   Origin: 1987   Attendance: 25,000

The **South by Southwest Music and Media Conference** proves that Austin ain't just whistlin' Dixie when proclaiming itself "live-music capital of the world." All you need is an **SXSW** admission wristband to get free rein on scores of citywide music events, highlighted by dynamic crowds at nightly performances by some 900 bands from all over the world, from Austin to Australia.

Many fans and industry types consider **SXSW** the pop-music world's most important gathering. While shopping around for favorite artists playing in forty bars and clubs downtown (as well as alternative locations such as record shops, art galleries and garages), you might stumble upon rare, small-venue performances by well-known artists such as Johnny Cash, Sheryl Crow or Flaming Lips.

Once University of Texas students drain out of Austin for spring break, **SXSW** participants flood the city to attend seminars, panels and a trade show, in addition to live performances. Most important for industry people, **SXSW** offers the chance to make connections and sign contracts. Musicians, hoping to be discovered, perform with special vigor. Off-stage, Austin is charged with intense networking and the conspicuous presence of celebrity entertainers.

The state capital, with a population of just more than 500,000, Austin is the "misfit" of Texas, defined more by openness, university culture and creativity than by oil rigs and cattle ranches. Per capita, it has more artists than any other Texas city, and more bars and restaurants than any other American city (many Austin clubs feature live music throughout the year). Its live-music scene centers around Sixth Street. There, more than seventy venues, restaurants and shops occupy the Victorian buildings that play host to all types of music, from hip hop to tears-in-your-beer country.

To make the most of a three-day itinerary, visitors can combine two nights at **SXSW** with a visit to nearby San Antonio (page 160), Houston (page 156) or, as in this chapter, Dallas/Fort Worth. The Dallas metroplex is known primarily as a commercial center, but a day there makes for a great beginning to a musical weekend.

On the Calendar

Official Event Dates
Five days in March, during spring break

Best 3 Days To Be There
Thursday-Saturday

☽ 48°/71° (9°/21°)

Texas

Day-by-Day Plan

DAY 1 Thursday

10:00 am Start your journey through the Old West, or what's left of it, in Fort Worth's **Stockyards National Historic District** (although it's more fun at night when the clubs are open). Then head downtown to Sundance Square for a look at its array of architectural styles, from art deco to glass-and-steel.

Noon Head to **Mi Cocina** for well-prepared ❌ Mexican food. Fajitas are a Texas favorite at almost any Mexican place.

1:30 pm Drive to the cultural district and spend a few hours at two small but wonderful museums. The **Kimbell Art Museum** has a range of painted masterpieces. Across a pretty park, The **Amon Carter Museum** has a good collection of American art.

3:30 pm Cap off the one-hour drive to Dallas with a cocktail and another tower view from the 50th floor of **Reunion Tower**.

5:30 pm Stop at the **Beau Nash Bar**, an upscale meeting place in the magnificent Hotel Crescent Court.

8:30 pm **Sipango** is a trendy-crowd restaurant ❌ with Italian-inspired dishes, a lively bar scene, music and a disco, the Rio Room (open only on Fridays and Saturdays).

11:30 pm Drive to Deep Ellum, Dallas' popular area for funky shops, galleries, restaurants and music venues. Try **Sambuca** for jazz.

DAY 2 Friday

9:30 am After a hotel breakfast, head down- ❌ town to the **Sixth Floor Museum**, the site where Lee Harvey Oswald supposedly fired the shots that killed President John F. Kennedy. It's now a powerful exhibit about the president, the times and the assassination, including film clips and memorabilia.

11:30 am Drive through downtown Dallas, notable for architecture and sculptures that dot the landscape, especially Robert Summer's longhorns in Pioneer Plaza.

12:30 pm Lunch at **Arcodoro & Pomodoro**—it ❌ serves contemporary Italian dishes for the casually elegant crowd—before leaving for Austin (a thirty-minute flight or a three-hour drive).

4:30 pm In Austin, pick up the special edition of the *Austin American-Statesman*. It has a complete list of bands and venues for the week.

5:00 pm Walk along Auditorium Shore to the memorial statue of guitar legend Stevie Ray Vaughan. No blues or rock fan should miss this one.

6:00 pm Enjoy an outdoor concert on Sixth Street. You'll be a few hours early for the incredible sea of people that fill this area.

7:00 pm The **Cafe at the Four Seasons** serves ❌ New Texas cuisine in one of the city's only five-star restaurants. Make reservations in advance to get a view of Town Lake at sunset and you may see more than a million bats emerge from under the Congress Avenue bridge.

8:30 pm If you can't decide which band to see, walk to **Antone's** for what promises to be one of the best *SXSW* lineups. Willie Nelson celebrated his sixtieth birthday here, Stevie Ray Vaughan was a regular and major blues acts frequently play at this diverse and popular venue.

11:00 pm For a change of scenery, walk to **Momo's** for live funk, rock or blues with a sophisticated crowd. It's not affiliated with *SXSW*, but always books talented musicians. After dancing, have a late-night Reuben sandwich from **Katz's Deli**, which serves food in its twenty-four-hour diner below the club.

DAY 3 Saturday

9:30 am Stroll to the modern Southwestern- ❌ style **Little City Cafe** for light, home-baked blueberry muffins.

11:00 am Walking up Congress Avenue, you can't miss the distinctive **State Capitol**— it's the country's tallest. After the original limestone version burned down in 1881, it was rebuilt with Texas' own red granite. Take a free guided tour, and don't miss the awesome rotunda.

DAY 3 · Saturday (cont.)

1:00 pm Lunch at nearby **Cafe Serranos** at ✪ Symphony Square for good Tex-Mex food with a view that takes advantage of its location in the historic square.

2:30 pm Continue north to the **University of Texas at Austin** visitor information center to get a map of the campus. Since it's Saturday and spring break, you'll see few students as you explore the grounds and its nineteenth-century Texas architecture. Visit the **Lyndon B. Johnson Library and Museum**.

7:00 pm Have dinner at **Mezzaluna**. It's ✪ known for Italian cuisine and a fun bar atmosphere.

9:00 pm Jump into the scene at the 2,900-capacity **Austin Music Hall**, *SXSW*'s largest venue. Long lines might lead you a block away to the brightly painted **La Zona Rosa**, a renovated garage that always hops with cutting-edge sounds from alternative country to punk polka.

11:00 pm Stomp around the wood-plank dance floor at the **Broken Spoke**, a honky-tonk with solid *SXSW* lineups.

12:30 am Stay a little bit country at the **Continental Club**, a small, smoky Austin classic. Or head to **Maggie Mae's**, a club with a great lineup of rock bands and beer, two things that *SXSW* is all about.

2:00 am Stroll down Sixth Street for a final hit of musical energy, ignited by *SXSW*'s collision of the music industry's art, business and fun.

■

More Time, More Choices

Threadgill's was the first live-music club to open in Austin after the repeal of Prohibition in 1933 and it's where Janis Joplin got her start. The chicken-fried steak is good. **Emilia's** chef was named one of the top ten best new chefs in America by *Food & Wine* magazine. In

Dallas, **Star Canyon**, which serves upscale Southwestern cuisine, attracts a people-watching crowd. **Abacus**, serving Pacific Rim-American food, is warm and inviting with a theater kitchen. Fort Worth's **Lonesome Dove**, a western bistro, offers urban western food in a restored 1921 building built with Old Chicago brick.

For a different type of evening, try multi-clubbed **Dallas Alley** in Dallas' West End Historic District. The main draw is its Alley Cats dueling-pianos venue. Or try the **Samba Room** for some lively Latin music. A night in Fort Worth means **Billy Bob's Texas**—the world's largest honky-tonk (100,000 square feet), complete with an indoor rodeo arena, dance floor and concert stage.

Accommodations

You're part of the action at the modern Southwest-style **Four Seasons Hotel Austin**. It's the unofficial *SXSW* headquarters, popular with conference participants and performers who meet up and hang around the lobby. The **Four Seasons Austin** fills up a year in advance. You might try the **Driskill Hotel**. It's located in a renovated nineteenth-century building located right in the action on Sixth Street. The **Omni Austin**, part of a large office complex, is a more modern alternative. In Dallas, **The Mansion on Turtle Creek** is beautiful and refined. The **Worthington** is the place to stay in Fort Worth.

Event & Ticket Info

South by Southwest: A festival wristband ($105) gives you second-priority (after convention-goers, before pay-at-door) admission to all SXSW-sponsored performances. You may have to wait in line at some venues. Wristbands, which sell out by Friday morning, must be picked up in person in Austin. For more information, contact *SXSW Headquarters* (512-467-7979).

Hotels	Phone	Address	Price	Fax	Rooms/Best
Driskill Hotel	512-474-5911 800-252-9367	604 Brazos St.	$$$	512-474-2188	188/Senate rms
Four Seasons Austin	512-478-4500 800-332-3442	98 San Jacinto Blvd.	$$$	512-478-3117	291/Town or lake vw
Hotel Crescent Court	214-871-3200 800-654-6541	400 Crescent Court	$$$	214-871-3272	220/Dlx w/court vw
The Mansion on Turtle Creek Rosewood Hotels & Resorts	214-559-2100 800-527-5432	2821 Turtle Creek Blvd.	$$$$	214-528-4187	142/Courtyard vw
Omni Austin	512-476-3700 800-843-6664	700 San Jacinto Blvd.	$$	512-397-4888	375/Atrium vw
Worthington	817-870-1000 800-433-5677	200 Main St.	$$$	817-338-9176	504/Downtown vw

Restaurants	Day	Phone	Address	Price	Rec	Food
Abacus	A	214-559-3111	4511 McKinney Ave.	$$$	D	American, Pacific Rim
Arcodoro & Pomodoro	2	214-871-1924	2708 Route St.	$$	L/D	Italian
Cafe at the Four Seasons	2	512-685-8300	see Four Seasons hotel	$$$	D/BL	Nuvo Texas
Cafe Serranos	3	512-322-9080	1111 Red River St.	$$	L	Tex-Mex
Emilia's	A	512-469-9722	600 East 3rd St.	$$$	D	New American
Katz's Deli	2	512-472-2037	618 W. 6th St.	$	T/BLD	Deli
Little City Cafe	3	512-476-2489	916 Congress Ave.	$	B/LD	American bistro
Mezzaluna	3	512-472-6770	310 Colorado St.	$$	D/L	Italian
Lonesome Dove	A	817-740-8810	2406 N. Main St.	$$$	LD	Urban Western
Mi Cocina	1	817-877-3600	509 Main St.	$	L/D	Mexican
Sipango	1	214-522-2411	4513 Travis St.	$$$	D	Italian, New American
Star Canyon	A	214-520-7827	3102 Oaklawn Ave.	$$$	LD	Southwestern
Threadgill's	A	512-451-5440	6416 N. Lamar Blvd.	$$	LD	Southern

Nightlife	Day	Phone	Address	Cover	Rec*	Music
Antone's	2	512-474-5314	213 W. 5th St.	MP	$$	Blues
Austin Music Hall	3	512-495-9962	208 Nueces St.	M	$$$	Blues, jazz, swing, rock
Beau Nash Bar	1	214-871-3240	see Hotel Crescent Court	None	M(F)	Jazz
Billy Bob's Texas	A	817-624-7117	2520 Rodeo Plaza	$	MP	Country
Broken Spoke	3	512-442-6189	3201 S. Lamar Blvd.	$	MP(F)	Country
Continental Club	3	512-441-2444	1315 S. Congress Ave.	$	MP	Country, blues, rock
Dallas Alley	A	214-720-0170	Dallas Alley	$	MP(F)	Sing-a-long
La Zona Rosa	3	512-472-2293	612 W. 4th St.	$$	M	Blues, jazz, rock
Maggie Mae's	3	512-478-8541	325 E. 6th St.	$	MP(F)	Rock
Momo's	2	512-479-8848	618 W. 6th St.	$	MP	Funk, blues, rock
Samba Room	A	214-522-4137	4514 Travis St.	None	M(F)	Latin
Sambuca	1	214-744-0820	2618 Elm St.	None	M(F)	Jazz

* M=Live music; P=Dancing (Party); R=Bar only; S=Show; (F)=Food served. For further explanation of codes, page 12.

Sights & Attractions	Day	Phone	Address	Entry Fee
The Amon Carter Museum	1	817-738-1933	3501 Camp Bowie Blvd.	None
Kimbell Art Museum	1	817-332-8451	3333 Camp Bowie Blvd.	None
LBJ Library and Museum	3	512-478-0098	2313 Red River St.	None
Reunion Tower	1	214-651-1234	300 Reunion Blvd.	$
Sixth Floor Museum	2	214-747-6660	411 Elm St.	$
State Capitol	3	512-463-0063	11th St. & Congress Ave.	None
Stockyards Nat. Hist. Dist.	1	817-624-4741	Main and Exchange Sts.	None
University of Texas at Austin	3	512-471-1655	2300 Red River St.	None

Austin CVB	**800-926-2282**	**201 E. 2nd St.**
Dallas CVB	**800-232-5527**	**100 S. Houston**
Fort Worth CVB	**800-433-5747**	**415 Throckmorton**

Austin area code: 512   Dallas area code: 214   Fort Worth area code: 817

 NYC -1   Dallas/Fort Worth (DFW) <45 min./$35
Mueller Municipal (AUS) <30 min./$10    Yes   Map Code: A36

Texas

Dickens on the Strand

Key Month: Dec   Ratings: Event ★ ★ ☆ ☆ ☆   **H**   City ★ ★ ★ ☆ ☆   Origin: 1974   Attendance: 50,000

What do Charles Dickens and the Texas coast have in common? Not a thing, except for North America's largest Victorian Christmas celebration. Every year in the beachside city of Galveston, tens of thousands of revelers don period clothes and hoist cups of cheer to the literature and culture of nineteenth-century England.

What started as a potluck dinner to promote the city's historic venues has now become one of Texas' top winter events. Along with a day spent in search of the Ghost of Christmas Past, there are plenty of opportunities to enjoy Christmas present and future, thanks to a full schedule of attractions in nearby Houston. An array of nightclubs—with atmospheres ranging from spring break to elegant—round out the weekend of Texas partying.

Mention Galveston and Houston, the fourth-largest city in the United States, and two things come to mind: oil money and sandy beaches. Long the capital of the Texas oil "bidness," Houston, which earned the nickname Bayou City because it was founded near a creek (*bayou* is Southern for "creek"), is still dotted with high-dollar hangouts. The food scene is cosmopolitan, with a meaty Texas influence. The choice of fun ranges from highbrow art museums and quiet botanical gardens to Texas-size nightclubs. December is a good time for a weekend that involves hopping into a car and driving from spot to spot—an activity best avoided during Houston's hellishly humid summers.

When you're ready for seaside fun, do what Houston's high rollers do: Head to Galveston Island, fifty miles to the southeast. In summer, all the fun takes place along its thirty-two miles of shoreline, but during winter, the party heads to the historic district of the city, The Strand.

The spirits of Oliver Twist, David Copperfield and Queen Victoria come to this seaside party, where visitors are encouraged to take part in the period fun and dress the part as well. But whether you wear a cowboy hat, top hat or no hat, you'll have a tough time topping this warm December weekend.

On the Calendar

Official Event Dates
First Friday-Saturday in December

Best 3 Days To Be There
Thursday-Saturday. Party-night Thursday in Houston and two days of Dickens meets Great Expectations.

☽ 43°/66° (6°/13°)

Texas

Day-by-Day Plan

DAY 1 — Thursday

10:30 am Start in downtown Houston to get a sense of how oil money can be spent. Stop for a lofty perspective from the observation deck at **Chase Tower**.

Noon Lunch in the Montrose area, a funky neighborhood filling up with hip restau-
❌ rants such as **Urbana**. The eclectic food is beautifully presented. If the weather cooperates, sit on the patio.

1:30 pm View the **Menil Collection** of contemporary art, medieval pieces and tribal artwork. The building itself is a work of art, designed by architect Renzo Piano of Italy. Nearby is the **Rothko Chapel**, which contains fourteen site-specific paintings.

6:00 pm For fine dining, try **Ruggles Grill**,
❌ which remains trendy, noisy and hip.

7:30 pm It's a holiday tradition and most fitting for this weekend—a production of Dickens' *A Christmas Carol*, performed by one of the nation's leading (and most underrated) theater companies, the **Alley Theater**. The theater itself is almost worth the price of admission.

10:00 pm In the Theater District is the state's largest entertainment facility, **Bayou Place**. The $22 million nightclub-and-restaurant complex sprawls over 150,000 square feet. Stop by for a drink and sushi at **Sake Lounge**. It has a retro look and is the perfect place to end the day listening to Frank Sinatra. Or ...

11:00 pm Stop at **Solero** for tapas, then head upstairs to its **Czar Bar** for music and a nightcap.

DAY 2 — Friday

10:00 am After breakfast in your hotel, choose one of two museums that are close to each other. The **Holocaust Museum Houston** was designed by the same person who created the one in Washington, D.C., and it is a similarly moving exhibit. The **Museum of Fine Arts, Houston** has one of the nation's largest collections of art. It spans many centuries and cultures.

1:00 pm Head to the Galleria area for a fine
❌ pan-American lunch at **Americas**.

2:30 pm Although shopping isn't usually on the itinerary, it is Christmas, and this is an amazing shopping center, so go to **The Galleria** to check out holiday decorations. This two-million-square-foot mall will be decked out with holiday decorations that include a Texas-size tree that rises from the middle of an ice-skating rink.

7:00 pm For good Italian food and a great
❌ atmosphere, head to **Brother's Petronella** for the one of the best dining views of downtown. Be sure to get a window seat. Enjoy the view and live blues and jazz music while you dine.

10:00 pm Continue down Richmond Avenue. The hippest part of the thoroughfare is between the 5600 and 6600 blocks. Take your pick of bars featuring live rock, country and blues. Check out **City Streets**, a "superclub" that's home to nightclubs for every interest: The Rose for country (all under a thirty-five-foot replica of the Alamo); Blue Monkey for karaoke (guarded by a blue gorilla); the nautical-themed Atlantis for '70s and '80s hits; Cages for house music; and Stray Cats, a sing-along bar with dueling pianos.

12:30 am For an upscale, late-night alternative, try **Club Sempers** for dancing in a refined atmosphere.

DAY 3 — Saturday

8:00 am Enjoy a traditional Tex-Mex break-
❌ fast at the **Spanish Flowers**, a star that stands out in a city that knows good south-of-the-border fare. Make sure to order extra tortillas—they come hot off the griddle.

9:00 am Drive out to Clear Lake, about twenty minutes south of the city, for a look at the interactive visitor center for the **Space Center Houston**. This complex (created by Disney) brings the technology of space travel to a level that any visitor can enjoy.

DAY 3 — Saturday (cont.)

9:00 am (cont.) You can also eavesdrop on the crew of the space shuttle at Mission Status Center or take a behind-the-scenes tour.

1:30 pm ✖ Continue driving south to Galveston. Have some faire food and get in position for the *Queen's Parade*, led by a bagpipe band and the Queen's Guard of Beefeaters. The elegant procession of carriages and coaches is filled with men and women in Victorian finery and viewed by a heavily costumed crowd (there's free admission for those in period garb). The best viewing is from the second-floor balconies, but you'll have to quickly join the Galveston Historical Foundation to snag one of these aeries.

4:00 pm Stroll The Strand, once called The Wall Street of the Southwest, to view the iron-front buildings that now house restaurants, pubs and shops. Hear hand-bell choirs at Trafalgar Square, listen to carolers at Windsor Castle and watch jugglers and magicians at Piccadilly Circus.

6:00 pm When the last rays of sun fade, gas lanterns light up The Strand, marking the route of *Pickwick's Lanternlight Parade*. Costumed lantern-bearers escort parade wagons through streets in another salute to Christmas past.

7:30 pm ✖ A short walk from the bustle brings you to **Fisherman's Wharf** for dinner—they serve delicious seafood with a view.

9:00 pm Back in the thick of the party, choose from twenty-seven draft beers at **Connolly's** and enjoy local rock bands. Make a stop at **Yaga's Cafe & Bar** for live reggae music. Have a nightcap at **The Old Cellar Bar** and quietly reflect on Christmas past, present and future.

■

More Time, More Choices

In Houston, you could try the ribs at **Goode Co. Barbecue** or have what many consider to be the finest meal in town at **Cafe Annie**.

It's hard to choose among top-notch restaurants, but **La Griglia** is among the most hip in town. In Galveston, **Gaido's** serves up seafood fresh from the Gulf.

In Galveston, **Club 21** is an upscale martini bar that features cover bands and good dancing music.

If you overnight in Galveston, have the *Scottish Country Breakfast* at 1859 Ashton Villa, an Italianate house and museum. You'll get typically British fare: fresh scones with marmalade, grilled tomatoes and egg-and-cheese tarts. You can also enjoy the sounds of Christmas carols.

The **Houston Ballet** offers its version of *The Nutcracker* in the Wortham Center.

Accommodations

The **Hyatt Regency Houston** is the city's largest hotel and has easy access to downtown attractions. In Houston, those looking for plenty of pampering will find it at the **Houstonian Hotel Club & Spa**, which has a full-service spa. Check into the European-style **Tremont House**, located in the heart of the festival action and within walking distance of most activities. The **Hotel Galvez**, with a commanding view of the Gulf, is a longtime Galveston favorite.

Event & Ticket Info

Dickens on the Strand (The Strand and 25th Street): Tickets ($10) are available at the gates. For information, contact *The Galveston Historical Foundation* (409-765-7834).

Scottish Country Breakfast (1859 Ashton Villa, 2328 Broadway): Tickets ($20) are available from *The Galveston Historical Foundation* (409-765-7834).

Galveston (Houston)

Hotels	Phone	Address	Price	Fax	Rooms/Best
Hotel Galvez	409-765-7721 800-996-3426	2024 Seawall Blvd.	$$$	409-765-5623	225/Gulf of Mexico vw
Houstonian Hotel Club & Spa	713-680-2626 800-231-2759	111 N. Post Oak Ln.	$$$	713-680-2992	291/Corner rm
Hyatt Regency Houston	713-654-1234 800-233-1234	1200 Louisiana St.	$$	713-951-0934	965/City vw
Tremont House	409-763-0300 800-996-3426	2300 Ships Mechanic Row	$$	409-763-1539	117/(none)

Restaurants	Day	Phone	Address	Price	Rec	Food
Americas	2	713-961-1492	1800 Post Oak Blvd.	$$	L/D	South American
Brothers Petronella	2	409-766-7266 713-223-0119	2301 The Strand at 23rd St./1000 Prairie St.	$$	L/D	Continental, seafood
Cafe Annie	A	713-840-1111	1728 Post Oak Blvd.	$$$$	LD	Continental, Southwestern
Fisherman's Wharf	3	409-765-5708	Pier 22, Harborside Dr.	$$$	D/L	Seafood
Gaido's	A	409-762-9625	3800 Seawall Blvd.	$$$	LD	Seafood
Goode Co. Barbecue	A	713-522-2530	5109 Kirby	$	LD	Barbecue
La Griglia	A	713-526-4700	2002 W. Gray	$$	LD	Italian
Ruggles Grill	1	713-524-3839	903 Westheimer Rd.	$$$	D/L	American bistro, Southwestern
Sake Lounge	1	713-228-7253	550 Texas Ave.	$$	T/LD	Japanese
Solero	1	713-227-2665	910 Prairie St.	$	T/LD	Tapas
Spanish Flowers	3	713-869-1706	4701 N. Main St.	$	B/LD	Mexican
Urbana	1	713-521-1086	3407 Montrose	$$	L/D	Creole, Southwestern

Nightlife	Day	Phone	Address	Cover	Rec*	Music
Alley Theater	1	713-228-8421	615 Texas Ave.	$$$	S	
City Streets	2	713-840-8555	5078 Richmond Ave.	$	MP	Rock, blues, country
Club 21	A	409-762-2101	2102 Post Office St.	$	MP	Cover bands, jazz
Club Sempers	2	713-785-0978	2727 Crossview	$	P(F)	R&B, hip hop
Connolly's	3	409-762-8894	215 22nd St.	$	MP	Rock
Czar Bar	1	713-227-0459	see Solero restaurant	$	P(F)	Latin
Houston Ballet	A	800-828-2787	Wortham Center	$$$	S	
The Old Cellar Bar	3	409-763-4477	2013 Post Office St.	None	R	
Yaga's Cafe & Bar	3	409-762-6676	2314 Strand	$	MP	Reggae, blues, funk

* M=Live music; P=Dancing (Party); R=Bar only; S=Show; (F)=Food served. For further explanation of codes, page 12.

Sights & Attractions	Day	Phone	Address	Entry Fee
Chase Tower	1	713-223-0441	600 Travis St.	None
Holocaust Museum Houston	2	713-942-8000	5401 Caroline St.	None
Menil Collection	1	713-525-9400	1515 Sul Ross	None
Museum of Fine Arts, Houston	2	713-639-7300	1001 Bissonnet St.	$
Rothko Chapel	1	713-524-9839	3900 Yupon	None
Space Center Houston	3	281-244-2100	1601 Nasa Rd. 1	$$

Other Sights, Shops & Services				
Bayou Place	1	713-230-1666	520 Texas Ave.	None
The Galleria	2	713-621-1907	5075 Westheimer Rd.	None

Greater Houston CVB   **713-227-3100**   **801 Congress**

Houston area code: 281   Galveston area code: 713

 NYC -1   Houston Intercontinental (IAH) <60 min./$35 Hobby (HOU) <30 min./$20   Yes   Map Code: A37

Texas

Fiesta San Antonio

Key Month: Apr   **Ratings:** Event ★ ★ ★ ★ ☆   City ★ ★ ☆ ☆   Origin: 1891   Attendance: 3,500,000

Throw together a whopping dose of Texas pride, the partying spirit of Old Mexico, plenty of cerveza and tequila, and what have you got? Nothing less than *Fiesta San Antonio*, the annual fete that wakes up this South Texas city and draws party lovers from across the United States and Mexico.

While the event may have been founded for the purpose of commemorating Texas heroes and April 21, the anniversary of the Battle of San Jacinto (which won Texas independence from Mexico), today the emphasis is on Texas-size fun and the recognition of San Antonio's entire cultural heritage. Events begin at about ten every morning, although most of the dedicated partying takes place much later in the day.

Music festivals, elaborate parades and serious noshing with everything from Tex-Mex to German to Cajun offerings appeal to cowboys and *caballeros*, ranch hands and city slickers. The food and music reflect the cultural pride of the more than one million people living in metropolitan San Antonio. While most events wrap up by midnight, the party continues at crowded nightclubs along the Riverwalk until about 2 a.m. Mariachi music floats through the air, often punctuated with the kinds of hoots and hollers Texas made famous.

On the Calendar

Official Event Dates
Ten days covering two weekends, including San Jacinto Day (April 21)

Best 3 Days To Be There
Three days beginning April 20. Catch the three best moments: River Parade, Night in Old San Antonio (NIOSA) and the special tour of the Alamo.

☀ 59°/79° (15°/26°)

Crowds are thickest along the Riverwalk, or *Paseo del Rio*, the meandering arm of the San Antonio River that winds through downtown. Located below street level, this is ground zero for out-of-towners, a shady walkway lined with hotels, sidewalk cafes, bars and colorful nightlife. During *Fiesta*, the busiest stretch lies between La Mansion del Rio hotel at Navarro Street and around the horseshoe-shaped stretch of the river to La Villita historic area at Presa.

The Riverwalk stretches for two-and-a-half miles, so, away from the partying crowds, there's plenty of opportunity for touring, walking or relaxing beneath a riverside cypress tree enjoying the perfect antidote to a fiesta—a siesta. This will give you a chance to ponder how San Antonio has managed to keep one of America's greatest parties a secret for so long.

For links to most current web sites for cities and events, go to www.funrises.com

DAY 1 — April 20

10:30 am Head to **The Alamo**, a mission that became the scene of a bloody battle in the fight for Texas independence. Walk through what's called the cradle of Texas liberty, a quiet attraction tucked in a bustling commercial district.

Noon Cab to the Mission Trail and the **Mission San José**, once called the Queen of the Missions. Attend a San Antonio tradition: Mariachi Mass. Or go to the **McNay Museum**, which has unusual paintings in a beautiful mansion.

1:30 pm Cab to the Riverwalk and stroll to ✖ **Rio Rio Cantina** for Tex-Mex favorites and some of the best margaritas in town. Snag an outdoor table with a view of the river and passing tourist barges.

3:00 pm Tour the Riverwalk by barge. Hop aboard near the kiosk at Rivercenter Mall or across from the Hilton Palacio del Rio.

7:00 pm Head to **Le Rev** for an intimate two ✖ to three hour dining experience of contemporary French cuisine. You had to make reservations for this place a week in advance, remember?

11:00 pm End the evening with Dixieland jazz at **Jim Cullum's Landing** at the Hyatt.

DAY 2 — April 21

9:00 am Walk to the King William District for ✖ breakfast at the **Guenther House**. Built in 1860, the restaurant serves breakfast favorites plus a Texas standby—biscuits and gravy.

10:30 am Stroll through the King William District, home of stately mansions built during the nineteenth century. You can tour the most opulent one, the **Steves Homestead**, which boasts a natatorium (or "swimming pool" to the less well-bred).

1:00 pm Head to the Riverwalk for lunch at ✖ **Zuni Grill**. Selections start with blue-corn nachos and progress to breaded Anaheim chili pepper filled with crab and sweet corn.

> **D**uring **Fiesta**, there's no escape from *cascarones*, dyed eggshells filled with confetti and covered with tissue paper. Sold in many stores, everyone's a target for these little bombs.

3:30 pm See the story of the Alamo at the **IMAX Theatre at Rivercenter**. From a rolling thunderstorm over the rugged Texas landscape to the daybreak siege by Santa Ana's troops, this forty-five-minute movie wonderfully re-creates the fateful battle.

4:45 pm Do as visitors have done since 1925 and make the pilgrimage to **The Alamo**, a tribute to the heroes of that battle. A special ceremony today includes costumed participants walking up to the former mission where the name of each of the Alamo defenders is called out.

5:30 pm Try **Boudro's**, many San Antonians' ✖ favorite Riverwalk eatery. Arrive early for a good chance at a riverside table. Start with a cactus margarita, a frozen concoction with a jolt of red-cactus liqueur. Follow with an appetizer of duck tamales. Save room for the specialties— coconut shrimp, pecan-grilled fish fillet or blackened prime rib.

6:00 pm Thousands pack the river bank, but you can beat the madness by enjoying the parade from your table. *The Texas Cavaliers' River Parade* features more than forty floats, each with musicians, singers and celebrities.

10:30 pm On a Monday night, **Sunset Station** may be the best place to dance or just hang out.

12:30 am Get a nightcap at **Dick's Last Resort**, one of the rowdiest places on the river. The wait staff likes to crack jokes and toss out matchbooks decorated with old photos of topless women. Ladies can check out restroom walls decorated with more photos of scantily clad hunks.

DAY 3 **April 22**

8:00 am Breakfast at **Schilo's Delicatessen**, ❌ which opened as a saloon in 1917, but became a deli with the coming of Prohibition.

9:00 am Head to the **Institute of Texan Cultures** to explore the twenty-plus ethnic cultures that settled Texas. Costumed docents mosey through the museum, ready to explain the role of a chuck-wagon cook on a cattle drive or the rigors of life as a frontier woman.

11:00 am Walk to the **Tower of the Americas**, the symbol of the 1968 HemisFair world's fair and a landmark of San Antonio. The tower soars 750 feet, but visitors view the city from the observation deck at 579 feet.

12:30 pm Head to **Mi Tierra**, the restaurant ❌ that never sleeps. Twenty-four hours a day, 365 days a year, this San Antonio institution serves some of the city's best Tex-Mex in a festive eatery garnished with Christmas decorations. Strolling troubadours take requests for Mexican ballads.

2:00 pm Start partying at **Fiesta del Mercado**, where five stages showcase mariachi, Tejano, jazz and rock. Pop inside El Mercado, the largest Mexican marketplace in the United States.

5:30 pm Party away the evening at the biggest **Fiesta** event. **A Night in Old San Antonio** is better known by its nickname, NIOSA (*nie-o-sa*). The party, featuring fifteen elaborate cultural areas, takes place in La Villita, a restored eighteenth-century village on the Riverwalk. Dance to Western, *conjunto*, oompah or mariachi ❌ music. Dine on-the-fly at food booths that sell everything from *escargot* to German sausage to tacos.

8:00 pm Walk to the **Mariachi Festival**, one of the oldest in the country. Amateurs and pros battle for the spotlight.

10:30 pm Follow the Riverwalk to **Howl at the Moon**, a sing-along bar that features dueling pianos. Not for quiet types, the bar is filled with folks singing to show tunes and classic-rock songs. Next door, finish the evening with jazz and cocktails at **Swig**.

After

The **Fiesta** continues through the following weekend, when there is a **Battle of Flowers** street parade. On that Sunday, you can bus to the Sunken Gardens in Brackenridge Park for **A Taste of New Orleans**.

More Time, More Choices

Biga offers oak-roasted antelope and other exotic dishes. Try **Paesano's** steak Florentine with spaghetti. **Presidio** has good food and a happening ambience.

The Atrium has a variety of music including merengue and salsa. If you're into cages and fur, check out the jungle-themed **Savages Surf and Safari Club**.

Accommodations

Check out **La Mansion del Rio**. With south-of-the-border elegance, this historic hotel is within walking distance of much of the action, and dining. **The Fairmount** hotel is a small property that pampers guests. The recently opened **Havana Riverwalk Inn** is housed in a historic building. The **Hyatt Regency on the River** is perfectly located with great views.

Event & Ticket Info

Fiesta San Antonio: Many events, including **Fiesta del Mercado**, **Mariachi Festival**, **The Alamo** ceremony and **the Battle of the Flowers** are free. For more information, contact *Fiesta San Antonio Commission* (877-723-4378).

Texas Cavaliers' River Parade (Riverwalk): Tickets for riverside viewing ($8-$20) sell out and are available after January 1 (you don't need a ticket if you have dinner at a riverside restaurant). Contact *Texas Cavaliers' River Parade* (210-227-4837).

Night in Old San Antonio (La Villita, Alamo and Nueva streets): Tickets ($8) are available at the gate. Contact *NIOSA* (210-226-5188).

A Taste of New Orleans (Sunken Garden Theater, Brackenridge Park): Tickets ($5) available at the gate. For information, contact *San Antonio Zulu Association* (210-225-2331).

Hotels	Phone	Address	Price	Fax	Rooms/Best
The Fairmount	210-224-8800 800-996-3246	401 S. Alamo	$$$	210-475-0082	37/City vw
Havana Riverwalk Inn	210-222-2008 888-224-2008	1015 Navarro St.	$$	210-222-2717	27/River vw
Hyatt Regency on the River	210-222-1234 800-233-1234	123 Losoya St.	$$$$	210-227-4925	632/Alamo vw
La Mansion del Rio	210-225-2581 800-292-7300	112 College St.	$$$$	210-226-0389	337/River vw

Restaurants	Day	Phone	Address	Price	Rec	Food
Biga	A	210-225-0722	203 S. St. Mary's St.	$$$	D	American fusion
Boudro's	2	210-224-8484	421 E. Commerce St.	$$	D/L	Southwestern, Tex-Mex
Guenther House	2	210-227-1061	205 E. Guenther St.	$	B/L	Texas breakfast
Le Rev	1	210-212-2221	152 E. Pecan	$$$$	D	Contemporary French
Mi Tierra	3	210-225-1262	218 Produce Row	$	L/BD	Tex-Mex
Paesano's	A	210-828-5191	555 E. Basse St.	$$$	L/D	Italian
Presidio	A	210-472-2265	245 E. Commerce St.	$$	LD	New American
Rio Rio Cantina	1	210-226-8462	421 E. Commerce St.	$$	L/D	Tex-Mex
Schilo's Delicatessen	3	210-223-6692	424 E. Commerce St.	$	B/LD	Deli
Zuni Grill	2	210-227-0864	511 Riverwalk	$$	L/BD	Southwestern

Nightlife	Day	Phone	Address	Cover	Rec*	Music
The Atrium	A	210-822-1912	8505 Broadway	$	MP(F)	Varies
Dick's Last Resort	2	210-224-0026	406 Navarro St.	None	MP(F)	R&B, Motown
Howl at the Moon	3	210-212-4695	111 W. Crockett St.	$	M	Piano sing-along
Jim Cullum's Landing	1	210-223-7266	see Hyatt Regency hotel	$	MP(F)	Jazz
Savages Surf & Safari Club	A	210-641-7827	5500 Babcock St.	$	MP	R&B
Sunset Station	2	210-222-2017	1174 E. Commerce	$	MP	Varies
Swig	3	210-476-0005	111 W. Crockett St.	None	M	Jazz

* M=Live music; P=Dancing (Party); R=Bar only; S=Show; (F)=Food served. For further explanation of codes, page 12.

Sights & Attractions	Day	Phone	Address	Entry Fee
The Alamo	1,2	210-225-1391	300 Alamo Plaza	None
IMAX Theatre at Rivercenter	2	210-225-4629	849 E. Commerce St.	$
Institute of Texan Cultures	3	210-458-2300	801 S. Bowie St.	$
McNay Museum	1	210-824-5368	6000 New Braunfels Ave.	None
Mission San José	1	210-932-1001	6701 San José Dr.	None
Steves Homestead	2	210-225-5924	509 King William	$
Tower of the Americas	3	210-207-8615	600 HemisFair Park	$

San Antonio CVB   **210-225-4636**   **317 Alamo Plaza**

 NYC -1   San Antonio (SAT) <30 min./$15    No   Map Code: A38

Texas

Sundance Film Festival

Key Month: Jan   Ratings: Event ★ ★ ★ ★ ☆   City ★ ★ ★ ☆ ☆   Origin: 1978   Attendance: 18,000

You'll be at the hottest film festival in the country and the coolest spot in the West when you land at Robert Redford's **Sundance Film Festival**. Be sure not to miss the opening three days, when Park City's population (6,000) doubles with independent directors, producers, agents and actors trying to start, revive or expand their careers.

Think of your favorite independent films and chances are it premièred at **Sundance**—*sex, lies and videotape, Four Weddings and a Funeral, Breaking the Waves, The Big Lebowski, The Full Monty*—they're all **Sundance** originals. Directors have broken out from here, too. Quentin Tarantino, Michael Moore and Steven Soderbergh got their starts at the world-class festival. Foreign films, American originals, plays from the Sundance Institute theater project and sightings of Ordinary Bob (Redford won his Oscar for directing *Ordinary People*, ergo the nickname) are all part of the action.

Make sure to leave time for the town. There's good gallery browsing—art, jewelry and clothes are the mainstays—and some fun pubs in the not quite sober Beehive State. But "the greatest snow on earth" is what the winter is all about here. Take the new gondola up the backside of Deer Valley Resort and ski in knee-deep powder among native deer.

The worst thing you can do in any movie town—and Park City definitely becomes a movie town each January—is not dress the part. Fortunately, dressing right is pretty easy: jeans, turtlenecks, parkas, hats, gloves and warm footwear. This is not a place where you need to make any huge fashion statements, but shivering people are immediately spotted as outsiders and nobody comes to this insider event to be an outsider.

Park City consistently ranks among the world's top ski destinations, and during the festival, the fun is notched up to even higher levels. With cutting-edge films, incredible snow and celebrities at every turn, **Sundance** is the place to star in your own fun vacation.

On the Calendar

Official Event Dates
Ten days beginning third Thursday in January

Best 3 Days To Be There
Thursday-Saturday, beginning opening day. Opening Day gala is best, but film buffs may prefer final-night awards.

☀ 19°/40° (-7°/4°)

Utah

For links to most current web sites for cities and events, go to www.funrises.com

Day-by-Day Plan

DAY 1 — Thursday

10:00 am Stop first in Salt Lake City, which has the closest major airport to Park City. Long blocks make Salt Lake a tough walking city, so head to **Temple Square**, which houses the headquarters of the Church of Jesus Christ of the Latter-day Saints and the Mormon Tabernacle Choir. Daily tours of the gorgeous temple run every ten minutes.

Noon With an art-deco interior, linen cloths, black and white tiles, big mirrors and award-winning food, lunch at **The New Yorker** is a must. Their fresh desserts are worth saving room for.

2:30 pm Grab a film guide at the hotel and decide which movies you want to see. If a film is sold out, get in the waiting line, anyway. Almost everybody who waits gets in. Your best chance any day or time is at the 1,270-seat George S. and Dolores Dore Eccles Center for the Performing Arts. Other venues seat between 170 and 460, so tickets can be harder to come by.

5:00 pm Head to Salt Lake City for the **Opening Night Gala**. If you're lucky enough to nab an invitation for the shuttle, you can catch it to Salt Lake City (forty-five minutes) from The Kimball Art Center. Festival directors have a flair for picking a great yet-to-be-discovered film to première at the event. Afterward, cruise the party, where you can't throw a popcorn kernel without hitting an industry biggie. There are lots of bright lights, rolling cameras and energetic dancers at this gathering, which always begins the festival on a high note.

12:30 am Avant-garde people and projects tend to show up for midnight screenings at several venues. But you may want to have a drink at **Lakota**. At Stein Eriksen Lodge, you can enjoy brandy and the fireplace in the bar. Nicolas Cage, Madonna, Keifer Sutherland and other celebrities have been known to hang out here.

DAY 2 — Friday

9:00 am If you can tear yourself away from your down comforter, head back to Main Street for breakfast at **The Eating Establishment**, known as the Double E to locals. The Miner's Dawn is an eggs-fries-and-cheese dish served in a cast-iron skillet.

10:00 am Head to the Town Lift to ride up Treasure Mountain at **Park City Mountain Resort**. Ski where Olympians raced in 2002. Park City is generally blessed with great weather and what the ski magazines love to call "champagne powder" snow.

1:00 pm Lunch at the historic **Mid Mountain Lodge**, where beef dominates the menu. Or ski at the **Deer Valley Resort**, also Olympic terrain, where runs are groomed like putting greens. You can valet-check your skis when you lunch at **Silver Lake Lodge**, which has some of the finest food of any North American ski resort.

6:00 pm Craving another cutting-edge film? At almost any hour in this schedule, you can insert a movie. But you've gotta eat sometime. For an Old Tuscan dinner experience, get a table at **Grappa**, complete with hand-thrown pottery dishes, hand-painted walls and an ebullient staff who love to cook and serve. Don't miss the ravioli-and-butternut-squash winter soup.

9:30 pm The late première screening at the Eccles Center includes the directors, writers, producers and stars of the film, who show up for a question-and-answer session afterward. Attending means you'll have to miss some of the partying hosted by movie companies and producers. Don't worry, the parties won't finish up too early. The one you go to will depend on whom you've met in the last twenty-four hours and whether or not your *Sundance* ticket gets you in the door.

12:30 am Head up Main Street to **Cisero's**, where live music—usually dance-type rock—is always featured.

DAY 3 Saturday

9:00 am Morning Ray Cafe and Bagel Shop is ✖ a good way to start the day, if you don't mind waiting in line. Afterward, grab a (very fast) bobsled ride at the **Utah Olympic Park**.

Noon Enjoy the cozy charm of **Zoom** ✖ (Ordinary Bob's place) at the bottom of Main Street. Roaring fireplaces and wooden floors inside this historic train depot are offset by photos of festival winners and celebs. The open grill allows you to watch the stylish chefs at work. The greatest number of sightings of the rich and famous take place here—most of them come for the legendary garlic mashed potatoes.

3:00 pm Look at the movie schedule and pick the most off-the-wall documentary. Odds are good it will grab a fistful of awards come Oscar time. Filmmakers and casts hang out with their movies, and they want to talk about them. Find a question-and-answer session and become part of the experience. You're likely to learn more about movies than you thought possible at an industry schmooze fest.

6:00 pm Bundle up under blankets and let the huge Clydesdale horses at the Victorian **Snowed Inn Sleigh Company** take you through nearby meadows, where you may see moose, elk and golden eagles. Back at the barn, you ✖ can dig into some tapas from **Picasso**, where the colorful décor includes a wall-size faux Picasso done by a local artist.

10:00 pm Main Street is hopping at this time, and if you wander into **The No Name Saloon**, you can do the shuffle—shuffleboard, that is. This is the kind of Old West hangout that inspires set designers, as well as fans of the Duke.

Midnight It's Saturday night in one of the world's best ski towns during a festival where the second most important reason for being is to have fun—you shouldn't need cue cards for this one.

More Time, More Choices

Former Swiss ski racer Adolph Imboden serves cosmopolitan fare, from veal to escargot, at his restaurant, **Adolph's**. His flaming desserts are legendary. The sushi chefs know their fish at **Mikado Restaurant** on lower Main. The **Riverhorse Cafe** is a hip restaurant that gets booked up by major players, but if there's an opening, try the New American fare. **Wahso** is a hot place to go with its Asian fusion cuisine and '30s Shanghai décor. **Texas Red's** has the best ribs in town.

At the top of Main Street, sample beers at the best microbrewery around, **Wasatch Brew Pub**. Two hot spots for jazz are **Renee's Bar** and **Mother Urban's Ratskellar**.

You can visit one of the few remaining territorial jails in the basement of the **Park City Museum**. Local buzz has it that the secluded cell below street level offers enough privacy for adventuresome paramours to engage in at least misdemeanor behavior (handcuffs not included).

Accommodations

Check out the **Stein Eriksen Lodge**. Named for the Norwegian Olympic-gold-medal skier who lives in town, it's considered one of the most elegant ski lodges in North America, with awards for exquisite design, comfort and gourmet food and wine. **Shadow Ridge Hotel** and **The Yarrow Resort Hotel** are two good, centrally located accommodation options. Both are full-service hotels with all the amenities you'd expect from a top-draw ski resort. The best chain stay is the **Radisson Inn Park City**.

Event & Ticket Info

Sundance Film Festival: All ticket packages are obtained via mail. The best option for Film Festival Opening Parties is Festival Package A ($650). Daily screening tickets are available each morning. For information, call the *Sundance Institute* (801-328-3456).

The Hot Sheet

Hotels		Phone	Address	Price	Fax	Rooms/Best
Radisson Inn Park City		435-649-5000 800-649-5012	2121 Park Ave.	$$	435-649-2122	131/Mtn vw
Shadow Ridge Hotel		435-649-4300 800-451-3031	50 Shadow Ridge Rd.	$$	435-645-9132	150/Dlx Park City vw
Stein Eriksen Lodge		435-649-3700 800-453-1302	7700 Stein Way	$$$$+	435-649-5825	170/Lux rm w/everything
The Yarrow Resort Hotel		435-649-7000 800-327-2332	1800 Park Ave.	$$$	435-645-7007	181/Mtn vw

Restaurants	Day	Phone	Address	Price	Rec	Food
Adolph's	A	435-649-7177	1500 Kearns Blvd.	$$$	D	European, American
The Eating Establishment	2	435-649-8284	317 Main St.	$$	B/LD	American
Grappa	2	435-645-0636	151 Main St.	$$$	D	Northern Italian
Mid Mountain Lodge	2	435-649-8111	Park City Mountain Resort	$$	L	American
Mikado Restaurant	A	435-655-7100	738 Main St.	$$	D	Japanese
Morning Ray Cafe and Bagel Shop	3	435-649-5686	268 Main St.	$	B/L	American eclectic
The New Yorker	1	801-363-0166	60 W. Market St.	$$	L/D	American
Picasso	3	435-658-3030	900 Main St.	$$	D	Spanish tapas
Riverhorse Cafe	A	435-649-3536	540 Main St.	$$	D	American
Silver Lake Lodge	2	435-649-1000	Deer Valley Resort	$$	L	American
Texas Red's	A	435-649-7337	440 Main St.	$$	LD	Barbecue
Wahso	A	435-615-7300	577 Main St.	$$$	D	Asian fusion
Zoom	3	435-649-9108	660 Main St.	$$	L/D	American eclectic

Nightlife	Day	Phone	Address	Cover	Rec*	Music
Cisero's	2	435-649-5044	306 Main St.	$	MP(F)	Rock
Lakota	1	435-658-3400	751 Main St.	None	R(F)	
Mother Urban's Ratskellar	A	435-615-7200	625 Main St.	$	M(F)	Jazz
The No Name Saloon	3	435-649-6667	447 Main St.	None	R(F)	Rock, blues
Renee's Bar	A	435-615-8357	136 Heber Ave.	None	M(F)	Jazz
Wasatch Brew Pub	A	435-649-0900	250 Main St.	None	R(F)	

* M=Live music; P=Dancing (Party); R=Bar only; S=Show; (F)=Food served. For further explanation of codes, page 12.

Sights & Attractions	Day	Phone	Address	Entry Fee
Temple Square	1	801-240-2534	50 W. North Temple St., Salt Lake City	None

Other Sights, Shops & Services				
Deer Valley Resort	2	435-649-1000	2250 Deer Valley Dr. S	
Park City Mountain Resort	2	435-649-8111	1310 Lowell Ave.	
Park City Museum	A	435-649-6104	528 Main St.	None
Snowed Inn Sleigh Company	3	435-647-3310	3770 N. Hwy. 224	$$$$+
Utah Olympic Park	3	435-658-4200	3000 Bear Hollow Dr.	$$$$+

Park City CVB		**800-453-1360**	**528 Main St.**	

 NYC -2   Salt Lake City (SLC) <60 min./$45   Yes/No Map Code: A39

Utah

Bumbershoot

Bumbershoot, The Seattle Arts Festival

Key Month: Aug/Sep   Ratings: Event ★ ★ ☆ ☆ ☆   **ⓟ**   City ★ ★ ★ ★ ☆   Origin: 1971   Attendance: 250,000

There's a buzz in Seattle and it isn't from the coffee. It comes from **Bumbershoot** (slang for "umbrella"), an annual Labor Day weekend celebration that's become one of the largest arts festivals in the United States. Set against the stunning backdrop of Puget Sound and the Olympic Mountains, this food, culture and music explosion runs twelve hours a day for four days, attracting top local and international bands as part of an awesome program.

Nestled among dark-green pine trees, embraced by fresh ocean breezes, shadowed by the 605-foot Space Needle and loaded with as many as twenty-eight indoor and outdoor stages, **Bumbershoot** attracts a fun-loving and usually mellow crowd. More than 2,500 artists, authors, filmmakers, poets and musicians give praise to the human spirit in the seventy-four-acre Seattle Center—a legacy of the 1962 Seattle World's Fair and now the festival's home. Barbecued salmon, Northwest art, experimental films, ballet and opera provide the subtext, but the real draw here is music. Crowds as large as 20,000 often gather to watch music-world legends bring familiar and cutting-edge sounds to music-crazy Seattle. While listening, fans work on tans during the day and watch the stars at night. Forty food and beverage booths appease the hungry.

On the Calendar

Official Event Dates
Friday-Monday of Labor Day (first Monday in September) weekend

Best 3 Days To Be There
Friday-Sunday

☀ 52°/69° (11°/21°)

When **Bumbershoot** festivities end at 11 p.m. each night, party-goers walk a few blocks to hip Belltown, or farther, to the music scene in historic Pioneer Square. During the days, visitors can hop ferries for ten-minute rides to West Seattle or two-hour trips to Victoria, British Columbia. Hikers can visit the nearby Olympic and Cascade mountains and wander among old-growth forests. City attractions include the Seattle Art Museum and Pike Place Market, the oldest farmers market in the United States.

Twenty years ago, Seattle was a sleepy city known for timber and salmon. These days, music, food, coffee and computer-culture booms continue to make this Northwest gem—with an area population of 2.3 million—one of the country's most visited cities. **Bumbershoot** collects the best of Seattle into one glorious weekend.

Day-by-Day Plan

DAY 1 — Friday

10:30 am Dressed in comfortable clothing, walking shoes and a lightweight jacket (you now blend with the locals), stop into one of Seattle's famed coffeehouses and order an energy-boosting latte, Seattle's drink of choice.

11:30 am Walk to Westlake Shopping Center and the Monorail at the top of the mall. After a two-minute elevated-train ride, you'll be at Seattle Center, site of **Bumbershoot**. Your ticket admits you to all performances and exhibitions on a first-come-first-served basis.

12:30 pm Select from a multitude of ❌ regional food and drink specialties for lunch and grab a seat on the grass. Study the festival program. More than 2,000 acts, performances and spectacles take time to sort out.

3:00 pm Stroll the grounds and get your bearings at the gigantic international fountain. With sprays of cooling water, it serves as a central meeting place. Meander around the art market, taking mental note of which piece of Northwest art to buy later. Locate the Opera House, Budweiser Mainstage, Literary Stage, rock arena, and playhouse, where continuous screenings of independent short films are held.

6:30 pm Exit at the Space Needle gate and ❌ hop into the elevator bound for the **Sky City Restaurant**. At 520 feet, the observation deck offers a 360-degree view of Puget Sound, bays, lakes, rivers and snow-capped Mount Rainier. Have dinner at a window table in the revolving restaurant while watching a spectacular sunset unfold.

8:30 pm Catch the last show at the festival. If the performer is well-known, be prepared to wait in line for thirty minutes or more.

11:00 pm Exit at the Broad Street gate and walk ten minutes to Belltown, where there's no shortage of night-life options. **Queen City Grill** is known for its Friday singles scene. **The Crocodile Cafe** is a hot spot for the sounds Seattle made famous—grunge and alternative rock.

While **Bumbershoot** captures the spirit of the city's reputation for wet weather, according to the Seattle-King County News Bureau, Seattleites buy more sunglasses per capita than residents of any other city in the United States.

DAY 2 — Saturday

9:00 am Stroll ten blocks to **Le Panier Bakery** ❌ at **Pike Place Market**. If you're lucky, you'll be able to snag a window table, watch the crowd and enjoy a homemade pastry with a steaming bowl of French-style coffee.

10:00 am Join the Pike Place Market crowd browsing past fresh produce, flowers, restaurants and gift shops. Be prepared to duck the flying fish heads being thrown as you walk past the Pure Food Fish Market.

11:00 am Walk six blocks to gracefully restored Pioneer Square, where loggers built the original Skid Road to slide logs downhill to the waterfront. (As Seattle's economic center migrated north, Skid Row was abandoned to the homeless and indigent.) Meet at Doc Maynard's public house for the humorous **Underground Tour**, a walk through subterranean Seattle.

1:30 pm A local favorite since 1938, **Ivar's** ❌ **Acres of Clams** has fresh seafood and stunning views of Elliott Bay.

3:00 pm Walk along the water and up the 16,000-square-foot staircase-turned-park called the Harbor Steps. At the top you'll find the spectacular Robert Venturi-designed **Seattle Art Museum**. Enjoy outstanding collections of African, Pacific Northwest and contemporary American art.

6:00 pm Head back to **Bumbershoot** for the ❌ Saturday-night headliner. Food concessions dot the stadium, so you won't go hungry.

11:00 pm Stop at **Dmitriou's Jazz Alley** to catch the last nationally renowned jazz act of the evening. **The Ballard Firehouse** has live rock or blues.

1:00 am If you're not ready for the party to end, cab to **13 Coins** for a late-night snack. It's been a Seattle institution for thirty-five years.

DAY 3 · Sunday

10:00 am Walk to the Four Seasons Olympic ❌ hotel for its famous Sunday brunch among the palms at **The Garden Court**.

11:30 am Instead of more *Bumbershoot*, board a tour boat at Piers 55 and 56 to **Tillicum Village** for a four-hour visit to Blake Island. Your trip will include a buffet featuring Pacific salmon, baked Northwest Coast Native American-style on cedar stakes over alder fires.

4:30 pm Have a final cup of Seattle coffee at the original **Starbucks** at Pike Place Market.

7:00 pm Watch the sun set behind the Olympic Mountains while sampling from one of Seattle's most honored wine lists at **Ray's Boat House**, a local favorite for leisurely boaters and high-powered business types.

9:00 pm Dress smartly for dinner at **El** ❌ **Gaucho**, Seattle's trendiest elegant restaurant. It's known for flaming steaks. After dinner, be part of Seattle's casual social scene at its big bar or in the cigar lounge.

■

More Time, More Choices

You'll probably eat lots of stall food at *Bumbershoot*, but you can also try the acclaimed **Sazerac** restaurant in the Hotel Monaco, where dishes are accompanied by sparkling city views. **McCormick and Schmick's Seafood Restaurant** is a regional favorite. The largest outdoor deck in Seattle, overlooking Elliott Bay, is at **Anthony's Bell Street Diner**. Order from a wide range of food that includes Northwest seafood delicacies such as charcoal-grilled salmon with sun-dried tomato butter. Small, neighborhood restaurant **Zoe** has a lively atmosphere and signature dishes such as scallops with corn-and-smoked-bacon risotto.

I Spy is a great dance club with three levels if you're ready to hit the dance floor (or three). If hip hop or reggae is more to your liking, check out **Bohemian Backstage**.

The aircraft industry's presence can be enjoyed at the **Museum of Flight** where you'll see more than fifty full-size aircraft. The **Washington Park Arboretum** is a huge park with a unique collection of plants from around the world, along with a gorgeous **Japanese Garden**. Go to Victoria, B.C. via *The Victoria Clipper*, a turbo-jetted ferry. Victoria harbor is pretty, but the fountains and flowers at **The Butchart Gardens, Ltd**. are the island's highlight and well worth the short bus ride. End your visit with high tea (starting at 3:30 p.m.) at the luxurious **Empress Hotel**.

Accommodations

Snazzy characterizes the **Hotel Monaco**. Enjoy the lobby mural and Mediterranean-eclectic interior design. Opened in 1997, the Monaco has fast become the happening hotel for travelers. The **Four Seasons Olympic**, three blocks from Westlake Center, has been fully restored to its original '20s Renaissance Revival splendor—it may be Seattle's most elegant hotel. Another older hotel, the **Mayflower Park Hotel**, adjacent to the Westlake Shopping Center, could not be more convenient to *Bumbershoot*.

Event & Ticket Info

Bumbershoot, The Seattle Arts Festival (Seattle Center): Daily adult tickets ($14) are available at the Seattle Center during the festival. For advance tickets, call *Ticketmaster* (206-628-0888) beginning in August. For more information, call *One Reel Special Events Hotline* (206-281-8111).

The Hot Sheet

Hotels	Phone	Address	Price	Fax	Best/Rooms
Four Seasons Olympic (Regent Hotels)	206-621-1700 800-223-8772	411 University St.	$$$$	206-682-9633	450/Dlx corner rms w/ prt wtr vw
Hotel Monaco (Kimpton Hotels)	206-621-1770 800-945-2240	1101 4th Ave.	$$$	206-621-7779	189/Corner rm w/city vw
Mayflower Park Hotel in Westlake Center	206-382-6990 800-426-5100	405 Olive Way	$$$	206-382-6997	171/Corner rm w/city vw

Restaurants	Day	Phone	Address	Price	Rec	Food
13 Coins	2	206-682-2513	125 Boren Ave. N	$$	BLD	Varied
Anthony's Bell Street Diner	A	206-448-6688	2201 Alaskan Way	$$	LD	Seafood
The Garden Court	3	206-621-1700	see Four Seasons Olympic hotel	$$$	BLD	Continental
El Gaucho	3	206-728-1337	2505 1st Ave.	$$$$	D	American, steaks
Ivar's Acres of Clams	2	206-624-6852	Pier 54	$$	L/D	Seafood
McCormick and Schmick's Seafood Restaurant	A	206-623-5500	1103 1st Ave.	$$	LD	Seafood
Le Panier Bakery	2	206-441-3669	1902 Pike Pl.	$	B/L	French
Sazerac	A	206-624-7755	1101 4th Ave.	$$	D/BL	Southern American
Sky City Restaurant	1	206-443-2100	400 Broad St.	$$$$	D/L	American
Starbucks	3	206-448-8762	1912 Pike Pl.	$	T	Coffee, pastries
Zoe	A	206-256-2060	213 2nd Ave.	$$	D	American w/ Mediterranean influences

Nightlife	Day	Phone	Address	Cover	Rec*	Music
The Ballard Firehouse	2	206-784-3516	5429 Russell Ave. NW	$	M(F)	Blues, rock, reggae
Bohemian Backstage	A	206-447-1514	111 Yesler Way	$	MP(F)	Reggae, R&B
The Crocodile Cafe	1	206-448-2114	2200 2nd Ave.	$	M(F)	Alternative, rock
Dmitriou's Jazz Alley	2	206-441-9729	2033 6th Ave.	$$	M(F)	Jazz, blues, Latin, African
I Spy	A	206-374-9492	1921 5th Ave.	$	MP(F)	
Queen City Grill	1	206-443-0975	2201 1st Ave.	None	R(F)	
Ray's Boat House	3	206-789-3770	6049 Seaview Ave. NW	None	R(F)	

* M=Live music; P=Dancing (Party); R=Bar only; S=Show; (F)=Food served. For further explanation of codes, page 12.

Sights & Attractions	Day	Phone	Address	Entry Fee
The Butchart Gardens Ltd.	A	250-652-4422	800 Benvenuto Ave.	$$
The Empress Hotel	A	250-384-8111	721 Government St.	$$$
Japanese Garden	A	206-684-4725	1502 Lake Washington Blvd.	$
Museum of Flight	A	206-764-5720	9404 E. Marginal Way S	$
Pike Place Market	2	206-682-7453	1st Ave.	None
Seattle Art Museum	2	206-654-3100	100 University St.	$
Tillicum Village, Blake Island	3	206-933-8600	2992 SW Avalon Way	$$$$+
Underground Tour	2	206-682-4646	Pioneer Square	$
Washington Park Arboretum	A	206-543-8800	2300 Arboretum Dr. E	None

Other Sights, Shops & Services				
The Victoria Clipper	A	800-888-2535	Pier 69 in Seattle	$$$$+

Seattle-King CVB	206-461-5840	Convention Center, 8th Ave. and Pike	

 NYC -3 Seattle/Tacoma (SEA) <60 min./$35  Yes   Map Code: A40

Washington

Summerfest

Key Month: Jun/Jul   Ratings: Event ★ ★ ☆ ☆ ☆   **P**   City ★ ★ ☆ ☆ ☆   Origin: 1968   Attendance: 940,000

Milwaukee, the self-proclaimed City of Fabulous Festivals, hails *Summerfest* as The Big Gig. They might as well call it The Biggest Gig—with eleven stages, more than 2,500 local, regional and international acts, and about a million spectators, it's arguably the world's largest music festival.

Fans of Hungarian folk opera might be disappointed, but almost no one else will. Each *Summerfest* stage is dedicated to a different musical genre: alternative, rock, jazz, blues, country, folk, big band, zydeco, reggae and just about anything else you can think of or hum to. All shows are free, with the exception of daily concerts in the 24,000-capacity Marcus Amphitheater that feature some of the biggest names in music.

But *Summerfest* stands for more than music. For eleven days in late June and early July, it jumps with dancing, music, food, fireworks and Milwaukee's best-known commodity: beer. Opening day is the best day to attend, when the city empties into the lakeside festival grounds to ring in the party with a bang that would make Milwaukeans' Bavarian forebearers proud. *Summerfest* ranks with Munich's legendary Oktoberfest as one of the world's premier beer blowouts.

Milwaukee has been making beer since about 1822, when founder Solomon Juneau started brewing a frontier pilsner here. Business thrived as the area filled with waves of thirsty immigrants—mostly Germans. Beer quickly became a central factor in Milwaukee's economy and culture, and before long, the city was a prosperous, industrial giant. It attracted immigrants from around the globe, making Milwaukee a surprisingly cosmopolitan, land-locked island of cultures. Pabst, Blatz, Stroh's, Schlitz and, of course, the monolithic Miller were all born and raised in Milwaukee, aka Brew City.

Milwaukee's beer-loving, northern European heritage remains conspicuous in its night life, which is synonymous with its pub life. Milwaukee's cuisine sways toward steak, cheese, potatoes and heavy Teutonic platters relished by the city's founders. There are also enough attractions in this city of more than 600,000 to keep you hopping when you're not enjoying one of the biggest and best music festivals in the world.

On the Calendar

Official Event Dates
Eleven days (Thursday-Sunday), including July 4

Best 3 Days To Be There
First three days (Thursday-Saturday). Both weekends are huge, but there are better places to be on the Fourth of July.

☽ 59°/80° (15°/27°)

Wisconsin

Day-by-Day Plan

DAY 1 Thursday

10:30 am Wander around your hotel's neighborhood, then head to Lake Michigan and the **Milwaukee Art Museum** for its noon opening. The 20,000-piece collection is strong in nineteenth-century German art and American sculpture, photography and painting, including two of Andy Warhol's soup cans.

1:45 pm Not far away, *Summerfest* is already crawling with party-goers. Before entering the Henry W. Maier Festival Grounds, walk through the parking lots closest to the entrance. Milwaukee's own Harley-Davidson company commandeers them for the arrival of thousands of Harleys in an unofficial, thundering opening-day parade of leather and chrome.

2:00 pm The booths of more than forty-five restaurants sell foods that include bratwurst, pizza, braised-beef medallions and focaccia sandwiches. *Summerfest* stages and dancing areas are surrounded and separated by crafts peddlers, games of chance and carnival rides. There are also corporate-sponsored activities, including in-line skating exhibitions, volleyball games and tents where you can spend cash on CDs and other music stuff.

6:30 pm Cab to the popular **Coerper's Five O'Clock Club**, a diamond-in-the-rough dinner spot with dim lighting, dark accents and vinyl booths. You can choose from one entree: steak (it's the best in Milwaukee). A well-balanced meal here means a brandy old-fashioned before and after the main course.

8:30 pm Catch one more show—and, of course, one more beer—at the *Fest*. Everywhere you look, a banner, decorated tent or a three-stories-high inflated can reminds you of Milwaukee's drink of choice. But there's no sign of the so-called King of Beers in this town. This is Brew City, where local flavors rule. Wrap your hands around a cold one and join the dancing and people-watching. Or sit by the lake and enjoy the melodies from the many stages blending together into a symphony.

10:35 pm Day One finishes with a fireworks extravaganza—the *Big Bang* at the Big Gig. You can see the show from anywhere on the grounds, but people start gathering at 9:30 p.m. for spectacular lakeside views.

11:30 pm When **Summerfest** closes, follow the crowd and walk five minutes to the historic Third Ward. On Water Street, stop into the **Milwaukee Ale House**, the place to continue the **Summerfest** celebration. Patrons quaff house-brewed beer, dance and sing on a two-level deck over the Milwaukee River.

DAY 2 Friday

10:00 am For breakfast, **Lakeside Inn Café** serves great omelets in a cozy atmosphere.

10:30 am Walk along the Milwaukee Riverwalk toward a cluster of interesting shops on Old World Third Street. Sample some of Wisconsin's homemade cheeses, honeys and mustards at the Wisconsin Cheese Mart. Stop into Milwaukee landmark Usinger's Famous Sausage. They've been making "America's finest sausage" since 1880. Between shops, duck into **Buck Bradley's Saloon & Eatery** to pull up one of forty stools to the gorgeous cherry-wood and rose-granite bar—it's the longest one east of the Mississippi River.

Noon Cross the street to **Mader's Restaurant**, which has kept its German cuisine and atmosphere authentic since 1902. Feast like a Bavarian prince on specialties such as sauerbraten, surrounded by an impressive collection of medieval armor and art. Mader's adjacent **Knight's Bar** serves the same menu and more than 200 beers. Dark wood, stained glass and furniture from Baron von Richthofen's castle emanate Old World ambience.

2:00 pm The **Milwaukee Public Museum**, with walk-through exhibits including the "Streets of Old Milwaukee," is the star of a three-museum complex that includes the Humphrey IMAX Dome Theater and Discovery World-The James Lovell Museum of Science, Economics and Technology.

6:30 pm Walk or cab to dinner at **Louise's Trattoria** for a California-comes-to-Milwaukee dinner.

8:30 pm **Taylor's** has a nice bar. Or head to **Eagan's on Water** to order your favorite cocktail, concocted from among the more than 400 liquors displayed behind the bar.

10:00 pm Close the day back on Old World Third Street at one of Milwaukee's better clubs—the retro-chic **Velvet Room** dance club.

DAY 3 Saturday

9:30 am Take a walk to the contemporary ❌ **Cafe Knickerbocker**. On the outdoor patio, soak up the sun while you eat light and tasty pancakes, waffles or omelets.

10:30 am It's a worthwhile cab ride to **America's Black Holocaust Museum**, which provides a history of racial injustice in a thought-provoking exhibit.

Noon There are spectacular views of St. John's Cathedral and to-die-for burgers at the swank but inviting ❌ lunch spot, **Elsa's on the Park**.

1:30 pm Back to *Summerfest* to catch anything you may have missed Thursday—such as the windsurfing or water-ski shows. You can try winning a car in the Hole-In-One golfing contest in between musical performances. Or shop around for more music.

7:30 pm After dressing up a bit, stop into Pfister's elegant **Lobby Lounge** for an aperitif among *Summerfest* musicians.

8:30 pm Cab to Brady Street, the eclectic epicenter of Milwaukee's East Side neighborhood. Among Milwaukee's ❌ upper echelon of eateries, **Sanford Restaurant** is a cozy hot spot offering impeccable contemporary American cuisine created by an award-winning chef. A good alternative for Italian food is **Mimma's Cafe**.

10:30 pm **Up & Under Pub** has been popular since long before the East Side's current renaissance, attracting renowned blues acts from across the country. The new **Hi Hat Lounge** has a jazzier feel. If you still haven't had enough music, you could always stay another day—along with summer, *Summerfest* is still just getting started.

More Time, More Choices

If you can't get a table at Coerper's, **Butch's Old Casino Steak House** is great for steak, as well as beautiful pork chops and succulent lamb shanks. One of the city's only true late-night restaurants is **Pizza Man**, home to the largest collection of wines in the city—all available by the glass—and a menu that surpasses pizza, with treats such as wild-boar ravioli and *escargot* in a white-wine sauce. For an excellent German restaurant, look no further than **Karl Ratzsch's**. Two restaurants located in the historic Third Ward worth checking into are **Nanakusa** for Japanese cuisine and **Coquette Café**, a French bistro.

If you just gotta dance, head to **Tom Tom Club**, a contemporary Chicago-style dance club. Start or end your night on the town with a drink at **Blu**, a live jazz club showcasing the best views of the city from atop the Pfister Hotel.

Accommodations

Rich with Old World charm and elegance, the **Pfister Hotel** is a twenty-minute walk from *Summerfest*. It's even closer to the nightlife of the historic Third Ward and Milwaukee's East Side. Musicians playing the festival tend to stay here, so check the lobby for familiar faces. The **Wyndham Milwaukee Center Hotel**, located in the heart of downtown's Theater District, is an attractive old building, with rooms decorated in what it calls Flemish-Renaissance style. The newly developed art-deco, all-suite **Hotel Metro** is another good downtown choice.

Event & Ticket Info

Summerfest (Henry W. Maier Festival Park): Tickets ($10 Friday/Saturday, $9 other days) are available at the gate. For more information, contact *Milwaukee World Festival, Inc.* (414-276-4545). For headliner shows at the Marcus Amphitheater, an additional ticket (prices vary) should be ordered in advance through *Ticketmaster* (414-276-4545).

Hotels	Phone	Address	Price	Fax	Rooms/Best
Hotel Metro	414-272-1937	411 E. Mason St.	$$$	414-223-1158	65/Spa suite
Pfister Hotel	414-273-8222 800-558-8232	424 E. Wisconsin Ave.	$$$	414-273-0747	307/Lake vw
Wyndham Milwaukee Center Hotel	414-276-8686 800-996-3426	139 E. Kilbourn Ave.	$$$	414-276-8007	221/Grand king city vw

Restaurants	Day	Phone	Address	Price	Rec	Food
Butch's Old Casino Steak House	A	414-271-8111	555 N. James Lovell St.	$$	D	American
Cafe Knickerbocker	3	414-272-0011	1030 E. Juneau Ave.	$	B/LD	International
Coerper's Five O'Clock Club	1	414-342-3553	2416 W. State St.	$$	D	American
Coquette Cafe	A	414-291-2655	316 N. Milwaukee St.	$$	LD	French
Elsa's on the Park	3	414-765-0615	833 Jefferson St.	$	L/D	American
Karl Ratzsch's	A	414-276-2720	320 E. Mason St.	$$$	D	German
Knight's Bar	2	414-271-3377	see Mader's Restaurant	$	L/D	German
Lakside Inn Café	2	414-276-1577	801 N. Cass St.	$	BLD	American
Louise's Trattoria	2	414-273-4224	801 N. Jefferson St.	$$	D/L	Italian
Mader's Restaurant	2	414-271-3377	1037 N. Old World 3rd St.	$	L/D	German
Mimma's Cafe	3	414-271-7337	1307 E. Brady St.	$$$	D	Italian
Nanakusa	A	414-223-3200	408 E. Chicago St.	$$$	LD	Japanese
Pizza Man	A	414-272-1745	1800 E. North Ave.	$$	LD	Italian
Sanford Restaurant	3	414-276-9608	1547 Jackson St.	$$$$	D	Contemporary American

Nightlife	Day	Phone	Address	Cover	Rec*	Music
Blu	A	414-273-8222	see Pfister Hotel	None	M	Jazz
Buck Bradley's Saloon & Eatery	2	414-224-8500	1019 N. Old World 3rd St.	None	R(F)	
Eagan's on Water	2	414-271-6900	1030 N. Water St.	None	R(F)	
Hi Hat Lounge	3	414-225-9330	1701 N. Arlington St.	None	M(F)	Jazz
Lobby Lounge	3	414-273-8222	see Pfister Hotel	None	M(F)	Piano
Milwaukee Ale House	1	414-226-2337	233 N. Water St.	$	MP(F)	Swing, rock, blues, folk
Taylor's	2	414-271-2855	795 N. Jefferson St.	None	R	
Tom Tom Club	A	414-291-5555	618 N. Broadway	$	MP	Dance
Up & Under Pub	3	414-276-2677	1216 E. Brady St.	$	M(F)	Blues
Velvet Room	2	414-319-1190	730 N. Old World 3rd St.	None	MP(F)	Jazz, swing

* M=Live music; P=Dancing (Party); R=Bar only; S=Show; (F)=Food served. For further explanation of codes, page 12.

Sights & Attractions	Day	Phone	Address	Entry Fee
America's Black Holocaust Museum	3	414-264-2500	2233 N. 4th St.	$
Milwaukee Art Museum	1	414-224-3200	700 N. Art Museum Dr.	$
Milwaukee Public Museum	2	414-278-2700	800 W. Wells St.	$

| Greater Milwaukee CVB | | 800-554-1448 | 400 W. Wisconsin Ave. | |

Wisconsin

 NYC -1 General Mitchell (MKE) <30 min./$<20  Yes/No Map Code: A41

Cheyenne Frontier Days

Key Month: Jul   Ratings: Event ★★★☆☆   🅗   City ★★☆☆☆   Origin: 1897   Attendance: 400,000

Cowboys have figured out a lot of cool things to do with cattle—wrangle 'em, rope 'em, ride 'em, rustle 'em, eat 'em—but **Cheyenne Frontier Days** has to be the best thing they've come up with so far. Justly known as "the daddy of 'em all," **Frontier Days** is a century-old rawhide rodeo, Wild West show and summertime hoedown rolled into one rowdy spectacle that's unlike any other American gathering. Real cowboys and cowgirls still exist and it seems like every last one of 'em rides into town for this annual buckskin bacchanal.

With $500,000 in prize money at stake, the competition and personal rivalries grow fierce as more than 1,000 top-ranked cowboys compete in the world's largest outdoor rodeo arena. Tension builds through roping events, bull riding, barrel racing, steer wrestling, bulldogging, bronco riding and the absolutely bizarre chuck-wagon races. Crowds roar as teams load wagons with a stove and grub, race on a figure-eight course and pound down the track to the finish line—often on two wheels. This is the only rodeo in the United States to which Canadian teams bring their unique, home-grown racing tradition. Then comes the **Frontier Days Wild Horse Race** climax. Mayhem prevails as twelve three-man teams try to saddle and race horses judged too wild for the arena events.

On the Calendar

Official Event Dates
Ten days, beginning Friday, including two weekends in July

Best 3 Days To Be There
Final weekend (Thursday-Saturday). The Sunday finals are exciting, but there's more action within and without the rodeo Thursday through Saturday on the final weekend.

☾ 50°/85° (10°/29°)

Sleepy Cheyenne's tourist attractions are mostly found in the nearby Rocky Mountains. But during **Frontier Days**, Cheyenne's modest head count of 55,000 more than doubles, so there's plenty more to chew on when the broncs aren't bucking.

The **Frontier Days Parade** is a cavalcade of history that rolls from the state capitol to the Union Pacific tracks, where Cheyenne began as a prairie outpost. Along the midway, neon lights illuminate the careening rides, side shows and games of chance that surround a giant merchandise mart where everything western is bartered. Country-music stars and rodeo-circuit favorites mount stages around town nightly to make cowpokes and visitors feel at home with laughin', hollerin' and dancin'.

Wyoming

For links to most current web sites for cities and events, go to www.funrises.com

Cheyenne Frontier Days

DAY 1 Thursday

11:00 am Yoked shirts and cowboy boots are *de rigueur* this weekend. **The Wrangler** and **Just Dandy** are top spots to shop for dude gear hip enough to wear after the *Frontier Days* weekend.

12:30 pm At the fairgrounds, rodeo tickets ✪ and hearty grub are found at **The Cowboy Cafeteria**, where cowboys and families feast on 'cue, beans, buns and corn on the cob.

1:15 pm The *Grand Entry Parade* passes the grandstands signaling the start of a full day of *rodeo* events, where cowboys demonstrate the skills and courage that helped tame the West and introduced words such as *broncobusting* and *lassoing* to the English language.

5:00 pm While post-rodeo traffic thins, visit the *Frontier Park Indian Village*, where the Wind River Dance Group lives and performs Native American dances daily.

7:30 pm Drive to **Los Amigos** Mexican restau-✪ rant, where Carroll Leger smothers just about every item on the menu with his specialty—green chile and pork.

9:00 pm A mile north at **The Horn's Cowboy Bar**, winners of the Wild Horse Races keep tradition alive by literally drinking from their victory boots. Hundreds pack this combination Bavarian beer hall/*Animal House*/Old West saloon to two-step to regional bands. Go ahead and close down the joint, since—as Waylon sings it—"the girls all get prettier at closing time." (And the guys get louder, if nothing else.)

DAY 2 Friday

7:00 am Hit the free pancake breakfast ✪ (7–9 a.m.) in downtown's city center parking lot. No after-church Sunday social, this is where 10,000 locals and visitors sit on hay bales enjoying hotcakes and ham fresh from the griddle. Entertainment is provided by The Chugwater Philharmonic String Quartet—a fast-moving country-music-and-comedy show that's an annual crowd favorite.

9:00 am If you're willing to forgo the rodeo, make the seventy-mile drive on I-80 to the Snowy Range of the Rocky Mountains. After crossing an 8,640-foot pass, take Highway 130 west to Centennial (population 100) for a look at the boxcar museum and a public library consisting of a rack of paperback novels.

Noon Have lunch at **The Old Corral** in the ✪ town's newest building (which is still old enough to have housed The Old Corral for seventy-five years). The steak and chicken dinners are excellent, but there's also a cowpoke surprise: the state's best salads. Continue on scenic Highway 130, passing wildflowers, the sapphire waters of Lake Marie and good spots for midsummer snowball fights.

5:00 pm Back in Cheyenne, proceed to the ✪ popular **Lexie's** for an early dinner of American favorites.

7:00 pm *The Cheyenne Frontier Days Night Show* features western-music concerts in front of the grandstands get boots stompin' and hands clappin'. It can get cool and breezy at night, so consider bringing a coat or blanket.

10:30 pm Get your boots to the dance floor at the **Hitching Post Inn** or **The Horn's Cowboy Bar**.

DAY 3 Saturday

9:30 am A cannon blast signals the long and strong *Frontier Days Parade*. Find a place a block south of the capitol building where you can sit in the shade on the grass. Thousands of spectators enjoy more than 1,000 horses, marching bands, historic vehicles and antique autos. Ladies costumed in turn-of-the-century finery ride in the world's largest collection of horse-drawn vehicles. Floats carry folks dressed in the traditional wear of Native Americans, cowboys, cowgirls, gamblers and gunslingers.

Noon Walk down Capitol Avenue to **The** ✪ **Albany**, a local favorite and Cheyenne's oldest cafe. The prime-rib roast-beef sandwich is among the more popular lunch orders.

Day-by-Day Plan

DAY 3 — Saturday (cont.)

1:15 pm Head back to the stands for the *rodeo semi-finals* or take the two-hour **Cheyenne Street Railway Trolley** tour. Retired teachers dish up details of Cheyenne's history as you cruise past famous and infamous sights, buildings, homes and museums, including the **Cheyenne Frontier Days Old West Museum** at Frontier Park.

3:00 pm Cross the road from the Frontier Park complex to **Lions Park**, where you can take a dip in Sloan's Lake, Cheyenne's original swimmin' hole with beach and paddle-boat rentals. Don't leave without visiting **Cheyenne Botanic Gardens and Solar Conservatory**. The lush oasis retreat seems far away from the heat and dust of the rodeo arena.

7:30 pm About ten minutes south of town on I-25, the Terry Bison Ranch serves delicious buffalo steaks and lamb chops in ✪ its **Senator's Steak House**.

9:30 pm Don't miss the *Frontier Days'* party finale (and highlight) starring Ricky and the Red Streaks at **The Coach Room**. Ricky's bawdy humor and cookin' band have made this hilarious act the *Frontier Days* favorite since the '70s. Rodeo royalty and the cattle corporate crowd drink Black Velvet and rest their $1,000 boots on the bar's brass rail. Mix with directors of other Western shows, Frontier Days committeemen and various Western celebs before saying "happy trails" and riding off into the sunset.

■

After

If you can manage to stay until Sunday, be sure to catch the *rodeo finals*. The events are basically the same, but the excitement level tends to be higher when most of the prize money is on the line.

More Time, More Choices

Cheyenne folks know meat, and local restaurants tend to focus on it—**The Little Bear Inn** is yet another solid option. But for a change from Western meals, **The Twin Dragons** restaurant has a lunch buffet featuring Mandarin and Szechwan specialties. Or, try **Botticelli Ristorante Italiano** for fresh seafood or steak—Italian style. The Hitching Post Inn also houses two good beef restaurants, the **Carriage Court Restaurant** and the **Cheyenne Cattle Company**. Both have earned awards from the Wyoming Beef Council.

Cheyenne's nightlife is mostly downtown. If you've already become a regular at the Hitching Post or The Cowboy Bar, check out the **Cheyenne Club** for kit-shickin' live music. **The Outlaw Saloon** opens the patio bar for *Frontier Days*—mechanical bull included. Even during the day, the **Wigwam** is a popular watering hole and meeting place.

An hour's drive northwest of Cheyenne, the **Diamond Guest Ranch** offers horseback riding, trout fishing, teakhouse, bar and cabins. The **Wyoming Hereford Ranch** is a cattle-breeding operation that has produced world-renowned stock since 1883. **Terry Bison Ranch** has more than 2,500 bison on a 27,000-plus acre ranch. It also has camels, llamas, emus, ostriches, peacocks and turkins, which are half turkey, half chicken.

Accommodations

Little America Hotel's charm and views make it the prime place to stay on the frontier, but the newly built and conveniently located **Holiday Inn** is a good option. Also suited to the *Frontier Days* experience is the **Hitching Post Inn**, which combines Old West style with a good selection of amenities.

Event & Ticket Info

Cheyenne Frontier Days (Frontier Park, Carey Ave. and 8th Ave.): $2 gets you admission to the park, the parades, *Frontier Park Indian Village* or the *Pancake Breakfast* (Lincoln Way and Carey Ave.). Tickets for reserved seating for the rodeo ($10-$20) and *The Cheyenne Frontier Days Night Show* ($18) go on sale in January. The best seats for the rodeo, which are over or close to the chutes, sell out months in advance. Some Night Shows sell out in advance. For tickets or information, contact *Frontier Days* (800-227-6336).

Hotels		Phone	Address	Price	Fax	Room/Best
Hitching Post Inn Resort and Conference Center Best Western		307-638-3301 800-221-0125	1700 W. Lincolnway	$$	307-778-7194	169/New section, Bldg 4 or 5
Holiday Inn		307-638-4466 800-465-4329	204 Fox Farm Rd.	$$	307-638-3677	245/Laramie Range vw
Little America Hotel		307-775-8400 800-445-6945	2800 W. Lincolnway	$$	307-775-8425	188/Facing golf course

Restaurants	Day	Phone	Address	Price	Rec	Food
The Albany	3	307-638-3507	1506 Capitol Ave.	$	L/D	Beef
Botticelli Ristorante Italiano	A	307-634-9700	300 E. 17th St.	$$	LD	Northern Italian
Carriage Court Restaurant	A	307-638-3301	see the Hitching Post Inn	$$	LD	Beef
Cheyenne Cattle Company	A	307-638-3301	see the Hitching Post Inn	$$	LD	Beef
The Cowboy Cafeteria	1	307-778-7222	Frontier Park	$	L/D	Burgers, hot dogs
Lexie's	2	307-638-8712	216 E. 17th St.	$$	D/BL	American, International
The Little Bear Inn	A	307-634-3684	Little Bear Road N, I-25N, Exit 16	$$	D	Steak
Los Amigos	1	307-638-8591	620 Central Ave.	$	D/L	Mexican
The Old Corral	2	307-745-5918	2750 Hwy 130, Centennial	$	L/BD	Chicken, steak
Senator's Steak House	3	307-634-4994	I-25, 51 Service Rd. E	$$	D/L	Chuck-wagon dinner
The Twin Dragons	A	307-637-6622	1809 Carey Ave.	$	LD	Chinese

Nightlife	Day	Phone	Address	Cover	Rec*	Music
Cheyenne Club	A	307-635-7777	1617 Capitol Ave.		MP	Country
The Coach Room	3	307-638-3301	see the Hitching Post Inn	$$	MP	Country, oldies
The Horn's Cowboy Bar	1,2	307-637-3800	312 S. Greeley Hwy.	None	MP	Country
The Outlaw Saloon	A	307-635-7552	3839 E. Lincolnway	None	MP	Country
Wigwam	A	307-635-9096	1600 Central Ave.	None	MP	Country

* M=Live music; P=Dancing (Party); R=Bar only; S=Show; (F)=Food served. For further explanation of codes, page 12.

Sights & Attractions	Day	Phone	Address	Entry Fee
Cheyenne Botanic Gardens and Solar Conservatory	3	307-637-6458	710 S. Lions Park Dr.	Donation only
Cheyenne Frontier Days Old West Museum	3	800-778-7290	4610 N. Carey Ave.	$
Cheyenne Street Railway Trolley	3	800-426-5009	309 W. Lincolnway	$
Diamond Guest Ranch	A	800-932-4222	40 mi. no. of Cheyenne, Chugwater (I-25)	None
Lions Park	3	307-637-6429	520 W. 8th St.	None
Terry Bison Ranch	A	302-634-4171	51 I-25 Service Rd. E	None
Wyoming Hereford Ranch	A	307-634-1905	1600 Hereford Ranch Rd., east of Cheyenne	None

Other Sights, Shops & Services				
Just Dandy	1	307-635-2565	212 W. 17th St.	None
The Wrangler	1	307-634-3048	1518 Capitol Ave.	None

The Cheyenne Area CVB	800-426-5009	309 W. Lincolnway

 NYC -2   Cheyenne (CYS) <30 min./$5 Denver (DEN) <120 min./NA   Yes   Map Code: A42

Two Much Fun

Any one of the destinations in this book makes for a great trip, but some dates and locations make it possible to double or even triple your fun and minimize travel hassles with back-to-back events at nearby locations. Some indefatigable readers are figuring out ways to attend all 96 events on *The Fun Seeker's Gold List* (Hooray!), but if that's not possible, combining just two can turn a great vacation into an unforgettable epic.

1. **The Sporting Life**
   Phoenix Open (page 14, map A01) and **Super Bowl Weekend** (page 116, map A26)

   Unless you feel compelled to see the final rounds of a golf tournament, you can start partying in Phoenix/Scottsdale on Wednesday, then take the short trip to Las Vegas on Saturday for its biggest weekend of the year! (Golf diehards can always watch the tournament on a big screen in Vegas.)

2. **Bikers with Salsa**
   Bike Week (page 46, map A09) and **Calle Ocho** (page 62, map A12)

   It's an easy drive from Daytona Beach to Miami Beach, but the flavor of these two cities and events couldn't be more different. Drive south on Saturday—you'll miss a bit of the excitement of **Bike Week**, but it doesn't get much better than Saturday night in South Beach (Miami Beach).

3. **Fiesta! Fiesta! Fiesta!**
   Party Acapulco (page 199, map A47), **Feria de San Marcos** (page 202, map A48), and **Fiesta San Antonio** (page 160, map A38)

   You can party in Acapulco almost anytime (although Thursdays through Saturdays are usually the best days), so it's easy to combine the Feria with a short, one-stop flight to or from Acapulco. Then, another one-stop flight gets you to San Antonio. Warning—only very serious fun seekers should attempt this!

4. **Elegance Times Two**
   Black and White Ball (page 30, map A05) and **Napa Valley Wine Auction** (page 22, map A03)

   The **Black and White Ball** in San Francisco is held only every other year, but those years provide an incredible opportunity to experience two of the most elegant events on *The Fun Seeker's Gold List*. The drive to Napa from the city takes less than 90 minutes.

5. **Food and Music or Music and Food?**
   Summerfest (page 172, map A41) and **Taste of Chicago** (page 78, map A17)

   Milwaukee is only 90 minutes by car from Chicago, giving you a chance to overload on great bands and food. Both events take place over two weekends, so there's plenty of opportunity to make room on your schedule for both.

6. **The Florida Blitz**
   Fantasy Fest (page 50, map A10); **Cruise: Carnival** (page 58, map A12); **Do: Disney World** (page 54, map A11); **Bike Week** (page 46, map A09); and **Calle Ocho** (page 62, map A12)

   Carnival Cruise and **Disney World** can be enjoyed year 'round, making it easy to combine them with one of three other Florida events. Miami, the departure port for the **Carnival Cruise**, is a short flight or couple hours drive from Key West, so a cruise can be easily combined with **Fantasy Fest**. **Disney World** is just outside of Orlando, a short drive from Daytona (**Bike Week**). It's also within driving distance of Miami, home to **Calle Ocho**. In other words, you could make the trip from **Disney World** to **Bike Week** to **Calle Ocho** to a **Carnival Cruise** in a very short amount of time—a sure-fire way to get into Fun Seeker heaven!

Of the 96 events and destinations
*(**The Fun Seeker's Gold List**) that*
every fun seeker should experience,
four are in Canada. Read on ...
amusez vous bien!

Events and Destinations in
Canada

Calgary Stampede

Calgary, Alberta

Key Month: Jul   Ratings: Event ★★★★☆   **H**   City ★★☆☆☆   Origin: 1912   Attendance: 1,100,000

If you've ever wanted to watch a full-size chuck wagon bite the dust in a blaze of glory, or hear a defeated cowboy swear a blue streak at a two-ton piece of twisting livestock, the **Calgary Stampede** is the place to be. At this annual Western bash, visitors get so close to the action—on the grounds and on the city streets—that there really are no spectators here, just participants.

For ten days every July, Calgary— one of the most underrated cities in North America—becomes the world's biggest and best party town. The celebration of Old West spirit is highlighted by a world-class rodeo, but public gatherings for pancake feasts, square-dancing, two-stepping, beer-guzzling and all-night partying are the real purpose (and fun).

Each day, the afternoon rodeo and evening *Rangeland Derby* showcase the dangerous world of the professional cowboy. The rodeo equivalent of an auto-race crash is a cowpoke getting booted in the head by a bronc or bull. Only lunatics really want to see that sort of thing, but the possibility of calamity will keep you nervously clutching your seat bottom.

Away from the Stampede grounds, the Western spirit rages. Day and night, country bands belt out tunes all over town. Two-steppers and line dancers congregate at outdoor hoe-downs. Those too shy to dance gather nerve by joining local saloons and clubs that spill over with ten-gallon hats and the cowboy's drink of choice—a shot of whiskey with a beer chaser.

During *Stampede*, denim rules this otherwise-cosmopolitan city of 800,000. Cowboy-clad customs and immigration officers work the airport. Hotels put up Western-themed façades. Local business types get to ditch their suits for jeans in the office, proving that cowboy garb can be *très* chic.

An hour outside Calgary, Banff National Park is the country's best place to view the majestic beauty of the Canadian Rockies, and see for yourself why the Winter Olympics were held here. Lake Louise, possibly the most beautiful lake in the world, is the centerpiece of this stunning park, making the scenic drive a perfect topper to a weekend at one of the world's great events.

On the Calendar

Official Event Dates
Ten days, beginning first Friday in July

Best 3 Days To Be There
Final weekend (Friday-Sunday). By the time the final Friday arrives, people are excited, cowboy-ized and two-steppin' uncontrollably.

☾ 47°/76° (8°/24°)

Canada

Day-by-Day Plan

DAY 1 — Friday

9:00 am For a genuine **Western Breakfast**, ❌ grab some free flapjacks from a chuck wagon on Stephen Avenue Walk, along the Eighth Avenue Mall, one block from The Palliser. This is your first chance to get an idea of what *The New York Times* meant when it said the **Stampede**'s two million visitors create "a raucous party that turns the entire city into a Western theme park."

10:30 am Stroll down the mall to **Lammle's Western Wear** and ditch your city-slicker ensemble for dude duds. This upscale store carries boots, Western shirts and vests, denim, cowboy hats, bolo ties, skirts, dresses and beaded shirts.

Noon In Eau Claire Market, lunch in the Big Skye Dining Room or on the outdoor ❌ deck at **Whiskey Creek**, an eatery with the ambience of a Western movie set. Try a bowl of red-hot chili, ribs grilled with barbecue sauce or aged Alberta steak or prime rib. For the less easily satisfied, ostrich is also on the menu.

1:00 pm Cab to the hotel, drop off your purchases. A trip to the observation terrace of the **Calgary Tower**, just a block from The Palliser, gives a great panoramic view of Calgary and the Rockies.

1:30 pm Walk the few blocks to the **Stampede** grounds and take your seat for the **Rodeo**. This is the tension-building warm-up for the finals.

4:30 pm Check out the *Daily Events Schedule*. It lists all free exhibits, shows, entertainers and activities. Make your way down the incredibly clean midway, with its neon cacophony, barkers and games of chance. Pig races and livestock competitions are the draw here. Or take your chances on the Ejection Seat (an amazing bungee contraption).

7:00 pm Have a cold beer and chow down ❌ on a barbecue steak, beef-on-a-bun or all-you-can-eat, Western buffet.

8:00 pm With thundering hooves and flying dust, the **Rangeland Derby** pits four chuck wagons and sixteen outriders in a race down the Half Mile of Hell. **The Grandstand Show** follows with energetic song, dance and comedy routines.

11:30 pm Don't miss the fireworks show, an awe-inspiring pyrotechnic light-and-laser spectacle.

11:45 pm Still on the fairgrounds, party to live country music at Nashville North or Top 40 music at the outdoor Coca-Cola stage. Close out the night with a swing through the casino.

DAY 2 — Saturday

9:00 am Walk to Olympic Plaza for entertainment in Rope Square. Grab a coffee and only enough chuckwagon grub to stave off your appetite until brunch.

10:30 am Drive ninety minutes to Banff National Park. Mountain weather can change quickly, so take extra clothing and, of course, extra film.

12:15 pm At your reserved table in the Banff ❌ Springs Hotel's **Bow Valley Grill**, take in staggering views while enjoying an excellent buffet brunch.

2:00 pm Ride the **Sulphur Mountain Gondola** to the "top of the world." Walk off your brunch along the Vista Trail walkway to Sanson's Peak. Then soak in the natural mineral waters of the **Banff Upper Hot Springs.**

6:30 pm Try the **Grizzly House**, which features ❌ fondue specialties and wild game, including rattlesnake.

10:00 pm Check out **Cowboys Dance Hall**, which you'll have heard about by this time. A favorite nightspot, its vast arena-like structure may be packed, but there's also an outside keg party. Slipping $20 to the doorman should get you past the line.

DAY 3 — Sunday

10:30 am Stroll to breakfast at the **1886** ❌ **Buffalo Cafe**. Established long before the surrounding trendy Eau Claire Market, this tiny restaurant is known for omelets with a choice of nineteen fillings. If there's a line, hang tough—it's worth the wait.

Sunday (cont.)

12:30 pm Grab a cab and head for the **Stampede** grounds. The 1:30 p.m. rodeo finals are filled with thrills and spills, as cowboys and cowgirls compete for $300,000 in prize money. Choose from ❌ a variety of carnival-style food and beverages on sale throughout the grounds.

7:00 pm Change into your new Western wear at the hotel. Since the Stampede is on, you'll be appropriately dressed, even for an evening in tonight's tony establishments.

8:00 pm If you're hooked on chuck-wagon races, stay for the finals. Otherwise, cab to Eau Claire and unwind as you dine on ❌ the patio of the **River Cafe** in Prince's Island Park, along the Bow River. This chic cafe features Canadian wood-fired cuisine and an extensive selection of Northwestern wines.

11:00 pm Wrap up the evening at **The Palace Nightclub** on Stephen Avenue Walk. The popular Palace retains its classy flair, while exchanging its usual Egyptian theme for Stampede style and country bands.

■

More Time, More Choices

La Caille on the Bow is a terrific place for dinner with a river view, an outdoor patio and both casual and elegant dining rooms. Another great choice is **Mescalero**, a cozy, local favorite specializing in Southwestern wood-grilled entrees presented with artistic flair. If you can't get enough cowboy fare, pay a visit to **Buzzards Cookshack**. Surrounded by Western memorabilia, you can try prairie oysters (calves' testicles sautéed in herbs, lemon juice and white wine). **Teatro** features Italian-inspired regional cuisine. Popular for lunch and dinner is **Rococco**, which has tremendous service and a good wine list. For breakfast, **Break The Fast Cafe** has a fun atmosphere. **The Palliser** offers a wonderful weekend brunch.

The Palliser's **Oak Room** features live bands and a Western buffet. **Desperadoes** is just a couple of blocks from the Stampede grounds, and as western as you can get.

Six blocks away is **Roxy's**, a sushi bar—emphasis on bar—which has a best-dressed man and woman contest every Saturday night with a $500 prize.

Accommodations

Upon entering **The Palliser**, you'll get a "Howdy ma'am, sir," from the doorman. Built in 1914, The Palliser is *Stampede* central. West-facing rooms provide breathtaking views of the mountains. The **Calgary Marriott Hotel**, just a block from The Palliser, is probably the best modern hotel in town and within walking distance of the *Stampede* grounds. The **Sheraton Suites Calgary Eau Clair** is close to the action in Eau Claire. The all-suite hotel delivers terrific amenities. If you stay in Banff, the **Banff Springs Hotel** is the grande dame of the area.

Event & Ticket Info

Calgary Exhibition and Stampede (Stampede Park, Olympic Way and 14th Ave. SE): Tickets ($15-$35) should be ordered close to one year in advance for good seats. A limited number of "rush seat" tickets ($6) go on sale each day ninety minutes prior to show time. Contact *Calgary Stampede* (800-661-1767).

Rangeland Derby and Grandstand Show: Tickets ($15-$35) for the grandstand are best for the chuck-wagon races. Contact *Calgary Stampede* (800-661-1767).

Stampede Park has a separate admission charge for those not already holding tickets for the Rodeo or the Rangeland Derby. Contact *Calgary Stampede* (800-661-1767).

The Hot Sheet

Hotels	Phone	Address	Price	Fax	Rooms/Best
Banff Springs Hotel	403-762-2211 800-441-1414	405 Spray Ave.	$$$$	403-762-4447	770/Valley vw
Calgary Marriott Hotel	403-266-7331 800-228-9290	110 9th Ave. SE	$$	403-231-4523	383/Downtown vw
The Palliser	403-262-1234 800-441-1414	133 9th Ave. SW	$$$	403-260-1260	405/Mtn vw
Sheraton Suites Calgary Eau Clair	403-266-7200 888-784-8370	255 Barclay Parade SW	$$	403-266-1300	323/River valley vw

Restaurants	Day	Phone	Address	Price	Rec	Food
1886 Buffalo Cafe	3	403-269-9255	187 Barclay Parade SW	$	B	Breakfast
Bow Valley Grill	2	403-762-6860	see Banff Springs Hotel	$$	L/BD	Buffet lunch
Break The Fast Cafe	A	403-265-5071	516 9th Ave. SW	$	BL	Ukrainian
Buzzards Cookshack	A	403-264-6959	140 10th Ave. SW	$$	LD	Steakhouse
Grizzly House	2	403-762-4055	207 Banff Ave.	$$$	D/L	Fondue
La Caille on the Bow	A	403-262-5554	100 La Caille Pl. SW	$$	LD	Contemporary, continental
Mescalero	A	403-266-3339	1315 1st St. SW	$$	LD	Contemporary Southwestern
The Palliser	A	403-262-1234	see The Palliser hotel	$$	BLD	Brunch
River Cafe	3	403-261-7670	in Prince's Island Park	$$$	D/L	Organic game
Rococco	A	403-233-2265	125 8th Ave. SW	$$$	LD	International
Teatro	A	403-290-1012	200 8th Ave. SE	$$$	D/L	Italian
Whiskey Creek	1	403-262-9378	151 Eau Claire Market	$$	L/D	Regional American

Nightlife	Day	Phone	Address	Cover	Rec*	Music
Cowboys Dance Hall	2	403-265-0699	826 5th St. SW	$$$	MP(F)	Country, pop
Desperadoes	A	403-263-5343	1088 Olympic Way SE	$	MP(F)	Country
Oak Room	A	403-262-1234	see The Palliser hotel	None	MP(F)	Country
The Palace Nightclub	3	403-263-9980	219 8th Ave. SW	$$	MP	Varies
Ranchman's Restaurant	3	403-253-1100	9615 Macleod Trail	$	MP(F)	Country
Roxy's	A	403-214-7699	219 17th Ave. SW	$	P(F)	Top 40

* M=Live music; P=Dancing (Party); R=Bar only; S=Show; (F)=Food served. For further explanation of codes, page 12.

Sights & Attractions	Day	Phone	Address	Entry Fee
Banff Upper Hot Springs	2	403-762-1515	Mountain Ave.	$
Calgary Tower	1	403-266-7171	101 9th Ave. SW	$
Lammle's Western Wear	1	403-266-5226	211 8th Ave. SW	None
Sulphur Mountain Gondola	2	403-762-2523	End of the Mountain	$$

Calgary CVB	800-661-1678	220 8th Ave. SW

 NYC -2  Calgary (YYC) <30 min./$20   Yes   Map Code: A43

Montréal Jazz Festival

Festival International de Jazz de Montréal

Key Month: Jun/Jul Ratings: Event ★★★☆☆ **P** City ★★★★☆ Origin: 1979 Attendance: 1,500,000

In a city calling itself the City of Festivals, the **Montréal Jazz Festival** is the biggest and most joyful fete of the year. Often called the best jazz festival in the world—2,000 musicians from twenty-five countries get crowds moving at 400 shows—this event rates as one of Canada's best annual shindigs.

The *Jazz Fest* really ought to be called the *Montréal Music Festival and Street Party*. From noon until the early-morning hours, 1.5 million music lovers and social animals pack six square blocks, all of them closed to vehicular traffic. Musicians play free concerts on eight outdoor stages, turning the area into a party that reverberates with the sounds of jazz, blues, world beat, African, zydeco, rhythm and blues and most other party-music genres. Every night, concerts and galas crank up eight indoor venues, which range from elegant theaters in Place des Arts, to some downright weird and very alternative nightclubs. Bands aren't the only acts in town—jugglers, unicyclists, illusionists, mimes and performance artists help fill the festival site with sights. Throughout the area, jazz bars and food kiosks keep energy levels high.

So much happens at the festival that it's tempting to linger at party central. But by breaking away from the festival scene, you'll be able to enjoy cosmopolitan Montréal's beauty and vitality. Whether in Old Montréal, the Latin Quarter or amid striking downtown architecture, Montréal is a great walking city. Old Montréal, with its narrow cobbled streets, is an especially worthwhile side trip. Don't forget to take part in the most popular local sport—people-watching from the city's sidewalk cafes.

Montréal is actually two cities, one above ground, one below. During summer you may never see the eighteen miles of subterranean pedestrian malls, but you will enjoy plenty of restaurants and bars with 3 a.m. closing times. Nearly three-quarters of metropolitan Montréal's 3.5 million citizens are French, making it the largest French population outside Paris. And as in Paris, although English is spoken, the language you'll understand best here is the local *joie de vivre*. (*For more on jazz festivals, see page 218.*)

On the Calendar

Official Event Dates
Eleven days beginning last Thursday in June

Best 3 Days To Be There
Tuesday-Thursday. Don't miss the huge outdoor concert on Tuesday. Otherwise, either weekend is good.

Other Times To Go
Perhaps the best comedy festival in the world (with at least some English spoken), *Just For Laughs* (514-790-4242) takes place right after the *Jazz Festival*.

☽ 61°/80° (16°/27°)

Day-by-Day Plan

DAY 1 — Tuesday

10:30 am Explore the Old Port. Then hire a *calèche* (a type of horse-drawn carriage), for a tour of Old Montréal's quaint cobbled streets. More than any other place in North America, Old Montréal really feels like Europe.

12:30 pm Cab to lunch at the very French ❌ **L'Express**, marked only by its name painted on the sidewalk. Mingle at the bar with Montréalers drenched in style—from their attitudes to their designer ensembles—before having delicious bistro fare.

2:00 pm Do some window-shopping on Rue St-Denis, then sit, have coffee and people-watch from one of the street-front terraces. The sidewalk traffic—Montréalers are very fashion conscious—is excellent for those who appreciate contemplating the better half of the human condition.

4:00 pm The **Musée d'Art Contemporain** is one of Montréal's most worthwhile attractions. Enter from Place des Arts and browse through shows featuring artists working on the latest edge of modern art, many of whom tend to come from Québec.

6:00 pm Leaving the museum, you'll be in the thick of *festival activity*. Grab some ❌ festival food and find a place to watch the main event, an outdoor concert for 100,000 people. Music themes change each year, but the outdoor extravaganza practically guarantees a good time.

11:00 pm Walk to **Shed Café** for excellent late-night food and drink. Afterward, if there's a crowd outside, follow it to one of the many clubs in the area. You'll be excused for not playing on, however, since tomorrow promises to be an even-busier day.

DAY 2 — Wednesday

9:00 am Montréal is famous for its bagels. Find out why by ordering a bagel with ❌ cream cheese and lox at **Eggspectation**.

10:30 am Cab to one of the city's top attractions, the **Montréal Biodôme**, an environmental museum that allows you to enter the Amazon rainforest, the Arctic or two other climate areas filled with so much flora that you'll believe you're really there.

12:30 pm It's a short ride to **Schwartz's** ❌ **Montréal Hebrew Delicatessen** to enjoy Montréal's famous smoked meat—which is similar to corned beef—and an old-fashioned cherry Coke. It's a long way from posh, but it's a visitor's don't-miss, and Montréalers flock there, too.

2:00 pm Today's *free concerts* have started. Pick up a copy of The Gazette for the complete performance schedule and the paper's picks for the day. You can watch outdoor concerts from stageside tables until around 6:30 p.m., when crowds become larger and denser. Scope out the area to familiarize yourself with all eight stages before the crowds show up.

6:00 pm On your way back to your hotel, stop up, way up, at one of the best terrace bars in Montréal, **737**. You'll get a great view from its forty-fifth-floor perch.

8:00 pm Allow enough time to find the theater showing your choice of headliner concerts, which is probably at Place des Arts. If you choose one of the concerts at Salle Wilfrid-Pelletier, book a seat near the front for the best view or—for optimal acoustics—in the middle of the first row under the balcony overhang. In Théâtre Maisonneuve, home of Les Grand Concerts, all seats offer good views, but sit toward the rear of the first section for the best acoustics.

10:15 pm Cab to dinner at **Ferreira Café** ❌ **Trattoria** for an unusual Portuguese-inspired meal with an attractive crowd and setting.

12:15 am Afterward, walk to **Thursdays**, where you can have a nightcap in the bar upstairs or dance until 3 a.m. in the club below.

DAY 3 Thursday

9:30 am At **Chez Cora**, along with basic breakfasts such as bacon and eggs and fruit, you can try *cretons*, a Québecois dish made from ground pork.

10:30 am The **Montréal Museum of Fine Arts** has one of the best permanent collections in North America. Its great range of works spans centuries and disciplines.

12:30 pm Have lunch at **Globe**, where the casually attractive atmosphere perfectly suits the healthy lunch menu.

2:00 pm It should be an afternoon of great jazz at the *festival*, capped with a drink at **Jello Bar**. Have one or two of the many martini concoctions and bask in the '50s-style sophistication of its lounge.

7:30 pm Dinner is at **Mediterraneo**, where you'll find Montréal's hip crowd eating California-Italian cuisine.

9:30 pm If you crave a cigar or that type of atmosphere, try **Wax** above the restaurant Primadonna.

11:00 pm When you're ready, catch a cab to L'Hôtel de la Montagne, where, until as late as 3 a.m., you can dance to a live orchestra amid starry skies near the rooftop swimming pool at **Terrasse Magnétic**.

More Time, More Choices

If you like what you eat at **L'Epicier**, you can go to the gourmet shop in the restaurant and buy some of the products or ingredients to take home. Hip dinner alternatives are **Ristorante Primadonna** and **Buona Notte**. Another popular restaurant is **Weinstein and Gavino's**. Many people consider **Toqué!** to be Montréal's finest restaurant, where the clientele is surprisingly animated amid expensive surroundings.

Funkytown is the hot club downstairs from the Restaurant Alexandre. The young and the beautiful can be found at **Electric Avenue**, which features '80s music in an intimate setting. Check out Formula One driver Jacque Villeneuve's **New Town**, which

includes a restaurant and disco on its four levels. The **Casino de Montréal** provides a complete evening of entertainment—dinner, nightclub show, gaming—in elegant surroundings. Just in case you can't get enough, Montréal's best-known jazz club is **Biddle's Jazz & Ribs, Inc.**, where you can have chicken and ribs while listening to the music of veteran bassist Charlie Biddle and his illustrious sidemen.

Mont-Royal Park, with its lighted cross atop the peak, dominates the island city's skyline. Its natural area is a favorite with locals as a place to exercise, picnic or just sit and enjoy nature. A taxi can take you partway up the mountain to enjoy wonderful views, day or night. The **Montréal Botanical Garden**, next to the Biodôme, has the largest Chinese Garden outside of Asia, and a creepy but cool collection of bugs and other small, scary things at its renowned Insectorium.

Accommodations

If you're coming to Montréal primarily for jazz, consider **Hotel Wyndham Montréal**. This is the hotel where the festival's jazz musicians traditionally stay, and where some of them meet to jam from midnight to 4 a.m. in the hotel lounge. All you have to do is walk out the door to be in the middle of the free-concert area. The attractive **L'Hôtel de la Montagne** has a posh lobby, intricately detailed marble and artwork and rooms that offer nice views of the beautiful Mont-Royal Park. Another option is the recently redecorated **Omni Mont-Royal** hotel. Its spacious rooms—only twelve to a floor—include living rooms.

Event & Ticket Info

Montréal International Jazz Festival
(Rue Ste-Catherine between Jeanne-Mance and Boulevard St-Laurent): Of 400 performances, almost 300 are free. Tickets for selected shows ($10-$50) can be ordered from *Admission Ticket Network* (800-361-4595). For more information, contact *Montréal International Jazz Festival* (888-515-0515).

The Hot Sheet

Hotels	Phone	Address	Price	Fax	Rooms/Best
L'Hôtel de la Montagne	514-288-5656 800-361-6262	1430 rue de la Montagne	$$	514-288-9658	135/Queen Suites
Hôtel Wyndham Montréal	514-285-1450 800-996-3426	1255 Jeanne-Mance	$$	514-285-1243	600/Mtn vw
Omni Mont-Royal	514-284-1110 800-843-6664	1050 rue Sherbrooke Ouest	$$$	514-845-3025	300/Above 8th fl, mtn or city vw

Restaurants	Day	Phone	Address	Price	Rec	Food
Buona Notte	A	514-848-0644	3518 blvd. St-Laurent	$$	LD	Italian
Chez Cora	3	514-286-6171	1425 Stanley	$	B/L	International breakfast
Eggspectation	2	514-278-6411	198 av. Laurier	$	B/LD	Breakfast
L'Epicier	A	514-878-2232	311 St. Paul Ouest	$$$	LD	French w/ Asian, Italian influence
L'Express	1	514-845-5333	3927 rue St-Denis	$$	L/BD	French
Ferreira Café Trattoria	2	514-848-0988	1446 rue Peel	$$$	D/L	Mediterranean, Portuguese
Globe	3	514-284-3823	3455 blvd. St-Laurent	$$	D	California fusion
Mediterraneo	3	514-844-0027	3500 blvd. St-Laurent	$$	D	Mediterranean
Ristorante Primadonna	A	514-282-6644	3479 blvd. St-Laurent	$$$	LD	Italian, sushi
Schwartz's Montréal Hebrew Delicatessen	2	514-842-4813	3895 blvd. St-Laurent	$	L/BD	Deli
Shed Café	1	514-842-0220	3515 blvd. St-Laurent	$	T/BLD	Continental
Toqué!	A	514-499-2084	3842 rue St-Denis	$$	D	French
Weinstein and Gavino's	A	514-288-2231	1434 rue Crescent	$	LD	Italian

Nightlife	Day	Phone	Address	Cover	Rec*	Music
737	2	514-397-0737	Place Ville Marie, Penthouse 2	None	P(F)	Varies
Biddle's Jazz & Ribs Inc.	A	514-842-8656	2060 rue Aylmer	$	M(F)	Jazz
Casino de Montréal	A	514-392-2746	1 av. de Casino	None	MS(F)	Cabaret
Electric Avenue	A	514-285-8885	1469 rue Crescent	$	P	'80s
Funkytown	A	514-282-8387	1454 rue Peel	$	P	Disco
Jello Bar	3	514-285-2621	151 rue Ontario Ouest	$	MP	Jazz, swing
New Town	A	514-284-6555	1476 Crescent St.	$	P(F)	Jazz, disco, house
Terrasse Magnétic	3	514-288-5656	see L' Hôtel de la Montagne	None	MP	Dance
Thursdays	2	514-288-5656	see L' Hôtel de la Montagne	None	P	Pop, R&B, rock
Wax	3	514-282-0919	3481 blvd. St-Laurent	$	P	Soul, R&B, house

* M=Live music; P=Dancing (Party); R=Bar only; S=Show; (F)=Food served. For further explanation of codes, page 12.

Sights & Attractions	Day	Phone	Address	Entry Fee
Mont-Royal Park	A	514-843-8240	Av. du Royal and Av. du Parc	None
Montréal Biodôme	2	514-868-3000	4777 Pierre de Coubertin	$
Montréal Botanical Garden	A	514-872-1400	4101 rue Sherbrooke E	$
Montréal Museum of Fine Arts	3	514-285-2000	1379-1380 rue Sherbrooke Ouest	$
Musée d'Art Contemporain	1	514-847-6226	185 rue Ste-Catherine Ouest	$

Greater Montréal CTB   514-844-5400   1001 Square Dorchester

 NYC Dorval (YUL) <30 min./$20   No   Map Code: A44

Canada

Québec Winter Carnaval

Québec City,
Québec

Carnaval de Québec

Key Month: Jan/Feb Ratings: Event ★★★☆☆ **P** City ★★☆☆☆ Origin: 1894 Attendance: 1,000,000

It's one of the world's biggest carnivals, but with one big difference that separates it from the pack: snow. You won't see anyone sporting a bikini, except for a few nuts taking snow baths. And instead of dazzling clouds of tinsel, the streets more often swirl with sparkling snow. It's the **Québec Winter Carnaval**, a three-week samba in padded parkas.

Deep in the heart of winter, the oldest walled city north of Mexico defies hypothermia by becoming a pulsing conga line, with parades, balls, snow sports and parties. Lit by millions of pinpoint lights stretching from the snow-banked suburbs to the heart of Old Québec, the celebration is fueled by 18,000 liters of local Caribou (a wicked libation made of port and grain alcohol). Presiding over the festivities is Bonhomme, a seven-foot walking, talking snowman in a red toque. He's the city's ambassador of bonhomie and his massive ice palace—with fortified defense walls, crowded medieval alleys, huge ancient monasteries, burghers' stone homes and reminders of battles lost and won—is a Québec legend.

Although **Québec's Winter Carnaval** wasn't officially established until 1894, it originated 390 years ago, when French explorer Samuel de Champlain threw a party for settlers.

During the bitter January of 1608, they were hungry, sick with scurvy, freezing and depressed. Champlain decreed the "Order of Good Times" and a festival filled with wine, food and dancing. Suicidal spirits soared. From a celebration born of despair, **Carnaval** has become a lusty salute to *joie de vivre* and the world's biggest blast in the snow.

With its beautifully preserved historic buildings, Québec City is a UNESCO World Heritage site—one of only two in North America. Such a distinction hasn't fossilized the vibrancy of a populace proud to celebrate its roots, culture, art, gastronomy, sports, snow and ice. During the carnival, Québec demonstrates its exuberance with endless rounds of **Carnaval**'s signature song: "*Car-na-val ... Mardi Gras ... Car-na-val!*" It's a refrain that will echo through your sleep—if you're lucky enough to get any.

On the Calendar

Official Event Dates
Three weekends beginning last Friday of January

Best 3 Days To Be There
Friday-Sunday of last weekend. Includes two don't-miss events— Bal de Bonhomme and the Night Parade.

Other Times To Go
Quebec City Summer Festival (418-692-5200) in early July is a first-class music gathering.

☀ 04°/20° (-16°/-7°)

For links to most current web sites for cities and events, go to www.funrises.com

Day-by-Day Plan

DAY 1 Friday

9:30 am Purchase a Bonhomme figurine, your pass for outdoor **Carnaval** venues. Another must-buy is a hollow Bonhomme walking cane to fill with Caribou. If your cane should run empty, shots are sold at makeshift bars everywhere. Also pick up multicolored, traditional *ceinture fléchées* (sashes) from weavers working their looms in the lobby of Le Château Frontenac.

10:00 am Then have breakfast at the
✖ hotel's **Café de la Terrasse** while watching strollers on the historic Dufferin Terrace boardwalk.

11:00 am Walk two minutes to rue du Trésor. In this picturesque open-air gallery, local artists display and sell their paintings—snow or shine.

Noon The **Québec Experience**, a 3-D sound-and-light show, gives an overview of the city's some 400-year history.

1:30 pm Stroll three minutes to lunch at the fabled site of North America's first French kiss, across from the
✖ château. Built in 1679, **Auberge du Trésor** claims to be the continent's oldest continuously inhabited dwelling. Specialties include beef Wellington and rabbit in mustard sauce.

4:00 pm Walk five minutes and take a one-horse open-sleigh ride across the Plains of Abraham, adjacent to the château.

6:00 pm Dressed in evening finery, descend to the resplendent château ballroom for the **Bal de Bonhomme**. You and 300 others in fancy gowns or suits
✖ dine on five gourmet courses and dance to a full orchestra.

11:30 pm Cap the night in the oak-paneled **Le Bar Saint-Laurent** for one last whirl on its tiny dance floor.

DAY 2 Saturday

10:00 am Walk fifteen minutes to a hearty,
✖ outdoor **flapjack breakfast**. Canada's cowboy city, Calgary, hosts 5,000 appetites on Place Loto-Québec in front of the Parliament building.

11:00 am Nearby is the striking **Bonhomme's Palace**, a glittering fantasy of 6,000 ice blocks weighing 225 tons. Visit rooms with ice furniture and mementos from Bonhomme's world tours. Meet some Knuks—merry dancers and pranksters from the Arctic Circle.

Noon Lunch on authentic Québecois cuisine—pea soup, *tourtière* and maple-syrup pie—
✖ at the historic **Aux Anciens Canadiens**.

1:00 pm Head to Place Desjardins for the **canoe race preliminaries**; competitors practice on snow for tomorrow's treacherous river crossing on the ice floes. If athletically inspired, you can tube down a glissade, climb a forty-foot ice mountain, play minigolf en glace or snowboard. Laid-back pleasures include a dog-sled ride and an igloo village, with igloo-building lessons. On Côte de la Fabrique, fifteen-minutes away, watch the fast and colorful **Normandin Soapbox Derby**.

3:30 pm Order a bowl of French onion soup or *moules et frites* (mussels and fries) at one of the Old City's many bistros. Or choose one of **Portofino**'s charcoal-baked pizzas.

4:30 pm Head to your room for even warmer clothes for the night's outdoor activities.

7:00 pm Cane reloaded, take the hotel shuttle to Charlesbourg and join the **Night Parade** throng. Floats and bands wend their way through snowy streets, while about 180,000 chant "*Car-na-val ... Mardi Gras ... Car-na-val,*" until it's forever imbedded in your head.

8:30 pm Back on Grande Allée—the Champs-Elysées of North America—bistros and nightclubs shimmer with ice sculptures and tiny white lights. Dine at the award-winning French ✪ restaurant **Bonaparte**, as fine an establishment as you'll find with mitts, toques and boots steaming by the fire. The specialty is local lobster from Sept-Îles.

10:00 pm Stroll along crowded Grande Allée. Two happening spots are **Chez Dagobert**, where 1,500 people pulsate on a stainless-steel floor, and **Le Charlotte Lounge**, a mellower nightclub. **Maurice Salon-Bar** has cognac and cigars.

2:00 am Stop by Place Desjardins to watch *The Night of the Long Knives*—sculptors stay up all night carving massive blocks of snow into art for tomorrow's 9 a.m. judging.

DAY 3 — Sunday

10:00 am Take the funicular from Dufferin Terrace to the Quartier Petit-Champlain. The oldest commercial district in North America, it bustles with one-of-a-kind craft shops.

11:30 am Brunch at **Le Lapin Sauté**, a ✪ country-style nook warmed by a fireplace.

1:30 pm Carnaval events change from year to year and often involve some form of entertaining competition. Get details from the official program and go.

3:30 pm Visit **Musée de la Civilisation**. Exhibits range from American Indian civilization to "Diamonds."

5:00 pm Stop into **Pub Thomas Dunn** for a choice of more than 150 brews and seventy-five brands of single-malt Scotch.

8:00 pm Cross to the Gare du Palais, a train station resembling a small castle, which holds two local hot spots. Dine at the hip ✪ **L'Aviatic Club**. Its menu includes sushi and Tex-Mex.

10:00 pm Cap off the night at **Société Cigare**, a plush cigar bar or at **Jules et Jim**, a bar with an intimate French ambience.

More Time, More Choices

Café du Monde is a lively hangout and a good brunch spot on Sunday. Popular **Initiale** is known for its *foie gras* and rack of lamb specialties. For a unique dining experience, try **Le Champlain** where employees don seventeenth-century velvet costumes. The city's top maitre d's listed these eating spots among the best: **Laurie Raphaél** for tartares and desserts; **Marie Clarisse** for seafood dishes; **Louis-Hébert** for French cuisine; and **a la Bastille chez Bahuaud** for unique appetizers and entrees such as stingray.

Call before catching a packed dinner show at **Le Capitole de Québec**. Have a digestif at the trendy **Ristorante Il Teatro**.

Montmorency Falls is 114 feet higher than Niagara Falls. Cable car to the top for lunch at opulent **Manoir Montmorency**.

Accommodations

The romantic and elegant **Le Château Frontenac** is based close to *Carnaval* action. This turreted, copper-topped castle towers above the walled city and is the world's most photographed hotel. Rooms have hosted Churchill, Roosevelt, De Gaulle, Princess Grace or any of eighteen monarchs. **Loews Le Concorde** is a modern hotel popular partly for its revolving restaurant and central location. In historic Quartier Petit-Champlain are **Hôtel Dominion 1912**, a cozy boutique hotel, and **Auberge Saint-Antoine**, a charming small hotel.

Event & Ticket Info

Québec Winter Carnaval: A Bonhomme figurine ($5) is your pass for outdoor *Carnaval* venues. Some events have an additional, minimal fee. *Bal de Bonhomme* ($50) tickets sell out and should be purchased before Christmas. For tickets and a program, contact *Carnaval de Québec* (418-626-3716).

Hotels	Phone	Address	Price	Fax	Room/Best
Auberge Saint-Antoine	418-692-2211 / 888-692-2211	10 rue St-Antoine	$$	418-692-1177	31/St. Lawrence River vw
Le Château Frontenac	418-692-3861 / 800-441-1414	1 rue des Carrières	$$$	418-692-3820	651/St. Lawrence River vw
Hôtel Dominion 1912	418-692-2224 / 888-833-5253	126 rue St-Pierre	$$$	418-692-4403	60/Old Town vw
Loews Le Concorde	418-647-2222 / 800-463-5256	1225 place Montcalm	$$	418-647-4710	409/City vw

Restaurants	Day	Phone	Address	Price	Rec	Food
Auberge du Trésor	1	418-694-1876	20 rue Ste-Anne	$$	L/BD	French
Aux Anciens Canadiens	2	418-692-1627	34 rue St-Louis	$$	L/D	Québecois
L'Aviatic Club	3	418-522-3555	450 de la Gare du Palais	$$	D	International
a la Bastille chez Bahuaud	A	418-692-2544	47 av. Ste-Geneviève	$$$	D	French
Bonaparte	2	418-647-4747	680 Grande Allée E	$$$$	D/L	French
Café de la Terrasse	1	418-692-3861	1 rue des Carrières	$$	B/LD	Continental
Café du Monde	A	418-692-4455	57 rue Dalhousie	$$	L/BD	French bistro
Initiale	A	418-694-1818	54 St. Pierre	$$$	D	French
Laurie Raphaél	A	418-692-4555	117 rue Dalhousie	$$$	LD	Québecois
Le Champlain	A	418-692-3861	see Le Château Frontenac	$$$$	D	French
Le Lapin Sauté	3	418-692-5325	52 Petit Champlain	$$	B/LD	French
Louis-Hébert	A	418-525-7812	668 Grande Allée E	$$	BLD	French, seafood
Manoir Montmorency	A	418-663-3330	490 av. Royale	$$$	L	Québecois
Marie Clarisse	A	418-692-0857	12 Petit Champlain	$$$$	LD	Seafood
Portofino	2	418-692-8888	54 rue Couillard	$$	L/D	Italian
Ristorante Il Teatro	A	418-694-4040	972 rue St-Jean	$$	BLD	Italian

Nightlife	Day	Phone	Address	Cover	Rec*	Music
Chez Dagobert	2	418-522-0393	600 Grande Allée E	$	MP	Alternative
Jules et Jim	3	418-524-9570	1060 av. Cartier	None	R	
Le Bar Saint-Laurent	1	418-692-3861	see Le Château Frontenac	None	R	
Le Capitole de Québec	A	418-694-9930	972 rue St-Jean	$$$	S	
Le Charlotte Lounge	2	418-647-2000	575 Grande Allée E	$	P	Rock, Latin
Maurice Salon-Bar	2	418-640-0711	575 Grande Allée E	None	R	
Pub Thomas Dunn	3	418-692-4693	369 rue St-Paul	None	R(F)	
Société Cigare	3	418-575-7588	575 Grand Allée E	None	R	

* M=Live music; P=Dancing (Party); R=Bar only; S=Show; (F)=Food served. For further explanation of codes, page 12.

Sights & Attractions	Day	Phone	Address	Entry Fee
Montmorency Falls	A	418-663-3330	2490 av. Royale	$
Musée de Civilisation	3	418-643-2158	85 rue Dalhousie	$
Québec Experience	1	418-694-4000	8 rue du Trésor	$

Québec City Tourism	**418-649-2608**	**835 av. Wilfrid Leurier**

Canada

 NYC   Jean-Lesage (YBQ) <30 min./$20 Dorval (YUL) 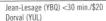 No   Map Code: A45

Caribana

Key Month: Jul/Aug   Ratings: Event ★ ★ ☆ ☆ ☆   **P**   City ★ ★ ★ ★ ★   Origin: 1967   Attendance: 1,500,000

Like snow in June, like peanut butter and chocolate, the great joy of Toronto's **Caribana** is the mind-boggling combination of two seemingly disparate elements. When hard-core Caribbean partying plows head first into hard-core Anglo culture, the result is one of the most exciting blends of opposites since Bob Dylan discovered electricity.

One of North America's largest and most exuberant street parties, **Caribana** takes place in Toronto, a city with a history of straight-laced refinement. Over the past few decades, however, immigration from every corner of the globe has dramatically changed the face of the Ontario capital. To celebrate the heritage of the largely Caribbean and Latin influx, **Caribana** gathers more than a million happy people to grind to traditional calypso, steel-drum music and. soca, a calypso offshoot originally called soul calypso that pumps up the energy and volume.

The carnival traditions of the Carib and Latin worlds are well-known, and **Caribana** evokes them all. Musical competitors vie for the Calypso Monarch crown and the trophy for best steel band. Others opt for jump-ups, sunset cruises or the mas (short for "masquerade") drama of the king-and-queen competition. Excitement peaks at the **Caribana Parade**. Flatbed trucks jammed with brightly costumed dancers and bands follow a two-mile lakeside route, cheered on by half a million drinking, dancing spectators. On the water side of Lakeshore Boulevard, crowds gather around food stands to sample traditional island fare such as *roti* and patties. Liberal use of the beer tents is a favorite way to beat the afternoon heat.

Since most **Caribana**-weekend activities are held close to Lake Ontario, it's easy to slip away to find out what else makes Toronto tick. The city's world-renowned restaurants, ethnic neighborhoods, museums, galleries and live theater have been touted by *National Geographic*, *Fortune* and the *Utne Reader*. Just beyond the city limits lies one of the world's most awe-inspiring natural sights: Niagara Falls. The city is clean, the locals are friendly and for this weekend at least, dancing in the streets is the top priority. Who says Canada and the Caribbean have nothing in common?

On the Calendar

Official Event Dates
Seventeen days, beginning third Friday in July

Best 3 Days To Be There
Thursday-Saturday of final weekend. Thursday and Friday prepare you for the parade (climax) on Saturday.

Other Times To Go
Held in early September
The Toronto Film Festival
(416-968-3456) is growing into one of the biggest, most user-friendly film events (may make the next edition of the *Fun Seeker's Gold List*).

☾ 59°/79° (15°/26°)

Canada

Day-by-Day Plan

DAY 1 Thursday

10:30 am Take a tour of **Casa Loma**, a mock-medieval castle built in 1914 with an intriguing mix of furnished suites, secret passages, underground tunnels and magnificent gardens.

12:30 pm Lunch at **Prego della Piazza**, an ✖ oasis of calm in midtown surrounded by boutiques, towering office blocks and old churches. Exquisitely prepared meals earn consistently high ratings.

2:30 pm Walk to the **Royal Ontario Museum**, commonly known as ROM. Famous for its East Asian collection, new additions include a wing dedicated to European decorative arts and a working paleontology lab.

6:00 pm Join the financial-district crowd for a drink at a popular after-work spot, **Jump Cafe & Bar**.

8:00 pm **Boba** serves up original and tasty ✖ dishes such as rice-paper-wrapped chicken breast on Thai black rice or big-eye tuna grilled rare with coconut noodles, mango and avocado salsa and black bean frites.

10:00 pm For dancing, try the jazzy **Easy & The Fifth**. Downstairs there's a DJ, upstairs there's jazz.

DAY 2 Friday

8:00 am Have breakfast at the **Studio Cafe** in ✖ the Four Seasons hotel. Designed to evoke the atmosphere of an artist's loft, the dining room is adorned with pieces from notable Canadian artists.

9:00 am Set off to **Niagara Falls**, a ninety-minute drive. Park on the Niagara Parkway. Walk or take the People Mover to Table Rock House for great views of Horseshoe Falls and the smaller American Falls. Ride on *Maid of the Mist*, an open boat that carries you into the maelstrom at the base of Horseshoe Falls. (You'll be issued waterproof gear.) The Table Rock Scenic Tunnels are a drier but equally dramatic alternative, opening onto viewing portals right under the falls.

1:00 pm Take Winston Churchill's advice and follow the prettiest afternoon drive in the world to historic Niagara-on-the-Lake. Along the way, a good lunch stop ✖ is the **Queenston Heights Restaurant**. It has a varied menu—seafood, chicken, beef, etc.—but the restaurant sits high on the Niagara Escarpment, and the real draw is its spectacular view of the Niagara River.

2:00 pm In Niagara-on-the-Lake, Fort George is a fascinating reconstruction of the original (which was destroyed in 1812) and there are plenty of stores, cafes and restaurants along Queen Street.

6:00 pm Return to Toronto to join the crowd at the ferry terminal beside your hotel for the **Sunset Cruise**. Remember, Toronto is on island time for **Caribana**, so go with the flow and be prepared for a late start. Most of your fellow passengers will have Caribbean roots and will definitely know how to have a party. Once on board, live bands—local and from the West Indies—drive up the tempo. Rum drinks and beer are plentiful, and there's a tasty Caribbean spread.

11:30 pm A number of Caribbean dance parties dot the city, most of them put on in association with **Caribana**. Check the local newspaper. Or hit the entertainment district and check out **Limelight** or **Whiskey Saigon**.

2:00 am Late-night hunger pangs can be ✖ assuaged at **Pearl Court**, where very good Cantonese and Szechwan dishes are served until 4 a.m.

DAY 3 Saturday

9:00 am Take the hotel shuttle to Union Station and walk to the **CN Tower**, the world's tallest tower at 1,815 feet. At the observation level, you can step on to the glass floor and see the ground beneath your feet—a frightening 1,122 feet below. Half the fun is seeing the traumatizing effect this has on folks of all ages. The Space Deck, at 1,464 feet, has the world's highest observation gallery.

Day-by-Day Plan

DAY 3 — Saturday (cont.)

10:30 am Head for **Masquerade Caffè Bar**. ✖ Steaming bowls of latte, flaky croissants, fresh fruit and yogurt are standard breakfast fare.

11:30 am Armed with sunscreen, a hat and comfortable shoes, get to Lakeshore Boulevard West and the *Caribana Parade* route. Crowds don't build until several hours later, but the earlier you arrive, the better the chance you'll have of finding a spot in the shade. By late afternoon, you'll thank yourself.

Noon Wander through the marketplace and ✖ lunch on whatever suits your mood—fresh coconut, hamburgers, sweet corn, *roti*, jerk chicken and pilau are all available. Exotic bevies include *mauby*, ginger beer and sorrel. Around you, people will not be shy about whooping it up, greeting long-lost friends and acquaintances, exchanging shouts and hugs, waving to Moko Jumbies (traditional African characters who walk on stilts) and singing and dancing to the live calypso, soca, steel-drum, reggae and samba bands. By 6 p.m., the parade is usually finished and all of the day's winners will have been announced.

7:30 pm Have a great meal on your last night ✖ in Toronto at **Zoom Caffè & Bar**. The décor, presentation and clientele are all top-notch.

9:30 pm Get back in the Caribbean mood at **The Bamboo**, a hip nightclub with live bands—tonight will be reggae—and people-watching upstairs at its Treetop Lounge.

11:30 pm If you want to slow down a bit, head to the **Top o' the Senator** for a nightcap and some of the best jazz around. Have a final drink and reflect on a city that can be as energetic, stimulating or relaxed as suits its mood. If you haven't yet discovered Toronto's charm and sophistication, a *Caribana* weekend is the most fun way to get to know this fascinating and diverse city.

■

More Time, More Choices

Bistro 990 offers a superior kitchen with bistro informality, and its décor creates a sophisticated yet comfortable atmosphere. A hip alternative lunch or dinner spot is Splendido. **Canoe** restaurant is fifty-four floors up and has food equal to its exquisite views. The Annex, one of Toronto's trendiest residential neighborhoods, boasts some of the city's best ethnic shopping and dining. In a cozy Markham Street house you'll find **Southern Accent**, where Cajun and Creole dishes are excellent. **Mildred Pierce** is a groovy restaurant renowned for its Sunday brunch and over-the-top décor.

After a long day, **The Eleventh Hour** is an intimate and comfortable place to relax or dance away any leftover energy. An icon on the Toronto bar scene, the **Roof Lounge** at the Park Hyatt Hotel Toronto is a longtime haunt of literary types.

The **Art Gallery of Toronto** has the world's largest public collection of Henry Moore sculptures and a fabulous accumulation of Inuit and contemporary Canadian art. It also often hosts large touring exhibits. For somewhat quirkier edification, the **Bata Shoe Museum** has the world's most comprehensive collection of shoes, spanning some 4,500 years. It includes everything from eighteenth-century French chestnut-crushing clogs to space boots.

Accommodations

The **Westin Harbour Castle**'s twin, modern high-rises have a prime location, central to the festivities and convenient to downtown. Make sure to ask for a room with a view of the lake or city. **Sheraton Centre Toronto** and the **Royal York** are conveniently located downtown for easy access to most *Caribana* activities. Both hotels are also popular with weekend-getaway travelers. In midtown's trendy Yorkville, it's difficult to beat **The Four Seasons Toronto** for luxurious rooms and always-dependable service.

Event & Ticket Info

Caribana: Most of the events are free. For more information, contact *Caribbean Cultural Committee/Caribana* through the www.funrises.com link.

Caribana Sunset Boat Cruise (Ferry Dock, at foot of Bay Street): Tickets ($40) should be ordered in advance through your hotel concierge.

The Hot Sheet

Hotels	Phone	Address	Price	Fax	Rooms/Best
The Four Seasons Toronto	416-964-0411 800-332-3442	21 Avenue Rd.	$$$	416-964-2301	380/Lake vw
Royal York	416-368-2511 800-828-7447	100 Front St. W	$$	416-368-9040	1,549/Lake vw
Sheraton Centre Toronto	416-361-1000 800-325-3535	123 Queen St. W	$$	416-947-4874	1,377/City Hall vw
Westin Harbour Castle	416-869-1600 800-228-3000	1 Harbour Sq.	$$$	416-869-0573	980/South Tower harbor vw

Restaurants	Day	Phone	Address	Price	Rec	Food
Bistro 990	A	416-921-9990	990 Bay St.	$$$	LD	French
Boba	1	416-961-2622	90 Avenue Rd.	$$$	D	Fusion
Canoe	A	416-364-0054	66 Wellington St. W	$$$	LD	New Canadian
Masquerade Caffè Bar	3	416-363-8971	181 Bay St.	$	B/LD	Pastries
Mildred Pierce	A	416-588-5695	99 Sudbury St.	$	BLD	American
Pearl Court	2	416-463-8778	633 Gerrard St.	$	T/BLD	Chinese
Prego della Piazza	1	416-920-9900	150 Bloor St. W	$	L/D	Italian
Queenston Heights Restaurant	2	905-262-4274	14184 Niagara Parkway	$	L/D	American
Southern Accent	A	416-536-3211	595 Markham St.	$$	D	Cajun, Creole
Splendido	A	416-929-7788	88 Harboard St.	$$	D	Continental
Studio Cafe	2	416-928-7330	see The Four Seasons Toronto hotel	$$	B/LD	Continental
Zoom Caffè & Bar	3	416-861-9872	18 King St. E	$$	D/L	World fusion

Nightlife	Day	Phone	Address	Cover	Rec*	Music
The Bamboo	3	416-593-5771	312 Queen St. W	$	MP(F)	Reggae
Easy & The Fifth	1	416-979-3000	225 Richmond St. W	$	P	Top 40, Latin, jazz, blues
The Eleventh Hour	A	416-599-4687	184 Pearl St.	$	H(F)	Dance
Jump Cafe & Bar	1	416-363-3400	Commerce Court E, Yonge and Wellington sts.	None	R(F)	
Limelight	2	416-593-6126	250 Adelaide St. W	$	P	Top 40, '70s, '80s
Roof Lounge	A	416-924-5471	4 Avenue Rd.	None	R	
Top o' the Senator	3	416-364-7517	253 Victoria St.	$	M(F)	Jazz
Whiskey Saigon	2	416-593-4646	250 Richmond St. W	$	P	House, Top 40

* M=Live music; P=Dancing (Party); R=Bar only; S=Show; (F)=Food served. For further explanation of codes, page 12.

Sights & Attractions	Day	Phone	Address	Entry Fee
Art Gallery of Toronto	A	416-979-6648	317 Dundas St. W	None
Bata Shoe Museum	A	416-979-7799	327 Bloor St. W	$
Casa Loma	1	416-923-1171	1 Austin Terrace	$
CN Tower	3	416-360-8500	301 Front St. W	$$
Niagara Falls	2	905-356-6061	80 mi. south of Toronto	None
Royal Ontario Museum	1	416-586-8000	100 Queen's Park	$$

Metropolitan Toronto CVB   **800-363-1990**   **207 Queen's Quay W**

 NYC Lester B. Pearson (YYZ) <30 min./$20  Yes/No Map Code: A46

Canada

*Of the 96 events and destinations (**The Fun Seeker's Gold List**) that every fun seeker should experience, two are in Mexico. Read on ... diviertase!*

Events and Destinations in
Mexico

Party: Acapulco

Key Month: n/a   Ratings: Event n/a **V**   City ★ ★ ★ ★ ☆   Origin: n/a   Attendance: n/a

All night, the bright lights of crowded bars and flashy *discotecas* twinkle and glow along the gentle arc of the bay. Since the inception of its fame in the 1950s, **Acapulco** has been known as a party town. But after reigning over sun-seekers, beach bums and mind-blowing nocturnal fiestas for more than four decades, Acapulco, the glamour queen of the Pacific, was finally due for a facelift. An extensive revitalization project has now put sexy Acapulco back on the map.

Bordered by the verdant Sierra Madre mountains on the east and the crystal waters of Acapulco Bay on the west, this coastal paradise is a vision from all directions. With a rapidly growing population of two million, Acapulco is quaint yet cosmopolitan, a place that offers everything you could want from a beach town—quiet escape, raucous parties, sun-soaked siestas, watersport adventure. But one thing it doesn't offer is a trendy carbon copy of home. Despite its historic popularity among American jet-setters, Acapulco never stopped being Mexican. Unlike the gringo-saturated scenes in Cancún and Cabo, Spanish still dominates the streets here, and traditional eateries and markets prevail in Acapulco's Old Town.

On the Calendar

Best 3 Days To Be There
Thursday-Saturday
is official party time.

☾ 74°/89° (23°/31°)

Though the high season explodes from December to March, Acapulco rocks any time of the year. The city's most prevalent daytime activity is baking in the sun with a margarita in hand, but boating, kayaking, scuba diving, parasailing and deep-sea fishing are all popular pastimes. In a spot where more than 360 days of the year are sunny and clear, simply taking in the beauty of (and on) the beaches can be a full-time occupation.

The languor of the day dissolves after sunset, when tanned, scantily dressed vacationers flock to nightclubs with names like Baby 'O and Enigma. There's no need to hurry. Acapulco's nightlife doesn't start until after 11 p.m.—and of course there's always mañana.

Mexico

Hotels

Most of Acapulco's recent hotel development and revitalization has been along Diamond Acapulco (from Las Brisas to the airport) where Acapulco's swankiest hotels and resorts are found. The largest of the luxury resorts, the **Acapulco Princess** has more than 1,000 rooms on 480 lush acres, as well as several fabulous swimming pools and one of the best beach scenes around. Sharing the beach with the Princess is its sister resort, the somewhat more exclusive and quieter **Pierre Marques**. The **Hyatt Regency**, located in town, also has a great beach with private *palapas* (palm-thatched beach huts) for guests, and an ongoing party around its giant pool. For more subdued, private accommodations, try **Las Brisas**, set high on a hill, or the stunning **Camino Real Acapulco Diamante**, which has its own small private beach.

Restaurants

Each of the recommended hotels has restaurants that are consistently good and convenient. When you're ready to venture out, your first choices should be **El Olvido**, whose nouveau-continental cuisine is served on an open-air patio overlooking the beach, and **Restaurante Kookaburra**, which specializes in seafood, steaks and ceviche. Also good is the Italian cuisine at **Ristorante Casanova** and **Spicey**'s exotic amalgamation of flavors from Asia, Africa, India and Mexico. If you feel like exploring the distant reaches of Acapulco, try **La Cabaña** on Caleta Beach for good seafood in a vivacious atmosphere. For a more romantic setting with sophisticated international dishes, head to the elegant **Coyuca 22**. A former hillside villa, Coyuca 22 is considered one of the most beautiful restaurants in world.

Nightlife

Nightlife action centers in two areas: the southern end of the bay's hotel zone and the La Vista area, on the way to the Marques and Princess hotels. In the hotel zone, two clubs reign. The elaborately designed **Andromeda's**, which has two aquariums, a stage for big-name acts and a small swimming pool with an exotic mermaid show, is the current rage. **Baby 'O** lacks the dramatic décor of Andromeda's but more than makes up for it with a faithful following and always-crowded dance floor. In the bustling La Vista area, **Enigma** (formerly Extravaganzza) attracts a slightly older crowd with house and techno beats in one room and a piano bar in another. It's hard to miss the sexy shaking at the **Palladium** next door, where passersby get a look at dancers through a giant glass wall.

If you need a breather from the club scene, try **Pepe's Piano Bar**, which attracts an uninhibited, upbeat crowd that vies for the microphone in piano sing-alongs. In the same complex, **Señor Frog's** has a college-age crowd, group-party atmosphere and casual, funky design. Also in the same complex is **Succa**, one of the hottest dance clubs in town.

Other Attractions

The torch-wielding cliff divers at **La Quebrada** are a sight to behold. These courageous, buff men make crucially timed dives from a 135-foot precipice into the rising surf. Sunset or evening is the most dramatic time to view these plunging Adonises. **La Perla Restaurant** (for a drink or dinner) at Hotel El Mirador Plaza Las Glorias is the best place to watch them—it's just a fifteen-minute walk up the hill from the middle of town.

Before the arrival of tourists, life in Acapulco centered around Old Town, with its narrow, winding streets filled with charming shops and strolling musicians. By contrast, the *zócalo*, aka Plaza Juan Alvarez, in the heart of town bears testament to Acapulco's less-than-traditional past. Nearby is the interesting **El Fuerte de San Diego**, a fort built in 1616. Today it contains a museum dedicated to Acapulco's history.

Hotels	Phone	Address	Price	Fax	Rooms/Best
Acapulco Princess	69-1000 800-223-1818	Playa Revolcadero	$$	69-1012	1019/Dlx ocean vw w/balc
Camino Real Acapulco Diamante	66-1010 800-722-6466	Baja Catita	$$	66-1111	156/Supr rm w/balc and ocean vw
Hyatt Regency	69-1234 800-233-1234	1 Av. Costera Miguel Alemán	$$	84-3087	645/21st fl w/ocean vw
Las Brisas	69-6900 800-223-6800	5255 Carretera Escénica Clemente Mejía	$$$$	84-6071	265/Royal Beach rm, 4th level
Pierre Marques	66-1000 800-223-1818	Playa Revolcadero	$$	66-1046	344/4th fl w/ocean vw

Restaurants	Phone	Address	Price	Rec	Food
Coyuca 22	82-3468	22 Avenida Coyuca	$$$$	D	International
El Olvido	81-0214	Pl. Marbella, Costera Miguel Alemán	$$$	D	International
La Cabaña	83-7121	Caleta Beach, Lado Oriente	$	BLD	Seafood
La Perla Restaurant	83-1155	74 c/ La Quebrada in	None	R(F)	Seafood
Restaurante Kookaburra	46-6020	Carretera Escénica, Las Brisas	$$$	D	International, seafood
Ristorante Casanova	46-6237	5256 Carretera Escénica	$$$$	D	Italian
Spicey	46-6003	Carretera Escénica, Fracc. Marina de Las Brisas	$$	D	International, Asian, fusion

Nightlife	Phone	Address	Cover	Rec*	Music
Andromeda's	84-8815	Av. Costera Miguel Alemán, Lomas de Costa Azul	$$$	P	Pop, techno, house, Latin
Baby 'O	84-7474	22 Av. Costera Miguel Alemán	$$$	P	Disco, pop, Latin
Enigma	46-5711	Carretera Escénica, Las Brisas	$$$	PM	House, techno, Latin, piano bar
Palladium	46-5490	Carretera Escénica	$$$	P	Techno, pop, house, Latin
Pepe's Piano Bar	46-5736	28 Carretera Escénica in La Vista center	None	M(F)	Piano
Señor Frog's	46-5734	28 Carretera Escénica in La Vista center	None	P	Disco
Succa	46-5690	28 Carretera Escénica	$$	P	'70s, '80s, '90s

* M=Live music; P=Dancing (Party); R=Bar only; S=Show; (F)=Food served. For further explanation of codes, page 12.

Sights & Attractions	Phone	Address	Entry Fee
El Fuerte de San Diego	82-3828	c/ Hornitos y Morelos, Colonia Centro	$
La Quebrada	83-7228	c/ La Quebrada	$

| **Tourism Office** | **81-1168** | **Miguel Alemán, Lower fl. in Convention Center** | |

Mexico country code: 52   Acapulco city code: 74

Mexico

 NYC-1   Acapulco (ACA) <45min./$20   Yes/No   Map Code: A47

Feria de San Marcos

Feria Nacional de San Marcos

Key Month: Apr/May   Ratings: Event ★★★☆☆   **ⓟ**   City ★☆☆☆☆   Origin: 1848   Attendance: 1,600,000

Mexico's wild nightclubs and beauty-packed beaches provide plenty of opportunities to party. But year in and year out, the country's largest and most famous fiesta, **Feria de San Marcos**, wins new converts with three rowdy weeks of dancing, carousing and tequila baptisms.

Music fills every side street and blasts out of temporary discos and bars, as the event engulfs Aguascalientes' stone-paved pedestrian plazas. Street-food choices abound, and roving mariachi bands spark enthusiasm on corners throughout town. But music and food aren't the only draws. Makeshift clubs with indoor and outdoor dance floors stay open until dawn. The tequila companies do such a good job of getting everyone *borracho* (drunk) in their tent bars that even confirmed wallflowers drop their inhibitions and become lost in *baile* (dance). Mexico's only legal casino operates during the event.

During the festival, local laws are relaxed, making it legal to stumble through the streets with a spicy *carne asada* taco in one hand and a bottle of tequila in the other. Fireworks extravaganzas flare up nightly along with theater performances, poetry readings, dance shows

and other spectacles. Bullfights, horse shows and a rodeo highlight the day time activities. Those who need more than tequila and livestock to get excited can bungee-jump or test the thrill rides in the carnival area.

Named for its thermal springs, Aguascalientes (hot waters) has few city attractions, so the only time you're likely to want to visit is during **Feria de San Marcos**. The capital of the small central Mexico state of the same name isn't normally the place to go to paint the town red— a more appropriate color would be the faded sepia of the worn floorboards at one of the town's few cantinas. Over the course of the festival, however, the town's 900,000 residents play host to some of their country's top musicians, bullfighters and party animals, making Aguascalientes the ultimate fiesta destination as hot as its name.

On the Calendar

Official Event Dates
Second Saturday in April
to first Sunday in May

Best 3 Days To Be There
Middle weekend (Friday-Sunday).
Middle weekend is biggest, with
all events (and people) in
full-swing.

☀ 35°/99° (1°/37°)

Mexico

DAY 1 Friday

10:45 am While it's still cool, stroll to the colonial heart of the city. Begin at the fair's *paseo*, the wide avenue that runs north to San Marcos church and garden. Follow Carranza Street—foot traffic only—where you'll find the artists section and folk-art shops.

11:45 am At the main square, Plaza de la Patria, admire the renovated interior of the **Catedral**. On an adjacent corner, pick up *Feria* programs at the Tourist Information Office in the **Palacio de Gobierno**, the state capitol. The building houses colorful murals by Chilean artist Osvaldo Barra Cunningham, whose mentor was Diego Rivera. Don't miss the humorous one of the fair on the second floor.

1:30 pm Opposite the cathedral, in the pink palace (which formerly housed ✖ the opulent Hotel Francia), **Sanborn's** provides air-conditioned bliss in its upstairs restaurant—perfect for a cold beer and lunch.

3:00 pm Do as the locals do—lie low until around 5 p.m. With the mile-high altitude, a siesta will be welcome. Or hang out in a shady corner of your hotel's pool and study the fair program.

5:00 pm As you head to the plaza, you can watch the bull and bullfighter emerge from the Fiesta Americana hotel clock as it chimes the hour.

6:00 pm Don't miss the *voladores de Papantla*, six fearless flying Indians who whirl around and around a sturdy maypole that soars 150 feet above ground. It's best to scout around the fairgrounds before the big crush begins at dusk. Then stop in at **Merendero Don Chendo** for appetizers and drinks.

8:30 pm Stake out a table at Fiesta ✖ Americana's outdoor patio, **Café Plaza**. It's a great spot to do cocktails and dinner as you watch the parade of humanity go by. When the urge strikes, feel free to join in.

9:30 pm Talk about the ultimate sign of a nonstop fiesta—the *Feria* has a daycare center that operates 7 p.m.-7 a.m.! And where are the parents? A good bet is the nearby **Casino**, where gambling is legal only during the fair. It may be the only casino in the world where a priest circles the craps table asking for donations.

11:30 pm The city's nightclubs and discos move to temporary quarters at the fairgrounds, and dancing and drinking go on until early morning. Most places are open-air. Mariachi groups and *tambora* (big drum) bands play amid the throngs of partyers, so there are plenty of chances to dance.

DAY 2 Saturday

10:00 am Have a room-service breakfast before heading for the fascinating **Hacienda de Chichimeco**, a ranch noted for breeding spirited bulls. Brave souls can even take a crack at bullfighting.

2:00 pm If you didn't get lunch at the ✖ Hacienda, grab a bite at **VIP's**. Or try one of the restaurants near the fair.

4:00 pm Take the twenty-minute stroll past the bullring, the carnival and the cow exhibits to the Lienzo Charro, site of the equestrian events. At the *charreada* (rodeo), dashing *charros* (cowboys) in wide-brimmed sombreros dazzle the crowd with their horseback skills, bronco riding and roping talents.

6:30 pm Take a siesta, or walk around the fairgrounds, stopping for a tequila in preparation for dinner.

8:00 pm Dine at the elegant **Los Murales** in ✖ the **Quinta Real** hotel, a colonial-style building furnished with antiques, original art and Mexican handicrafts. Try the *huachinango a la Veracruzana*, a regional red-snapper specialty. Or go to **El Campeador**, one of the better steakhouses in town.

11:30 pm Some of the biggest names in Mexican show-business are scheduled for the headliner concerts at the Palenque. Allow at least half an hour before show time to make your way through the crowd.

1:30 am By now the *Feria's* discos should be hopping, especially at the Cuervo tent.

DAY 3 Sunday

10:00 am Start your day with an international ❌ breakfast buffet at **Argentina**.

Noon Museum-hop, first to the **Museo José Guadalupe Posada**. Guadalupe Posada was a political cartoonist at the turn of the twentieth century. Then, hit the **Museo de Aguascalientes**, which houses a permanent exhibition of Mexican modernists. Afterward, peek inside the ornate **Church of San Antonio** across the street.

3:15 pm Finish your cultural tour at the De Andrea Alameda hotel with a late lunch ❌ at **Los Cisnes.** This palatial hotel is the traditional home away from home for the top bullfighters, and you'll be there when they make an appearance at the restaurant en route to the ring.

5:30 pm It's a five-minute walk from Fiesta Americana to the Plaza de Toros Monumental, the second-largest bullring in Mexico. Top Mexican and Spanish matadors show off their skills for their adoring fans at the bullfight.

9:00 pm Have an Argentine-style barbecued ❌ steak at **Rincón Gaucho**, one of the fair's popular restaurants. Or try *cabrito al pastor* (goat) at **La Majada**, across from Fiesta Americana.

11:00 pm This is your last chance to dance in the *Feria* discos, so max out your energy reserves and salsa your way into Mexican heaven.

Before

If you arrive earlier in the week, enjoy *San Marcos Day* (April 25), celebrated with a lively and colorful parade.

More Time, More Choices

The fair program is loaded with activities. In addition to itinerary listings, there are concerts by jazz groups, rock bands, dance troupes and the Aguascalientes Symphony Orchestra. Other entertainment includes mariachi competitions, a circus and a carnival.

Although closed during *Feria*, the center of nightlife from Wednesday to Saturday is **Ios**, where DJs spin for a full house. Also closed during *Feria* is **The Station**, one of the best dance clubs in Aguascalientes.

Accommodations

The first-class, four-story **Fiesta Americana's** Mexican-colonial architecture features terra-cotta-colored stucco walls, balconies and stone archways. The **Quinta Real** has Old World charm accented with contemporary Mexican furnishings. **Gran Hotel Hacienda de la Noria** offers a taste of traditional elegance. Bullfighting aficionados can headquarter at the **De Andrea Alameda**, where many matadors make their home during the *Feria*.

Event & Ticket Info

Feria de San Marcos (Various locations in Aguascalientes): Admission to see the *voladores de Papantla* (fairgrounds), *Casino* (San Marcos Garden) and parade is free. Tickets are needed for the *Headliner Concerts* ($10-$40, in person at the Palenque), *bullfights* ($20-$30, Plaza de Toros) and the *charreada* ($3-$5, Lienzo Charro). It is recommended to purchase tickets in advance for the Headliner Concerts and Bullfights from *Ticketmaster* (52/5-325-9000).

Hotels	Phone	Address	Price	Fax	Rooms/Best
De Andrea Alameda	78-3800	Av. Tecnológico	$$	18-3759	48/Gdn vw
Fiesta Americana	18-6010 800-343-7821	c/ Laureles	$$$$	18-5118	192/Plaza vw
Gran Hotel Hacienda de la Noria	18-4343	1315 Héroe de Nacozari S.	$$$	18-4343	50/Poolside
Quinta Real	78-5818	601 Avenida Aguascalientes S.	$$	78-5616	85/Gdn vw

Restaurants	Day	Phone	Address	Price	Rec	Food
Argentina	3	78-2005	407 Republica de Argentina	$	BL	Buffet
Café Plaza	1	18-6010	see Fiesta Americana hotel	$$	D/BL	International, Mexican
El Campeador	2	16-9886	517 Cinco de Mayo	$$	LD	Steakhouse
La Majada	3	no phone	Arturo J. Pane, Expo Pl. near Fiesta Americana hotel	$	D	Goat barbecue
Los Cisnes	3	18-4417	see De Andrea Alameda hotel	$$	L/BD	International, Mexican
Los Murales	2	78-5818	see Quinta Real hotel	$$	D/BL	International, regional Mexican
Rincón Gaucho	3	15-9313	110 Arturo J. Pane N.	$	D/L	Argentinian barbecue
Sanborn's	1	12-4002	Pl. de la Patria	$	L/BD	International, Mexican
VIP's	2	18-4260	c/ Commercial, Expo Pl.	$	L/BD	International, Mexican

Nightlife	Day	Phone	Address	Cover	Rec*	Music
los	A	12-6576	1821 Blvd. Miguel de la Madrid	None	P	Dance
Merendero Don Chendo	1	16-1680	130 Arturo J. Pane N.	None	R(F)	
The Station	A	12-0991	129 Don Also Colosio	None	P(F)	House, techno, dance

* M=Live music; P=Dancing (Party); R=Bar only; S=Show; (F)=Food served. For further explanation of codes, page 12.

Sights & Attractions	Day	Phone	Address	Entry Fee
Catedral	1	15-1052	Pl. de la Patria	None
Church of San Antonio	3	15-2898	Pedro Parga and Zaragoza	None
Hacienda de Chichimeco	2	16-2008	Carretera Jesús María à Valladolid	$
Museo de Aguascalientes	3	15-9043	505 Zaragoza	$
Museo José Guadalupe Posada	3	15-4556	Jardín del Encino	$
Palacio de Gobierno	1	15-9504	Pl. de la Patria	None

Tourist Information		15-1155	Office in Palacio de Gobierno

Mexico country code: 52   Aguascalientes city code: 49

 NYC -1   Aguascalientes (AGU) <15 min./$10   Yes/No   Map code: A48

Mexico

*Only the best of the best events make it to the **Fun Seeker's Gold List**—but what about the many other fun events?*

*The **Hot Sheets** identify the best things to do in a city—but what are some of the other attractions that contribute to the fun seeker's enjoyment of a destination?*

***JUNOs** (short for "Did you know?") answer some of these questions and make the fun seeker's picture complete.*

JUNOs (More Fun Things)

G-Wiz, You Call This Fun?

About Amusement Parks

The modern age of the amusement park began in 1884 when the world's first roller coaster was built at New York's Coney Island. By today's standards, the first coaster was about as exciting as a Congressional filibuster. Coney's Switchback Railway ride stood 15 feet tall and ran a heart-stopping four mph. Well, you gotta start somewhere.

In the old days, people looking for amusement were likely to take stately rides to the country or, if they really wanted a wild time, organize picnics. Today's fun-lover is looking for more: sensory intensity, excitement, and an adrenalin rush that puts one's concentration squarely on the moment at hand. After all, it's hard to let your mind wander when you're hurtling downhill on a pair of skinny tracks at nearly 90 mph.

Newer and faster rides began to evolve at the early amusement parks, which were called trolley parks because they were operated and serviced by trolley companies. By the 1950s, though, automobiles had put most trolley companies out of business. Only the best, most well-run amusement parks struggled on and even they appeared to be on their last legs.

Then the amusement gods sent a savior to Earth. Walt Disney took old ideas of fun and dressed them up in modern 1955 concepts, combining rides, shows, restaurants, and, most important, a theme. Disneyland became an immediate smash. Other companies soon expanded on Disney's idea. Now, enormous theme parks such as Six Flags and Great America set the definition for amusement parks. (Walt Disney World in Florida has become a category unto itself, page 54.) The latest twist, water parks, sends nearly 10 million people a year laughing and screaming down water-filled tubes and slides.

The 250 million people who visit amusement parks each year don't need the word fun in the park's name—although it's used more than any other adjective—to know that the sights, smells, sounds, and action promise a good time. Some go for the entertainment. Most get pleasure from just being out with lots of people. But for those not lucky enough to be astronauts or fighter pilots, there may be no better source for an instant adrenalin rush than a roller coaster.

Speed, force, and velocity are natural allies for destruction, making roller coasters the maximum thrill you can get in a safe environment.

Today's coasters often take off with riders standing or hanging from the bottoms of the rails. They make loops and corkscrews and heart-stopping drops. They provide lots of heart-in-the-mouth "air time" that lifts riders off their seats. Veteran riders know that front seats give smoother rides, but more extreme G-forces. Third seats on nonlooping coasters are best for negative Gs (weightless "hang time"). Back seats offer the most severe force of the drops. Sitting over the wheels gives rougher jolts.

Many parks also use propellers, bungee cords, swings, and other devices to create the G-forces and sudden drops thrill-seekers crave. But no matter what the method, for most of us, amusement parks still provide the mental and physical challenge thrill-seekers call the ultimate fun.

Top Ten Best-Attended U.S. Theme Parks
(annual attendance)

Disneyland, Anaheim, Calif.—15,000,000
The Magic Kingdom, Walt Disney World, Lake Buena Vista, Fla.—13,800,000
Epcot, Walt Disney World, Lake Buena Vista, Fla.—11,235,000
Disney-MGM Studios, Walt Disney World, Lake Buena Vista, Fla.—9,975,000
Universal Studios Florida, Orlando, Fla.—8,400,000
Universal Studios Hollywood, Universal City, Calif.—5,400,000
Sea World of Florida, Orlando, Fla.—5,100,000
Busch Gardens, Tampa, Fla.—4,170,000
Six Flags Great Adventure, Jackson, N.J.—4,000,000
Sea World of California, San Diego, Calif.—3,890,000

More Barbeque to Chew On

About Barbeque

Memphians consider themselves the nation's purveyors of "true" barbecue—they emphasize pork, not beef; pay rigid attention to achieving the right culinary combination of smoke, heat and time; and specialize in dry-rubbed seasoning (not that gooky stuff most of us call barbecue sauce).

But barbecue is a strong part of American culture everywhere, inspiring nostalgia, patriotism, zeal and deep divisions in spelling preference. The word barbecue was first used around 1666. It derives from French-speaking pirates who called this type of pork feast *de barbe et queue*, which means "from head to tail."

 Seventy-five percent of American households own a barbecue grill; these are used an average of five times per month.

 Forty-two percent of consumers say the most popular form of home entertaining is a barbecue or cook-out party.

 Men do 59 percent of the barbecuing, but women decide to have 57 percent of barbecues.

 The United States is home to about 11,000 barbecue restaurants.

 The most popular occasions for a barbecue and the percentage of the population that participates: Fourth of July (81 percent), Labor Day (70 percent), Memorial Day (66 percent).

Top Barbecue Competitions (in prize order)

There are more than 400 barbecue contests held annually in the United States.

Name	Month	Location	Phone	Prizes	Attend.	Teams
Memphis in May World Championship Barbecue Cooking Contest	May	Memphis, Tennessee	901-525-4611	$56,000	100,000	248
American Royal Barbecue Contest	Oct.	Kansas City, Kansas	816-221-9800	$50,000	77,000	375
World Pork Expo The Great Pork BarbeQlossal	Jun.	Des Moines, Iowa	515-223-2622	$25,000	60,000	102
Best in the West Nugget Rib Cook-Off	Sep.	Sparks, Nevada	800-648-1177	$13,500	200,000	23
Pro Football Hall of Fame Festival Ribs Burnoff	Jul.	Canton, Ohio	800-533-4302	$4,000	110,000	35
Great Lenexa Barbecue Battle	Jun.	Lenexa, Kansas	913-541-8592	$2,425	25,000	165
World's Championship Bar-B-Que	Feb.	Houston, Texas	713-791-9000	Trophy	162,000	341

Running of the Bowls

About Bowl (Football) Games

The great thing about football is you don't have to know a fullback from a hole in the ground to enjoy the party atmosphere that has grown up around this most American of pastimes. Once second fiddle to major league baseball, professional and college football now dominate the American sports scene from the National Football League's preseason in August to its top-rated Super Bowl finale on the last Sunday of January, a game that draws more than 100 million television viewers worldwide.

In between there's the weekly *Monday Night Football* ritual—a 1970s invention that has single-handedly recast once-quiet Monday nights into big business in the bar and tavern world—and Thanksgiving, a day now associated with professional football as well as turkey and American history. On the amateur level, Americans devote an entire autumn of Saturdays to watching the best collegiate players in the nation. The last two weekends in November are usually saved for intense intrastate games—Washington and Washington State, for example, play for state pride and the Apple Cup each year—and settling legendary regional and national rivalries for another year. Georgia and Tennessee universities' Battle Between the Hedges is always one of the most anticipated games of the year, as are matchups between Auburn and Alabama, Texas and Oklahoma, Ohio State and Michigan, Army and Navy, Notre Dame and the University of Southern California, Stanford and the University of California at Berkeley, and dozens of other teams.

Since college football's inaugural year in 1869 (Princeton University was the national champ), the system for determining the national champion has been inexact and protean. New Year's Day once provided college football's biggest showcase, when top teams would vie for the media-elected national championship by competing in major bowls attended and watched by millions. Traditional bowl games are still important, but the system for deciding upon a national champion has been restructured around the major conferences and the BCS (Bowl Championship Series), a complex, computer-aided formula that sets up title games on a rotating basis between the Rose, Fiesta, Sugar and Orange bowls. Depending on the calendar, the final game pairing the country's top two teams usually takes place a few days after January 1. The highly controversial and imperfect BCS system, however, will likely be replaced by the end of the decade.

One thing the pro and college games have in common is the tailgater, a ritual that's now a fixture at virtually all football stadiums across the country. How do eager fans build entire weekends around games that last only a few hours? Simple. They bring their parties to the stadiums—in cars, trucks, vans and rented RVs—set up camp in the parking lot, and start cracking cold ones. For dedicated tailgaters, the outcome of the game is never as important as the outcome of the party.

To the uninitiated, a football tailgater might appear to exude all the charm and subtlety of a village raid by Viking berserkers. And it's true, having fun at a tailgater depends on participants' willingness to suspend certain standards of normal behavior. Liberate yourself from your prejudices and you'll soon understand the joy of tailgating: Where else but a tailgater is it acceptable to hang around a parking lot drinking Southern Comfort from a flask at 10:30 in the morning? Where else is it okay to, just for the hell of it, cut loose with a rebel yell in front of 2,000 strangers (not counting a Metallica concert)? Where else is one at complete liberty to verbally abuse any passerby who happens to be wearing the logo of an opposing team?

Okay, getting away with crazy behavior isn't all that tailgaters are about. In fact, it's best to think of football parties—whether indoor or outdoor—as autumn's answer to the summer picnic. The props are the same—chips, dip, burgers, dogs and beer—but more important are the surrounding faces of friends and family who gather in increasing numbers each year to laugh, eat, drink and cheer together in a distinctly American tradition now in its third century of play.

Start Your Engines

About Car Racing

The more than 400,000 spectators whose idea of fun is raw speed, horsepower and noise, make the Indianapolis 500 the largest-attended single-day sporting event on the planet. Auto racing is, in fact, one of the most popular spectator sports in the world, with a long list of car designs and styles of racing to suit every type of fan. To the neophyte, most racing cars might look similar, but track types and sanctioning organizations that govern various races dictate fundamental differences in each design.

Three of the races on our list of the world's most fun places to be—Indy 500, Macau Grand Prix, Monte Carlo Grand Prix—feature similar cars. Each is a mid-engined, open-wheeled, single-seat racer unsuitable for anything but competition. All are referred to as Formula cars because of certain technical criteria determined by racing's governing bodies. Typically, these criteria restrict the power of the engine in order to limit development costs and top speeds. Also, restrictions make the races more dependent on driver skill, thus avoiding a competition between design technologies.

The Indianapolis 500 is sanctioned by the IRL (Indy Racing League), an organization formed in 1996. IRL races are run on oval tracks, with an emphasis on top speed. A competing organization, CART (Championship Auto Racing Teams), runs open-wheeled racers, but top speeds may be considerably less, because most CART events are held on curvy road courses that slow down drivers.

Formula One (F1) racing is similar to CART racing, but it's generally concentrated in Europe. F1 racing is sanctioned by the Paris-based FIA (International Automotive Federation). Races are run exclusively on road courses, placing more emphasis on adhesion and traction than on sheer speed. The most famous of the European road races is at Monaco, where drivers blast through the streets of Monte Carlo on a narrow, dangerous course that has remained largely unchanged since the race's inception in 1929. F1 racing is tremendously expensive, but, for manufacturers, the prestige of a championship is worth the expense, giving rise to a kind of macho snob appeal. When Indy and CART speeds rise, F1 engineers typically up the ante,

working feverishly to make sure their cars remain the fastest.

Formula Three (F3) racing is essentially F1's baby brother. The cars are similar in design, only smaller and less powerful. Its main distinction is as a proving ground for racers, so it's common for F3 champions to graduate to F1 status.

The most popular and still fastest-growing form of auto racing in the United States is stock-car racing sanctioned by NASCAR (National Association of Stock Car Auto Racing). With forty major races at tracks primarily in the Southeast, NASCAR features American cars and American drivers. The term stock, however, is a misnomer. Stock cars may display the names of their showroom counterparts, but the similarity ends there. Like IRL events, NASCAR races are held primarily on oval tracks, and its cars are designed to reach obscenely high speeds. At the speedway in Daytona, with its long straights and high banks, speeds of more than 220 mph have been recorded.

One of the world's most historically significant races is the 24 Hours of Le Mans endurance race. As the oldest race in Europe—run continuously since 1923—the prestige of winning Le Mans is immeasurable. Endurance races involve several classes of automobile, such as world sports cars (single-seat, open-top) and GT-1s (grand-touring cars), which tend to look like street cars, but are far more sophisticated. A lower class is GT-2, which includes heavily modified BMW M3s and Porsche 911s. Most endurance cars are designed for one race and one track only, and are completely rebuilt after each race. An endurance race is a grueling test to prove that a car can handle the punishment and speeds of a racetrack over a long period. If you've ever driven your car on a long road trip, imagine the strain of maintaining that endurance for not only three times as long, but at three or four times the speed.

Also popular in Europe is *rallying*, considered by some to be the most dangerous and exciting form of racing in the world. Rallying involves hurtling heavily modified sedans through all types of terrain, sometimes on dirt roads and through small towns, even at night. Each car contains a driver and a navigator who has carefully plotted the course for maximum speed and must dictate each directional nuance to the driver. The special stages (closed sections of public roads) sometimes use narrow dirt roads that involve great elevation changes, numerous hard turns and plenty of bumps and ruts. The responsibility for victory weighs heavier on the driver and navigator than on the design of the car.

Amateur *vintage-car racing*, a hobby rather than a professional sport, is gaining popularity. Vintage racing involves driving older, usually obsolete race cars and road cars around existing road courses. Vintage race cars are often individually owned, races emphasize fun, and trophies are rarely awarded. In order to ensure safe competition that injures neither drivers nor their extremely valuable toys, cars are grouped in terms of age, type and engine displacement. It wouldn't be much of a race if a 1920s Morgan were pitted against a mid-'70s Ferrari. Another distinction in vintage racing regards modifications. Some sanctioning groups insist that cars must be raced exactly as they were in their original time period, while others accept some technological upgrades, usually for safety or reliability.

A *concours d'elegance* event is based entirely on originality, style and appearance. A car must have all of its original equipment and it must be operable, but the similarities to racing end there. It's a pure beauty contest, where the paint must shine, the seats must have no cracks, the engine must be spotlessly clean, the body work must be flawless, the wheels and tires must be polished and the exhaust pipe must be clean of soot or rust. For a collector, the awarding of a Concours ribbon can immortalize a car, sometimes doubling its value.

The World's Top Races and Auto Competitions

IRL
- Indianapolis 500, Indianapolis, Indiana; May
- Longhorn 500, Fort Worth, Texas; Jun.
- UAW-GM 500, Charlotte, North Carolina; Jul.

NASCAR
- Daytona 500, Daytona Beach, Florida; Feb.
- Brickyard 400, Indianapolis, Indiana; Aug.
- Coca-Cola 600 at Charlotte Motor Speedway, Charlotte, North Carolina; May

CART
- Toyota Grand Prix of Long Beach, Long Beach, California; Apr.
- Gran Premio Telmex-Gigante Autodromo Hermanos Rodriguez, Mexico City, Nov.
- Honda Indy 300, Queensland, Australia, Oct.
- G.I. Joe's 200, Portland, Oregon; Jun.
- Grand Prix of Cleveland, Cleveland, Ohio; Jul.

Formula One
- Monte Carlo Grand Prix, Monte Carlo, Monaco; May
- Belgian Grand Prix, Spa-Francorchamps, Belgium; Aug.
- Italian Grand Prix at Monza, Monza, Italy; Sep.

Rallying
- Network Q Rally of Great Britain, England; Nov.
- 1,000 Lakes of Finland, Finland; Feb.
- New Zealand Rally/Australia Rally; Oct. and Nov.

Endurance Racing
- 24 Hours of Le Mans, Le Mans, France; Jun.
- 24 Hours of Daytona, Daytona Beach, Florida; Feb.
- 12 Hours of Sebring, Sebring, Florida; Mar.

Formula Three
- Macau Grand Prix, Taipa Island, Macau; Nov.
- Marlboro Masters of Formula 3, Zandvoort, Holland; Aug.
- British Championship Race, Brands Hatch, England; Sep.

Vintage Racing
- Monterey Historic Races, Monterey, California; Aug.
- Brian Redman International Challenge, Elkhart Lake, Wisconsin; Jul.
- Goodwood Festival of Speed, Sussex, England; Jul.

Concours d'Elegance
- Pebble Beach Concours, Pebble Beach, California; Aug.
- Meadow Brook Concours, Rochester, Michigan; Aug.
- Louis Vuitton Classic, New York, New York; Sep.

Living Fantasies

About Fantasy Camps

"Life," as John Lennon said, "is what happens when you're making other plans." Despite how great things may have worked out, there comes a time when you find yourself wondering, What if ... ?

What if you'd kept playing baseball? Kept practicing music and taken that club gig? Run away and become a cowboy? Whatever it is, what if you'd followed that dream? Now, how can you tell without abandoning the life you've worked so hard to build?

Fantasy camps started in the 1980s with baseball camps for people who wanted to play as hard as they worked. Now, many other sports and interests have camps. Some, such as golf, tennis and gourmet-chef fantasy camps, may be only onetime deals. But many return each year, running from a few days to a week or more.

Whether you save the day with a home run, winning basket or miraculous touchdown, there's a camp that lets you join some of the top athletes in the game in daily practices and "championship" games. You can also be an umpire, coach, scorekeeper or announcer. Sports camps not your passion? Then live the life of a jazz great, fighter pilot, astronaut or brewmeister.

Baseball Camps

Imagine you're up with the bases loaded, playing for your favorite pro team. The crowd's chants turn to a roar as you send a dinger into the cheap seats, bringing home three of the game's greatest heroes and winning the game. Your home-run trot is a thing of beauty. Your all-star teammates mob you at the plate.

Most baseball teams hold fantasy camps, although not always every year. Camps usually are held in Florida or Arizona and include several team members and legends of the game. Call your favorite baseball team's headquarters for more information.

The Doubleday Country Inn and Farm near Harrisburg, Pennsylvania (717-789-2456), re-creates "the olden days" when one could ride horses on the wooded hillsides and play baseball on converted cornfields. At the camp, former major leaguers join you in twilight games.

Other baseball fantasy camps include:

Cal Ripken Jr.'s Adult Baseball Vacation 800-486-0850
Cooperstown Baseball Camp 800-726-7314
Diamond Dreams 888-333-1881
Left and Center Field of Dreams 800-443-8981
Heroes in Pinstripes Fantasy Camp 606-474-2514
Los Angeles Dodgers Baseball Fantasy Camp . . . 800-334-7529

Other Sports Camps

Maybe you'd rather be standing at the free-throw line, score tied, no time left on the clock. Your pro-basketball teammates, legends all, watch anxiously as you take your shot—then burst into wild cheers as, no sweat, you drain the winning charity toss. If you're a hoops junkie, try **Sports Legends Fantasy Camp** (Dallas, Texas; 800-937-5107), or the **Washington Wizards-Wes Unseld Fantasy Camp** (Washington, D.C.; 202-661-5000).

You can also score touchdowns at the **Green Bay Experience** fantasy football camp (800-945-7102) or put your opponent in the dreaded camel clutch at the **Mark Curtis Memorial Pro Wrestling Fantasy Camp** (513-771-1650).

Beyond Sports

Not all fantasies center on sports. You can jam with jazz greats at **Jazz Fantasy Camp** (Rhinelander, Wisconsin; 715-369-1500) or Moravian College's **July Jazz Getaway** (Bethlehem, Pennslyvania; 610-861-1650). Pump adrenaline as a military fighter pilot at **Aviation Challenge Camp** (Huntsville, Alabama; 800-637-7223) or aim for the stars at the **Space Academy's Fantasy Astronaut Camp** (Huntsville, Alabama; 800-637-7223). Drive those doggies home on an **American Wilderness Experience Cattle Drive** (800-444-0099). Or kick back and savor classic suds at the **American Brewer's Guild's Homebrewers Fantasy Camp** (800-636-1331).

If It's Tuesday, It Must Be Alligator Lasagna ...

About Food Festivals

Eating well gives joy to life and food festivals in North America leave no aspect of that joy unexplored. From a few hundred invitation-only attendees to millions gorging together, from regional cuisine to the truly exotic, from fast food to gourmet—food festivals cover the gastronomic gamut. Festivals may honor one type of food with a smorgasbord of endless variations. They may showcase an ethnic cuisine. They may feature amateur cook-off competitions or samples from high-class restaurants. Some, such as the **Taste of Chicago**, America's biggest food and music festival, may feature top entertainment, rides and exhibits, in addition to dozens of food vendors and gourmet restaurants. Whatever your preference, delicious events await you throughout the year.

You could build a complete meal traveling to U.S. food festivals, awakening to the world's largest pancake breakfast in Springfield, Massachusetts, with syrup from either Vermont's or New York's maple festivals. Add South Carolina's **World Grits Festival** before a spicy Creole lunch at Louisiana's gumbo or jambalaya festivals. For dinner, start with appetizers at the **Great Wisconsin Cheese Festival** and **Alabama's National Peanut Festival**, where the streets are paved with peanuts for the big parade. Make chili your next course at the **Republic of Texas Chilympiad**, as 500 contestants dazzle festival-goers in the North American Open chili cook-off. Grab your main course from the world's largest skillet at **Kentucky's World Chicken Festival**, garnished with garlic from the Gilroy (California) **Garlic Festival** ("the smelliest party on the continent") or honey from the **Ohio Honey Festival**, where possibly deranged volunteers sport living-bee beards.

For vegetables, try artichokes from the Castroville (California) **Artichoke Festival**, potatoes from North Dakota's **Potato Bowl** or Vidalia onions from Georgia's festival. Choose fruit from Michigan and South Carolina peach festivals. At the latter, you can also exercise away calories in the *Tour de Peche* bicycle race. Prefer strawberries? The succulent fruit inspires festivals all over the country—from Tennessee to Texas to California—drawing enormous crowds. The **Florida Strawberry Festival** is one of the best, where nearly a million visitors savor strawberries along with the finest country-music entertainers in the business.

If you're more of an old salt than a landlubber, you won't want to miss Maryland's **St. Mary's County Oyster Festival**. If you're terminally devoted to oysters, get tickets (only 2,700 are available) to **Virginia's Chincoteague Oyster Festival**. Other festivals across the country celebrate scallops, clams, lobsters, crawfish, catfish, mullet and more.

Dessert addicts, don't despair. Wisconsin's **Chocolate City Festival** or the chocolate-chile ice cream at Arizona's **La Fiesta de los Chiles** may convince you to skip dinner altogether.

This all too tame for you? Then you're ripe for the **Sweetwater (Texas) Rattlesnake Roundup**, where you can eat western diamondback rattlesnakes that can grow to eight feet. Or head to Kansas, where women in the **Pit Hissers** roundup crew welcome men's help in gathering dinner at the **Rattlesnake Roundup and Prairie Folk Festival**. You may prefer Anahuac, Texas, where a three-to-one alligators-to-people ratio doesn't stop townspeople from chowing down on their amphibian friends at their **Gatorfest**.

There are also some decidedly weird food festivals. About 100,000 visitors delight in slimy okra-eating contests at the **Okra Strut** in South Carolina. You can catch the *Product Costume Style Show* at the **Texas Citrus Fiesta**, where clothes are made with seed buttons, onionskin collars, pulverized tangerine rinds and other local agricultural products. Or dine on emu kebabs at the **Texas Watermelon Thump** and dandelion wedding soup at the **Dandelion Mayfest** in Ohio.

About Food Festivals (cont.)

Then there are the organic Viagras: Horseradish, chiles, artichokes, tomatoes, yams and Georgia's rampant kudzu vine (it grows a foot a day) have all been regarded at one time or another as aphrodisiacs. The Stockton (California) **Asparagus Festival** and a number of oyster fests claim libidinous side effects. But don't confuse erotic seafood with Montana's **Rocky Mountain Oyster Feed**, where brave souls, delirious from nonstop country music, feast on calf testicles, just like those at Oklahoma's **Calf Fry Festival**.

After all this, you may swear off down-home events for more refined festivals, where gourmet restaurants treat visitors to their most exquisite fare. Cities all over the United States hold "Taste" festivals that showcase top area restaurants. Santa Fe's **Wine & Chile Fiesta** features cooking demonstrations by nationally-recognized chefs, horseback rides to mesa-top campfire breakfasts and delicacies from more than sixty of the town's renowned restaurants. In the Northwest, 450,000 people know a good thing when they taste it at the **Bite of Seattle**, which showcases dozens of local restaurants. In California, the **La Jolla Festival of the Arts and Food Faire** combines chowings by more than 190 award-winning artists with a variety of cuisine from more than twenty international gourmet restaurants. Nearby, the **Taste of San Diego** is part of the state's largest annual food-and-music festival.

Gastronomically speaking, it's possible to travel the world without leaving the States. One of the biggest international cuisine festivals is the **Bronx Caribbean Festival**, with millions eating curried goat, conch and other delicacies. Ohio's **Oktoberfest-Zinzinnati** is one of the largest German festivals in the world (so big a whole chapter of this book is dedicated to it). **Kutztown's German Festival**, in the heart of Pennsylvania Dutch country, strives for authenticity in every detail. Sophia Loren once said, "Everything you see I owe to

Gastronomically speaking, it's possible to travel the world without leaving the States.

spaghetti," so if you want a figure like hers, go to Buffalo, New York, for its **Italian Heritage & Food Festival**. Of course, as somebody else once pointed out, "The trouble with eating Italian food is that five or six days later you're hungry again." Solve that at Arizona's **Matsuri Festival of Japan**, where spaghetti turns into yaki soba (pan-fried noodles). Stay for the prestigious **Heard Museum Guild Indian Fair & Market**, where you can sample Native American fry bread, Hopi stew, or piki, a thin Hopi bread made with blue cornmeal and rabbit brush plant. If you still can't decide, there are plenty of multiethnic food festivals. You may want to spend the summer in Milwaukee, where the **United Festivals** run from June to September, celebrating first Polish, then Italian, and on through German, African, Irish, Mexican and Native American.

You might also travel the continent to plan your day's menu. Start with syrup-filled pancakes from the **Beauce Maple Festival** in Saint-Georges, Canada, then grab lunch at the **Shellfish Festival** in Charlottetown, Canada. Or, if you've ever wondered how to cook up a cactus, check out the **Festival de Nopales** in Puebla, Mexico, where the noble nopal is stewed, stuffed and even made into ice cream. Make dinner a succulent steak from the **Actopan Barbecue Fair** in Hidalgo, Mexico, with a fiery side dish from Mexico's **Radish Fiesta**. For dessert you can sample the giant pie featured at **Mistassini**, Canada's Blueberry Festival. There's also the **Vanilla Festival** in Veracruz, Mexico, which celebrates this fragrant and erotic flavor by selling vanilla bean plant flowers, dolls and sculptures, as well as vanilla liqueurs and plenty of sumptuous fare.

No matter what your taste, there are enough culinary events out there to satisfy the appetite of even the hungriest festival-goer.

About Food Festivals—The Menu (cont.)

Event Name	City	State	Phone	Month	#Days	Att. (000)	
Central New York Maple Festival	Marathon	NY	607-849-3278	Apr.	3	60	BREAKFAST
World Grits Festival	St. George	SC	803-563-3255	Apr.	3	45	
Vermont Maple Festival	St. Albans	VT	802-524-2444	Apr.	3	40	
Gumbo Festival	Bridge City	LA	504-436-4712	Aug.	3	100	LUNCH
Jambalaya Festival	Sorrento	LA	504-622-2331	Apr.	3	25	
Republic of Texas Chilympiad	San Marcos	TX	512-396-5400	Sep.	n/a	n/a	
National Peanut Festival	Dothan	AL	334-793-4323	Nov.	9	136	
Heard Museum Guild Indian Fair & Market	Phoenix	AZ	602-252-8840	Mar.	2	20	
Kudzu Takeover Day and Crafts Fair	Lumpkin	GA	912-838-6262	Aug.	1	14	
Rattlesnake Roundup & Prairie Folk Festival	Sharon Springs	KS	913-852-4473	May	3	2	AFTERNOON SNACK
Rocky Mountain Oyster Feed	Clinton	Mt	406-825-4968	Sep.	5	13	
Dandelion Mayfest	Dover	OH	216-932-2145	May	2	10	
Calf Fry Festival	Vinita	OK	918-256-7133	Sep.	2	10	
Gatorfest	Anahuac	TX	409-267-4190	Sep.	3	25	
Sweetwater Rattlesnake Roundup	Sweetwater	TX	915-235-5466	Mar.	3	30	
Fiery Food Festival	Pasco	WA	509-545-0738	Sep.	2	50	
Great Wisconsin Cheese Festival	Little Chute	WI	414-788-7390	Jun.	3	15	
Matsuri Festival of Japan	Phoenix	AZ	602-262-5071	Feb.	2	40	
The Great Monterey Squid Festival	Monterey	CA	408-649-6544	May	2	30	
Boggy Bayou Mullet Festival	Niceville	FL	850-678-1615	Oct.	3	175	
World Chicken Festival	London	KY	606-878-6900	Sep.	4	20	
Mudbug Madness	Shreveport	LA	800-551-8682	May	3	120	
St. Mary's County Oyster Festival	Leonardtown	MD	301-863-5015	Oct.	2	25	DINNER
Maine Lobster Festival	Rockland	ME	800-562-2529	Aug.	5	10	
Yarmouth Clam Festival	Yarmouth	ME	207-846-3984	Jul.	3	150	
Bourne Scallop Festival	Bourne	MS	508-759-6000	Sep.	3	50	
World Catfish Festival	Belzoni	MS	800-408-4838	Apr.	1	20	
Bronx African-American and Caribbean Heritage Festival	Bronx	NY	718-367-1754	Sep.	1	15	
Italian Heritage & Food Festival	Buffalo	NY	716-874-6133	Jul.	5	100	
Oktoberfest-Zinzinnati	Cincinnati	OH	800-246-2987	Sep.	2	n/a	
Chincoteague Oyster Festival	Chincoteague	VA	804-336-6161	Oct.	n/a	n/a	
Gilroy Garlic Festival	Gilroy	CA	408-842-1625	Jul.	3	123	GARNISHES
International Horseradish Festival	Collinsville	IL	618-344-2884	Jun.	2	10	
Phelps Sauerkraut	Phelps	NY	315-548-5691	Aug.	4	10	
Ohio Honey Festival	Oxford	OH	513-868-5891	Sep.	2	20	
Castroville Artichoke Festival	Castroville	CA	408-633-2465	Sep.	2	n/a	
Stockton Asparagus Festival	Stockton	CA	209-467-8001	Apr.	3	80	SIDE DISHES
Vidalia Onion Festival	Vidalia	GA	912-538-8687	Apr.	4	60	
Potato Bowl	Grand Forks	ND	800-866-4566	Sep.	7	n/a	
Okra Strut	Irmo	SC	803-781-9878	Sep.	2	60	
East Texas Yamboree	Gilmer	TX	903-843-2413	Oct.	3	100	
Tomato Festival	Jacksonville	TX	903-586-2217	Jun.	1	10	
Florida Strawberry Festival	Plant City	FL	813-752-9194	Mar.	11	850	
Peach Festival	Romeo	MI	810-752-4436	Sep.	4	n/a	FRUITS
South Carolina Peach Festival	Gaffney	SC	864-489-5721	Jul.	2	25	
Texas Citrus Festival	Mission	TX	956-585-9724	Feb.	4	800	
Texas Watermelon Thump	Luling	TX	830-875-2082	Jun.	3	35	
La Fiesta de los Chiles	Tucson	AZ	520-326-9686	Oct.	2	12	
Boston Scooper Bowl	Boston	MA	617-632-3300	Jun.	6	25	DESSERTS
Kutztown Pennsylvania German Festival	Kutztown	PA	800-963-8824	Jun.	9	50	
Chocolate City Festival	Burlington	WI	414-763-6044	May	3	100	
La Jolla Festival of the Arts and Food Faire	La Jolla	CA	619-456-1268	Jun.	n/a	n/a	
Taste of San Diego	San Diego	CA	619-236-1212	Sep.	3	85	ADDITIONAL
Taste of Chicago	Chicago	IL	312-744-3315	Jun.	11	3,650	
Santa Fe Wine & Chile Festival	Santa Fe	NM	505-438-8060	Sep.	5	2	
Bite of Seattle	Seattle	WA	206-232-2982	Jun.	11	n/a	
United Festivals	Milwaukee	WI	414-273-3950	Jun.	n/a	n/a	

Real Swingers

About Golf

The Scots have invented many things, including the Edinburgh Festivals, bagpipes and Scotch—all of which are covered in the international companion edition to this book. But you'll have to agree, the world would be a lesser place without the most addictive, intriguing and implausible Scottish invention of them all: golf.

One of the Scots' best-loved contributions to the civilized world, The British Open, the world's oldest golf tournament, remains among the sport's greatest annual events. It's been played for almost a century and a half, and is always contested on one of England's or Scotland's hallowed venues. Watching this tradition-filled tournament unfold in person at Turnberry, Muirfield or St. Andrews (the birthplace of golf) is an unforgettable life experience.

As with so much else from the Old World, a lot of the money and excitement associated with golf has crossed the ocean. The United States has left its indelible imprint on the sport, and today, even for nonplayers, professional golf tournaments are a ball. Some spectators plant themselves at one hole and break out their lawn chairs for the day. Others follow a favorite golfer. The surroundings are always lush, lovely and perfect for an invigorating walk in the park. Hospitality tents and refreshment areas present great opportunities to meet people and discuss everything from missed putts to latest mergers or takeovers.

With increasing media coverage, golf has become one of the most popular sports on the planet—more than fifty million people worldwide now pronounce themselves golfers. But the skill level may not have changed much since Scottish shepherds first played with sticks and stones more than 300 years ago—most of us are still woeful on the links. Still, there's a whole lot more hacking going on these days.

With pro tours and events all over the world, hitting a tournament is easy. The best male players congregate on three tours:

The Professional Golfers' Association Tour (PGA Tour), the Japan Professional Golfers' Association Tour (JPGA Tour) and the European Professional Golfers' Association Tour (EPGA Tour). The best females play on the Ladies Professional Golf Association Tour (LPGA Tour). The best players over fifty compete on the Senior Professional Golfers' Association Tour (Senior PGA Tour).

The format for most tournaments is "stroke play," which simply means that the golfer with the lowest aggregate score at the end of the designated number of holes (usually 72) wins the tournament. A "skins game" is typically played between four golfers, and each hole is worth a certain number of dollars. If no one wins the hole, the value is carried over to the next hole. Particularly at televised skins games featuring a quartet of golf's biggest stars, a single hole can be worth $500,000 or more. "Match play" pits one golfer against another. Whichever player wins the most holes wins the match. This format is often used in nail-biting international competitions, such as the Ryder Cup or The Presidents Cup.

The Senior PGA Tour is fun to watch because many of the golfers ham it up for the crowds. Über-stars such as Jack Nicklaus and the "Merry Mex" Lee Trevino still make occasional appearances, but popular hot shots such as Hale Irwin and Fuzzy Zoeller ensure that the level of play is top-notch. Even so, the vibe on this tour is more laid back. Players are often master showmen who have as much fun as the spectators.

The LPGA is loads of fun, too. At most ladies tournaments the galleries are smaller, making it easier to get close to players and hear what they're discussing with their caddies. If you want to improve your own swing, pattern it after an LPGA player. The women are widely held to have the best swings in the game.

The PGA Tour is where you'll find Tiger Woods and colleagues. From year to year, there are about fifty official events on the PGA Tour, with prize money totaling more than $100 million. Over the course of the year, the most successful golfers on tour will pocket a few million bucks in prize money and endorsements (not counting Tiger, whose earnings are off the charts). Are players worth it? Did Henry Ford's assembly line increase profits?

The professional tours travel from one end of the globe to the other. Each host city has its charm, and each tournament its distinct personality. Some are downright fun, such as the AT&T Pebble Beach National Pro-Am, which draws top celebrities as well as top golfers into the field. Bill Murray and Clint Eastwood are regulars here. Others, such as the Masters and U.S. Open—two of the four prestigious "majors" played each year—are more serious. Winning one of these tournaments boosts a golfer to a new level of respect and accomplishment.

If you've ever taken narrow stick to dimpled spheroid and tried to manipulate its course of flight toward a hole in the ground 450 yards away marked by a half-inch diameter flagpole, you know that golf is more aggravating than do-it-yourself plumbing. Par on most courses is 72; the average golfer doesn't break 100. If you were this successful in your job, you'd be fired! Once, when asked which single factor contributed most to his success, Jack Nicklaus, along with Tiger perhaps the greatest golfer ever to play the game, remarked, "I miss better than anyone else." The Golden Bear wasn't kidding.

But, for all its infamous aggravation, golf remains mysteriously fun. Watching a perfectly hit ball as it floats magically against a solid blue sky produces a feeling like no other. A twenty-foot putt dropping exquisitely into the cup makes a uniquely graceful sound. A hole-in-one is like a grand slam, three-point buzzer beater and long-bomb touchdown all rolled into one.

To enjoy watching a golf tournament, you don't have to paint your face in team colors. There's no "dawg pound" in the visiting team's end zone taunting and heckling. Golf is a civilized sport with skilled athletes playing a game of honor. See for yourself at a professional tournament and you'll be a better hacker for it.

Keeping Your Eye On The Ball

The Majors

The Masters (April)
Augusta National (706-667-6000)

U.S. Open (June)
U.S. Golf Association (800-345-8742)

The British Open (July)
The Ticket Office, Royal & Ancient Golf Club (011-44-1334-478-478)

The PGA Championship (August)
PGA of America (800-742-8258)

Most Fun U.S. Tournaments

The Phoenix Open (January)
Phoenix, Arizona (602-870-4431)

Worldcom Classic—The Heritage of Golf (April)
Hilton Head Island, South Carolina (800-234-1107)

The AT&T Pebble Beach National Pro-Am (January)
Pebble Beach, California (800-541-9091)

Nabisco Championship (March)
Rancho Mirage, California (760-324-4546)

Most Fun International Tournaments

Ryder Cup (U.S. team vs. European team; biennial, alternating sites)
PGA of America (800-742-8258)

The Presidents Cup (U.S. team vs. international team; biennial, alternating sites)
PGA of America (800-742-8258)

All That Jazz

About Jazz Festivals

What exactly is a jazz festival? Usually the event features multiple bands on multiple stages on multiple days, but that can vary. The **Jazz & Image Festival** in Rome has only one stage, tucked into a hill above the Coliseum, but presents jazz every summer night. Audiences sip Brunello with their pasta as they listen to the music on warm Italian evenings. In contrast, the **North Sea Jazz Festival** in the Netherlands squeezes 70,000 audience members into the Hague Congress Center for hundreds of performances on fifteen stages in just three days. The fare? Herring and beer, naturally. But, if the Dutch event is one of the largest and the Roman one of the longest, one of the smallest might be the two-day, ten-act **Jazz in the Sangres**, presented in a tent on the town green in tiny Westcliffe, Colorado, each August.

There's no shortage of jazz holidays—from France to Finland, from Cuba to California—literally thousands of festivals celebrate the beloved American art form each year. The millions of pilgrims who attend these events attest to the prominence of jazz in twenty-first-century culture. Although the music sprang up in the American South, the jazz-festival tradition reaches back to jazz-mad France in 1948, when the high priests of the Hot Club of France produced the first such affair—the **Nice Jazz Festival**, still one of the best in the world—headlined by Louis Armstrong. The following year, Paris hosted the Festival International du Jazz with performances by Charlie Parker and Miles Davis, among others.

In 1954, just five years after the bash in Paris, came the jazz event that would set the standard for all to come—the Newport Jazz Festival, in Newport, Rhode Island (which continues today as the **JVC Jazz Festival Newport**). Since its inception, just about every jazz star has performed at Newport. Its genre-bending affairs of thirty years ago featured Frank Sinatra, Led Zeppelin and Frank Zappa, alongside Duke Ellington, Dave Brubeck and Sarah Vaughan. Nowadays, you can hear superstars and young lions, while soaking up a New England ambience, redolent of clam chowder and lobster, and full of beachfront mansions and elegant sailboats.

Two California events round out the selection of great American jazz festivals. **The Monterey Jazz Festival**, founded in 1958, takes place near the scenic coastline, 120 miles south of San Francisco, and always features the best mainstream jazz. Many world-première performances have been presented here over the years, including Duke Ellington's "Suite Thursday." The **Playboy Jazz Festival** sells out the huge Hollywood Bowl each year with stellar performers in classic and contemporary styles. Bring a picnic basket, settle in for some great listening, and you might get a bonus—jazz fan Bill Cosby is often the master of ceremonies.

The French jazz connection has wound its classic way to the present-day **Jazz Festival in Antibes**, commonly known as the Jazz a Juan, on the famous topless beaches of the country's southern coast. Farther north, the **JVC Jazz Festival Paris** presents concerts in venues such as the Théâtre Champs d'Élysées, Salle Pleyel and Elysee Montmartre. In the Parisian early hours, you can catch a set at the New Morning jazz club after the French cuisine of your dreams at restaurant Flo (Rue Fauborg St-Denis). In addition to these notable events, France hosts more than eighty other jazz festivals each year.

Jazz festivals are as diverse as the music itself. Experimental and avant-garde styles are well represented at **Moers Festival** (Germany), while Dixieland, swing and other early forms can be heard at **The Great Connecticut JazzFest**. But, how about a festival high in the Japanese Alps? The **Newport Jazz Festival in Madarao** has been swinging Japanese audiences since 1984 on the grassy summer slopes of the Madarao ski area in Nagano, site of the 1998 Winter Olympics. Twenty-thousand-plus jazz lovers picnic on barbecued squid and yaki soba (fried noodles) while enjoying the festival's unique jam sessions, with musicians from different ensembles improvising together.

Romance is everywhere at the **Umbria Jazz Festival** in the hilltop city of Perugia, Italy. As you stroll through the narrow, spiraling streets, you may find a big band playing in the ruins of a medieval church, a piano solo at an outdoor restaurant, a guitar trio beneath an Etruscan arch, or a duet serenading a crowd from a vista that overlooks the rolling vineyards of Umbria and Tuscany. For northern ambience, check out the **Pori Jazz Festival** in Finland. In a birch grove in the city park, you can hear top international musicians as the sun sets—at 1 a.m.!

No legitimate review of jazz festivals could neglect New York City, christened the Big Apple by swing-era musicians sixty years ago. The Apple hosts a dozen jazz fests each year, but the biggest is the **JVC Jazz Festival New York**. Often voted Best Jazz Festival by *Jazz Times* magazine readers, the event takes place not only at such hallowed venues as Carnegie Hall and the Lincoln Center, but also around Harlem, Greenwich Village and Bryant Park in the heart of the city.

Salty types can dig their jazz while riding the high seas aboard the *Queen Elizabeth II.* **The QE2 Newport Jazz Festival at Sea** cruises up the Atlantic coast with world-class musicians performing onboard. When the liner anchors in Newport two days later, passengers are ferried directly to the granddaddy of them all—the **JVC Jazz Festival Newport**. This idea has proven so popular that similar jazz-theme excursions abound worldwide, adding a little bit of "rock and roll" to the rich heritage of the jazz festival.

Name	Location	Telephone	Month	Attendance
The World's Most Fun Jazz Festivals				
Montréal Jazz Festival	Montréal	888-515-0515	Jun-Jul	1.7 million
Montreux Jazz Festival	Montreux, Switzerland	41-848-800-800	Jul	220,000
New Orleans Jazz Festival	New Orleans	504-522-4786	Apr-May	618,000
More Great Jazz Festivals				
Nice Jazz Festival	Nice, France	33-49-214-4800	Jul	45,000
International Jazz Festival in Antibes (Juan les Pins)	Antibes, France	33-49-290-5300	Jul	24,000
The Great Connecticut Jazz Festival	Guilford, Connecticut	800-468-3836	Jul	17,000
JVC Jazz Festival	New York, New York	212-501-1390	Jun	65,000
JVC Jazz Festival Newport	Newport, Rhode Island	401-847-3700	Aug	16,000
JVC Jazz Festival Paris	Paris, France	33-14-621-0837	Oct	11,000
Jazz & Image Festival	Rome, Italy	39-06-5897-807	Jun-Aug	110,000
Jazz in the Sangres	Westcliffe, Colorado	303-794-4170	Aug	1,500
Moers Festival	Moers, Germany	49-2-841-7741	Jun	25,000
Monterey Jazz Festival	Monterey, California	831-373-3366	Sep	42,000
Newport Jazz Festival in Madarao	Nagano, Japan	81-269-64-3081	Aug	20,000
North Sea Jazz Festival	The Hague, Netherlands	31-15-214-8900	Jul	70,000
North Sea Jazz Festival	Cape Town, South Africa	27-21-418-5614	Mar	70,000
Playboy Jazz Festival	Los Angeles, California	310-449-4070	Jun	35,000
Pori Jazz Festival	Pori, Finland	35-82-626-2200	Jul	115,000
QE2 Newport Jazz Festival at Sea	New York, New York	800-728-6273	Aug	1,700
Umbria Jazz Festival	Perugia, Italy	39-75-573-2432	Jul	200,000

Larger Than Life

About Movies, Giant Screen

You're a bird, soaring above the parched Serengeti as massive herds of wildebeests ripple across the grasslands below. You're a dolphin, gliding through glittering coral reefs, then shooting up in exhilarating somersaults high above the waves. You hear and feel the thundering roar of rockets as you and your international crew of astronauts and cosmonauts blast off from Kennedy Space Center to rendezvous with the international space station, 220 miles above the earth's surface.

This is fun? Yes, because you're in the midst of large-format movies, films so huge and crisp they almost literally bring you into the experience. While this book emphasizes participation rather than passive observation, virtually all of the destinations include giant-screen movie theaters that occasionally provide a worthy diversion from the main attractions suggested.

Projected onto screens as high as eight stories or domes up to 88 feet in diameter, large-format films extend beyond viewers' fields of peripheral vision. Specially designed theaters with steeply raked seating provide a "best" seat for everyone, and multichannel, multispeaker sound systems enhance the effects. In certain theaters, viewers can dive into these three-dimensional films with the aid of electronic liquid-crystal shutter glasses (a far cry from those goofy, plastic 3-D glasses of the 1950s). Some film centers add audience motion. The combination of these effects brings viewers into the action so realistically that they often walk out of films such as *Everest* expecting to buckle up their boots and tackle snow and ice outside.

So, what makes these panoramic illusions possible? Basically, it's the larger-size film and a revolutionary projection system pioneered by a group of Canadian filmmakers and entrepreneurs who were inspired by the multiscreen films that amazed audiences at Montreal's Expo '67. Their 15/70 film frames are ten times larger than conventional 35mm frames and three times greater than 70mm ones.

Today, the Imax Corporation dominates in 15/70 technology and number of theaters, but other companies, such as Iwerks Entertainment, also feature theaters and cutting-edge technology, which includes the somewhat-smaller 8/70 film format. Originally found most often at museums, science centers, world fairs and expositions,

large-format film theaters are now just as likely to be built at theme parks and, increasingly, as part of commercial developments. Since its opening in November 1994, the Sony Imax theater at New York's Lincoln Square has been one of the highest-grossing single movie screens in the United States.

Filmmakers who lease special cameras and equipment from companies such as Imax and Iwerks make many of the films shown on these oversize screens. In 1976, MacGillivray Freeman Films thrilled audiences with *To Fly!* at the Smithsonian Institution's National Air and Space Museum in Washington, D.C. Their haunting 1998 film *Everest* led to an explosion of public interest in large-format films. Destination Cinema in cooperation with National Geographic Television produces films specific to its theaters at tourist destinations such as the Grand Canyon and Niagara Falls.

For fans of this new technology, the good news is large-format movies are getting ever better. Imax teamed up with NASA to develop cameras for launch into space, where astronauts show *Space Station*, a 3-D film about the building of the International Space Station. Imax's digital remastering (DMR) technology which converts 35mm movies such as *Apollo 13* and *Star Wars II: Attack of the Clones* into Imax's big-screen format, may have the most far-reaching implications.

With public demand increasing, large-format films will continue to develop. As Imax co-founder Graeme Ferguson observes, "One of the things you discover when you invent a medium that you yourself don't know all of its potential. It's only when a large number of artists start using it that they start to astonish those who invented it."

See and be Seen

About Parades

Whenever someone says, "They don't make 'em like they used to," you can be certain they're not talking about parades. In recent years, parades have become so extravagant that people spend entire years preparing for them.

For millions of people around the world, New Year's Day is synonymous with parades, the most extraordinary being The Tournament of Roses Parade in Pasadena, California—a typical float includes more flowers than the average florist uses in five years. Balloons in New York City's Macy's Thanksgiving Day parade dwarf even the skyscrapers of Manhattan. Tens of thousands of devotees swear that New Orleans' infamous Mardi Gras parade is the single most fun event of any kind in the world.

From military might to flower power, parades cover hundreds of different themes, but the best ones have a single element common to virtually every event in this book: participation. While there are no parades without spectators, shared experience is the key. Whether in the streets or on the sidewalk sidelines, the parade atmosphere prevails as communities join together to sing, dance, eat, drink and smile together as the spectacle passes by.

Today's parades are descendants of religious processions, holiday festivals and military parades. Marching bands have replaced fife-and-drum corps and civic groups, police and firefighters have replaced soldiers. But, even today, parades often are shows of patriotism and strength. One of the best all marching-unit parades is New York City's St. Patrick's Day Parade, where more than two million spectators cheer on firefighters, police and other might-and-muscle units.

Most parades have moving mechanical parts—floats—that fall into one of three categories for judging (in order of prestige): floral, motorized disguising what propels the float and visible-motorized. The Tournament of Roses Parade, which showcases Southern California's mild winter with flowers and fruit, is the world's most famous. One million curb-side spectators are joined by tens of millions of television viewers in more than 100 countries. Every inch of every phenomenal float is covered with flowers or other natural materials.

Philadelphia starts the New Year with its Mummers Parade, complete with comic brigades and marching string bands. The Fourth of July is parade day in towns across the United States—Philadelphia turns the whole city into a patriotic celebration (page 136). Milwaukee's Great Circus Parade relives old-time, circus street processions, complete with circus wagons and wild animals. Dancing dragons herald Chinese New Year's parades in San Francisco, New York and other cities. New York's ethnic communities parade in a different language every week during summer. San Francisco's Lesbian, Gay, Bisexual, Transgender Pride Parade is the largest annual lesbian/gay event in the world. New York's Greenwich Village Halloween Parade invites everybody in costume to join thousands of wild dancers, artists and bands. Pasadena's silly Doodah Parade—celebrated around Thanksgiving—includes marching units such as The BBQ & Hibachi Marching Grill Team and the Synchronized Precision Briefcase Drill Team.

No matter what kind of parade, where you stand makes a difference. Units perform before judging stands and cameras, so be near those for the best views. Walking a parade route backward makes the parade go by faster. If crowds are too large, bring a footstool to raise yourself above the crowd for a good view—at least until everybody else takes our advice.

Meet Me at the Fair

About State Fairs

The thrill of the midway, blue-ribbon competitions, stellar entertainment and remnants of "grandfather's farm"—these still draw 150 million people to more than 3,200 county, state and regional fairs and expositions across the United States and Canada. Although these events lack pizzazz, nearly every community has a fair appealing to local interests, and lots of people consider them a great place to have fun.

The York (Pennsylvania) Fair, one of the oldest in the country, started in 1765, eleven years before the Declaration of Independence was signed. Back then, neighboring farmers got together once a year to show off their best livestock and skills and everyone went home with tips to improve their farms. Today's fairs still center on agriculture, even though ninety-eight percent of the country's population is now urban.

But fairs also have adapted to city interests. Now there may be ostriches, llamas and angora goats as well as cows, pigs and rabbits. The Orange County (California) Fair's "sheep to shawl" exhibit connects farm animals to modern couture, the Ozark Empire (Missouri) Fair's highly popular Birthing Center welcomes dozens of calves into the world to audience acclaim, and excitement runs high as competitors bet on powerful frog legs at the Calaveras County (California) Fair and Jumping Frog Jubilee. Not content with only apple-pie contests, the Utah State Fair adds chili cook-offs and salsa competitions, and the Del Mar (California) Fair rates the best home-brew in its beer-making contest. Multimedia computer exhibits, complete with virtual-reality games, are just as likely now as livestock exhibits.

Fairs increasingly feature top entertainment. Country stars such as Randy Travis and Sawyer Brown join old rock stars such as the Doobie Brothers, Pat Benatar, Huey Lewis and the News and The Neville Brothers. Rodeos, big-top circuses, stock-car races, horse-and-harness racing and boxing add to the excitement.

The midway, with its games and Ferris wheels, adds daring thrill rides. The Minnesota State Fair has featured the 125-foot-high Ejection Seat towers, while California State Fair-goers have thrilled to the Skycoaster, which holds up to three people who are strapped to a bungee cord and sent off a 140-foot tower in a pendulum swing that reaches speeds of fifty-five mph.

Fairs reflect local cultures. The Los Angeles County Fair meets a particularly complex challenge by including the usual butter-churning and husband-calling contests, then adding the Asian and Pacific Islander Festival, Plaza de las America, Mexican village, Trinidad Steel Drum Band and Mariachi U.S.A. Fiesta. Even the Arizona State Fair reflects its region—its UFO Encounters puts participants through an interactive re-creation of four types of alien abductions.

Why do fairs have such staying power? One reason is money. Minnesota estimates the total economic impact of its state fair at $150 million annually. That's quite an increase from the first Hopkinton (New Hampshire) State Fair in 1915 which reported net profits of less than five dollars. Fairs make history, too. In 1955, a vendor distributed flying disks the Los Angeles County Fair. These days, who doesn't own a Frisbee?

Top Ten Best-Attended U.S. Fairs

1. State Fair of Texas, Dallas — 3,000,000
2. Minnesota State Fair, Minneapolis-St. Paul — 1,706,486
3. Houston Livestock Show and Rodeo, Houston, Texas — 1,563,662
4. Los Angeles County Fair, Pomona, California — 1,288,056
5. Illinois State Fair, Springfield, Illinois — 1,264,750
6. Western Washington Fair, Puyallup, Washington — 1,184,671
7. Del Mar (California) Fair — 1,169,384
8. Eastern States Exposition, West Springfield, Massachusetts — 1,165,224
9. Arizona State Fair, Phoenix — 1,025,000
10. Erie County Fair and Exposition, Hamburg, New York — 1,013,110

Beautiful People

About Supermodels

Supermodel hasn't made it into Webster's Dictionary yet, but, as a cultural reference point, few of us are unaware of the weighty (and not so weighty) impact this group of beautiful people has had on modern society. We talk about them. We track their careers. We buy the clothes they wear. Mostly, though, we just want to look at them.

Most supermodels have unpredictable schedules, but there are times of the year when many are guaranteed to be in the right place at the right time. If you know the pattern, it's possible to schedule a lunch with Heidi, Giselle or stalwarts such as Cindy, Tyra, and Claudia. Well, at least at the same cafe or restaurant.

Milan is the queen of style and Fashion Week is its crown jewel. Paris and Rome present most of the women's couture showings, with winter and fall designs on the runways in January, and spring designs in July. These are the times to book into grand hotels such as The Ritz, which host the luxurious shows. In Paris, you're likely to spot models in Marais-district restaurants in the evenings, especially after big shows. (Supermodels prepare by skipping food for days before the shows.)

Designers follow the couture made-to-order extravaganzas with separate shows in Milan, Paris and New York, then make the rounds again for spring ready-to-wear fashions in September. There are more ready-to-wear shows than couture shows, so Paris supermodel sightings in March are even more likely than in January.

Not all beautiful models have "supermodel" status. Catch glimpses of up-and-coming beauties at high-fashion catalog photo shoots—Miami in February is the favorite backdrop. Miami shines with models in April, too, when photographers shoot designer campaigns and fall magazine layouts. Cuba and Cape Town, South Africa, are April favorites, as well.

Male models congregate in Paris for January shows following the women's couture collections, then move to Milan for the Italian menswear shows. They return to Paris in July for the spring menswear collection.

Since only the fashion elite is invited to see the runway shows that make headlines, where do you find supermodels when they're not on the job? Paris is a decent spot year-round, but New York is the best bet. Even if they hail from Australia, Germany, London or Los Angeles, most models have homes in the Big Apple. They want proximity to the larger magazines and advertising firms, as well as designers such as Calvin Klein and Donna Karan in the garment district on Sixth Avenue.

Models generally take vacations in August, but in only the most glamorous and exclusive locales: Majorca, Monte Carlo and obscure islands in the Caribbean. Good bets in the Caribbean are St. Martin, Virgin Gorda and Mustique.

Following supermodels' schedules gives you a good chance of sighting one. And even if you don't get lucky, there are worse places to hang around waiting than Paris, London and New York.

The Beautiful Calendar	
Jan.:	Paris couture, Paris menswear, Milan menswear, Rome couture
Feb.:	New York, London, Milan starts
Mar.:	London Fashion Week, Milan ready-to-wear, Paris ready-to-wear
Apr.:	Miami, Cape Town, Cuba designer campaigns
Jul.:	Paris couture, Paris menswear (Milan in June menswear), Rome couture (women)
Aug.:	Holidays: Caribbean, Monte Carlo, Majorca
Sep.:	New York men and women, London ready-to-wear, Milan
Oct.:	Milan ready-to-wear, Paris ready-to-wear
Nov.:	New York ready-to-wear (no formal shows)
Dec.:	Holiday
All year:	New York, Paris, Milan

High Times

About Tall Buildings

Observation decks on towers and tall buildings are a feature common to most cities in this book. When travelers ascend these universally popular landmarks, they're continuing a tradition thousands of years old. Early human always surveyed their surroundings from high vantage points—watching for enemies, looking for food, waiting for loved ones to come home. Trees and hills were the first lookouts. Towers built of wood, stones and bricks followed.

The development of steel and steel-beam construction, however, revolutionized builders' capabilities. Adding high-strength concrete provided compression resistance and minimized vibration. With the addition of elevators, telephones and electric lights, even the sky no longer seemed the limit.

Built in Chicago in 1885, the first skyscraper was a monument to an insurance company. The Home Insurance Building, at 180 feet tall, employed a totally different concept from traditional towers, with its eleven floors built to be occupied, not just used as lookout posts. It was soon obvious that skyscrapers were a natural in New York City, too, where the best way to maximize scarce and expensive urban land was to build straight up. Surprisingly, several of its tallest skyscrapers were built during the Great Depression, with the Empire State Building taking the "highest" crown in 1931 at 1,250 feet.

The New York/Chicago skyscraper competition heated up a few decades later with the John Hancock Center and Amoco Building in Chicago and the World Trade Center towers in New York. Chicago's Sears Tower took the crown in 1974, at 1,450 feet (not counting twin antennae more than 250 feet tall), and held the "world's tallest" title until the 1997 opening of the Petronas Towers in Kuala Lumpur, Malaysia.

Determining the world's tallest building seem straightforward, but recognized criteria now include four categories. The Sears Tower qualifie for three of the "top" honors (height to rooftop, height to antennae and highest occupied floor). The Petronas Towers are highest in the world to the architectural top. The Chinese have built many huge, space-age-style towers and building in the Pudong area of Shanghai, intentionally turning it into a showcase of twenty-first-centur architecture. Australia reportedly plans to build the tallest structure in the world, a half-mile-hig energy tower in the middle of the Outback. Builders in Tokyo continue to salivate over sever fantasy plans for a city-within-a-building, one of which is two-and-a-half miles high!

CN tower in Toronto at 1,815 feet, though not technically a building, is North America's tallest structure with an observation floor. But even cities with more modest skylines boast high points with incredible views, often with restaurants added. Seattle's Space Needle, San Francisco's Embarcadero Skydeck, Houstor Chase Tower Skylobby, St. Louis' Gateway Arch and Boston's Prudential Tower Skywalk all provide thrills to visitors who come to see the sight

The Five Tallest Buildings in North America						
				Height		Floor of
Building	City	Year Built	Stories	Structural Top	Spire/Ant.	Obs. Deck/Rest.(R
Sears Tower	Chicago	1974	110	1,450'	1707'	103
Empire State Building	New York	1931	102	1,250'	1472'	86
Amoco Building	Chicago	1973	83	1,136'	No spire	80R
John Hancock Center	Chicago	1969	100	1,127'	No spire	94/95R
Chrysler Building	New York	1930	77	925'	1,046'	(no obs. deck)

Christmas Nuts

About The Nutcracker Ballet

Ask enough people what they do for fun during the holidays and you're likely to hear stories about dancing snowflakes, flying Christmas trees and battles in which multiheaded mouse kings are felled by a girl's slipper. Maybe you dipped into the eggnog one time too many, but more likely, you'd be hearing a description of *The Nutcracker* ballet, the annual holiday-season drama that, for roughly two million fans each year, is as traditional as fruitcake and family gatherings.

The production that introduces many to classical dance, *The Nutcracker* is the most widely performed ballet in the world. Dance companies offer performances from Thanksgiving through New Year's, with several productions competing in large metropolitan areas. *The Nutcracker* is so beloved that it provides significant chunks of most ballet companies' budgets.

Based on the book *The Nutcracker and the Mouse King* (written by E.T.A. Hoffmann and revised by Alexandre Dumas), the legendary Marius Petipa, first ballet master to His Imperial Majesty, the Russian Tsar, created a detailed story and commissioned his friend Peter Ilyich Tchaikovsky to compose the music. Despite the weighty credentials of its writers, *The Nutcracker* was not well received when it debuted in St. Petersburg in 1892.

But the show survived and, in 1944, the San Francisco Ballet brought *The Nutcracker* to the United States, offering its own choreography. It wasn't until 1954, however, that Americans fell in love with the production, when Russian George Balanchine created his signature full-length staging for the New York City Ballet. Now, many different versions are performed worldwide, including performances featuring the original choreography. In the United States, more than 550 dance companies perform *The Nutcracker*, with the biggest audiences in Boston and the most versions to choose from in the San Francisco Bay Area.

Attempts to widen audience appeal and translate the old-fashioned German setting into modern scenarios have produced increasingly novel adaptations. Ballet Arts Minnesota features rat armies on Rollerblades hurling cheese bombs. New Jersey's Suburban Dance Force cruises Clara, the heroine, through a Lemonade Sea to the classic surf-rock tune "Wipeout." The Pacific Northwest Ballet uses sets designed by off-the-wall children's author Maurice Sendak. The Baton Rouge Ballet Theatre sets its "Bayou Nutcracker" in the antebellum South, complete with plantations and a hot-air balloon grand entrance to the Land of Sweets. A "Southwest Nutcracker" in Tucson replaces Clara with Maria Martinez and includes Indian princesses and Clara's godfather dressed as Zorro. New York City's Mark Morris Dance Group throws the classical ballet out the window, but keeps the music in its "Hard Nut," replacing jetés and pliés with the frug, watusi and hokey-pokey. Several companies, including Donald Byrd/The Group's "Harlem Nutcracker," translate the whole production to jazzy modern dance. San Francisco has the "Dance-Along Nutcracker," sponsored by the Lesbian/Gay Freedom Band—after some basic ballet instruction beforehand, sold-out performances feature hundreds of kids and adults, many in rented tutus, dancing to their own creative drummers, with some pas de deux looking suspiciously more like polkas.

Even without eccentric interpretation, the original *Nutcracker* is zany, with mouse-army battles and Clara arriving in fantasy lands riding sleighs, owls and unicorns. No wonder that in the end she's surprised to wake up in her own bed. Was it real or all a dream? Clara's mother tells her, "If you love something very much it is always alive." The same sentiment can inarguably be applied to *The Nutcracker* ballet.

Tourist Boards

State and Provincial Tourist Boards in the United States, Canada and Mexico

Just in case you want to explore more of the states and provinces in which there are FSG events and destinations, here are some useful telephone numbers:

USA

Arizona	800-842-8257
California	800-862-2543
Colorado	800-265-6726
Washington, D.C.	800-635-6338
Florida	888-735-2872
Georgia	800-847-4842
Hawaii	800-353-5846
Illinois	800-226-6632
Indiana	800-289-6646
Kentucky	800-225-8747
Louisiana	800-261-9144
Maryland	800-543-1036
Massachusetts	800-227-6277
Michigan	800-543-2937
Nevada	800-237-0774
New Mexico	800-545-2040
New York	800-225-5697
Ohio	800-282-5393
Pennsylvania	800-237-4363

South Carolina	800-868-2492
Tennessee	800-462-8366
Texas	800-888-8839
Utah	800-200-1160
Wisconsin	800-372-2737
Wyoming	800-225-5996

CANADA

Alberta	800-661-8888
Montréal	877-266-5687
Ontario	800-668-2746
Québec	800-363-7777

MEXICO

Aguascalientes	800-446-3942
Guerrero	800-446-3942

"Every week of the year there's a fun place to be. And every fun place to be has a best time to be there."

The Fun Seeker's Gold List
The Most Fun Places To Be In The World At The Right Time!

This section is dedicated to the event organizers, their staffs and the thousands of volunteers who create extraordinary environments that allow us to escape into fun.

Making The Fun Seeker's Gold List

Goals, Rules, Results, Exceptions

The Fun Seeker's Gold List

Our goal is to create a list of the world's 100 most fun events and destinations, which together cover every week of the year.

There are currently 96 events and destinations. We're hoping our readers will help us find the remaining four—contact us at **www.funrises.com**.

Events tend to bunch up seasonally, especially the large number that are tied to pre-Lenten celebrations. But with the help of destinations that are not tied to specific events, including the *Cruise: Carnival* which takes in two weekends, the occasional gaps in the calendar are filled. The result: Fun seekers have something to do every week of the year!

Selection Criteria for Events

The list must include a wide variety of events that appeals to a broad array of people (i.e., one doesn't have to be an aficionado to have fun at the event). An event is selected for one of five reasons, not necessarily mutually exclusive:

1. It is a totally unique fun experience (Burning Man is unlike anything else).
2. It is the best event of its kind (there are hundreds of jazz festivals throughout the world— only the three most fun ones were chosen).
3. The combination of the event and city makes for an incredible three-day visit (Memphis in May Barbecue and the attractions of Memphis combine for a non-stop weekend).
4. It is the best event in a city that has to be on a fun seeker's calendar (Boston is a must-visit, and Harborfest is the best time to experience the city).
5. It is the best thing happening in a particular week (the Detroit Auto Show is the only event good enough to fill its January time slot).

In addition, there are a few rules.

Rule: Events must take place every year in the same location.

> **Two Exceptions:** San Francisco's biennial Black and White Ball, and the Inauguration held every four years.

Rule: Events must have a total attendance of at least 10,000.

> **Two Exceptions:** The smallest event is the Napa Valley Wine Auction (2,000), followed by the Vienna Opera Ball (5,000).

Total attendance at all 86 events (ten on the list are destinations not tied to specific events) is more than 62 million. More than two-thirds of these events have an attendance greater than 50,000. The three most-attended events are Carnaval Rio (10 million), Munich's Oktoberfest (6 million) and Stuttgart's Volkfest (5 million). The most-attended events in North America are Fiesta San Antonio, Mardi Gras and Taste of Chicago (each 3.5 million).

Rule: There should be no more than one event per destination.

> **Five Exceptions:** San Francisco, New Orleans, Las Vegas, London and Edinburgh. These world-class cities (★★★★★ or ★★★★) have two world-class events and warrant second visits. Miami also gets a second listing because it's the port for the Carnival cruise.

Events and destinations are rated based on a three-day visit.

Rating the Events

Each of the events is given a FUN rating based on:

Participation - The outrageous parties of Mardi Gras are a great example.

Transformation - During Calgary's Stampede, the entire city gets a Western makeover.

People-watching - From celebrities in Los Angeles during the Academy Awards to bikers at Daytona's Bike Week, this is always rewarding.

Uniqueness - There's nothing like the Exotic Erotic Ball in San Francisco.

Spectacle - New Year's Eve in Times Square is tough to beat.

Scenic surroundings - Hawaii's Aloha Festival comes to mind.

Scenery of a more human variety - Rio's Carnaval is the big winner here.

Personal release - Events like Key West's Fantasy Fest coax people into being more crazy and daring than they'd normally be.

The World's Top Events

★★★★★

Burning Man	Running of the Bulls
Carnaval Rio	Trinidad Carnival
Mardi Gras	Venice Carnival
Munich's Oktoberfest	Vienna Opera Ball

★★★★

Bike Week	Kentucky Derby
Calgary Stampede	La Tomatina
Cannes Film Festival	Las Fallas
Cowes Week	Palio
Edinburgh Fringe Festival	Pushkar Camel Fair
Fantasy Fest	Royal Ascot
Fiesta San Antonio	Songkran Water Festival
Galway Oyster Festival	St. Patrick's Day
Hogmanay	Streetparade
Hookers' Ball/Halloween	Sundance Film Festival
Inauguration	Sydney Gay and
Karneval	Lesbian Mardi Gras

What Event Ratings Mean

★★★★★ and ★★★★

Must do. These events are worth making a special trip for, even planning your life around.

★★★ and ★★

Should do. These are events you should attend if you're already planning to visit the region, or if you're just looking for something fun to do on a given weekend.

★

These events, though not worth a special trip, are the times when it's most fun to be in a city.

The Perfect Combination

★★★★★ / ★★★★★

Four events/destinations scored a perfect 10 (Five-star events in Five-star cities):

Carnaval in Rio

Mardi Gras in New Orleans

Venice Carnival

Vienna Opera Ball, in Vienna, Austria.

The World's Top Cities

★★★★★

Amsterdam	New Orleans
Barcelona	New York City
Berlin	Paris
Cannes	Rio de Janeiro
Chicago	San Francisco
Disney World	Stockholm
Las Vegas	Tokyo
London	Toronto
Los Angeles	Venice
Madrid	Vienna
Miami	

★★★★

Acapulco	Monte Carlo
Aspen	Montréal
Athens	Munich
Boston	Philadelphia
Buenos Aires	St. Moritz
Copenhagen	St. Tropez
Dublin	Seattle
Edinburgh	Sydney
Ibiza/Majorca	Washington, D.C.
Melbourne	

Rating the Destinations

Each of the destinations is given a FUN rating based on the quality and quantity of its nightlife and restaurants, with secondary consideration given to attractions, hotels and overall aesthetic.

What City Ratings Mean

★★★★★ and ★★★★

These are the world-class FUN cities, worth a visit any time (though they're most fun during the recommended event).

★★★ and ★★

These are fun places to visit, but only worth a special trip during the recommended event.

★

Save going here for the recommended event.

The Fun Seeker's Gold List

Event Name (Official Name)	City State, Country	Event Description
Academy Awards Weekend	Los Angeles California, USA	Los Angeles is the North American destination for glitz and glamour, but with film-biz luminaries, screen superstars and major media clamoring about, the buzz is deafening.
Aloha Festival	Honolulu Hawaii, USA	Honolulu is where Hawaiians party and the state rolls out all its clichés—hula girls, mai tais, perfect beaches, tropical breezes—for this celebration.
Ati Atihan	Kalibo (Manila) Philippines	Filipinos take to the streets of Kalibo in a wildly costumed religious festival that celebrates dancing, shaking, foot-stomping and noise-making.
Balloon Fiesta (Kodak Albuquerque International Balloon Fiesta)	Albuquerque New Mexico, USA	With nearly 1,000 multicolored balloons ascending into the Southwestern sky, the world's largest ballooning event transforms Albuquerque into one big fiesta.
Berlin Carnival (Karneval der Kulturen)	Berlin German	Caribbean music and exotic costumes in one of Europe's great capitals—the exotic jumble of cultures fuels an enormous street party.
Bike Week	Daytona Beach (Orlando) Florida, USA	Thousands of bikers thunder into Florida, and Daytona becomes Harley heaven during an extraordinary week of motorcycle worshiping and partying.
Black and White Ball	San Francisco California, USA	This biennial event turns the streets of San Francisco into a set from a glamorous black-and-white movie for the world's largest indoor-outdoor black-tie ball.
Boston Harborfest	Boston Massachusetts, USA	Bostonians commemorate their city's first party (something about tea being thrown in a harbor) with a celebration that blends history with spectacle.
Bumbershoot (Bumbershoot, The Seattle Arts Festival)	Seattle Washington, USA	One of the largest music-and-arts festivals in the United States attracts top international talent to this beautiful city known for its music, coffee and computers.
Burning Man	Black Rock City Nevada, USA	The latest attempt at utopia is a mix of offbeat art and cultural experimentation—free spirits create a perfect (and wild) temporary city in the Nevada desert.
Calgary Stampede	Calgary Alberta, Canada	Calgary, the home of wild chuck-wagon races, hosts one of the world's biggest and best country-style parties, with a world-class rodeo as its centerpiece.
Calle Ocho (Carnaval Miami)	Miami (Miami Beach) Florida, USA	While other carnivals are moving into Lent, Miami's is cranking up two weeks of Latin music and dancing in the streets of North America's hottest destination.
Calle San Sebastián	San Juan Puerto Rico	Wall-to-wall people mingle, dance and drink together along the closed-off streets of San Juan at Puerto Rico's biggest fiesta.
Cannes Film Festival (Festival International du Film)	Cannes France	The world's most important film festival transforms this resort town into a nonstop cast party, where glamour and attention-getting stunts reign supreme.
Caribana	Toronto Ontario, Canada	One of the largest and most exuberant street parties—a million revelers celebrate Toronto's Caribbean and Latin populations with dance and music.
Carnaval Rio	Rio de Janeiro Brazil	The world's *numero uno* biggest party features outrageous costumes, the best dance music on the planet and more fun than some continents have in an entire year.
Cheyenne Frontier Days	Cheyenne Wyoming, USA	Real cowboys and cowgirls still exist and nearly every last one of 'em rides into town for this century-old rodeo, Wild West show and summertime hoedown.
Country Music Fan Fair (International Country Music Fan Fair)	Nashville Tennessee, USA	This five-day orgy of fan appreciation pulls in more than 20,000 die-hards for thirty-five hours of performances and face time with their beloved stars.
Cowes Week	Cowes Isle of Wight, England	The world's largest international yacht regatta transforms the small town of Cowes into a wild gathering of sailors and a frenzied meet market.

The 96 Most Fun Places to be in the World at the Right Time!

Key Month U.S. Holiday	Weather Origin / Attendance	Event Rating City Rating	Mating Rating	Event Type What To Wear	Map # * Page # **
Feb/Mar	49/69 (9/21)	★★☆☆☆	V	Film festival	A02
	1929 / n/a	★★★★★		Sexy	18
Sep	73/87 (23/31)	★★☆☆☆	P	Street party	A16
	1947 / 300,000	★★★☆☆		Hawaiian shirts	74
Jan	69/86 (20/30)	★★★☆☆	V	Carnival	D97
MLK Jr. Day	1212 / 200,000	★★★☆☆		Parade costume	I
Oct	44/71 (7/22)	★★★☆☆	H	Hot air balloons	A28
Columbus Day	1972 / 1,500,000	★★★☆☆		Casual or Western	120
May/Jun	50/69 (10/21)	★★☆☆☆	P	Street party	B60
	1996 / 200,000	★★★★★		Casual	I
Feb/Mar	53/75 (12/24)	★★★★☆	V	Motorcycle party	A09
	1937 / 500,000	★★★☆☆		Tattoos	46
May	50/69 (10/21)	★★★☆☆	H	Party	A05
	1956 / 12,000	★★★★★		Formal, or fun black & white	30
Jul	65/81 (18/28)	★★☆☆☆	H	Music with fireworks	A23
Fourth of July	1982 / 2,500,000	★★★★☆		Casual	100
Aug/Sep	52/69 (11/21)	★★☆☆☆	P	Music (all)	A40
Labor Day	1971 / 250,000	★★★★☆		Casual	168
Aug/Sep	39/82 (4/28)	★★★★★	V	Gathering	A25
Labor Day	1986 / 20,000	n/a		Suntan lotion	108
Jul	47/76 (8/24)	★★★★☆	H	Rodeo	A43
	1912 / 1,100,000	★★☆☆☆		Boots and white hat	182
Mar	63/80 (17/27)	★★★☆☆	V	Street party	A12
	1978 / 1,000,000	★★★★★		Beach	62
Jan	70/80 (21/26)	★★☆☆☆	P	Street party	C90
MLK Jr. Day	1970 / 50,000	★★★☆☆		Casual	I
May	52/71 (11/22)	★★★★☆	P	Film festival	B56
Memorial Day	1939 / 31,000	★★★★★		Hollywood chic	I
Jul/Aug	59/79 (15/26)	★★☆☆☆	P	Carnival	A46
	1967 / 1,500,000	★★★★★		Erotic Caribbean	194
Feb/Mar	73/85 (23/29)	★★★★★	V	Carnival	C87
	1930 / 10,000,000	★★★★★		Parade costume	I
Jul	50/85 (10/29)	★★★☆☆	H	Rodeo	A42
	1897 / 400,000	★★☆☆☆		Boots and black hat	176
Jun	66/88 (19/31)	★★★☆☆	P	Music (Country)	A35
	1972 / 125,000	★★☆☆☆		Country	148
Jul/Aug	55/70 (13/23)	★★★★☆	V	Sailing	B55
	1812 / 30,000	★☆☆☆☆		Paul Shark (sailing)	I

* Map A is on page 7; maps B, C, D are on page 251.
** I - Itineraries for international events can be found in the companion guide, *The Fun Seeker's International*.

The Fun Seeker's Gold List

Event Name (Official Name)	City State, Country	Event Description
Crop Over Festival	Bridgetown Barbados	This Carnaval-style event is an all-island jubilee that celebrates the end of the sugar-cane harvest with great music and molten energy.
Cruise: Carnival Victory (The Most Fun Cruise)	Miami Florida, USA	There are sailboats, motorboats, lifeboats and love boats—but when 2,700 fu seekers have a week-long party in Caribbean waters, this one becomes the Fun E
Detroit Auto Show (North American International Auto Show, NAIAS)	Detroit Michigan, USA	Detroit? Dead of winter? The motor city revs up for a great weekend during No America's premier auto show (complete with a black-tie preview).
Dickens on the Strand	Galveston (Houston) Texas, USA	Revelers don period clothes and hoist cups of cheer to the literature and cultu of 19th-century Britain in one of the nation's top yuletide parties.
Do: Disney World (Walt Disney World)	Lake Buena Vista Florida, USA	The world's best theme park and … party place for adults? Cartoon characters never lose their appeal, but often overlooked is this park's grown-up good time
Edinburgh Fringe Festival (Edinburgh Festival Fringe)	Edinburgh Scotland	You'd have to see it to believe it, but you can't see it all. The world's largest a festival has hundreds of daily performances of just about everything.
Exotic Erotic Ball/Halloween	San Francisco California, USA	The Castro street party competes with the Ball for San Francisco's legendary legion of free spirits who flood the town on Halloween night.
Fantasy Fest	Key West Florida, USA	Key West transforms itself for one of the world's most extravagant and wild costume balls, complete with legendary Florida weather and sunsets.
Feast of St. Anthony (Festas de Lisboa)	Lisbon Portugal	In every nook and cranny of Old Town, someone is barbecuing sardines, while people (packed like sardines) dance at outdoor concerts.
Féria de Nîmes (Feria de Pentecote)	Nîmes France	A completely packed town throws a street party that puts a French twist on everything Spanish, from bullfighting to paella.
Feria de San Marcos (Feria Nacional de San Marcos)	Aguascalientes Aguascalientes, Mexico	Hardly a tourist destination, Aguascalientes draws top-name musicians and bullfighters to Mexico's biggest national fair for a nonstop fiesta.
Fertility Festival (Kanamara Matsuri)	Kawasaki (Tokyo) Japan	They're not shooting *Attack of the Giant Phallus* in the streets, it just looks tha way when 10,000 people celebrate the biggest game in town.
Fête de la Musique	Paris France	Imagine the best of France—architecture, food, wine—then add music, in the streets, clubs, parks, everywhere. This is the best time to be in Paris.
Fiesta de Santa Fe	Santa Fe New Mexico, USA	The festival begins when a 40-foot-tall puppet is burned to banish gloom from the lives c 75,000 assembled partyers—the food, music and dancing that follow guarantee succes
Fiesta San Antonio	San Antonio Texas, USA	How have the 3.5 million people who annually attend this event kept secret one the nation's best festivals of music, food, parades and street parties?
Fiestas de San Isidro	Madrid Spain	The fiesta is celebrated with music and bullfighting, but this really just makes it the best time of year to visit one of the world's great cities.
Fourth of July (Sunoco Welcome America)	Philadelphia Pennsylvania, USA	The first and last words on Independence Day celebrations have always belonged to the City of Brotherly Love—2 million patriots keep coming back each year.
Galway Oyster Festival (Galway International Oyster Festival)	Galway Ireland	Oysters are simply the excuse for drinking lots of Guinness, which is simply th excuse for starting a party (not ending it) by dancing on the tables.
Gasparilla (Gasparilla Pirate Festival)	Tampa Florida, USA	Unruly pirate plunderers invade Tampa Bay to launch a parade, street party ar fireworks that would make any wench proud.

The 96 Most Fun Places to be in the World at the Right Time!

Key Month U.S. Holiday	Weather Origin / Attendance	Event Rating City Rating	Mating Rating	Event Type What To Wear	Map # * Page # **
Jul/Aug	74/87 (23/31)	★★★☆☆	(P)	Carnival	C86
	1974 / 100,000	★★★☆☆		Parade costume	I
n/a	n/a	n/a	(V)	Partying	A12
	1996 / 2,700	★★★★☆		Cruise	58
Jan	19/32 (-7/0)	★★☆☆☆	(H)	Car show	A24
	1907 / 790,000	★★★☆☆		Formal	104
Dec	43/66 (6/13)	★★☆☆☆	(H)	Street party	A37
	1974 / 50,000	★★★☆☆		Victorian	156
n/a	66/83 (19/28)	n/a	(H)	Entertainment	A11
	1971	★★★★★		Comfy	54
Aug	51/65 (10/18)	★★★★☆	(V)	Theater	B72
	1947 / 800,000	★★★★☆		Casual	I
Oct Halloween	52/70 (11/21)	★★★☆☆	(P)	Street party/Party	A05
	1979 / 15,000	★★★★★		Costume or nothing	34
Oct	76/84 (24/29)	★★★★☆	(V)	Carnival	A10
	1979 / 100,000	★★★☆☆		Body paint	50
Jun	60/76 (15/24)	★★☆☆☆	(P)	Street party	B71
	1232 / 300,000	★★★☆☆		Casual	I
May/Jun	59/79 (15/26)	★★★☆☆	(P)	Street party	B57
	1952 / 500,000	★★☆☆☆		Casual	I
Apr/May	35/99 (1/37)	★★★☆☆	(P)	Street party	A48
	1848 / 1,600,000	★☆☆☆☆		Casual	202
Apr	46/63 (8/17)	★★☆☆☆	(H)	Street party	D96
	c. 1750 / 2,000	★★★★★		Phallic-wear	I
Jun	54/70 (11/21)	★★★☆☆	(P)	Street party	B58
	1982 / 350,000	★★★★★		Casual	I
Sep	50/81 (10/27)	★★☆☆☆	(H)	Street party	A29
	1712 / 75,000	★★★☆☆		Casual or Western	124
Apr Easter	59/79 (15/26)	★★★★☆	(P)	Street party	A38
	1891 / 3,500,000	★★★☆☆		Casual	160
May	51/70 (10/21)	★☆☆☆☆	(H)	Street party	B76
	1622 / 25,000	★★★★★		Casual	I
Jul Fourth of July	67/87 (19/31)	★★★☆☆	(P)	Music with fireworks	A32
	1993 / 1,000,000	★★★★☆		Comfy	136
Sep	44/59 (6/15)	★★★★☆	(P)	Partying	B66
	1955 / 10,000	★☆☆☆☆		Formal	I
Jan/Feb	52/70 (11/21)	★★★☆☆	(V)	Street party	A14
	1904 / 400,000	★★☆☆☆		Pirate costume	66

* Map A is on page 7; maps B, C, D are on page 251.

** I - Itineraries for international events can be found in the companion guide, *The Fun Seeker's International.*

The Fun Seeker's Gold List

Event Name (Official Name)	City State, Country	Event Description
Hogmanay (Edinburgh's Hogmanay)	Edinburgh Scotland	This is New Year's Eve the way you'd like it to be. Europe's largest organized year-end celebration closes off its streets for musical entertainment and partying.
Inauguration (Presidential Inauguration)	Washington D.C., USA	The world's most important capital throws a party that sets the tone for the ne four years. From cowboy to intellectual, this blowout always swings.
Indy 500 (The 500 Festival)	Indianapolis Indiana, USA	The actual race may be "the greatest spectacle in racing," but the days leadin up to the main event are geared as much to party fans as to racing fans.
Junkanoo	Nassau Bahamas	Kick off your day at 2 a.m. with a parade of elaborately costumed dancers and Caribbean music that keeps the party spirit alive past the break of dawn.
Karneval	Köln Germany	Not everyone in Köln is dressed like a clown, it just seems like it. This surreal three-day gathering of clowns is about as organized as debauchery gets.
Kentucky Derby (Kentucky Derby Festival)	Louisville Kentucky, USA	Forget about the 20 horses—it's the 70-event festival, 80,000 mint juleps and the city that's the crown jewel of Southern style that make the Derby a winner.
La Tomatina	Buñol (Barcelona) Spain	The world's largest food fight lasts just 60 minutes, but where else can you joi 10,000 people throwing tomatoes at each other on a hot summer day?
Las Fallas	Valencia Spain	Gorgeous papier-mâché tableaux are constructed in Europe's fireworks capital, then burned while firefighters nervously stand by and fireworks explode overhea
Las Vegas Rodeo (National Finals Rodeo)	Las Vegas Nevada, USA	The Wild West takes over the town during the world championship National Finals Rodeo, where the hootin' and hollerin' are as big as the $4 million purse
Macau Grand Prix	Macau (Hong Kong) China	Macau is a let-your-hair-down town for the Chinese—even after the Portugues gave it back to China—and this formula-racing event is the largest of its kind
Mardi Gras	New Orleans Louisiana, USA	The event that's inspired 1,000 imitations could take place only here—Mardi Gras launches into a separate universe of costumes and uninhibited revelry.
Memphis in May Barbecue	Memphis Tennessee, USA	When disciples of blues and barbecue invade Memphis, how could the result b anything less than the world's greatest marriage of down-home food and fun?
Monaco Grand Prix (Grand Prix Automobile de Monaco)	Monte Carlo Monaco	Monte Carlo's streets are so tightly packed that spectators—many of them pa of Europe's beautiful-people crowd—can almost touch the racing cars.
Montréal Jazz Festival (Festival International de Jazz de Montréal)	Montréal Québec, Canada	Often called the best jazz festival in the world—2,000 musicians get crowds moving at 400 shows—this event rates as one of Canada's best annual shindi
Montreux Jazz Festival	Montreux Switzerland	Still the world's premier jazz event, the festival transforms the already beautifu town into one of the most hip spots in the universe.
Moomba (The Melbourne Moomba Festival)	Melbourne Australia	More than 1.5 million attend Australia's largest outdoor festival, which combines cultural and sporting events with native-arts displays and performances.
Napa Valley Wine Auction	Napa Valley (St. Helena) California, USA	Great food, great wine, great food, great wine, great food, great wine, great food, great wine—the nation's largest charity wine auction.
New Orleans Jazz Festival (New Orleans Jazz & Heritage Festival)	New Orleans Louisiana, USA	Some consider this the world's best jazz festival because of the talent lineup, but it's the backdrop of New Orleans nightlife that really makes it stand out.
New Year's Eve New York	New York New York, USA	New York has just about the best of everything but the city never gets closer to being the center of the universe than on New Year's Eve.

The 96 Most Fun Places to be in the World at the Right Time!

Key Month U.S. Holiday	Weather Origin / Attendance	Event Rating City Rating	Mating Rating	Event Type What To Wear	Map # * Page # **
Dec	35/44 (1/6)	★★★★☆	V	Street party	B72
New Year's	1993 / 400,000	★★★★★		Casual	I
Jan	27/42 (-3/6)	★★★★☆	P	Party	A08
	1809 / 15,000	★★★★☆		Formal	42
May	52/73 (11/23)	★★★☆☆	P	Car-racing party	A18
Memorial Day	1911 / 400,000	★★☆☆☆		Casual	82
Dec/Jan	59/78 (15/25)	★★★☆☆	V	Carnival	C85
Christmas, New Year's	c. 1800 / 10,000	★★★☆☆		Parade costume	I
Feb/Mar	31/42 (0/5)	★★★★☆	V	Carnival	B61
	1823 / 100,000	★★★☆☆		Clown costume	I
Apr/May	54/76 (12/24)	★★★★☆	P	Horse-racing party	A19
	1875 / 140,000	★★★☆☆		Formal and/or stylish w/hats	86
Aug	70/82 (21/27)	★★★★☆	P	Food fight	B74
	1957 / 25,000	★★★★★		Bathing suit under T-shirt	I
Mar	40/57 (4/13)	★★★★☆	P	Street party	B78
St. Patrick's Day	1497 / 500,000	★★★☆☆		Casual	I
Dec	34/57 (1/14)	★★★☆☆	P	Rodeo	A26
	1985 / 140,000	★★★★★		Boots and hat	112
Nov	77/86 (25/30)	★★☆☆☆	P	Car-racing party	D94
	1954 / 20,000	★★★☆☆		Casual	I
Feb/Mar	46/75 (8/24)	★★★★★	V	Carnival	A20
	1837 / 3,500,000	★★★★★		Beads	90
May	61/81 (16/27)	★★★☆☆	H	Barbecue festival	A34
	1976 / 80,000	★★★☆☆		Comfy, fun, porkish	144
May	56/67 (13/19)	★★★☆☆	P	Car-racing party	B69
Memorial Day	1942 / 75,000	★★★★☆		Chic	I
Jun/Jul	61/80 (16/27)	★★★☆☆	P	Music (jazz)	A44
Fourth of July	1979 / 1,500,000	★★★★☆		Casual	186
Jul	59/77 (15/25)	★★★☆☆	H	Music (jazz)	B80
	1967 / 220,000	★★☆☆☆		Casual	I
Mar	51/71 (10/21)	★★☆☆☆	P	Street party	D92
	1955 / 1,500,000	★★★★☆		Casual	I
Jun	52/86/ (11/30)	★★★☆☆	H	Wine party	A03
	1981 / 2,000	★★★☆☆		Formal	22
Apr/May	65/85 (18/29)	★★★☆☆	P	Music (jazz)	A20
	1970 / 480,000	★★★★★		Casual	94
Dec	30/41 (-1/5)	★★★☆☆	P	Party/street party	A30
New Year's	1904 / 500,000	★★★★★		Formal or dressy	128

*   Map A is on page 7; maps B, C, D are on page 251.
**   I - Itineraries for international events can be found in the companion guide, *The Fun Seeker's International*.

The Fun Seeker's Gold List

Event Name (Official Name)	City State, Country	Event Description
Notting Hill Carnival	London England	Europe's biggest street party, this Carnaval-style parade showcases an ethinic side of one of the world's most happening cities.
Oktoberfest	Munich Germany	The massive scale of the world's largest beer blowout is stunning, but it's the camaraderie in the huge beer tents that makes this one special.
Oktoberfest-Zinzinnati	Cincinnati Ohio, USA	From brats to Spaten to lederhosen, no place in America pumps up German culture as loud or as proud as the people of Cincy.
Palio (Palio di Siena)	Siena (Florence) Italy	The tension leading up to and at the world's most incredible horse race around the small town square is released in a centuries-old tradition.
Party: Acapulco	Acapulco Mexico	Cancún and Cabo are charging hard, but this is still Mexico's number-one party destination for adults. Great beaches and warm, wild nights.
Party: Athens	Athens Greece	Mykonos is great, but Greeks know that the action is in Athens, where the clubs are among the world's best and dance floors give way to table tops.
Party: Stockholm	Stockholm Sweden	The most "European" city in Europe is also its most underrated. A few days in this lively capital and you, too, will be tall, blonde and partied out.
Phoenix Open	Scottsdale (Phoenix) Arizona, USA	No golf tournament is more associated with fun and sun than this one. You don't need to be a golfer to enjoy the highlight of Phoenix's social season.
Preakness (Preakness Celebration)	Baltimore Maryland, USA	The second jewel in horse racing's Triple Crown is really an excuse for fun that combines let-it-all-hang-out revelry with quaint traditions.
Pushkar Camel Fair (Pushkar Mela)	Pushkar (Jaipur) India	The sight of thousands-strong caravans arriving from across the desert to the world's largest camel fair defies description.
Québec Winter Carnaval (Carnaval de Québec)	Québec City Québec, Canada	This three-week samba in parkas is fueled by happy throngs and ubiquitous sticks filled with Caribou (a libation made of port and grain alcohol).
Queen's Day (Koninginnedag)	Amsterdam Netherlands	The world's largest flea market turns into a party for 750,000—fireworks and Amsterdam's infamous pleasures are the calling cards of this unusual event.
Resort: Hedonism III (The Most Fun Resort)	Runaway Bay Jamaica	This activity-filled resort is divided by a walkway that separates the nude side from the prude side—as close to an anything-goes environment as a hotel gets.
Roskilde Rock Festival (Roskilde Festival)	Roskilde (Copenhagen) Denmark	Europe's largest annual rock festival is distinguished by the hearty audiences who brave consistently poor weather, and, of course, lots of music.
Royal Ascot (The Royal Meeting at Ascot Racecourse)	Ascot (London) England	The premier event of London's social season is racing, royalty, outrageous fashions and a demonstration that the upper crust can get down.
Running of the Bulls (Fiesta de San Fermín)	Pamplona Spain	This is it—the world's greatest 24/7 party! You don't have to run with the bulls to feel the spirit of the crowds, who come for fiesta, fiesta, fiesta!
Sailing Week (Annual Antigua Sailing Week)	St. John's Antigua	The premier Caribbean race-and-party week is always ranked among the top-five regattas, but it also has the number-one set of beaches.
Ski: Aspen	Aspen Colorado, USA	The Rocky Mountains may be perfect for skiing, but few places have a nightlife and social scene that compares to ritzy Aspen.
Ski: Zermatt	Zermatt Switzerland	Zermatt takes the European title for best ski-party town, adding its special touch of gorgeous scenery (the Alps aren't the only things worth looking at).

The 96 Most Fun Places to be in the World at the Right Time!

Key Month U.S. Holiday	Weather Origin / Attendance	Event Rating City Rating	Mating Rating	Event Type What To Wear	Map # * Page # **
Aug	55/70 (12/25)	★★★☆☆	P	Carnival	B53
	1965 / 1,500,000	★★★★★		Casual, Caribbean	I
Sep/Oct	36/75 (2/23)	★★★★★	V	Beer festival	B62
	1810 / 6,000,000	★★★★☆		Casual	I
Sep	57/80 (14/27)	★★☆☆☆	P	Beer festival	A31
	1976 / 500,000	★★★☆☆		Lederhosen	132
Jul/Aug	63/83 (17/28)	★★★★☆	H	Horse-racing party	B67
	c. 1600 / 50,000	★★★☆☆		Casual	I
n/a	74/89 (23/31)	n/a	V	Party destination	A47
	n/a	★★★★☆		Beach and party	199
n/a	60/74 (16/23)	n/a	V	Party destination	B64
	n/a	★★★★☆		Casual sexy	I
n/a	53/66 (11/18)	n/a	V	Party destination	B79
	n/a	★★★★★		Casual sexy	I
Jan	43/65 (6/18)	★★★☆☆	V	Golf party	A01
	1932 / 470,000	★★★☆☆		Golf attire	14
May	53/75 (12/24)	★★☆☆☆	P	Horse-racing party	A22
	1873 / 90,000	★★★☆☆		Casual	96
Nov	56/82 (13/27)	★★★★☆	H	Camel festival	D95
	1976 / 200,000	★☆☆☆☆		Camel attire	I
Jan/Feb	04/20 (-16/-7)	★★★☆☆	P	Party	A45
	1894 / 1,000,000	★★☆☆☆		Formal and the warmest clothes you have	190
Apr	38/55 (3/12)	★★★☆☆	P	Street party	B70
	1948 / 720,000	★★★★★		Casual	I
n/a	69/87 (21/31)	n/a	V	Party destination	C89
	1999 / n/a	★★★☆☆		Nothing	I
Jun	55/85 (12/30)	★★★☆☆	V	Music (rock)	B52
1971	90,000	★★★★☆		Casual	I
Jun	53/69 (12/20)	★★★★☆	P	Horse-racing party	B53
	1711 / 230,000	★★★★★		Morning coat, outrageous hats	I
Jul	63/86 (17/30)	★★★★★	V	Street party	B77
	c. 1600 / 100,000	★☆☆☆☆		All white, with red bandana	I
Apr/May	75/83 (23/28)	★★★☆☆	V	Sailing party	C83
	1967 / 10,000	★★☆☆☆		Beach / Sailing	I
n/a	n/a	n/a	V	Skiing party	A07
	n/a	★★★★☆		Chic aprés-ski	38
n/a	32/40 (0/4)	n/a	V	Skiing party	B81
	n/a	★★★★☆		Chic aprés-ski	I

* Map A is on page 7; maps B, C, D are on page 251.
** I - Itineraries for international events can be found in the companion guide, *The Fun Seeker's International.*

The Fun Seeker's Gold List

Event Name (Official Name)	City State, Country	Event Description
Songkran Water Festival (Songkran)	Chiang Mai (Bangkok) Thailand	This wild-and-wet festival commemorates the end of the dry season by staging a monsoon that soaks everybody in sight with pails of flying water.
South by Southwest (South by Southwest Music and Media Conference, SXSW)	Austin (Dallas/Ft.Worth) Texas, USA	The world's hippest music festival features 900 bands playing in a city that claims it has more bars and restaurants per capita than any other U.S. city.
Spoleto (Spoleto Festival USA/Piccolo Spoleto)	Charleston South Carolina, USA	One of the world's best performing arts festivals—neither drunken bacchanal nor hoity-toity gathering—has this beautiful city as its backdrop.
St. Patrick's Day Celebration	Savannah Georgia, USA	An improbable mix of Southern hospitality and Irish moxie makes this two-centuries-old party one of the world's biggest St. Patrick's Day celebrations.
St. Patrick's Festival	Dublin Ireland	Inspired by the Irish-American celebrations, Dubliners put on the world's most entertaining parade and follow it up with visits to—what else?—Irish pubs.
Street Scene	San Diego California, USA	Tans, tacos, tequila and tank tops—at this giant street party, you won't find a shortage of any of the local specialties.
Streetparade	Zurich Switzerland	650,000 partyers and ten times as many disco beats cram the streets of one of the most stunning cities in the world.
Stuttgart's Volksfest (Cannstatter Volksfest)	Stuttgart Germany	Not as famous, but almost as large as Munich's Oktoberfest, this beer bash proves that being number two can still be one heck of a good time.
Summerfest	Milwaukee Wisconsin, USA	With 11 stages, 2500 local, regional and international acts, and a million spectators, The Big Gig is arguably the world's largest music festival.
Sun: Ibiza/Majorca	Ibiza/Majorca Spain	The Spanish islands are full of the world's top beach destinations—fashionable crowds tan on beaches by day and hit the world's best discos by night.
Sun: St. Tropez	St. Tropez France	It doesn't get any sexier than this—the world's beautiful people converging (from their yachts) on the almost-exclusive beach clubs, restaurants and night clubs.
Sundance Film Festival	Park City Utah, USA	The glitterati schmooze, party, ski and even watch the world's best new films being unveiled at the hottest film festival in the U.S.
Super Bowl Weekend	Las Vegas Nevada, USA	Hotels and casinos unfurl red carpets for players who know that the football game is just a sidelight during the world's quintessential gambling weekend.
Sydney Gay and Lesbian Mardi Gras	Sydney Australia	Boas, leather, glitter, G-strings, rubber and Saran Wrap—lots of people (straights and gays) believe this to be the best human spectacle on earth.
Taste of Chicago	Chicago Illinois, USA	It's tough to decide which is better in Chicago: music or food. Fortunately, you don't have to take sides at the world's largest food party.
Trinidad Carnival	Port of Spain Trinidad and Tobago	Steel drums, wild costumes, calypso bands, no sleep and a 3 a.m. kickoff party that covers participants (there are no spectators) with mud and music.
Vendimia	Mendoza (Buenos Aires) Argentina	This wine festival is not a laid-back taste test—it turns the town into a party and makes a most convincing argument for the South American wine industry.
Venice Carnival (Carnevale di Venezia)	Venice Italy	The world's most beautiful city is transformed into a Fellini-esque scene of masked paraders and costumed street performers by day, and elegant balls by night.
Vienna Opera Ball	Vienna Austria	The best formal party in the world—the unparalleled Vienna Opera House is the setting for gorgeous debutantes, ties and tails.
Viña del Mar Song Festival (International Song Festival of Viña del Mar)	Viña del Mar (Santiago) Chile	The late-night crowd warms up with beaches and top-name acts at the world's largest Latin music festival.

The 96 Most Fun Places to be in the World at the Right Time!

Key Month U.S. Holiday	Weather Origin / Attendance	Event Rating City Rating	Mating Rating	Event Type What To Wear	Map # * Page # **
Apr	77/95 (25/35)	★★★★☆	P	Street party	D98
	c. 1300 / 200,000	★★★☆☆		T-shirt and shorts	I
Mar	48/71 (9/21)	★★★★☆	P	Music (all)	A36
	1987 / 25,000	★★★☆☆		Country or casual	152
May/Jun	61/83 (16/28)	★★★☆☆	P	Performing Arts	A33
	1977 / 72,000	★★★☆☆		Comfy	140
Mar St. Patrick's Day	47/70 (8/21)	★★★★☆	V	Street party	A15
	1813 / 300,000	★★☆☆☆		Green	70
Mar St. Patrick's Day	36/51 (2/10)	★★★☆☆	P	Street party	B65
	1996 / 850,000	★★☆☆☆		Green	I
Sep	62/76 (17/24)	★★★☆☆	P	Music (all)	A04
	1984 / 85,000	★★★☆☆		Fun costume	26
Aug	73/59 (21/5)	★★★★☆	V	Street party	B82
	1992 / 500,000	★★★☆☆		Casual	I
Sep/Oct	39/75 (3/23)	★★★☆☆	P	Beer festival	B63
	1818 / 5,000,000	★★☆☆☆		Casual	I
Jun/Jul	59/80 (15/27)	★★☆☆☆	P	Music (all)	A41
	1968 / 940,000	★★☆☆☆		Casual	172
n/a	63/86 (17/30)	n/a	V	Partying	B75
	n/a	★★★★☆		Beach chic	I
n/a	60/74 (16/23)	n/a	V	Partying	B59
	n/a	★★★★☆		Beach chic	I
Jan	19/40 (-7/4)	★★★★☆	V	Film festival	A39
	1978 / 18,000	★★★☆☆		Hollywood with snow boots	164
Jan	33/56 (1/13)	★★★☆☆	P	Partying	A26
	1967 / 200,000	★★★★★		Gold chains and pinky rings	116
Feb/Mar	63/76 (17/24)	★★★★☆	V	Street party	D93
	1978 / 500,000	★★★☆☆		Leather	I
Jun/Jul	57/79 (14/26)	★★★☆☆	P	Music (all) and food festival	A17
	1980 / 3,500,000	★★★★★		Casual	78
Feb/Mar	75/92 (21/33)	★★★★★	V	Carnival	C91
	c. 1750 / 100,000	★☆☆☆☆		Parade costume	I
Mar	60/79 (16/26)	★★☆☆☆	H	Wine festival	C84
	1936 / 300,000	★★★★☆		Casual	I
Feb/Mar	34/47 (1/8)	★★★★★	P	Carnival	B68
	1979 / 500,000	★★★★★		Elaborate Fellini-esque costume	I
Feb	30/40 (0/5)	★★★★★	H	Party	B51
	1877 / 5,000	★★★★★		Formal (white tie)	I
Feb President's Day	53/84 (12/29)	★★★☆☆	P	Music (Latin)	C88
	1959 / 110,000	★★★☆☆		Casual	I

* Map A is on page 7; maps B, C, D are on page 251.

** I - Itineraries for international events can be found in the companion guide, *The Fun Seeker's International*.

FSG: The Mating Rating

There are all kinds of fun events and destinations, but some are better than others for meeting someone with whom you can develop a relationship. Even if just for a three-day visit. Each of the FSG events is evaluated for the number of singles attending, sexual energy and opportunity to interact.

The list is divided into three sections. Since there's no such thing as a sure thing, the highest rating for the chance of finding a mate at an event is Hope, followed by Hope/Slight Chance. Then there are the No Chance events. The medications used to represent each rating are optional, but bring your best moves!

Hope (Viagra ⓥ)

North America

Event	City	State/Country	Key Month	Page #
Academy Awards Weekend	Los Angeles	California	Feb	18
Bike Week	Daytona Beach (Orlando)	Florida	Mar	46
Burning Man	Black Rock City	Nevada	Aug/Sep	108
Calle Ocho	Miami (Miami Beach)	Florida	Mar	62
Cruise: Carnival Victory	Miami (Port)	Florida	n/a	58
Fantasy Fest	Key West	Florida	Oct	50
Gasparilla	Tampa	Florida	Jan/Feb	66
Mardi Gras	New Orleans	Louisiana	Feb/Mar	90
Party: Acapulco	Acapulco	Mexico	n/a	199
Phoenix Open	Scottsdale (Phoenix)	Arizona	Jan	14
Ski: Aspen	Aspen	Colorado	n/a	38
St. Patrick's Day Celebration	Savannah	Georgia	Mar	70
Sundance Film Festival	Park City	Utah	Jan	164

International

Event	City	Country	Key Month
Ati Atihan	Kalibo (Manila)	Philippines	Jan
Carnaval Rio	Rio de Janeiro	Brazil	Feb/Mar
Cowes Week	Cowes/Isle of Wight	England	Jul/Aug
Edinburgh Fringe Festival	Edinburgh	Scotland	Aug
Hogmanay	Edinburgh	Scotland	Dec
Junkanoo	Nassau	Bahamas	Dec/Jan
Karneval	Köln	Germany	Feb/Mar
Oktoberfest	Munich	Germany	Sep/Oct
Party: Athens	Athens	Greece	n/a
Party: Stockholm	Stockholm	Sweden	n/a
Resort: Hedonism III	Runaway Bay	Jamaica	n/a
Roskilde Rock Festival	Roskilde (Copenhagen)	Denmark	Jun
Running of the Bulls	Pamplona	Spain	Jul
Sailing Week	St. John's	Antigua	Apr/May
Ski: Zermatt	Zermatt	Switzerland	n/a
Streetparade	Zurich	Switzerland	Aug
Sun: Ibiza/Majorca	Ibiza/Majorca	Spain	n/a
Sun: St. Tropez	St. Tropez	France	n/a
Sydney Gay and Lesbian Mardi Gras	Sydney	Australia	Feb/Mar
Trinidad Carnival	Port of Spain	Trinidad and Tobago	Feb/Mar

Hope, Slight Chance (Prozac ⊕)

North America

Event	City	State/Country	Key Month	Page #
Aloha Festival	Honolulu	Hawaii	Sep	74
Balloon Fiesta	Albuquerque	New Mexico	Oct	120
Bumbershoot	Seattle	Washington	Aug/Sep	168
Caribana	Toronto	Canada	Jul/Aug	194
Country Music Fan Fair	Nashville	Tennessee	Jun	148
Exotic Erotic Ball/Halloween	San Francisco	California	Oct	34
Feria de San Marcos	Aguascalientes	Mexico	Apr/May	202
Fiesta San Antonio	San Antonio	Texas	Apr	160
Fourth of July	Philadelphia	Pennsylvania	Jul	136
Inauguration	Washington	D.C.	Jan	42
Indy 500	Indianapolis	Indiana	May	82
Kentucky Derby	Louisville	Kentucky	Apr/May	86
Las Vegas Rodeo	Las Vegas	Nevada	Dec	112
Montréal Jazz Festival	Montréal	Canada	Jun/Jul	186
New Orleans Jazz Festival	New Orleans	Louisiana	Apr/May	94
New Year's Eve New York	New York	New York	Dec	128
Oktoberfest-Zinzinnati	Cincinnati	Ohio	Sep	132
Preakness	Baltimore	Maryland	May	96
Québec Winter Carnaval	Québec City	Canada	Jan/Feb	190
South by Southwest	Austin (Dallas/Ft.Worth)	Texas	Mar	152
Spoleto	Charleston	South Carolina	May/Jun	140
Street Scene	San Diego	California	Sep	26
Summerfest	Milwaukee	Wisconsin	Jun/Jul	172
Super Bowl Weekend	Las Vegas	Nevada	Jan	116
Taste of Chicago	Chicago	Illinois	Jun/Jul	78

International

Event	City	Country	Key Month
Berlin Carnival	Berlin	Germany	May/Jun
Calle San Sebastián	San Juan	Puerto Rico	Jan
Cannes Film Festival	Cannes	France	May
Crop Over Festival	Bridgetown	Barbados	Jul/Aug
Feast of St. Anthony	Lisbon	Portugal	Jun
Féria de Nîmes	Nîmes	France	May/Jun
Fête de la Musique	Paris	France	Jun
Galway Oyster Festival	Galway	Ireland	Sep
La Tomatina	Buñol (Barcelona)	Spain	Aug
Las Fallas	Valencia	Spain	Mar
Macau Grand Prix	Macau (Hong Kong)	China	Nov
Monaco Grand Prix	Monte Carlo	Monaco	May
Moomba	Melbourne	Australia	Mar
Notting Hill Carnival	London	England	Aug
Queen's Day	Amsterdam	Netherlands	Apr
Royal Ascot	Ascot (London)	England	Jun
Songkran Water Festival	Chiang Mai (Bangkok)	Thailand	Apr
St. Patrick's Festival	Dublin	Ireland	Mar
Stuttgart's Volksfest	Stuttgart	Germany	Sep/Oct
Venice Carnival	Venice	Italy	Feb/Mar
Viña del Mar Song Festival	Viña del Mar (Santiago)	Chile	Feb

No Chance (Hemlock ⊕)

The remainder of the events and destinations are fun, really, but they are not the best for finding a new mate.

Event Name	City State, Country	Travel Date 2004 Travel Date 2003	Event Dates 2004 Event Dates 2003	Event Rating City Rating	Mating Rating Origin / Attendance	Map # Page #*
JANUARY						
Detroit Auto Show	Detroit	1/8 Thu	Jan 10 - 19	★★☆☆☆	(H)	A24
	Michigan, USA	1/9 Thu	Jan 11 - 20	★★★☆☆	1907 / 790,000	104
Sundance Film Festival	Park City	1/15 Thu	Jan 15 - 25	★★★★☆	(V)	A39
	Utah, USA	1/16 Thu	Jan 16 - 26	★★★☆☆	1978 / 18,000	164
Ati Atihan	Kalibo (Manila)	1/16 Fri	Jan 12 - 18	★★★☆☆	(V)	D97
	Philippines	1/17 Fri	Jan 13 - 19	★★★☆☆	1212 / 200,000	I
Calle San Sebastián	San Juan	1/17 Sat	Jan 16 - 19	★★☆☆☆	(P)	C90
	Puerto Rico	1/18 Sat	Jan 17 - 20	★★★☆☆	1970 / 50,000	I
Phoenix Open	Scottsdale (Phoenix)	1/21 Wed	Jan 19 - 25	★★★☆☆	(V)	A01
	Arizona, USA	1/22 Wed	Jan 20 - 26	★★★☆☆	1932 / 470,000	14
Super Bowl Weekend	Las Vegas	1/23 Fri	Jan 23 - 25	★★★☆☆	(P)	A26
	Nevada, USA	1/24 Fri	Jan 24 - 26	★★★★★	1967 / 200,000	116
Inauguration	Washington	n/a	n/a	★★★★☆	(P)	A08
	D.C., USA	n/a	n/a	★★★★☆	1809 / 15,000	42
Ski: Zermatt	Zermatt	1/29 Thu	n/a	n/a	(V)	B81
	Switzerland	2/20 Thu	n/a	★★★★☆	n/a	I
FEBRUARY						
Gasparilla	Tampa	2/6 Fri	Jan 31 - Feb 7	★★★☆☆	(V)	A14
	Florida, USA	1/31 Fri	Jan 25 - Feb 1	★★☆☆☆	1904 / 400,000	66
Québec Winter Carnaval	Québec City	2/6 Fri	Jan 30 - Feb 15	★★★☆☆	(P)	A45
	Québec, Canada	2/7 Fri	Jan 31 - Feb 16	★★☆☆☆	1894 / 1,000,000	190
Viña del Mar Song Festival	Viña del Mar (Santiago)	2/14 Sat	Feb 11 - 16	★★★☆☆	(P)	C88
	Chile	2/15 Sat	Feb 12 - 17	★★☆☆☆	1959 / 110,000	I
Vienna Opera Ball	Vienna	2/17 Tue	Feb 19	★★★★★	(H)	B51
	Austria	2/25 Tue	Feb 27	★★★★★	1877 / 5000	I
Venice Carnival	Venice	2/20 Fri	Feb 15 - 24	★★★★★	(P)	B68
	Italy	2/28 Fri	Feb 23 - Mar 4	★★★★★	1979 / 500,000	I
Karneval	Köln	2/21 Sat	Feb 18 - 24	★★★★☆	(V)	B61
	Germany	3/1 Sat	Feb 26 - Mar 4	★★★☆☆	1823 / 100,000	I
Carnaval Rio	Rio de Janeiro	2/21 Sat	Feb 11 - 24	★★★★★	(V)	C87
	Brazil	3/1 Sat	Feb 19 - Mar 4	★★★★★	1930 / 10,000,000	I
Mardi Gras	New Orleans	2/22 Sun	Jan 5 - Feb 24	★★★★★	(V)	A20
	Louisiana, USA	3/2 Sun	Jan 6 - Mar 4	★★★★★	1837 / 3,500,000	90
Trinidad Carnival	Port of Spain	2/22 Sun	Feb 22 - 24	★★★★★	(V)	C91
	Trinidad and Tobago	3/2 Sun	Mar 2 - 4	★☆☆☆☆	c. 1750 / 100000	I
Sydney Gay and Lesbian Mardi Gras	Sydney	2/26 Thu	Feb 10 - Mar 3	★★★★☆	(V)	D93
	Australia	2/27 Thu	Feb 11 - Mar 5	★★★★☆	1978 / 500,000	I
Academy Awards Weekend	Los Angeles	2/27 Fri	Feb 29	★★☆☆☆	(V)	A02
	California, USA	3/21 Fri	Mar 23	★★★★★	1929 / n/a	18

Event sequence is determined by 2004 travel date. The travel date is the first day of a 3-day itinerary based on our selection of the absolute best time to be there. Event dates are the official opening and closing dates. *I - Itineraries for international events can be found in the companion guide, *The Fun Seeker's International*

Event Name	City State, Country	Travel Date 2004 Travel Date 2003	Event Dates 2004 Event Dates 2003	Event Rating City Rating	Mating Rating Origin / Attendance	Map # Page #*
MARCH						
Bike Week	Daytona Beach (Orlando)	3/4 Thu	Feb 27 - Mar 7	★★★★☆	**V**	A09
	Florida, USA	3/6 Thu	Feb 28 - Mar 9	★★★☆☆	1937 / 500,000	46
Moomba	Melbourne	3/5 Fri	Mar 5 - 8	★★☆☆☆	**P**	D92
	Australia	3/7 Fri	Mar 7 - 10	★★★★☆	1955 / 1,500,000	I
South by Southwest	Austin (Dallas/Ft.Worth)	3/11 Thu	Mar 11 - 15	★★★☆☆	**P**	A36
	Texas, USA	3/13 Thu	Mar 12 - 16	★★★☆☆	1987 / 25,000	152
Vendimia	Mendoza (Buenos Aires)	3/11 Thu	Mar 7 - 14	★★☆☆☆	**H**	C84
	Argentina	3/6 Thu	Mar 2 - 9	★★★★☆	1936 / 300,000	I
Calle Ocho	Miami (Miami Beach)	3/12 Fri	Mar 5 - 14	★★★☆☆	**V**	A12
	Florida, USA	3/7 Fri	Mar 1 - 9	★★★★★	1978 / 1,000,000	62
St. Patrick's Festival	Dublin	3/15 Mon	Mar 14 - 17	★★★☆☆	**P**	B65
	Ireland	3/15 Sat	Mar 16 - 19	★★★★☆	1996 / 850,000	I
St. Patrick's Day Celebration	Savannah	3/17 Wed	Mar 17 - 20	★★★★☆	**V**	A15
	Georgia, USA	3/15 Sat	Mar 14 - 17	★★☆☆☆	1813 / 300,000	70
Las Fallas	Valencia	3/17 Wed	Mar 12 - 19	★★★★☆	**P**	B78
	Spain	3/17 Mon	Mar 12 - 19	★★★☆☆	1497 / 500,000	I
Ski: Aspen	Aspen	3/25 Thu	n/a	n/a	**V**	A07
	Colorado, USA	3/27 Thu	n/a	★★★★☆	n/a	38
APRIL						
Party: Athens	Athens	4/3 Sat	n/a	n/a	**V**	B64
	Greece	4/4 Fri	n/a	★★★★☆	n/a	I
Fertility Festival	Kawasaki (Tokyo)	4/9 Fri	Apr 10 - 11	★★★★☆	**H**	D96
	Japan	4/11 Fri	Apr 12 - 13	★★★★★	c. 1750 / 2000	I
Songkran Water Festival	Chiang Mai (Bangkok)	4/13 Tue	Apr 13 - 15	★★★★☆	**H**	D98
	Thailand	4/13 Sun	Apr 13 - 15	★★★☆☆	c. 1300 / 200,000	I
Fiesta San Antonio	San Antonio	4/19 Mon	Apr 16 - 25	★★★★☆	**P**	A38
	Texas, USA	4/21 Mon	Apr 19 - 27	★★★☆☆	1891 / 3,500,000	160
Feria de San Marcos	Aguascalientes	4/23 Fri	Apr 10 - May 2	★★★☆☆	**P**	A48
	Aguascalientes, Mexico	4/25 Fri	Apr 12 - May 4	★☆☆☆☆	1848 / 1,600,000	202
Sailing Week	St. John's	4/25 Sun	Apr 25 - May 1	★★★☆☆	**V**	C83
	Antigua	4/27 Sun	Apr 27 - May 3	★★★☆☆	1967 / 10,000	I
Queen's Day	Amsterdam	4/28 Wed	Apr 30	★★★☆☆	**P**	B70
	Netherlands	4/28 Mon	Apr 30	★★★★★	1948 / 720,000	I
Kentucky Derby	Louisville	4/29 Thu	Apr 10 - May 1	★★★★☆	**P**	A19
	Kentucky, USA	5/1 Thu	Apr 12 - May3	★★★☆☆	1875 / 140,000	86
New Orleans Jazz Festival	New Orleans	4/29 Thu	Apr 22 - May 2	★★★☆☆	**P**	A20
	Louisiana, USA	5/1 Thu	Apr 24 - May 4	★★★★★	1970 / 480,000	94

Event Name	City State, Country	Travel Date 2004 Travel Date 2003	Event Dates 2004 Event Dates 2003	Event Rating City Rating	Mating Rating Origin / Attendance	Map # Page #*
MAY						
Party: Stockholm	Stockholm	5/6 Thu	n/a	n/a	V	B79
	Sweden	5/8 Thu	n/a	★★★★★	n/a	I
Preakness	Baltimore	5/13 Thu	May 10 - 18	★★☆☆☆	P	A22
	Maryland, USA	5/15 Thu	May 9 - 17	★★★☆☆	1873 / 90,000	96
Fiestas de San Isidro	Madrid	5/13 Thu	May 13 - 17	★☆☆ ☆☆	H	B76
	Spain	5/15 Thu	May 15 - 18	★★★★★	1622 / 25,000	I
Memphis in May Barbecue	Memphis	5/20 Thu	May 20 - 22	★★★☆☆	H	A34
	Tennessee, USA	5/15 Thu	May 15 - 17	★★★☆☆	1976 / 80,000	144
Cannes Film Festival	Cannes	5/20 Thu	May 12 - 23	★★★★☆	P	B56
	France	5/22 Thu	May 14 - 25	★★★★★	1939 / 31,000	I
Monaco Grand Prix	Monte Carlo	5/21 Fri	May 20 - 23	★★★☆☆	P	B69
	Monaco	5/30 Fri	May 29 - June 1	★★★★☆	1942 / 75,000	I
Indy 500	Indianapolis	5/27 Thu	May 8- 30	★★★☆☆	P	A18
	Indiana, USA	5/22 Thu	May 3 - 25	★★☆☆☆	1911 / 400,000	82
Féria de Nîmes	Nîmes	5/28 Fri	May 28 - 31	★★★☆☆	P	B57
	France	6/6 Fri	Jun 6 - 9	★★☆☆☆	1952 / 500,000	I
Berlin Carnival	Berlin	5/28 Fri	May 28 - 31	★★☆☆☆	P	B60
	German	6/6 Fri	Jun 6 - 9	★★★★★	1996 / 200,000	I
Black and White Ball	San Francisco	n/a	n/a	★★★☆☆	H	A05
	California, USA	5/29 Thu	May 31	★★★★★	1956 / 12,000	30
JUNE						
Napa Valley Wine Auction	Napa Valley (St. Helena)	6/3 Thu	June 3-6	★★★☆☆	H	A03
	California, USA	6/5 Thu	June 5-8	★★★☆☆	1981 / 2000	22
Spoleto	Charleston	6/11 Fri	May 28 - Jun 13	★★★☆☆	P	A33
	South Carolina, USA	6/6 Fri	May 23 - Jun 8	★★★☆☆	1977 / 72,000	140
Country Music Fan Fair	Nashville	6/10 Thu	Jun 10 - 13	★★★☆☆	P	A35
	Tennessee, USA	6/5 Thu	Jun 5 - 8	★★☆☆☆	1972 / 125,000	148
Feast of St. Anthony	Lisbon	6/12 Sat	Jun 12 - 29	★★☆☆☆	P	B71
	Portugal	6/12 Thu	Jun 12 - 29	★★★☆☆	1232 / 300,000	I
Royal Ascot	Ascot (London)	6/16 Wed	Jun 15 - 18	★★★★☆	P	B53
	England	6/18 Wed	Jun 17 - 20	★★★★★	1711 / 230,000	I
Fête de la Musique	Paris	6/19 Sat	Jun 21	★★★☆ ☆	P	B58
	France	6/19 Thu	Jun 21	★★★★★	1982 / 350000	I
Summerfest	Milwaukee	6/24 Thu	Jun 24 - Jul 4	★★☆☆☆	P	A41
	Wisconsin, USA	6/26 Thu	Jun 26 - Jul 6	★★☆☆☆	1968 / 940,000	172
Roskilde Rock Festival	Roskilde (Copenhagen)	6/24 Thu	Jun 24 - 27	★★★☆ ☆	V	B52
	Denmark	6/26 Thu	Jun 26 - 29	★★★★☆	1971 / 90,000	I
Taste of Chicago	Chicago	6/25 Fri	Jun 25 - Jul 4	★★★☆ ☆	P	A17
	Illinois, USA	6/27 Fri	Jun 27 - Jul 6	★★★★★	1980 / 3,500,000	78

Event sequence is determined by 2004 travel date. The travel date is the first day of a 3-day itinerary based on our selection of the absolute best time to be the Event dates are the official opening and closing dates. *I - Itineraries for international events can be found in the companion guide, The Fun Seeker's Internation

Travel Dates & Ratings

Event Name	City State, Country	Travel Date 2004 Travel Date 2003	Event Dates 2004 Event Dates 2003	Event Rating City Rating	Mating Rating Origin / Attendance	Map # Page #*
ILY						
Boston Harborfest	Boston	7/2 Fri	Jun 29 - Jul 4	★★☆☆☆	(H)	A23
	Massachusetts, USA	7/3 Thu	Jul 1 - 6	★★★★☆	1982 / 2,500,000	100
Fourth of July	Philadelphia	7/2 Fri	Jun 29 - Jul 4	★★★☆☆	(P)	A32
	Pennsylvania, USA	7/2 Wed	Jul 1 - 6	★★★★☆	1993 / 1,000,000	136
Montréal Jazz Festival	Montréal	7/6 Tue	Jul 1 - 11	★★★☆☆	(P)	A44
	Québec, Canada	7/1 Tue	Jun 26 - Jul 6	★★★★☆	1979 / 1,500,000	186
Running of the Bulls	Pamplona	7/6 Tue	Jul 6 - 14	★★★★★	(V)	B77
	Spain	7/6 Sun	Jul 6 - 14	★☆☆☆☆	c. 1600 / 100,000	I
Calgary Stampede	Calgary	7/9 Fri	July 2 - 11	★★★★☆	(H)	A43
	Alberta, Canada	7/11 Fri	July 4 - 13	★★☆☆☆	1912 / 1,100,000	182
Montreux Jazz Festival	Montreux	7/15 Thu	July 2 - 18	★★★☆☆	(H)	B80
	Switzerland	7/17 Thu	July 4 - 19	★★☆☆☆	1967 / 220,000	I
Cheyenne Frontier Days	Cheyenne	7/22 Thu	Jul 16 - 25	★★★☆☆	(H)	A42
	Wyoming, USA	7/24 Thu	Jul 18 - 27	★★☆☆☆	1897 / 400,000	176
Cowes Week	Cowes	7/28 Wed	Jul 31 - Aug 7	★★★★☆	(V)	B55
	Isle of Wight, England	7/30 Wed	Aug 2 - 9	★☆☆☆☆	1812 / 30,000	I
Caribana	Toronto	7/29 Thu	Jul 16 - Aug 1	★★☆☆☆	(P)	A46
	Ontario, Canada	7/31 Thu	Jul 18 - Aug 4	★★★★★	1967 / 1,500,000	194
Sun: St. Tropez	St. Tropez	7/29 Thu	n/a	n/a	(V)	B59
	France	7/31 Thu	n/a	★★★★☆	n/a	I
Crop Over Festival	Bridgetown	7/31 Sat	Jun 25 - Aug 2	★★★☆☆	(P)	C86
	Barbados	8/2 Sat	Jun 27 - Aug 4	★★☆☆☆	1974 / 100,000	I
UGUST						
Streetparade	Zurich	8/6 Fri	Aug 7	★★★★☆	(V)	B82
	Switzerland	8/8 Fri	Aug 9	★★★☆☆	n/a	I
Edinburgh Fringe Festival	Edinburgh	8/12 Thu	Aug 1 - 24	★★★★☆	(V)	B72
	Scotland	8/14 Thu	Aug 3 - 25	★★★☆☆	1947 / 800,000	I
Palio	Siena (Florence)	8/15 Sun	Aug 13 - 17	★★★★☆	(H)	B67
	Italy	8/15 Fri	Aug 13 - 17	★★★☆☆	c. 1600 / 50,000	I
Sun: Ibiza/Majorca	Ibiza/Majorca	8/19 Thu	n/a	n/a	(V)	B75
	Spain	8/21 Thu	n/a	★★★★☆	n/a	I
La Tomatina	Buñol (Barcelona)	8/25 Wed	Aug 25	★★★☆☆	(P)	B74
	Spain	8/27 Wed	Aug 27	★★★★★	1957 / 25,000	I
Notting Hill Carnival	London	8/28 Sat	Aug 29 - 30	★★★☆☆	(P)	B53
	England	8/23 Sat	Aug 24 - 25	★★★★★	1965 / 1,500,000	I
EPTEMBER						
Burning Man	Black Rock City	9/3 Fri	Aug 30 - Sep 6	★★★★★	(V)	A25
	Nevada, USA	8/29 Fri	Aug 25 - Sep 1	n/a	1986 / 20,000	108
Fiesta de Santa Fe	Santa Fe	9/2 Thu	Sept 3 - 5	★★☆☆☆	(H)	A29
	New Mexico, USA	9/4 Thu	Sept 5 - 7	★★★☆☆	1712 / 75,000	124
Bumbershoot	Seattle	9/3 Fri	Sep 3 - 6	★★☆☆☆	(P)	A40
	Washington, USA	8/29 Fri	Aug 29 - Sep 1	★★★★☆	1971 / 250,000	168

Event Name	City State, Country	Travel Date 2004 Travel Date 2003	Event Dates 2004 Event Dates 2003	Event Rating City Rating	Mating Rating Origin / Attendance	Map # Page #*
SEPTEMBER (cont.)						
Street Scene	San Diego	9/9 Thu	Sept 10 - 12	★★★☆☆	P	A04
	California, USA	9/4 Thu	Sept 5 - 7	★★★☆☆	1984 / 85,000	26
Aloha Festival	Honolulu	9/10 Fri	Sep 10 - 19	★★☆☆☆	P	A16
	Hawaii, USA	9/12 Fri	Sep 12 - 21	★★★☆☆	1947 / 300,000	74
Oktoberfest-Zinzinnati	Cincinnati	9/17 Fri	Sep 18 - 19	★★☆☆☆	P	A31
	Ohio, USA	9/19 Fri	Sep 19 - 21	★★★☆☆	1976 / 500,000	132
Oktoberfest	Munich	9/24 Fri	Sep 25 - Oct 3	★★★★★	V	B62
	Germany	9/26 Fri	Sep 27 - Oct 5	★★★★☆	1810 / 6,000,000	I
Galway Oyster Festival	Galway	9/25 Sat	Sep 23 - 26	★★★★☆	P	B66
	Ireland	9/26 Fri	Sep 25 - 28	★☆☆☆☆	1955 / 10,000	I
Stuttgart's Volksfest	Stuttgart	9/30 Thu	Sep 25 - Oct 3	★★★☆☆	P	B63
	Germany	10/2 Thu	Sep 27 - Oct 5	★★☆☆☆	1818 / 5,000,000	I
OCTOBER						
Balloon Fiesta	Albuquerque	10/7 Thu	Oct 2 - 10	★★★☆☆	H	A28
	New Mexico, USA	10/9 Thu	Oct 4 - 12	★★★☆☆	1972 / 1,500,000	120
Cruise: Carnival Victory	Miami	10/17 Sun	n/a	n/a	V	A12
	Florida, USA	11/23 Sun	n/a	★★★★☆	1996 / 2,700	58
Fantasy Fest	Key West	10/28 Thu	Oct 22 - 31	★★★★☆	V	A10
	Florida, USA	10/23 Thu	Oct 17 - 26	★★★☆☆	1979 / 100,000	50
Exotic Erotic Ball/Halloween	San Francisco	10/29 Fri	Oct 31	★★★☆☆	P	A05
	California, USA	10/29 Wed	Oct 31	★★★★★	1979 / 15,000	34
NOVEMBER						
Pushkar Camel Fair	Pushkar (Jaipur)	11/4 Thu	Nov 3 - 6	★★★★☆	H	D95
	India	11/6 Thu	Nov 5 - 8	★☆☆☆☆	1976 / 200,000	I
Do: Disney World	Lake Buena Vista	11/11 Thu	n/a	n/a	H	A11
	Florida, USA	10/16 Thu	n/a	★★★★★	1971	54
Macau Grand Prix	Macau (Hong Kong)	11/19 Fri	Nov 18 - 21	★★☆☆☆	P	D94
	China	11/14 Fri	Nov 15 - 16	★★★☆☆	1954 / 20,000	I
Party: Acapulco	Acapulco	11/25 Thu	n/a	n/a	V	A47
	Guerrero, Mexico	4/17 Thu	n/a	★★★★☆	n/a	199
DECEMBER						
Dickens on the Strand	Galveston (Houston)	12/2 Thu	Dec 5 - 6	★★☆☆☆	H	A37
	Texas, USA	12/4 Thu	Dec 6 - 7	★★★☆☆	1974 / 50,000	156
Las Vegas Rodeo	Las Vegas	12/10 Fri	Dec 3 - 12	★★★☆☆	P	A26
	Nevada, USA	12/12 Fri	Dec 5 - 14	★★★★★	1985 / 140,000	112
Resort: Hedonism III	Runaway Bay	12/16 Thu	n/a	n/a	V	C89
	Jamaica	12/19 Fri	n/a	★★★☆☆	1999	I
Junkanoo	Nassau	12/24 Fri	Dec 26, Jan 1	★★★☆☆	V	C85
	Bahamas	12/24 Wed	Dec 26, Jan 1	★★★☆☆	c. 1800 / 10,000	I
New Year's Eve New York	New York	12/29 Wed	Dec. 31	★★★☆☆	P	A30
	New York, USA	12/29 Mon	Dec. 31	★★★★★	1904 / 500,000	128
Hogmanay	Edinburgh	12/29 Wed	Dec. 29 - Jan 1	★★★☆☆	V	B72
	Scotland	12/29 Mon	Dec. 29 - Jan 1	★★★★★	1993 / 400,000	I

Event sequence is determined by 2004 travel date. The travel date is the first day of a 3-day itinerary based on our selection of the absolute best time to be the
Event dates are the official opening and closing dates. *I - Itineraries for international events can be found in the companion guide, The Fun Seeker's Internatia

The Fun Seeker's Gold List 2003 Calendar

The Most Fun Places to be in the World at the Right Time!

	Jan. 6	Jan. 13	Jan. 20	Jan. 27	
Jan.	• Detroit Auto Show	• Sundance Film Festival • Ati Atihan • Calle San Sebastián	• Phoenix Open • Super Bowl Weekend	• Gasparilla	

	Feb. 3	Feb. 10	Feb. 17	Feb. 24	
Feb.	• Québec Winter Carnaval	• Viña del Mar Song Festival	• Ski: Zermatt	• Vienna Opera Ball • Sydney Gay and Lesbian Mardi Gras • Venice Carnival • Karneval	• Carnaval Rio • Mardi Gras • Trinidad Carnival

	Mar. 3	Mar. 10	Mar. 17	Mar. 24	Mar. 31
Mar.	• Bike Week • Vendimia • Calle Ocho • Moomba	• South by Southwest • St. Patrick's Day Celebration • St. Patrick's Festival	• Las Fallas • Academy Awards Weekend	• Ski: Aspen	• Party: Athens

	Apr. 7	Apr. 14	Apr. 21	Apr. 28	
Apr.	• Fertility Festival • Songkran Water Festival	• Party: Acapulco	• Fiesta San Antonio • Feria de San Marcos • Sailing Week	• Queen's Day • Kentucky Derby • New Orleans Jazz Festival	

	May 5	May 12	May 19	May 26	
May	• Party: Stockholm	• Preakness • Memphis in May Barbecue • Fiestas de San Isidro	• Indy 500 • Cannes Film Festival	• Black and White Ball • Monaco Grand Prix	

	Jun. 2	Jun. 9	Jun. 16	Jun. 23	Jun. 30
Jun.	• Country Music Fan Fair • Napa Valley Wine Auction • Féria de Nîmes • Berlin Carnival • Spoleto	• Feast of St. Anthony	• Royal Ascot • Fête de la Musique	• Summerfest • Roskilde Rock Festival • Taste of Chicago	• Montréal Jazz Festival • Fourth of July • Boston Harborfest • Running of the Bulls

	Jul. 7	Jul. 14	Jul. 21	Jul. 28	
Jul.	• Calgary Stampede	• Montreux Jazz Festival	• Cheyenne Frontier Days	• Cowes Week • Caribana • Sun: St. Tropez • Crop Over Festival	

	Aug. 4	Aug. 11	Aug. 18	Aug. 25	
Aug.	• Streetparade	• Edinburgh Fringe Festival • Palio	• Sun: Ibiza/Majorca • Notting Hill Carnival	• La Tomatina • Burning Man • Bumbershoot	

	Sep. 1	Sep. 8	Sep. 15	Sep. 22	Sep. 29
Sep.	• Street Scene • Fiesta de Santa Fe	• Aloha Festival	• Oktoberfest-Zinzinnati	• Oktoberfest • Galway Oyster Festival	• Stuttgart's Volkfest

	Oct. 6	Oct. 13	Oct. 20	Oct. 27	
Oct.	• Balloon Fiesta	• Do: Disney World	• Fantasy Fest	• Exotic Erotic Ball/Halloween	

	Nov. 3	Nov. 10	Nov. 17	Nov. 24	
Nov.	• Pushkar Camel Fair	• Macau Grand Prix	• Cruise: Carnival Victory (begin)	• Cruise: Carnival Victory (end)	

	Dec. 1	Dec. 8	Dec. 15	Dec. 22	Dec. 29
Dec.	• Dickens on the Strand	• Las Vegas Rodeo	• Resort: Hedonism III	• Junkanoo	• New Year's Eve New York • Hogmanay

Events are listed according to the week in which the travel date takes place. Starting with January 5, all weeks begin on Monday.

The Most Fun Places to be in the World at the Right Time!

January

Jan. 5
- Detroit Auto Show

Jan. 12
- Sundance Film Festival
- Ati Atihan
- Calle San Sebastián

February

Feb. 2
- Gasparilla

Feb. 9
- Viña del Mar Song Festival
- Québec Winter Carnaval

March

Mar. 1
- Bike Week
- Moomba

Mar. 8
- South by Southwest
- Vendimia
- Calle Ocho

April

Apr. 5
- Fertility Festival

Apr. 12
- Songkran Water Festival

May

May 3
- Party: Stockholm

May 10
- Preakness
- Fiestas de San Isidro

June

Jun. 7
- Country Music Fan Fair
- Feast of St. Anthony

Jun. 14
- Royal Ascot
- Fête de la Musique

July

Jul. 5
- Montréal Jazz Festival
- Running of the Bulls
- Calgary Stampede

Jul. 12
- Montreux Jazz Festival

August

Aug. 2
- Streetparade

Aug. 9
- Edinburgh Fringe Festival
- Palio

September

Sep. 6
- Street Scene
- Aloha Festival

Sep. 13
- Oktoberfest-Zinzinnati

October

Oct. 4
- Balloon Fiesta

Oct.11
- Cruise: Carnival Victory (begi

November

Nov. 1
- Pushkar Camel Fair

Nov. 8
- Do: Disney World

December

Dec. 6
- Las Vegas Rodeo

Dec. 13
- Resort: Hedonism III

Jan. 19	Jan. 26	
enix Open	• Ski: Zermatt	
er Bowl Weekend		

Feb. 16	Feb. 23	
na Opera Ball	• Sydney Gay and Lesbian Mardi Gras	
ice Carnival	• Academy Awards Weekend	
neval • Mardi Gras		
naval Rio • Trinidad Carnival		

Mar. 15	Mar. 22	Mar. 29
Patrick's Festival	• Ski: Aspen	• Party: Athens
Patrick's Day Celebration		
Fallas		

Apr. 19	Apr. 26	
sta San Antonio	• Queen's Day	
a de San Marcos	• Kentucky Derby	
ing Week	• New Orleans Jazz Festival	

May 17	May 24	May 31
nphis in May	• Indy 500	• Napa Valley Wine Auction
nes Film Festival	• Féria de Nîmes	• Spoleto
naco Grand Prix	• Berlin Carnival	

Jun. 21	Jun. 28	
nmerfest	• Boston Harborfest	
kilde Rock Festival	• Fourth of July	
te of Chicago		

Jul. 19	Jul. 26	
yenne Frontier Days	• Cowes Week	
	• Caribana	
	• Sun: St. Tropez	
	• Crop Over Festival	

Aug. 16	Aug. 23	Aug. 30
: Ibiza/Majorca	• La Tomatina	• Burning Man
	• Notting Hill Carnival	• Fiesta de Santa Fe
		• Bumbershoot

Sep. 20	Sep. 27	
oberfest	• Stuttgart's Volkfest	
vay Oyster Festival		

Oct. 18	Oct. 25	
se: Carnival Victory (end)	• Fantasy Fest	
	• Exotic Erotic Ball/Halloween	

Nov. 15	Nov. 22	Nov. 29
au Grand Prix	• Party: Acapulco	• Dickens on the Strand

Dec. 20	Dec. 27	
kanoo	• New Year's Eve New York	
	• Hogmanay	

Events are listed according to the week in which the travel date takes place. Starting with January 5, all weeks begin on Monday.

The Fun Seeker's International Destinations

Map Code	Country	City	Event
Europe			
B51	Austria	Vienna	*Vienna Opera Ball*
B52	Denmark	Roskilde (Copenhagen)	*Roskilde Rock Festival*
B53	England	Ascot (London)	*Royal Ascot*
B55	England	Cowes	*Cowes Week*
B53	England	London	*Notting Hill Carnival*
B56	France	Cannes	*Cannes Film Festival*
B57	France	Nîmes	*Féria de Nîmes*
B58	France	Paris	*Fête de la Musique*
B59	France	St. Tropez	*Sun: St.Tropez*
B60	Germany	Berlin	*Berlin Karneval*
B61	Germany	Köln	*Karneval*
B62	Germany	Munich	*Oktoberfest*
B63	Germany	Stuttgart	*Stuttgart's Volksfest*
B64	Greece	Athens	*Party: Athens*
B65	Ireland	Dublin	*St. Patrick's Festival*
B66	Ireland	Galway	*Galway Oyster Festival*
B67	Italy	Siena (Florence)	*Palio*
B68	Italy	Venice	*Venice Carnival*
B69	Monaco	Monte Carlo	*Monaco Grand Prix*
B70	Netherlands	Amsterdam	*Queen's Day*
B71	Portugal	Lisbon	*Feast of St. Anthony*
B72	Scotland	Edinburgh	*Edinburgh Fringe Festival*
B72	Scotland	Edinburgh	*Hogmanay*
B74	Spain	Buñol (Barcelona)	*La Tomatina*
B75	Spain	Ibiza/Majorca	*Sun: Ibiza/Majorca*
B76	Spain	Madrid	*Fiestas de San Isidro*
B77	Spain	Pamplona	*Running of the Bulls*
B78	Spain	Valencia	*Las Fallas*
B79	Sweden	Stockholm	*Party: Stockholm*
B80	Switzerland	Montreux	*Montreux Jazz Festival*
B81	Switzerland	Zermatt	*Ski: Zermatt*
B82	Switzerland	Zurich	*Streetparade*
South America and the Caribbean			
C83	Antigua	St. John's	*Sailing Week*
C84	Argentina	Mendoza (Buenos Aires)	*Vendimia*
C85	Bahamas	Nassau	*Junkanoo*
C86	Barbados	Bridgetown	*Crop Over Festival*
C87	Brazil	Rio de Janeiro	*Carnaval Rio*
C88	Chile	Viña del Mar (Santiago)	*Viña del Mar Song Festival*
C89	Jamaica	Runaway Bay	*Resort: Hedonism III*
C90	Puerto Rico	San Juan	*Calle San Sebastián*
C91	Trinidad and Tobago	Port of Spain	*Trinidad Carnival*
Asia and Australia			
D92	Australia	Melbourne	*Moomba*
D93	Australia	Sydney	*Sydney Gay and Lesbian Mardi Gras*
D94	China	Macau (Hong Kong)	*Macau Grand Prix*
D95	India	Pushkar (Jaipur)	*Pushkar Camel Fair*
D96	Japan	Kawasaki (Tokyo)	*Fertility Festival*
D97	Philippines	Kalibo (Manila)	*Ati Atihan*
D98	Thailand	Chiang Mai (Bangkok)	*Songkran Water Festival*

The Fun Seeker's
International Maps

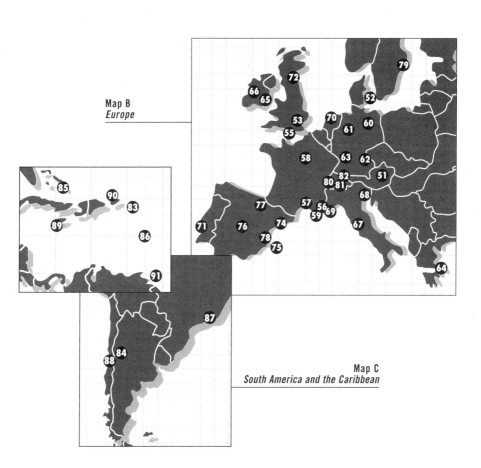

Map B
Europe

Map C
South America and the Caribbean

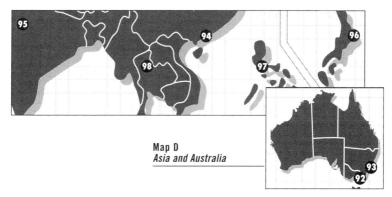

Map D
Asia and Australia

FSG: Changes Since 2000

The **Fun Seeker's Gold List (FSG)**, previously known as The FunGuide 100, has been reduced from 100 events to 96. We've raised our standards for including events and destinations, but we're hopeful that readers will make recommendations to help us bring the list back up to 100 (please contact us at **www.funrises.com**).

Below are changes from the Year 2000 list.

Additions

Berlin Carnival

Berlin has emerged as one of the hippest cities in Europe, and this is the city's major event (there is, of course, the Love Parade, but it's not recommended for adults).

Streetparade (Zurich)

A rave in the streets of Zurich! Things definitely do change, and Zurich is showing itself off by attracting some of the best party people on the planet.

Sun: St. Tropez

There are no noteworthy events in St. Tropez, but the town doesn't need one. This is one of the top-five party places in the world and must be on any fun seeker's calendar.

Replacements

Exotic Erotic Ball (San Francisco) has replaced **Hooker's Ball**.

The **Hooker's Ball** no longer exists, in part because the **Exotic Erotic Ball** has gotten bigger and better.

Fête de la Musique (Paris) has replaced **Bastille Day**.

Bastille Day is a terrific event, but it hasn't improved over the years. Meanwhile, the **Fête** has taken off as a truly unique and fun time in Paris.

Gasparilla (Tampa) has replaced **Guavaween**.

Guavaween is fun, but **Gasparilla** is a significantly larger, grander spectacle.

Inauguration (Washington, D.C.) has replaced **Taste of DC**.

The addition of **Taste of Chicago** makes **Taste of DC** pale in comparison. But D.C. deserves a spot on the list, and the **Inauguration** is worth making an exception to our rule requiring annual events.

Oktoberfest-Zinzinnati (Cincinnati) has replaced **Riverfest**.

Although **Oktoberfest** doesn't draw as large a crowd as the family-oriented **Riverfest**, the party spirit makes it a winner.

Replacements (cont.)

Party: Stockholm has replaced **Stockholm Water Festival**.

The greatest loss on the **FSG** list, the **Stockhoim Water Festival** has been terminated, probably because it was drawing too much business from restaurants and clubs during the busy summer season. Nevertheless, Stockholm is too much fun to be left off the list, and there are no other comparable events.

Skiing: Aspen has replaced **Skiing: Tahoe**.

There has been almost unanimous feedback that Aspen is as much fun as Tahoe and has greater buzz

Taste of Chicago has replaced **Chicago Blues Festival**.

Nothing should be better than a blues festival in Chicago, but the **Blues Festival** hasn't grown to match the size and fun of Taste.

Deletions

Aquatennial (Minneapolis)

Neither the city nor the event can meet the stricter standards of this year's list.

Big Muddy (St. Louis)

This festival has great potential, but needs a boost to make it back on the **FSG** list.

Cape Minstrel Festival (Capetown)

The event no longer draws the crowds to warrant inclusion on the **FSG** list.

Chinese New Year (Hong Kong)

The city's celebration hasn't managed to get local people out of their homes to celebrate communally. Capture, in the Macau itinerary, a more alive Hong Kong later in the year.

Concours d'Elegance (Carmel)

Although the preeminent event of its kind, compared to other events on our list, attendees at this one don't loosen up enough and there isn't enough going on in the Carmel area to merit inclusion on the **FSG** list.

Great American Beer Fest (Denver)

After re-tasting, it isn't great.

Nice Jazz Festival

There are already three jazz festivals on the **FSG** list (Montréal, Montreux and New Orleans), and the south of France was already well represented (St. Tropez, Cannes and Monte Carlo), so even a fun jazz festival like the one in Nice had to be cut.

Index

Academy Awards Weekend	18	Fantasy Fest	50
Acapulco	199	Feria de San Marcos	202
Aguascalientes	202	Festival International de Jazz de Montréal	186
Alberta	182	Fiesta de Santa Fe	124
Albuquerque	120	Fiesta San Antonio	160
Aloha Festival	74	Florida	46, 50, 54, 58, 62, 66
Arizona	14	Fourth of July	136
Aspen	38	Galveston	156
Austin	152	Gasparilla Pirate Festival	66
Balloon Fiesta	120	Georgia	70
Baltimore	96	Guerrero	199
Bike Week	46	Hawaii	74
Black and White Ball	30	Honolulu	74
Black Rock City	108	Houston	156
Boston Harborfest	100	Illinois	78
Bumbershoot, The Seattle Arts Festival	168	Inauguration	42
Burning Man	108	Indiana	82
Calgary Stampede	182	Indianapolis	82
California	18, 22, 26, 30, 34	Indy 500	82
Calle Ocho	62	International Country Music Fan Fair	148
Caribana	194	Kentucky Derby Festival	86
Carnaval de Québec	190	Key West	50
Carnaval Miami	62	Kodak Albuquerque International Balloon Fiesta	120
Charleston	140	Lake Buena Vista	54
Cheyenne Frontier Days	176	Las Vegas	112, 116
Chicago	78	Las Vegas Rodeo	112
Cincjnnati	132	Los Angeles	18
Colorado	38	Louisiana	90, 94
Country Music Fan Fair	148	Louisville	86
Cruise: Carnival Victory	58	Mardi Gras	90
Dallas/Ft.Worth	152	Maryland	96
Daytona Beach	46	Massachusetts	100
Detroit Auto Show	104	Memphis in May Barbecue	144
Dickens on the Strand	156	Miami	62
Disney World	54	Miami Beach	62
District of Columbia	42	Michigan	104
Exotic Erotic Ball/Halloween	34	Milwaukee	172

Montréal Jazz Festival	186
Napa Valley Wine Auction	22
Nashville	148
National Finals Rodeo	112
Nevada	108, 112, 116
New Mexico	120, 124
New Orleans	90, 94
New Orleans Jazz & Heritage Festival	94
New Year's Eve New York	128
North American International Auto Show, NAIAS	104
Ohio	132
Oktoberfest-Zinzinnati	132
Ontario	194
Orlando	46
Park City	164
Party: Acapulco	199
Pennsylvania	136
Philadelphia	136
Phoenix Open	14
Piccolo Spoleto	140
Preakness Celebration	96
Québec (province)	186, 190
Québec Winter Carnaval	190
San Antonio	160
San Diego	26
San Francisco	30, 34
Santa Fe	124
Savannah	70
Scottsdale	14
Seattle	168
Ski: Aspen	38
South by Southwest Music and Media Conference	152
South Carolina	140
Spoleto Festival USA	140
St. Helena	22
St. Patrick's Day Celebration	70
Street Scene	26
Summerfest	172

Sundance Film Festival	164
Sunoco Welcome America	136
Super Bowl Weekend	116
Tampa	66
Taste of Chicago	78
Tennessee	144, 148
Texas	152, 156, 160
The 500 Festival	82
Toronto	194
Utah	164
Walt Disney World	54
Washington, D.C.	42
Washington (state)	168
Wisconsin	172
Wyoming	176

JUNOs

Amusement Parks	207
Barbecue	208
Bowl (Football) Games	209
Car Racing	210
Fantasy Camps	212
Food Festivals	213
Gambling	115
Golf	216
Jazz Festivals	218
Movies, Giant Screen	220
Parades	221
State Fairs	222
Supermodels	223
Tall Buildings	224
The Nutcracker Ballet	225

Maps

Europe	251
North America	7
South America and the Caribbean	251
Asia and Australia	251

Alan S. Davis, Author

Alan, an entrepreneur, philanthropist, publisher and lecturer, began traveling professionally as a tour representative in 1967. This career path was interrupted by the pursuit of politically correct endeavors, but a fortune cookie set him back on the right path: "Preserve wild life—throw more parties." Since 1995 Alan has been to nearly 150 major events. He resides in one of the few places on earth where returning from these incredible journeys is not a letdown—San Francisco.

Chuck Thompson, Editor

Alan S. Davis met Chuck Thompson while both were on assignment at Carnival in Trinidad. How Davis convinced Thompson to give up such extraordinary assignments to spend months in front of a computer is a mystery for the ages, but great fortune for the readers of this book. Thompson is the former executive editor of *Travelocity* magazine, and contributing editor for *Escape* magazine. He's worked on assignment for a variety of magazines in more than thirty countries.

THINK OF *THE FUN SEEKER'S NORTH AMERICA* AS **3** EXTRAORDINARY GUIDEBOOKS IN **1**!

1 Travel Planner

THE FUN SEEKER'S NORTH AMERICA is the only guidebook that can answer all these travel questions:

Where should I go this year?

Where is the most fun place to be on *St. Patrick's Day, Halloween* or *New Year's Eve?*

How can we make a special occasion extra special?

Where should I go for *Memorial Day, Fourth of July* or the *Labor Day* holiday?

When would be the best time to go to ... ?

What is the best music, performing arts, food or film festival to go to?

How do we get tickets?

2 Day-by-Day Planner

THE FUN SEEKER'S NORTH AMERICA is the only guidebook that provides you with detailed, non-stop 3-day itineraries to the most fun events and destinations in the United States, Canada and Mexico!

3 City Guide

THE FUN SEEKER'S NORTH AMERICA is the only guidebook that provides you with quick-glance Hot Sheets for the hippest hotels, coolest restaurants and nightlife, and must-see attractions in more than 40 cities!

+ And more ...

The More Fun section of *THE FUN SEEKER'S NORTH AMERICA* gives you details on more than 200 other events, along with background tidbits on the best of fun seeking!

How Are Events Chosen for The Fun Seeker's Gold List?

The goal is to create a broad range (i.e., street parties, galas, rodeos, music festivals, etc.) of the world's most fun events and destinations, with at least one for every week of the year.

The rules (for which there are exceptions) are that the events must be held annually in the same location, with at least 10,000 people attending, and no more than one event per city.

Event Ratings

★★★★★ and ★★★★ *Must do.* These events are worth making a special trip to, even planning your life around.

★★★ and ★★ *Should do.* These are events you should attend if you're already planning to visit the region, or if you are just looking for something fun to do on a given weekend.

★ These events, though not worth a special trip, are the times when it is most fun to be at the destination.

Details about the ratings can be found on page 228.

In 1995 I set out on a journey to uncover the world's most fun places to be at the right time. The result is *The Fun Seeker's Gold List*—96 incredible events and destinations. With the information provided in the chapters on the 48 events and destinations in North America (the United States, Canada and Mexico), along with the essential details in the special *Fun Seeker's Gold List* section, I know you'll have some of the most fun vacations of your lifetime. – *Alan S. Davis*